Resurrection

Resurrection

Texts and Interpretation, Experience and Theology

Karl Olav Sandnes
AND
Jan-Olav Henriksen

◠PICKWICK *Publications* • Eugene, Oregon

RESURRECTION
Texts and Interpretation, Experience and Theology

Copyright © 2020 Karl Olav Sandnes and Jan-Olav Henriksen. All rights reserved. Except for brief quotations in critical publications or reviews, no part of this book may be reproduced in any manner without prior written permission from the publisher. Write: Permissions, Wipf and Stock Publishers, 199 W. 8th Ave., Suite 3, Eugene, OR 97401.

Pickwick Publications
An Imprint of Wipf and Stock Publishers
199 W. 8th Ave., Suite 3
Eugene, OR 97401

www.wipfandstock.com

PAPERBACK ISBN: 978-1-5326-9587-2
HARDCOVER ISBN: 978-1-5326-9588-9
EBOOK ISBN: 978-1-5326-9589-6

Cataloguing-in-Publication data:

Names: Sandnes, Karl Olav, author. | Henriksen, Jan-Olav, author.

Title: Resurrection : texts and interpretation, experience and theology / by Karl Olav Sandnes and Jan-Olav Henriksen.

Description: Eugene, OR: Pickwick Publications, 2020. | Includes bibliographical references and index.

Identifiers: ISBN 978-1-5326-9587-2 (paperback) | ISBN 978-1-5326-9588-9 (hardcover) | ISBN 978-1-5326-9589-6 (ebook)

Subjects: LCSH: Jesus Christ—Resurrection—Biblical teaching. | Bible. New Testament—Criticism, interpretation, etc. | Bible. New Testament—Theology.

Classification: BS2545.R47 R47 2020 (print) | BS2545.R47 (ebook)

Manufactured in the U.S.A. 04/15/20

Contents

Abbreviations | ix
Acknowledgments | xi

Introduction | 1
    Structure of the Book | 3

Part I. Theoretical Presuppositions

Resurrection is an Interpretative Category | 7
    Theoretical Building Blocks for the Claim that Jesus Did Rise from the Dead | 9
        Resurrection and Experience | 11
        Abduction and its Relation to Experience | 14
        The Semiotic Approach: Abduction at Work | 20
        On Stefan Alkier's Peircean Interpretation of the Resurrection | 28
    Empty Tomb (ET) and Appearances of Jesus/Visions of Jesus (AJ/VJ) as Religiously Significant: Ann Taves | 32

Part II. The New Testament Discourses on Resurrection

Mapping the Present-Day Terrain | 39
    Tradition-Critical Considerations: Early is Best | 40
    Psychological Attempts | 41
    Metaphorical Language: Meaning-Oriented Interpretations | 43
    "Orthodox" Faith | 44

Neither Witnessed nor Told: An Indescribable Event | 46
   The Gospel of Peter | 47
      Why this Detour | 51

What Does Belief in the Resurrection of Jesus *Do*? Pragmatic Contours of New Testament Theology of Resurrection | 53
   A Colloquium on the Resurrection | 54

Paul the Apostle: The First to Engage the Issue | 56
   A Divine Act | 57
   A Universal Perspective | 59
   The Risen Jesus and the Christ-Believer | 60
   God has not Given up on God's Creation | 63

The Acts of the Apostles | 65
   Evidentiary Presence | 65
   An Act of Restoration | 68

The Book of Revelation | 70
   Consolation | 70
   Confrontational | 71

Easter Faith Impacts | 74
   "The Day of the Lord" | 74
   Transformed Lives | 78
      Life Changing or Guilt Complex? | 80
      Celsus—Gerd Lüdemann's Ancient Like-Minded? | 84
   Summary | 86

1 Corinthians 15: Resurrection—Without an Empty Tomb | 89
   Tradition: Wording or Substance? | 91
      "Died for our Sins According to the Scriptures" | 92
      "He was Buried" | 93
      "He was Raised on the Third Day in Accordance with the Scriptures" | 96
      "He Appeared to Cephas and . . ." | 100
      No Empty Tomb? | 104

A Transformed Body or Another Body? | 109
    What Kind of Change Then? | 114
    Paul Muddling His Case? | 115
  Summarizing the Fomulaic Tradition | 118

The Easter Narratives | 120
  Mark 16:1–8: A Testimony of a Discovery | 120
    Mark 16:9–20: The Longer and Secondary Markan Ending | 124
  Matt 28:1–20: Excessively Present | 128
    The Matthean Inclusion: Emmanuel—"I am with You" | 131

Luke 24: Recognizing the Risen Jesus | 133
  Wrestling with Recognizing Jesus (vv. 13–35) | 134
  What Kind of Reality? (vv. 36–43) | 137
  John 20(–21): Initiating a New "Dispensation" | 140
    Narrating Creation Renewed | 144
  Women at the Tomb | 146
  Two Independent Traditions? | 153
  Summarizing Narrative Easter | 155
    Hole and Surplus | 157
    Conceptualizing Easter or the Resurrected Body | 159

Towards a New Testament Theology on the Resurrection of Jesus | 162
  Not so Credulous After All | 162
  An Abductively Interpreted Reality | 165
  An Eschatological Event—Narratively Hardbound | 168
  What Does the Empty Tomb and the Appearances Convey? | 172
  Why Insisting on Resurrection? | 177
  According to the Scriptures | 179
  Negotiating Creation | 183
  The All-Pervasive Resurrection | 186
  The Resurrected Body: Admitting and Grappling with Vagueness | 187

Part III. Resurrection Faith

Contributions to Resurrection Discourse:
Presentation and Analysis | 190
   Resurrection as a Saturated Phenomenon? Jean-Luc Marion on the Emmaus Story | 192
   "On Miracles" | 198

Engaging Key Voices | 207
   Rudolf Bultmann | 207
   Wolfhart Pannenberg | 212
   Peter Carnley | 219
   N. T. Wright | 234
   Dale C. Allison Jr. | 247
      Appearances: Allison's Contribution | 250
      Embodied and Transformed: Experiential Analogies/Parallels | 253

Part IV. Concluding Reflections

Resurrection from History to Theology | 256
   Resurrection and the Future: An Eschatological Event in the Present World | 259
   Remarks on the Resurrection, Individual Differences, and Disability | 267
   A Contemporary Approach to the Paulinian Core Argument | 271
   The Resurrection as Basis for Christology: Dirk-Martin Grube | 274
   Resurrection as Manifestation of Incarnation: Ingolf U. Dalferth | 277
   Conclusion: Resurrection as a Manifestation of God's Future for Creation | 282

Bibliography | 285
Author Index | 297
Subject Index | 299
Scripture Index | 301

Abbrevations

Abbreviations follow *The SBL Handbook of Style for Ancient Near East, Biblical, and Early Christian Studies*. Edited by Patrick H. Alexander et al. Peabody: Hendrickson, 1999. The following abbreviations are to be pointed out:

ANF   Ante Nicene Fathers, Grand Rapids: Eerdmans

BDAG   Walter Bauer, Frederick W. Danker, W. F. Arndt, and F. W Gingrich, *Greek-English Lexicon of the New Testament and Other Early Christian Literature*. 3rd ed. Chicago: Chicago University Press, 2000.

LCL   Loeb Classical Library, Cambridge, London: Harvard University Press

LSJ   Henry Georg Liddell, Robert Scott, and Henry Stuart Jones. *A Greek-English Lexicon*. 9th ed. Oxford: Clarendon

NETS   *A New English Translation of the Septuagint and the Other Greek Translations Traditionally Included under that Title*. Edited by Albert Pietersma and Benjamin G. Wright. New York, Oxford: Oxford University Press, 2007.

Nestle-Aland   Greek New Testament

NRSV   *The New Oxford Annotated Bibel with Apocryphal/Deuterocanonical Books*. Edited by Bruce M. Metzger and Roland E, Murphy. New York: Oxford University Press, 1991.

SC   Source Chrétiennes, Cerf: Paris

s.v.   *sub verbo* or under the word (specified) with reference to an entry in a dictionary

Acknowledgments

To WRITE ABOUT THE resurrection is a challenging task. We are not the first to do so, and probably not the last, either. However, not many have combined a historical and a contemporary systematic approach to this topic, as we attempt to do in the following. We have both benefited from entering into each other's disciplines and trying to look at why Christians speak about the resurrection and what it means today. This means that although we have had parts that each of us drafted on our own, we have discussed and commented on these drafts in such a way that it is not possible to say that one part is exclusively written by one of us.

Both of us have probably experienced something similar when writing this book as what we did when writing our previous book about *Jesus as Healer* (Eerdmans, 2016). It is both enjoyable and rewarding to do studies like the present one together. We hope the present book reflects this fact.

Many people deserve our thanks as this book comes to completion: The librarians, in Rome, Oslo, and Oxford, which were the places we worked on the book and found our sources. Our students, who listened, participated in discussions, and commented when we presented a preliminary manuscript in a lecture series in the Spring Term 2019. We owe thanks to our colleagues, Professors Ole Jakob Filtvedt and Asle Eikrem, who both commented helpfully on a draft. Anne Marie Hovland Aschim has improved our non-native English. Whatever flaws remain, are nevertheless on us. Our home institution, MF Norwegian School of Theology, Religion and Society, has provided us with the most valuable resource for doing research: Time. We are grateful to all. Finally, we express our gratitude to Pickwick Publications, and the editors with whom we have worked there.

Oslo, early September 2019

Karl Olav Sandnes   Jan-Olav Henriksen

Introduction

IT HAPPENS EVERY YEAR. Easter comes as an annual celebration, and in its wake follow resurrection debates. In our context, Norway, this happened in 2017 as well, and the debate was more intense than usual.[1] Discussions regarding Jesus's resurrection have taken place in many countries. In Germany, Gerd Lüdemann, formerly New Testament professor in Göttingen, caused debate when he denied the resurrection of Jesus and argued that it was a product of the apostle's hallucinations; a key notion in this interpretation is therefore "self-deception."[2] The German professor concluded that Christian faith should be based entirely on the *historical* Jesus, to whom resurrection is excluded. In the English speaking world, several debates, e.g., between John Dominic Crossan and N. T. Wright, have been staged on this topic, in which the former takes the view that this is metaphorical language while the latter holds a traditional viewpoint, namely that this is a real event that took place in time and place.[3]

A plethora of questions come into play in these discussions: Did Jesus rise from the dead? Is that really possible? Is resurrection language metaphorical or poetic rather than conveying history, something that took place? What kind of body did the resurrected Jesus have? What is the relationship between the risen Jesus and a general resurrection? To this, we add hermeneutical questions related to how this faith is situated within Christian doctrine generally, as it develops for example from the Apostolic Creed, cited in churches throughout the world regularly: "raised from the dead on the third day." This book is an attempt to think this through anew. We think that a dialogue between a New Testament scholar and a philosopher of religion, carried throughout every chapter of this book, may shed relevant and

---

1. See the Norwegian newspaper *Vårt Land* at the time of Easter 2017.
2. Lüdemann, *Resurrection of Jesus*; Lüdemann, *Resurrection of Christ*.
3. See, e.g., Stewart, *Resurrection of Jesus*.

new light on these perennial debates. We do think that this co-operation might prove fruitful in such a way that it is worthwhile rehearsing some of the questions anew. About our issue, Dale C. Allison rightly makes this dictum: "we require more than history if we are to find the truth of things."[4] We endorse this statement, and the immediate consequence of this insight is a cross-disciplinarian endeavor. It is precisely this inter-disciplinarian dialogue and approach that justifies yet another book on the resurrection of Jesus. The presentation can hardly avoid revolving around New Testament texts and their interpretation. The book about the Crossan—Wright dialogue, as well as the German book *Die Wirklichkeit der Auferstehung*,[5] include separate and individual contributions by scholars from other fields. A regular and continuous co-operation between scholars working in different fields—New Testament and Early Christian history, systematic theology, and philosophy—is rarely found relating to our topic. A cross-disciplinarian approach seems especially fit for the present topic.

For reasons of introductory simplicity, we embark upon the project by sketching two fundamental outlooks, often found on each end of a scale ranging from what is often labeled "conservative" to what is often labeled "liberal," albeit these labels are not very helpful. At the one end are those who emphasize the physical nature of Jesus's resurrection, underlining *continuity* and preservation of the past in the resurrected body. The resurrection of Jesus is primarily a matter of being revivified or resuscitated; that is, his being restored to life. At the other end of the scale are those who emphasize the *otherness* of the resurrection. The eschatological nature of the resurrection is emphasized in such a way that the event is hardly tangible to the present world. In the words of Hans Küng, the reality of the resurrection is "completely *intangible* and *unimaginable*."[6] To these advocates, the resurrection of Jesus is primarily a matter of a new world, and may also be a metaphor for a reality which is experienced primarily in a spiritual way.

An often used imagery in this debate is the surveillance camera. Imagine a camera placed right outside the tomb at the moment when Jesus was raised from the dead. What could the camera tell about the incident? Alternatively, would the camera let anything be seen or noticed at all? Some of the participants in these debates argue that a camera outside the tomb of Jesus would have shown *nothing* at all since the resurrection of Jesus was

---

4. Allison, *Resurrecting Jesus*, 351.

5. Eckstein, *Die Wirklichkeit der Auferstehung* and the debate volume, Copan and Tacelli, *Jesus' Resurrection: Fact or Figment?* The following issues are devoted to our topic: *Evangelische Theologie* 57.3 (1997); *Zeitschrift für Neues Testament* 19 (2007); *Journal for the Study of the Historical Jesus* 3.2 (2005).

6. Küng, *On Being a Christian*, 350. The italics are his.

an *eschatological* event, and hence special and not comparable to previous experiences. The illustration of the camera, albeit anachronistic, serves to put some important issues on the agenda: Was the resurrection of Jesus in any way noticeable? What kind of event was this? Was it an event at all? The New Testament sources relevant do not claim that the incident as such was witnessed by anybody (as we argue in the following chapters), but was what took place, in principle, something that could be witnessed or observed? Is it at all adequate to speak about something "taking place"? Would not even a reproduction of the event by the camera need an interpretation? These questions are historical and simultaneously highly theological and hermeneutical, as they pave the way for *what kind of reality* we are talking about, and on what conditions we can make sense of the experiences that led to the claims about Jesus's resurrection. Moreover, the image of the camera seems to downplay the importance of interpretative resources for saying something about what happened: as we will argue in the following, the event itself needs interpretation based on inferences that have been made abductively.

Taken together, the chapters of this book aim at discussing how it is possible to speak meaningfully and coherently about the resurrection of Jesus, when relevant texts and present-day hermeneutics are considered. In short, how do we *make sense* of the claim about the resurrection of Jesus within Christian theology and practice?

Structure of the Book

The book is divided into four main parts: Part I is a rather brief part that presents the theoretical and philosophical presuppositions on which the study builds and thus also the framework within which we interpret both the New Testament material and the contemporary discourse about the resurrection of Jesus. First, it presents an understanding of abductive inferences based in the semiotics of C. S. Peirce, and an understanding of religious experience based on practices of orientation and transformation. The understanding of experience builds on common elements in (Gadamer's) hermeneutics but is supplied with an understanding of how abduction plays a role in the interpretation of all experience. The main argument is that the concrete experiences that the New Testament witnesses to about the resurrection are the empty tomb and the appearances or visions of Jesus. These experiences are the foundation for the abductive inference that Jesus was raised from the dead by God. The flipside of this position is that nobody experiences the resurrection as such and that it, from a semiotic perspective, can be characterized as an interpretative category based on abduction from *other* experiences. Thus, the claim about the resurrection rests upon other experiences. This approach implies a rejection of positivistic interpretations such as "we would in principle be able to catch the resurrection on camera" since such positions ignore the need for inferences and abduction even if one could provide such material as "evidence." Second, and furthermore, the topic of *experience* is then added due to engagement with Ann Taves's understanding of religious experience, by her referred to as experiences deemed religious. Taves's contribution allows for understanding why the experiences referred to could take on a religious significance in the way that happened to the disciples.

These theoretical points of departure shape the approach that we develop in the subsequent analysis of the book.

Part II engages the New Testament scholarship and the sources we have about the resurrection. This part is rather comprehensive and covers all the relevant texts and positions that play a role in the contemporary debate. The focus is on the New Testament (NT) discourse on the resurrection of Jesus. Generally, NT is seen as kind of a colloquium, a "conference table," aimed at grasping what belief in the resurrection of Jesus is really about and what it brings about. From the very outset, it is emphasized that the resurrection itself is never described, thus leaving a hole in the stories. This implies an elusiveness which impacts on how it is possible to understand this phenomenon at all. Furthermore, the NT evidence is surveyed from a pragmatic perspective: how did belief in the resurrection of Jesus come into play in the genre of letters (Paul), a narrative (Acts) and an apocalypse (Revelation)?

Special attention is then given to the two main traditions; the formulaic tradition found in 1 Cor 15:3–11 in its context and the narrative traditions in the Gospels. As for 1 Cor 15, we question what has become almost a consensus, namely that Paul was unaware of the empty tomb. The narrative traditions are presented on an individual basis, thus confirming the "colloquium" mentioned above. This chapter also includes an entry relevant for all of them, namely the women at the tomb.

Part II is rounded off by summarizing the nature of belief in the resurrection. The NT evidence about our topic moves beyond discovery and justification in a way that makes the resurrection of Jesus an abductively interpreted reality. The hole in the stories and the fragmentariness of how this event is presented pave the way for theological considerations taking these observations into account. Furthermore, the resurrection of Jesus is narratively hardbound; it is at home in narratives about Jesus. Secondly, belief in the resurrection is itself a gift, not the sum of some so-called facts.

This paves the way for an understanding of his resurrection that is neither purely metaphorical nor an ordinary historical event.

Part III, Resurrection Faith, takes up the contemporary debate on the resurrection. This part is developed in two steps: First, by presenting J.-L. Marion's concept of a "saturated phenomenon" as a way to understand the richness and the diversity of interpretations about the resurrection, and then a short discussion of different positions regarding so-called "miracles." These introductory sections are followed by an analysis of the following positions found in recent literature, on which we offer new perspectives based on our theoretical approaches: R. Bultmann, W. Pannenberg, P. Carnley, I. Dalferth, N. T. Wright (with reference to his more philosophical arguments), and D. Allison. We here further advance the claim that the experiential basis on which resurrection faith rests (empty tomb, visions or appearances) are not in themselves without analogies, but that the faith in Jesus's resurrection calls for a further specification on what it is in resurrection faith that makes the inference about the resurrection the most plausible. In this regard, the theological tropes of God as creator, and the understanding of Jesus pre-Easter ministry becomes significant for understanding the content of the resurrection faith.

Part IV, From History to Theology, then advances further and develops an overall argument about the content and implications of resurrection faith with special attention to its contemporary significance, as well as a basis for the doctrinal understanding of Jesus (Christology). Here we also take up recent contributions of D.-M Grube and I. Dalferth, and touch upon recent discussions about resurrection and disability.

Hence, the overall argument of the book is that the resurrection is a part of Christian faith closely integrated with other theological aspects, related to both God as Creator and the redemptive ministry of Jesus. We argue that these elements are the most important of resurrection faith. Furthermore, we argue that there are good reasons for holding that the resurrection of Jesus was a historical event, while simultaneously also holding that it remains an open and, in many ways, indeterminate event—due to our lack of experiential access to it.

Part I: Theoretical Presuppositions

Resurrection is an Interpretative Category

IN ORDER TO EXPLORE the possible answers to the abovementioned questions, we have to recognize from the outset that *resurrection is an interpretative category*. The notion resurrection does not apply to any phenomenon that any human person has ever experienced (not even Jesus himself, as his capacity for experiencing a post-resurrection state presupposes that he had already been raised from the dead). The claims "Jesus has risen" or "God has resurrected Jesus"—both claims central to the Christian faith—are not based on any experience of the resurrection itself. These claims are based on other observations: the experiences of the empty tomb, and the appearances of Jesus after his death. It is the combination of these latter elements that makes it possible to claim that Jesus was resurrected.

When we speak of the resurrection as something unique, we, therefore, reserve this category for a specific interpretation *of the conditions for events* that have in principle been, at some point, observable by humans. To see resurrection as an interpretative category implies that it is based on an *abductive* inference[1] from experiences of other elements than the resurrection itself. The potential uniqueness of the resurrection of Jesus is, therefore, itself based on a decision about how to use this category: what people believe when they believe that Jesus was resurrected from the dead is that something happened to him that has not happened to anyone else. It is an exclusive category, applied to him only.

This use of the category "resurrection" as exclusive does not imply that the other experiences that caused the claim about Jesus's resurrection

---

1. We are not the only ones who have pointed to the abductive character in theological reflections on the resurrection, though. See also, e.g., Alkier, *Reality of the Resurrection* and Dalferth, "Volles Grab, Leerer Glaube?" The notion of abductive inferences is discussed extensively below.

are in the same manner unique or exclusive: It is likely that people could, for different reasons, have experienced empty tombs earlier and later, and not only in the case of Jesus. We also know that throughout history, a considerable amount of people have had visions of recently deceased persons and that this is still the case today.[2] In that regard, none of the experiential elements that constitute the claim that Jesus has risen are something to be considered as possible to apply exclusively to him. However, the claim that he is resurrected is. It is the claim that these experiences can be explained or interpreted as pointing to his resurrection that is the specific element that we must focus on if we want to speak about the exclusivity of what happened. The resurrection, therefore, does not depend only on the experiential content or the basis for the experiences people have, but also on how one relates these theologically to the ministry of Jesus before Easter. Hence, what Christians believe is that something *special* happened to Jesus that has not happened to any other human person, and the reason for this belief is a specific interpretation of the facts that Jesus's tomb was empty and that he appeared to his followers in the time following his crucifixion and burial. They saw these events as related to and confirming the truth and validity of Jesus's ministry before his death.

Keeping this in mind, we can proceed and ask on what grounds it is possible to claim that there is something unparalleled in the faith in the resurrection of Jesus that cannot be seen as in analogy with any other experience we can have? Surely, we know that it is possible that a tomb can be empty, and we have reasons to believe that people have had visions of Jesus after his death and did so in ways that may be seen as potentially parallel or analogous to how other dead persons may appear after death as well. In this regard, we move beyond the type of scholarship that restricts itself to stating things about Jesus only up until the time of his death: there is more than enough anthropological evidence to suggest that appearances of people after their death is something that actually takes place. Hence, there seems to be nothing impossible, unparalleled, or without analogy in the

---

2. For more recent studies of this in the contemporary world, see Austad, 'Passing Away—Passing by'; Hayes, "Experiencing the Presence of the Deceased"; as well as Hayes and Leudar, "Experiences of Continued Presence." Among New Testament scholars that takes this type of material seriously into consideration, one stands out: Allison, *Resurrecting Jesus*, whereas N. T. Wright more or less seems to dismiss this type of experience as relevant for the interpretation of the post-death visions of Jesus somewhat too quickly, in Wright, *Resurrection of the Son of God*. The percentage of people who have such experiences are between 50 and 80 percent, according to Hayes and Leudar. This might suggest that the experiences like those of the disciples may not be so unique, after all. See also for historical and contemporary examples Wiebe, *Visions of Jesus*.

actual experiences that constitute the background for the claim and belief that Jesus was raised from the dead.

What seems impossible is the content of the claim itself: that someone has risen from the dead and entered a new form of life. Despite mythological stories about such events, as well as some of the visions from the Old Testament (Ezekiel, chap. 37 in particular) this is not a likely thing to happen, and therefore unexpected and not anticipated. Against the backdrop of the above considerations, one has to admit that nothing seems to attest to the possibility or probability of a *resurrection* to happen in the actual experiences that humans have. That is so even when we know that sometimes dead people do appear, or tombs turn out as empty. However, the resurrection itself is not something that can be easily linked to our present world, emerging from present conditions of experience, and something likely to happen within reasonable horizons of expectation.[3]

In a way, that seems to be exactly the point about resurrection: when we see it in light of what happened on Good Friday, the resurrection is the total opposite, that for which all conditions of possibility are eradicated by the death of Jesus. Jesus manifested the powers of life, but when he was himself dead, these manifestations were no longer possible. The claim about resurrection nevertheless states that the power of life is still at work, still present, still operational. The question still remains: How can we understand the resurrection? What does it mean from a theological point of view? These are questions that will occupy us in this part of the book.

Theoretical Building Blocks for the Claim that Jesus Did Rise from the Dead

This chapter aims at clarifying some basic elements regarding how to understand experience and its conditions in general, in order to then, subsequently, say something about what it can imply for the understanding of the experiences that the disciples had after the death of Jesus.

When humans have a profound experience of something, it does not leave them unaffected. This claim goes for all kinds of experiences, including those of empty tombs or visions of the deceased. Such experiences can be confusing, and they may provide reasons for transformations in how you

---

3. Cf. Williams, *Resurrection*, 88: "[N]othing which occurred on Easter Day or after was anticipated. We read of fear, grief, doubt, ecstatic joy, but not of a simple sense of prophecy fulfilled." Hence, the element of dissociation with the past on the side of the disciples is one of the main obstacles when they are attempting to understand what happens.

live and what you think, in ways that entail a change in values, perceptions, ideas, and commitments that you have had hitherto.

From the outset, we need to distinguish between experiences and things that just happen. Whereas experiences in a qualified sense are what will occupy us in the following, mere occurrences that do not register any change in those to whom they befall are not what we have in mind here. In German, one can distinguish between these two categories of events by speaking about *Erfahrung* viz. *Erlebnis*. We will develop this distinction more thoroughly below.

We nevertheless first need to say here that we are not taking our point of view from a pre-established concept of "religious experience" as something that is set off from or can be easily distinguished from other types of experiences that humans have. We would even prefer to speak of "experiences with or by religion" instead, meaning that there are experiences in human life that are more likely to be interpreted in the framework of, or by means of, the semiotic resources that religious traditions offer for the interpretation of such. As we shall see below, this view is closely linked to our understanding of experience as the result of (abductive) semiotic processes. Our position means that we cannot place the experiences that lead to the claim about the resurrection in a realm that is separate from other types of human experiences or see it as unrelated to those.

Religious imagery and notions both mediate and are themselves mediated through concrete practices as these features express themselves in human lives. The stories surrounding the resurrection can contribute to practices that orient, transform, or instigate new reflection. Such practices thereby contribute to making sense of and interpreting what is happening. As *religious*, they point to things beyond the ordinary, and grounds human life in symbols, conceptions, and narratives that point us beyond the mundane and quotidian. Therefore, it makes sense to speak of religious signs as pointing toward the *superempirical*. Not so in the sense of something supernatural, meaning something belonging to a separate and inaccessible sphere of reality, but as something that is beyond what is at the forefront of our experience, and which, when presupposed, can help to make sense of it. Examples of such superempirical notions are not only assumptions about God, but also notions like "beauty," "society," "nation," "species," "truth," "goodness," etc. Such notions offer means for ordering and interpreting life (orientation) and may also point us in the direction of what change means or why it should take place.[4]

---

4. For further on this understanding of religion, see Henriksen, *Religion as Orientation and Transformation*.

Religious imaginaries thus provide means for orientation in pointing out what matters more than something else, be it God, love, goodness, community, hope, honor, etc. Furthermore, religious resources contribute to motivating and interpreting change and transformation in human life. Often, these two features are closely linked, as we can see, e.g., in how theology sometimes uses the story about the resurrection as an orientational point of view for the ethical life of believers and displays such a life in ways that may also imply changes in lifestyle and priorities.[5] The claim about Jesus as resurrected is a claim that works in the respects suggested here: it suggests that something happened that is of vital importance to human orientation, but it is, simultaneously, also something that transforms the basic perspectives on which the disciples acted and the way they chose to live from that point on.

Resurrection and Experience

From a phenomenological point of view, experience in a qualified sense establishes a temporal *before* and *after*, i.e., as something that takes place in *time*. Thus, the experience comes in between, as an event that makes the person who has it aware of what was before but now has changed. In this sense, the experience also makes us aware of the experienced in a way not recognized previously. Thus, to have an experience is not only to be aware of what happens or is going on—but this awareness also implies an awareness of *oneself* as changed by what is going on, compared to what was the case previous to the experience in question. In this sense, experience is also a *negation* of what was expected because someone took it for granted; it is the arrival of something new that transforms the consciousness of the one who experiences and creates an awareness of something that was not present beforehand. Accordingly, experiences imply the transformation of self-awareness and the content of consciousness.[6]

Gadamer[7] underscores the above points by pointing to how there is a *hermeneutical* dimension implied in an experience that makes us see something in a different light. Thus, since a real experience is a manifestation of change, it always expands and adds to the world as it hitherto has appeared. To experience means to undergo a transformation in such a way that nothing

---

5. See, e.g., Molnar, *Incarnation and Resurrection*, 144–46, 255–57.

6. Cf. Risser, *Hermeneutics and the Voice of the Other*, 89. According to this description, as well as what follows, it would be hard to say that God has experiences in the same way as humans do. Experience is a profoundly human mode of being, shaped and conditioned by finitude and time.

7. Gadamer, *Truth and Method*, esp. 340–55.

is quite like it was before. Such experience interrupts, destabilizes and changes the point of departure from which something previously was understood.[8] From this perspective, it is not hard to see why the experiences of the empty tomb and the appearances of Jesus were life-changing.

From a theological point of view, there are notable features in what Gadamer calls experience that has similarities with and may even be said to overlap with a notion of revelation: revelation is not merely conveying new information but is a specific mode in which God makes Godself known to us—in unexpected, surprising and uncontrolled ways. The event that we call resurrection is no exception in this regard: the interpretation of the events and conditions that leads to the claim about the resurrection contributes to the revelation of the situation as something that it was not beforehand. Theologically, it means that the events that are behind the claims about the resurrection disclose something about God, and about God's relationship with Jesus. Thus, the very notion "resurrection" itself disrupts already established modes of being in the world, ways of being self-conscious, as well as the ways the things that lead to the claim are experienced. Revelation can thus be seen as a disclosure of the empirical world that is not based on our existing anticipations about it, as there is nothing in the minds beforehand that determines how the experienced is understood and to what it is related.[9]

Accordingly, experience implies that we are confronted with the preliminary character of our concepts and our expectations and that we may find ourselves challenged to change them. It is worth noting that this is Gadamer's philosophical account of how we expand, transform, and develop our understanding, and not an apologetic move on behalf of a given theological position. Everyone is faced with the finitude of their mode of being in the world when they make experiences. Thus, in the experience of how the world represents an infinite array of possible options for experience, we also are confronted with our finitude.[10] We become aware of this finitude, however, when we are pointed beyond the limitations it implies. This fact is highly relevant for how we understand the claim about the resurrection as rooted in experience.

---

8. Gadamer, *Truth and Method*, 355.

9. Cf. for further on the interruptive element with relation to experience Boeve, "Theology and the Interruption of Experience," esp. 33–35.

10. As Risser says, with reference to Gadamer's *Truth and Method*, 357: "What we learn is the uncertainty of all predictions and the folly of attempting to master the future. Experience is the experience of human finitude, and 'genuine [eigentliche] experience is that whereby the human becomes aware of its finitude.'" Risser, *Hermeneutics and the Voice of the Other*, 91.

There are two possible ways to deal with the finite character of our experiences: one way is to absolutize it and say that there is nothing more to our experience than what is already contained in what we have experienced so far. This is a way of relating to oneself and the world which closes oneself off from the genuine meeting with the other, from possibilities for developing oneself further, and from the opportunity to have new experiences.[11] It manifests a type of (scientistic) dogmatism. This position has severe consequences for how we understand both God and the human self because it does not provide us with a genuine notion of an open future. The alternative is more promising: we become open to the infinite that is "surrounding" and conditioning finite experience by adopting an open approach to the world and possible experiences. It can be experienced in such a manner that the world in its richness and diversity occur because we can reckon with the possibility of being corrected or changed by the meeting with the other—with that which we have not so far experienced. Risser summarizes this in a manner that may also be relevant for the revelatory component in such genuine experience:

> The openness to experience itself is an openness to what is alien and other. It is to face what refuses my framework. Thus Gadamer concludes: "The hermeneutical consciousness culminates not in methodological sureness of itself, but in the same readiness for experience that distinguishes the experienced individual from the individual captivated by dogma. As we can now say more exactly in terms of the concept of experience, this readiness is what distinguishes historically effected consciousness."[12]

Gadamer's understanding of hermeneutical experience has, accordingly, consequences for how experiences are perceived as revelatory: they may not be seen as necessarily belonging to a specific mode of knowledge that is without connection to the ordinary features of human life and understanding. To the contrary, if theology says something about the new, about that which was not

---

11. Cf. Henriksen, *Finitude and Theological Anthropology*. Cf. also Pannenberg's more theological point here, regarding finitude: "Nor is the finitude of theological knowledge grounded only in the limitation of information about an object which the whole tradition information knows to be infinite, or in the limitation of what can be done with this information. It is grounded especially in the time-bound nature of the knowledge. According to the witness of the Bible the deity of God will be definitively and unquestionably manifested only at the end of all time and history. At every point in time it is a fact that what is lasting and reliable, and in this sense true, comes to light only in the future." Pannenberg, *Systematic Theology* 1:54.

12. Risser, *Hermeneutics and the Voice of the Other*, 94, with reference to Gadamer, *Truth and Method*, 362.

anticipated or expected (cf. 1 Cor 2:9), it is describing something that not only relates to how God may appear or become manifest in the world, but it is also about a feature of the human experience of the world.

Experience in this sense is then conditioned by a mode of relating to the world that is open to being corrected by and changed by the other. Hermeneutical experience (or revelatory experience, for that matter) does not consume that which is experienced, but allows instead the one who experiences to have his or her world expanded and opened up to something new that was not there previously in the same manner, or could be anticipated or fully controlled by the expectations in our already established relation to the world.

If we try to explicate these lines of reasoning with regard to the resurrection, we can say that in being open to new experiences, one can develop the capacity to re-frame one's life based on experiences such as those that led to the belief in it. Such re-framing is based on abductions that employ other contexts of interpretation than those that one had access to beforehand. Thus, to accept the *relative indeterminacy* of how one understands the features of the world is, simultaneously, to be open to experiencing the new, and it may also include (but need not, of course) the possibility that God can reveal Godself and that God can resurrect Jesus from the dead.

Abduction and its Relation to Experience

The lack of a directly accessible experiential reference in the case of the claim about the resurrection means that we have to see the claim that Jesus has risen as the result of *an abductive interpretation*. It results from an inference that is not necessary (deductive), but also not inductive, since there are no obvious experientially based parallels (although there are potential parallels in the literature[13]). No one has experienced that someone is resurrected from the dead. Hence, the inferences we can make on other topics that we try to understand are not in a similar way possible here.

This being said, however, there is nothing inferior in abductive reasoning: it is something we do all the time based on previous experiences and by engaging the different interpretative frameworks at our disposal. The challenge with regard to the resurrection, though, is that there are no previous and no later experiences accessible that allow us to make similar inferences,

---

13. The question about literary parallels will nevertheless not occupy us here, and accordingly, we make a decision already here about which context of interpretation is more relevant than others.

presupposing that this is something we already know something about, and therefore can fit into already existing frames of interpretation.

We need to stress from the outset that when we talk about the resurrection of Jesus, we enter a context in which *abductive reasoning is the only possible*. However, abductive reasoning operates on two levels: it is displayed in how the biblical authors engage their interpretative resources in order to deal with the experiences of the empty tomb and the appearances of Jesus, and it operates in the decisions that we, as contemporary interpreters of the reports (and their inherent abductive reasoning), make when we try to make sense of these reports. In both cases, decisions are made and operate against the backdrop of the interpreter's background beliefs (as these are expressed in their interpretative frameworks). To pretend otherwise is to ignore that we are here faced with a hermeneutical task that implies far more than just asking "what happened"—it opens for questions about *why* something happened, the *conditions* for the reported events, and finally, about what it can mean today—if it means something at all. This is one of the reasons why the example above about a camera recording is not very helpful, because none of these questions can be answered by mere observation.

Abduction is different from both *deduction* (inferring from a generic premise to statements about singular instances) in which nothing is contained in the conclusion that is not already present in the premise, and *induction* (inferring from singular cases to a generic statement). When carried out correctly, the first is always necessarily correct (under the condition that the premise is true). In inductive cases, the inference can always run the risk of being proven wrong due to later experience: not so by making a false inference, but by adding new cases (singular premises) to those that already function as warrants, in a way that jeopardizes the general inference. Thus, inductive inferences are always only about what we can infer due to our (plural) experiences *so far*. In this connection, it is important to note that what we call natural laws are based in induction, although they may in turn also provide a basis for deductive reasoning in which one infers about what would be likely to expect given that experiences are conform with what has hitherto happened.

However, in ordinary life, our experiences are normally of neither of these kinds. Abductive reasoning builds on previous experience, but is not strictly inductive or deductive, as it is mostly about understanding what happens in the present and with regard to the phenomenon in front of us, without the intent of making more generic statements or explicate how what we experience falls under an explanatory category we have established already.

The obvious way to interpret the claim about the resurrection is to see it as a case of abductive reasoning, also *called the inference to the (possibly) best explanation.*[14] It is not an event that falls under an already established category about which we can know something for sure, and it is not an event similar to others, which would justify that we could infer from it that "this is a case of resurrection." Hence, our analysis so far suggests that the resurrection is both unexperienced and unprecedented.

The *Stanford Encyclopedia of Philosophy* suggests that the best way to distinguish between induction and abduction is as follows:

> both are ampliative, meaning that the conclusion goes beyond what is (logically) contained in the premises (which is why they are non-necessary inferences), but in *abduction there is an implicit or explicit appeal to explanatory considerations,* whereas in induction there is not; in induction, there is only an appeal to observed frequencies or statistics.[15]

As we can see from this quote, the claim about the resurrection (hereafter: CR) would not fall under the category of induction for the reasons we have already suggested: there is, in this claim, no appeal to frequencies or statistical probabilities. There is, however, an implicit appeal to considerations that may explain the event, namely that it was God who raised Jesus from the dead, and that this explanation is what makes sense of the concomitant observations of Jesus and the empty tomb after his death.

At this point, it may be helpful to insert a consideration about how and why we trust people's testimony about events they have observed. It is relevant in the present context, since much of present historical scholarship, also regarding biblical sources, "has developed methods that make it possible to extract knowledge from sources without relying on those sources as testimony." However, as Wahlberg points out, there is a danger in "historians trying to *identify* historical knowledge with knowledge extracted without reliance on testimony." He, therefore, questions the established distinction between testimony and evidence and suggests that one

---

14. Although different in the way they do develop their conceptions, both Pannenberg and N. T. Wright's approaches to the claim about the resurrection can be seen as aiming at making a decision in which such an inference is the best explanation. See further on an analysis of their positions in Part III below. Moreover, their positions could also be seen as relying on abductive inference, understood as "a search strategy which leads us, for a given kind of scenario, in a reasonable time to a most promising explanatory conjecture which is then subject to further test." Schurz, "Patterns of Abduction," 205.

15. Douven, "Abduction." Our italics.

instead speaks of forensic viz. testimonial evidence. Both, he claims, can be a basis for historical knowledge.[16]

However, it is necessary to add to Wahlberg's point here that forensic and testimonial evidence both rely on abduction. In the case of forensic evidence, it depends on the abductions made by the investigator, whereas in the case of testimonial evidence, it relies on the abductions of the witness. However, there is more to say on this matter. As the *Stanford Encyclopedia* points out, trust in other people's testimony also rests on abductive reasoning. Normally, we assume that "'[t]he best explanation for why the informant asserts that P is normally that . . . he believes it for duly responsible reasons and . . . he intends that I shall believe it too,' which is why we are normally justified in trusting the informant's testimony."[17]

The most commonly used interpretation of abductive inferences in present use is the one we have presented above, meaning inference to the best (possible, accessible) explanation. The two words inserted in brackets here are not arbitrary, but they suggest significant qualifiers: to assess what is a possible explanation will always be dependent on the background beliefs held by the one who makes the inference. To speak of accessible explanations is a qualifier that suggests that we usually make abductive inferences based on the explanatory resources we already have at hand. However, to speak *only* of abductive inferences as relying on accessible explanations would mean that there would be no chances for coming up with *new* and original explanations to those hitherto in use. Hence, part of the discussions taking place in a scientific context is about the conditions for either employing established (accessible) explanatory strategies to the *explanandum*, or for introducing a new *explanans* to the phenomenon in question.[18]

---

16. Wahlberg, *Revelation as Testimony*, 175. It should be noted that the present discussion is an illustration of how these two types of evidence works hand in hand: we would not be able to speak about the resurrection unless there had been witnesses that made abductive inferences about it, but we are also trying to assess how the elements that constitute the resurrection faith can be assessed as forensic evidence as well, i.e., as evidence that is probable also independent of the witnesses. This being said, however, it is also important to acknowledge that the whole discussion about resurrection is not only dependent on the credibility of the witnesses; Ingolf Dalferth is probably correct when he identifies the core problem of the belief in the resurrection as not something that has to do with the credibility of the witnesses; it is the *content* of the claim that makes it difficult, namely that God raised Jesus from the dead. Cf. Dalferth, "Volles Grab, Leerer Glaube?," 388.

17. See Douven, "Abduction." To this can be added that "Testimony, rightly understood, invites trust by its very nature. An appropriate degree of trust is thus an epistemic virtue." Wahlberg, *Revelation as Testimony*, 172, with reference to Bauckham, *Jesus and the Eyewitnesses*, 478.

18. It can be added to the above considerations that inference to the best available

C. S. Peirce, who will occupy us in the following, introduces a further distinction that may be of help when we try to understand the role of abduction in how humans handle their experiences. In his view, abduction operates in two different contexts, both of which are important to know about, but also to keep separate, concerning the discussion about the resurrection. Hence, the inference to the best explanation as discussed above belongs in the *context of justification* of a given claim. However, Peirce sees abduction at work also in what we can call *the context of discovery*. Whereas the first context is the one concerned with the assessment of theories, the latter is "the stage of inquiry in which we try to generate theories which may then later be assessed."[19]

For Peirce, "[a]bduction is the process of forming explanatory hypotheses. It is the only logical operation which introduces any new idea."[20] This statement is important since it means that abduction is the only way in which we can gain any new knowledge. The other ways of inferring are at work in later stages than in the context of discovery: "deduction helps to derive testable consequences from the explanatory hypotheses that abduction has helped us to conceive, and induction finally helps us to reach a verdict on the hypotheses, where the nature of the verdict is dependent on the number of testable consequences that have been verified."[21] Thus, abductions cannot be reduced to inductions, because inductions cannot introduce new concepts or conceptual models; they merely transfer them to new instances. Abductions, on the other hand, can introduce new concepts,[22] and this point is not without bearings for the range of interpretative options when one considers the experiences of the empty tomb and the appearances of Jesus after his death. The claim that "God raised Jesus from the dead" is an obvious example that introduces something new that is not included in the mere statement about what could be observed and serve as an explanation for these observations. To understand the abductive process that leads to the claim about the resurrection helps us to understand how the disciples were reacting to the elements observed. They were not so much concerned with developing a

---

explanation may not be good enough: "Nobody knows all possible explanations for a given phenomenon, and therefore, what one really has instead of an IBE [inference to the best explanation] is an inference to the best available explanation, in short an IBAE." Nevertheless, "the best available explanation is not always good enough to be rationally acceptable. If a phenomenon is novel and poorly understood, then one's best available explanation is usually a pure speculation." Schurz, "Patterns of Abduction," 203.

19. See the appendix "Peirce on Abduction" in Douven, "Abduction."
20. Peirce, *Collected Papers* 5:172.
21. "Peirce on Abduction" in Douven, "Abduction."
22. Schurz, "Patterns of Abduction," 202.

scientific theory that could be assessed later (context of justification) as with the attempt to form a hypothesis that could make sense of their experiences (context of discovery). If we understand the claim "He is risen" in this way, we see that it is the result of an abduction that has led to the hypothesis that is intended to make sense of what happened. We can do this quite independently of how we later try to assess the warrants for this hypothesis—which then would be to relate it to a context of justification.[23]

Induction and abduction both aim at extending our present knowledge beyond observation but do so in different respects. Whereas induction infers something about the future course of events as they may be without our intervention, "abductions serve the goal of inferring something about the unobserved causes or explanatory reasons of the observed events."[24]

From what has been said so far, it should be clear that abduction is at work in different ways in the set-up of an explanation. Schurz classifies abductions along three different, although interdependent lines of reasoning:

1. Along the kind of *hypothesis* that is abduced, i.e., that is produced as a conjecture,

2. Along the kind of *evidence* that the abduction intends to explain, and

3. According to the *beliefs* or *cognitive mechanisms* that drive the abduction.[25]

If we apply these distinctions to the claims about Jesus as resurrected by God from the dead, the main claim serves here as the hypothesis and the visions and observations as the evidence in need of explanation. The beliefs that cause the interpretation presuppose that there is a God, that this God has the power to do what is claimed, and that God has good reasons for doing so. We shall see in our analysis of the different theological approaches to the resurrection in the following chapters how these distinctions may prove useful for analytic purposes.

In his thorough analysis of different kinds of abduction, G. Schurz identifies one of the kinds as "Unobservable-fact abduction." This type of abduction fits well with the claims about the resurrection. He writes:

> The typical case of unobservable-fact abductions are historical-fact abductions, in which the abduced fact is unobservable because it is located in the distant past. The abduced fact may also

23. The latter procedure is what N. T. Wright does when he discusses the sufficient and necessary conditions for the claim that Jesus is risen in part V of his extensive treatment of the topic. See Wright, *Resurrection of the Son of God*.

24. See the appendix "Peirce on Abduction" in Douven, "Abduction."

25. Schurz, "Patterns of Abduction," 205.

be unobservable in principle, because it is a theoretical fact [. . .] Historical-fact abductions are of obvious importance for all historical sciences.[26]

Historians conjecture explanations for their observations abductively, based on their accessible frameworks of interpretation. Although their explanatory hypothesis cannot be directly verified by observations, it does lead to a search for further empirical consequences that follow from the abduced conjecture plus background knowledge. When or if it is possible to verify further findings on this basis, the abductive conjecture is confirmed.[27]

Schurz thereby points to how hypotheses based on abduction need to be confirmed by observations and experiences that can be interpreted as such confirmations, and that the hypotheses also need such confirmation in order not to be merely speculative. There are nevertheless two points to be made about his reasoning on this point: Firstly, we need to note that the confirmation of the conjecture is always preliminary. Secondly and concomitantly, it implies that there can be observations and/or experiences that do not confirm the conjecture, and which call for its revision. An obvious example of this would be if someone were able to find a body that could be identified as Jesus from Nazareth. Thus, abductions are subject to the same criteria for falsification as other conjectures.[28]

The Semiotic Approach: Abduction at Work

Let us consider the reported appearances or visions of Jesus and the observation of the empty tomb. From a *semiotic* perspective, both these instances (hereafter abridged VJ, alternatively AJ and ET) will have to be interpreted in a specific way in order to make a claim about the resurrection (CR). From the perspective of inferences, the relations between these elements are established by abduction. Abduction and semiotic processes are two sides of the same coin: *The three elements we speak about here (ET, VJ, CR) are all the result of semiotic processes*, i.e., processes where something is interpreted as a sign of something for someone. Semiotic processes constitute, connect, transform, and engage signs in order to exchange information within and between different living beings. Humans are referred to such processes to interpret the experiences they have and to orient

---

26. Schurz, "Patterns of Abduction," 209.
27. Schurz, "Patterns of Abduction," 209.
28. Cf. for further on verification and falsification Popper, *Conjectures and Refutations*.

themselves. Andrew Robinson summarizes his interpretation of Peirce's semiotic along the following lines:

> Peirce suggested that signs consist of a relation between three elements: a sign-vehicle (sometimes referred to as the *representamen*, or simply the sign), which stands for an object, and to which a response may be made by an interpretant. The sign (or at least the interpreted sign) is thus a triadic relation. The sign-vehicle does not signify anything in itself, but is able to signify something (an object) to the extent that its relation to the object is such that an interpreting entity or agent may make a purposeful response to the sign, where the fulfillment of that purpose depends on a certain relation between the sign-vehicle and the object.[29]

An observation, as a sign, does not itself contain any fully determined meaning, and moreover, the meaning it has (as a sign) can be quite different depending on its actual use and the context in which it is employed. This point is not very controversial. Usually, it is *conventions* that establish the meanings of words. We need to keep this in mind, as it means that everything that functions as a sign (and that would, in fact, mean most "things") relies on conventions for its meaning or significance. It is against this backdrop that we can understand how unconventional language (metaphors) may also establish new meanings, as, e.g., in the notion of the resurrected crucified.

Common participation in common semiotic practices constitutes the conventions in which we agree about the use of signs. Often, the fact that there are already some established contexts for use and interpretation of signs makes it easier for us to engage signs. E.g., we use the sign "university" in many different contexts, although what constitutes a university is continuously under discussion. There are nevertheless some parallels or elements of family-resemblance that can make this easier for us.[30] More important here is nevertheless the fact that the conventional character that constitutes semiotic practices points to the dynamic character of religious interpretations of experiences in general: the dynamics that characterize semiotic processes also pertains to religious activity. This dynamic element is among the features that contribute to the relative semiotic indeterminacy of the events that constitute the basis for the claim about the resurrection.

---

29. Robinson, *God and the World of Signs*, 17–18.
30. On the notion of family-resemblance, including some of its historical background before Wittgenstein's more extensive introduction of it in modern philosophy, see Sluga, "Family Resemblance," 1–21.

It follows from the above that a sign's significance (what it signifies) is not given. Hence, we can speak about the relative semiotic indeterminacy of the events that constitute the claim for the resurrection, and even about the relative semiotic indeterminacy of the CR itself—as it can be interpreted in different ways, with different types of theological significance. It is not only a question about a possible empirical "fact," but also about in what context to interpret it so that it is given a specific theological significance.

Peirce's fundamental understanding of semiotics consists of a threefold system of "categories," which he calls Firstness, Secondness, and Thirdness. He sees these categories as interlinked, as irreducible, and as fundamental to understanding the process of semiosis.

> The First is that whose being is simply in itself, not referring to anything nor lying behind anything. The Second is that which is what it is by force of something to which it is second. The Third is that which is what it is owing to things between which it mediates and which it brings into relation to each other.[31]

Firstness can never be grasped or described adequately, Peirce holds. It is only present and immediate, so as not to be second to a representation. On the other hand, the category of Secondness is one that involves otherness or difference, as it "is precisely that which cannot be without the first." Here we can see the relevance of this analysis for the present topic immediately. Secondness "meets us in such facts as Another, Relation, Compulsion, Effect, Dependence, Independence, Negation, Occurrence, Reality, Result. A thing cannot be other, negative, or independent, without a first to or of which it shall be other, negative, or independent."[32]

It is worth noting here that when something is approached in its character as "second," it points to something else (First) which is not experienced, but to which the second points in its capacity as dependent, and in relation. Hence, when ET and VJ are seen as elements of "Secondness," they are so in relation to the Firstness which is not accessible, but which is articulated in CR as an abductive inference (thus CR is also an instance of Secondness, which presupposes the inaccessible Firstness as its condition). Thus, the three elements that constitute the cluster that is the warrant for the Christian belief in the resurrection are all instances of Secondness. It becomes clear that both the appearances and the observation of the empty tomb are instances of Secondness that require abductive reasoning in order to form a statement like "He is risen!" What is more, this statement

---

31. Peirce et al., *Essential Peirce*, 1:248.
32. Robinson, *God and the World of Signs*, 23.

cannot be made unless there is someone for whom these elements appear as a warrant for that statement (Thirdness, see below). In other words: *the semiotic process that leads to this statement or claim (CR) is one that is based on inference, not on observation of fact.* Thus, the Secondness of this claim is not constituted by instances similar to those of the empty tomb or the appearances of Jesus after his death.

However, the understanding of facts as having a specified character, and thereby relating to them as expressions of Secondness, requires what Peirce calls Thirdness. Thirdness is the mediator who engages in the world as a world of signs and thereby orients herself using signs that can denote what kinds of Secondness are at hand. For Peirce, Thirdness "comprises everything whose being consists in active power to establish connections between different objects."[33] It is this power that comes to the fore in abductive inference.

Now, how these abductions are made depend not only on the capacity to make such inferences but also on the resources that are accessible for making them. As we have already suggested, the amount of knowledge one has at hand, as well as one's background beliefs and the experiences of past personal history may all contribute such resources. Hence, abduction depends on historical and contextual conditions, and cannot be seen as independent of these.

From all of this follows that mediation of meaning is an activity dependent on the human being's relation to a world that she understands to be something specific. It is only possible if that which is First is mediated as Secondness for someone (Thirdness). In other words, what presents itself to us as humans in the world is a world that is mediated as something already—as signs of something—and we cannot get behind or beyond these mediations in order to relate directly to that which Peirce articulates by his category of Firstness. The theological significance of this point is that it helps us understand why we cannot think of God as an agent in a way that is similar to other agents in this world: God may be a name for a specific type of Firstness, the Firstness on which *everything ultimately depends, but which is not itself accessible.* How can we make such a claim?

If there is in all semiotic activity an element of Firstness that is only graspable through its manifestations in Secondness, it means that there is also inherent in all experience an element of transcendence—something that goes beyond the manifestations that are interpreted as something by someone. It is important to note that this transcendent dimension is not necessarily qualified as religious, but it means that there are common

---

33. Robinson, *God and the World of Signs*, 23.

reasons for arguing that transcendence is inherent in human experience—and not presupposed only by religiously inclined persons.

The abstract character of the above description notwithstanding, Peirce insists that all these categories are related to human experience, be it experiences of immediacy or mere presence (Firstness) or the "hard facts of reality" (Secondness). Robinson summarizes this point as follows: "while feeling is a manifestation of Firstness, and brute reaction is a manifestation of Secondness, intelligibility is a manifestation of the phenomenon of Thirdness."[34] It furthermore follows from his analysis that "the presence of one of the categories always carries with it the latent involvement of the others." In other words, to register what is present or going on is not simply a question of thinking but may involve the full range of human capacities for relating to the world, including the capacity to make abductive inferences.

Now, let us have a closer look at how to understand these abductive inferences. Abductive processes are active in two different ways: in C. S. Peirce's work, they belong to what theory of science calls the *context of discovery*; i.e., at the stage where we try to generate theories which may then later be assessed with regard to their validity in a context of justification.[35] To understand the process thus fits well with how we can see the disciples reacting to the elements observed: they were not so much concerned with developing a scientific theory that could be assessed later, as with the attempt to form a hypothesis that could make sense of their experiences. If we understand the claim "He is risen" in this way, we see that it is the result of an abduction that has led to the hypothesis that is intended to make sense of what happened. We can do this quite independent of how we later try to assess the warrants for this hypothesis—which then would be to relate it to a *context of justification*.[36] When it comes to the assessment of the biblical material, though, the distinction here made proves itself as having more analytic value than being something that can help us to distinguish between different materials.[37]

---

34. Robinson, *God and the World of Signs*, 26.

35. "Abduction is the process of forming explanatory hypotheses. It is the only logical operation which introduces any new idea" (Peirce, *Collected Papers* 5:172). Furthermore, abduction encompasses "all the operations by which theories and conceptions are engendered" (Peirce, *Collected Papers* 5:590).

36. The latter procedure is what N. T. Wright does when he discusses the sufficient and necessary conditions for the claim that Jesus is risen in part V of his extensive treatment of the topic. See Wright, *Resurrection of the Son of God*.

37. As we suggest below, even the biblical material seems to have both contexts in mind in the reports of what happened after Easter.

We can immediately apply the distinction between the contexts of discovery and justification when we consider the initial experiences that are the warrants for the resurrection. In order to see the appearances of Jesus as experiences of him, and thereby recognize him in a way that allowed them to use the notion *revelation*, the first-hand witnesses had to employ the accessible context of discovery that they had at hand. However, as soon as one moves from an assessment of the experiences to an assessment of their witnesses, and the content they convey, and thereby to a third-person perspective, one moves increasingly towards a context of justification.

At this point, it is important to point to the fact that the process taking place is not appearing out of thin air. We need to assume that the instance that Peirce calls "Thirdness"—the instance for whom the Secondness is interpreted as the result of resurrection—in principle have access to interpretative resources that allow for the development of the claim. However, again we need to point to the fact that the context that makes the interpretation possible is uncertain and under discussion. This complicates the matter significantly. Let us try to show what is at stake here by suggesting the decisions to be made, and by whom.

The disciples who observed the empty tomb or the appearances of Jesus had to find something in their own tradition and their cultural context that could help them develop this hypothesis. They have to employ a context of discovery that helps them to interpret their experiences, and thereby recognize what happens to them.[38] *The biblical authors* then had to decide not only which of the above interpretations to report, but they also had to address other possible explanations (that someone stole the body, Matt 27:64) and more deliberate theological elaborations about what took place. They still employ a context of discovery, but the New Testament also shows increasing signs that the claim about the resurrection must also be addressed within a context of justification.

The present reader who is interested in the historical question must decide which of the above historical contexts to select or emphasize and not, concerning their relevance: e.g., the instances of other dead people rising, and the visions of angels at the grave may be considered as literary additions, whereas other elements may not. Similarly, the context of interpretation may differ: some will point to Roman legends of risen gods, others to Ezekiel's visions of the valley of the dead, some may consider the appearances of Jesus as a parallel to what is often reported about such visions of

---

38. As Dirk-Martin Grube has recently argued, their interpretation thereby also implies a "paradigm shift" in comparison with what their previous understandings meant. Thus, it is more than a mere application of previously established contexts of understanding. See Grube, "Christian Theology," 178–93.

the dead,[39] whereas others may dismiss these as irrelevant, etc. All of this may be a part of decisions about the *context of justification* for the claim and is considered predominantly thus, although some of these approaches may also point to different contexts of discovery.

Finally, *the present critical reader* may also discuss the validity of the abductive inference in a contemporary context of justification. Much of the modern discussion of the resurrection is located in this area. The contemporary reader cannot ignore the fact that in the present context, it is hard to justify the claim "He is risen" with reference to the present stand of scientific knowledge.[40] She is then presented with different options:

a. She can accept this as a case. The present stand of scientific inquiry is taken to be a valid context of justification that makes the inference from the empty tomb and the appearances to the claim invalid. It can be done without rejecting the validity of the witnessed experiences of the empty tomb or the appearances as such. However, the central abduction made by the disciples and the biblical authors is then dismissed. The consequence of this is either that one concludes that Christianity is wrong altogether, or one has to make some hermeneutical moves in order to make sense of these stories without maintaining their content as historically adequate. The latter is the position that forms a basic part of Bultmann's approach to the resurrection.

b. She can adopt a strategy that counters how the present context of scientific justification is set up and argue along lines that suggest that there is no scientifically valid argument for saying that such things cannot happen in principle. Then, the possibility for the validity of the

---

39. Most strongly, this last point is developed in Allison, *Resurrecting Jesus*.

40. This point is also noted by Alkier and Moffitt, when they write that "Theories of accommodation, rationalism, and demythologizing posit different strategies for explaining the miraculous element of miracle stories. Nevertheless, they come together at this point—they agree with the scientific perspective regarding the possibility, or better, impossibility, of miracles. They do not, however, want to exclude them from the canon. They try instead to understand the miracle stories as theological messages that have to be decoded. The question, therefore, shifts from a scientific discussion to one of hermeneutics. The real issue for these interpreters becomes how one can understand miracle accounts as stories. Their goal is to produce readings of these (embarrassing) biblical narratives that can justifiably and simultaneously be held as true within the modern scientific and philosophical worldview, and as true for the Christian faith, which is based upon biblical texts. This hermeneutical conundrum is solved by appealing to a particular philosophical theory of history—the theory of development" (Alkier and Weissenrieder, *Miracles Revisited*, 319). In the following analysis, we analyze in more detail what this means.

claim "He is risen" is still maintained, but not necessarily justified. It is possible to read Pannenberg's position to be along such lines.

c. She can also argue that the resurrection, given the accessible evidence, is the best explanation of what the New Testament reports and that the statement "He is risen!" is in accordance with the best scholarly procedures we have for claiming this.[41] We can read N. T. Wright along these lines.

In all the three cases, the contemporary critical reader has to decide in what ways it may still be possible to interpret the stories about the resurrection as theologically significant. This significance is not a given but depends on the complicated relationship that the individual theologian has to the tradition, her community, and her background and skills.[42]

So far, we see that the abductive processes that lie behind a theological approach to the resurrection display what we have called the relative semiotic indeterminacy. Three different elements strengthen this indeterminacy. a) The assumed lack of parallels to this event, which may also include the sudden and unexpected experience for the disciples amid bereavement and shock that makes it difficult to establish—immediately—a clear interpretative context for the experiences. b) The multitude of material that can be used as the interpretative context in order to determine the significance of the instances of Secondness that is interpreted as evidence for the resurrection. c) The variety of decisions that has to be made among these about what their significance is for an actual someone who interprets them (Thirdness).

---

41. Gerhard Schurz's analysis of the different conditions for abduction seems to support this strategy. According to him, "the crucial function of a pattern of abduction . . . consists in its function as a search strategy which leads us, for a given kind of scenario, in a reasonable time to a most promising explanatory conjecture which is then subject to further test." See Schurz, "Patterns of Abduction," 205.

42. For more on this matter, see Henriksen, *Christianity as Distinct Practices*, 91–93. Thus, any notion of the resurrection implies a complicated relationship between the unique and singular on the one hand, and the common and generic on the other hand. What marks the resurrection is that as a saturated phenomenon, it presents us with a multitude of different contexts of both interpretation and of justification (and not), and the diversities, tensions and conflicts between these make it not only a contested topic, but also one that displays a certain semiotic indeterminacy, since it is not clear in what "part of the encyclopedia" it should be placed. The metaphor is intended: if the resurrection took place, it has bearings on many different parts of this encyclopedia, and requires a rewriting of several entries.

On Stefan Alkier's Peircean Interpretation of the Resurrection

There are two things that need to be underscored when we address the stories or texts about the resurrection from a semiotic perspective. First, a sign can only represent an object *in a certain respect*. No sign can represent the object in all respects, but only from a specific point of view.[43] Second, and concomitantly, this means that the relative indeterminacy mentioned above is something that also must be seen in relation to how these different aspects contribute to the whole, and thereby stabilize each other.

Thus, what we have called the relative semiotic indeterminacy in the previous section does not mean that the results of the semiotic process are arbitrary. Stefan Alkier, who has employed Peirce's semiotics for his analysis of texts about the resurrection, develops this semiotics further by employing Eco's notion of the *encyclopedia*. The reason is that a sign "needs at least two correlations in order to function: it must belong to a presently perceptible sign complex and at the same time to a culture as the totality of its virtual sign complexes." Alkier names the concretely perceptible sign complex the *universe of discourse*, whereas he calls the comprehensive cultural sign complex the *encyclopedia*.[44] These two instances would together provide us with an alternative articulation and specification of what we above have called contexts of interpretation.

Before we continue the presentation of Alkier's semiotic approach to the resurrection texts, we should note that what he calls the encyclopedia also comprises what hitherto has been called frameworks of interpretation. It is reasonable to see the encyclopedia as the instance that comprises all knowledge, and therefore also all the different frameworks we have at hand (accessible) for our interpretation of these texts as sign complexes. Hence, he contributes to the further theoretical development of what has been presented earlier.

The encyclopedia "encompasses the conventionalized knowledge of a given society and thus transcends the boundaries of individual sign complexes set by the concept of the universe of discourse. Every instance of sign production and sign reception must reach back to an encyclopedia of culturally conventionalized knowledge." Furthermore, we need to consider the encyclopedia as virtual because we cannot grasp it in its full complexity.[45]

---

43. Cf. Alkier, *Reality of the Resurrection*, 206.

44. Alkier, *Reality of the Resurrection*, 206.

45. Alkier, *Reality of the Resurrection*, 207. On the other hand, and nevertheless, "Every instance of sign production and sign reception must reach back to an encyclopedia of culturally conventionalized knowledge." Alkier, *Reality of the Resurrection*, 207.

Whereas the encyclopedia represents the virtual totality of possible and accessible knowledge, the universe of discourse of a given sign complex (text) cannot only be seen in relation to the encyclopedia but must be seen in relation to the world that this text presupposes or sets forth. This world determines to what extent a text or a statement can be said to have a plausible function.[46] This point can be seen as an expression of the fact that we always approach a text within a specific context of use, with regard to a certain respect, and not against the backdrop of *all* knowledge and all contexts, as that would make it impossible to determine what meaning or significance a text would have with regard to our purposes for approaching it.

Given the above, it becomes clear why Peirce distinguishes between the immediate, the dynamic, and the final interpretant:

- The immediate interpretant is the indeterminate, vague connection between two *relata*, which determines these as Sign and Object. Hence, the process of semiosis is engendered.
- The dynamic interpretant is what is drawn from the Sign by a given Individual Interpreter in a specific case of interpretation, where the sign is interpreted as expressing something in a certain respect.
- "The Final Interpretant is the ultimate effect of the Sign, so far as it is intended or destined from the character of the Sign, being more or less of a habitual and formal nature."[47]

It is the two first interpretants on this list that are given in every semiotic process. The notion of the final interpretant is more a regulative idea that expresses how a true interpretation offers the most comprehensive meaning of the word. "Its truth consists in the fact that it represents the dynamic Object in every respect." Accordingly, Alkier sees the strength of Peirce's semiotic theory "in the fact that it teaches one to conceive of the multiplicity of interpretations as necessary stations on the way to truth without propagating arbitrariness." However, such truth can only be achieved by a community on a long-term basis and effort.[48]

The relative openness on the level of the instances of Secondness implies that the dynamic object or interpretant that engenders the semiotic process cannot be identified as a revelation in any positivistic sense. Instead, the semiotic perspective that includes the category of Thirdness implies that "the resurrected Crucified One was conceived, at least by Paul as one who

---

46. Thus, Peirce seems to consider this relation in analogy with a correspondence theory of truth.

47. Peirce, here from Alkier, *Reality of the Resurrection*, 207.

48. Alkier, *Reality of the Resurrection*, 207.

had such an experience and expressed it in general as the final Interpretant." From this Alkier draws two important conclusions regarding the interpretation of Paul's experience of the risen Jesus:

> (1) The conviction concerning the resurrection of the Crucified One rests pre-critically on an experience that precipitated a sign process, and is emotionally anchored in this experience. (2) The conviction concerning the resurrection of the Crucified One is a conclusion of an abductive act, which co-originally [*gleichursprünglich*] assigns an immediate Interpretant to the perception of the experience of a Something and then determines that Interpretant with the dynamic Interpretant, "Jesus lives."[49]

Thus, Alkier contributes further to what we have developed in the above line of reasoning. He demonstrates that it is possible to use the tools that Peirce presents for a concrete reconstruction of the semiotic processes that led to the CR. Furthermore, the relative indeterminacy of the experiences that led to CR is displayed in the report about how Peter related to his observation of the empty tomb: for Peter, this was not considered a proof of the resurrection, although it made him wonder. Similar traits we find in the Gospel of Luke. Alkier sees Luke as "the one who is most strongly interested in an empirically verifiable proof of the resurrection, and again and again depicts the materially somatic dimension of the gospel and also of the resurrection of Jesus." Hence, he "regards the rational acceptance of the message of the resurrection as an occasion to examine it empirically."[50] However, as Alkier shows, the empirical approach is not sufficient to achieve the *immediate* plane of Firstness that can cause faith.

The theoretical reasons Alkier has for seeing the empirical approach as one that can lead to faith is that this approach relies on a dynamic interpretation in which the interpretant is determined in a certain respect, and hence does not appear in its immediacy. This immediacy is only given as *Firstness*.

As we see it, Alkier thereby uses Peirce's categories to make a specific theological point: faith is not grounded in interpretation of facts, but in the immediate relation to that which presents itself as Firstness and *then* causes further probing. Faith thus has an emotional component that goes beyond the mere cognitive. Alkier sees this point depicted in Luke's notion of the "burning hearts" of those traveling to Emmaus. He holds that the story about these men shows that in order for faith to come about, an emotional reaction and a hermeneutical key to interpreting the empirical elements in such a way

---

49. Alkier, *Reality of the Resurrection*, 211.
50. Alkier, *Reality of the Resurrection*, 213.

that they can engender faith are required. "These are encountered, however, precisely in the 'burning hearts' of the disciples on the road to Emmaus, who burn precisely at the moment when the Resurrected One speaks with them and 'opened the Scriptures' to them (24:32)."[51] Alkier continues his analysis of the Lukean material on the basis of Peirce's categories thus:

> Luke is so very interested in the empirical-material dimension, thus in the phenomenon of Secondness, that he very much precludes the misunderstanding of a hermeneutical automatism of empirical phenomena. The empty tomb can be understood at best as a sign of an event given to provoke thought, which breaks through the limits of the phenomena of Secondness. Even in Luke the body of the Resurrected One no longer obeys the laws of bodies of flesh, blood, and bone. *The truth of the message of the resurrection, however, according also to Luke, is to be felt and then interpreted only within the framework of the Scripture.* In any case, in his Acts of the Apostles Luke will employ the tomb no more as proof, indeed not once more, even for the sake of stimulating thought.[52]

Alkier here, in fact, develops an argument in which the category of Thirdness (i.e., the actual interpreter and her *reaction* to the perceived) is of crucial importance for the faith in the resurrection. At this point, it is important to distinguish between what he claims are points inherent in his reconstruction of what the New Testament says, and what can count as the insights of semiotics in general. As for the New Testament, he writes:

> According to the Scriptures of the New Testament, the foundation of Easter faith consists in a spontaneous feeling of truth driven by phenomena that cannot be reduced to the perception of the recipients. Easter faith is fundamental and is a phenomenon of Firstness, a pre-critical feeling of truth, before any critical examination and before any reflective encyclopedic connections, which is established [*sich einstellen*] as the dynamic Interpretant of a perception of something. According to the New Testament, Easter faith is not to be explained as an interior psychological construction that compensates for the cognitive dissonance between the experience of saving communion with Jesus in the Jesus movement before his death and then the experience of his horrific end through Jesus' execution.

---

51. Alkier, *Reality of the Resurrection*, 213.
52. Alkier, *Reality of the Resurrection*, 213. Emphasis added.

Easter faith is first and foremost the spontaneous answer to an overwhelming phenomenon.[53]

Thus, we see in this quote that Alkier reconstructs the concerns of the New Testament in accordance with the theoretical apparatus we have developed so far. However, he does more: he points to how Easter faith is a response to an *overwhelming* phenomenon. We need to highlight this point since this notion can be developed further using Marion's notion of the *saturated phenomenon* that we will develop later. This notion can help us to elaborate further both the contents of the experience of Firstness beyond an emotional response, and the relative indeterminacy, or rather, the richness of interpretative options on the level of Secondness (the dynamic interpretants) that the Easter experiences contain.

Alkier's approach to the resurrection thereby takes a theological turn which implies that he wants to avoid an empiricist approach to the resurrection as the basis for faith. Accordingly, he also underscores how it is not possible to determine the instances of Secondness like ET and VJ as final proofs for the resurrection.[54]

Empty Tomb (ET) and Appearances of Jesus/Visions of Jesus (AJ/VJ) as Religiously Significant: Ann Taves

Why and how is it that the experiences of the empty tomb and the visions of Jesus after his death came to be interpreted as religiously significant? Ann Taves has developed a theory about experiences that are given religious significance that can help us further in understanding how this can be the case.

The semiotic perspective presented above can substantiate Taves's theory, as her way of describing processes of "setting apart" experiences as religious implies that at a fundamental level one needs to interpret something *as something*. She holds that what one considers as religious is related to specific semiotic processes that identify specific features, events, or experiences as such. Hence, it is hardly possible to argue that we can identify something as religious experiences *per se*, or *sui generis*. Either we have experiences with religion, or the frameworks we have identified enable us to have experiences *by* means of what is defined as religious, be it symbols, rituals, or specific events, etc. Thus, to identify something as a religious experience depends on contextual factors and our ability to identify them as such. Experientially based frameworks of interpretation

---

53. Alkier, *Reality of the Resurrection*, 214–15.
54. Cf. Alkier, *Reality of the Resurrection*, 217.

come into play here, as do the personal ability to relate the experiences to diverse contexts of practice. Accordingly, something appears to us to be religious because we deem it so.[55]

Taves addresses religion as an integrated part of different dimensions of human life.[56] It has bearings on the approach to the resurrections as well. Taves focuses on *experience* in a way that may also help us to develop further the argument in the present chapter. She does not think that a notion of religious experience as *sui generis* is very helpful,[57] but understands religious experience to be the result of how the human mind "is both shaped by and shapes socio-cultural processes,"[58] processes of which religions are part. Her deliberate focus on "experiences deemed religious" allows her to see religious experiences as existing on many levels, from the intrapersonal to the intergroup levels.

Taves does not define some experiences as essentially religious or separate from experiences in other realms of human experience.[59] Human ordering and activity set apart "the sacred" from everything else. The sacred can be understood only in contrast with the profane and, therefore, is not *essentially* possible to characterize as sacred, but can only be characterized thus from a *relational* point of view.[60] The difficulties in defining religious experiences drive Taves to turn the tables and suggest the following:

> Rather than abandon the study of experience, we should disaggregate the concept of "religious experience" and study the wide range of experiences to which religious significance has been attributed. If we want to understand how anything at all, including experience, becomes religious, we need to turn our attention to the processes whereby people sometimes ascribe the special characteristics to things that we (as scholars) associate with terms such as "religious," "magical," "mystical," "spiritual," et cetera. Disaggregating "religious experience" in this way will allow us to focus on the interaction between psychobiological, social, and cultural-linguistic processes in relation to carefully specified types of experiences sometimes considered religious

---

55. These points are nuanced further in the way Asle Eikrem treats religious experiences as something that cannot be *explicated* independent of religious discursive practices. See Eikrem, *Being in Religion*, 161–63, 207, 216–17.

56. Taves, *Religious Experience Reconsidered*. Her work is presented more extensively in Henriksen, *Religion as Orientation and Transformation*, 37–49.

57. Taves, *Religious Experience Reconsidered*, 18–19.

58. Taves, *Religious Experience Reconsidered*, xiii.

59. Cf. Taves, *Religious Experience Reconsidered*, 16.

60. Taves, *Religious Experience Reconsidered*, 16.

and to build methodological bridges across the divide between the humanities and the sciences.[61]

Taves distinguishes between ascriptions and attributions to "things" in ways that make us deem them religious.[62] Thereby, it becomes possible to focus on what people *do* when they characterize something as religious, spiritual, mystical, magical, superstitious, etc. It is something they do during "processes of meaning-making and valuation, in which people deem some things special and set them apart from others."[63] This point can be elaborated further with reference to Peirce's semiotic theory, which was presented above. In other words, humans make something in their world religious by attributing or ascribing religious significance to them in semiotic processes.

A crucial element in Taves's argument is the phrase "*set apart,*" which enables her to use a non-religious and more generic approach to the processes at work. It is when people *set something apart* and thereby identify it as *special in some way* that things are deemed religious. To set something apart allows us "to sort out who is deeming things religious or characterizing them as special and on what grounds."[64] Moreover, she argues that if "we situate the processes whereby people characterize things as religious, mystical, magical, and so forth within larger processes of meaning-making and valuation (singularization), we are better able to analyze the contestations over the meaning and value of particular things and the way that those things are incorporated into and perpetuated by larger socio-cultural formations, such as religious traditions and spiritual disciplines."[65] One of the advantages of this approach is that it allows for ethic, and not only for emic descriptions of the "things" in question, be they acts, agents, artifacts, experiences, etc.

The notions of *attribution and ascription* play a crucial role in Taves's argument. Attribution is used to explain something resulting from casual connections, whereas ascription refers to how things are perceived to hold specific qualities.[66] *Explanation*, as Taves uses it, probably is not to be understood only in a strictly scientific and causal sense, as most religious "explanations" refer to *explananda* that are not easily identifiable or controllable—they rely on abductively established presuppositions.

---

61. Taves, *Religious Experience Reconsidered*, 16.
62 Taves, *Religious Experience Reconsidered*, 9–10.
63. Taves, *Religious Experience Reconsidered*, 12.
64. Taves, *Religious Experience Reconsidered*, 12.
65. Taves, *Religious Experience Reconsidered*, 14.
66. Cf. Taves, *Religious Experience Reconsidered*, 19.

Taves's theory of attribution offers the possibility of defining religion via the generic term *specialness*. When one attributes a religious quality to something, one sets it apart from other things and makes it special. Beliefs, things, rites, etc., are designated in ways that shape a specific order and identify the elements from which religions are built.[67] For our purpose here, it is not necessary to go into detail about how, and in what ways, things are set apart as religious. The main point is that Taves shows how the religious emerges from practices that imply specific ways of ordering the world and that thereby provide the means for orientation when it comes to the experiences that befall us. Concerning the resurrection, the attribution of specialness to the experiences of the ET and AJ/VJ makes it possible to use these in ways that warrant the unique claim about Jesus's resurrection.

The things that stand out as special in religions can be identified as being primarily the *ideal* and the *anomalous*.[68] The notion of the ideal points to what something (state, person, action, etc.) should be, and it thereby provides a basis for orientation and possible transformation to achieve the ideal. Taves employs the notion of the anomalous for those experiences that are crucial for human orientation, and experiences in a world no longer perceived as unproblematic. It is possible to see the notion of the resurrection as expressing the ideal (the glorified crucified) and the anomalous (that which does not usually happen).

When Taves describes the ideal and the anomalous in more detail, she does it along lines that follow from how we can identify each as distinct types of singularity: both can be placed on a continuum from the ordinary to the special. Things stand out as special because they seem ideal, perfect, or complete. They may do so in a relative sense or, "if they are thought to approach an ultimate horizon or limit, they may signal an ideal in an absolute sense." In the latter case, as absolutes, they "are no longer on a continuum with limited things, however special such things might be, but are fully set apart."[69] In any case, such ideals, either absolute or relative, provide means of orientation that are vitally important for the fulfillment of human life, be it in a religious sense or not. Taves makes concrete how such an orientation is possible by listing examples of these ideals: true, real, good, beautiful, pure, natural, and bad—these are all words that orient human life, and they can also be transformed into absolutes. None of these words can be substituted by others in order to bear the same meaning, and moreover, they all carry meaning only in relation to specific situations and practices.

---

67. Cf. Taves, *Religious Experience Reconsidered*, 26–27.
68. Taves, *Religious Experience Reconsidered*, 28.
69. Taves, *Religious Experience Reconsidered*, 36.

Taves allows us to identify a further step in *how* that which is set apart may serve as a *religious* ascription. She suggests: "The chief feature of the fully set-apart absolute [. . .] is its (postulated) existence apart from human perception and imagination."[70] Thus, she points to the fundamental process in which something can take on an important function for religious orientation, despite its supra-empirical character. Hence, she explains implicitly how the conception of the resurrection can have such bearings on human life, even when it refers to a non-observable event.

Taves's description of the anomalous substantiates further the understanding of *what* is set apart and points to material that allows us to consider more carefully the realms of experience to which religious orientation and transformation are related. She claims that the anomalous is that which is strange, unusual, contrary to, or violating our expectations. Thus, anything can be anomalous. However, in our context, it is not hard to see that such a definition may also be applied to ET and AJ/VJ. However, it is not possible to define beforehand what belongs in this category.[71] The anomalous is not necessarily mystical but may be unusual natural events (comets, earthquakes, eclipses, and solar auras) and things with an unusual appearance ("monstrous" births, faces in clouds, lifelike rock formations).

Moreover, Taves lists "phenomena thought to exceed scientific explanation, such as extrasensory perception, apparitions, out-of-body and near-death experiences, spiritual possession, immunity to pain and heat, psychokinesis ('mind over matter'), poltergeists, miraculous healing, and contact with the dead" in this category, and thus, her theory immediately shows the relevance to the present study. She also points to psychological studies of "anomalous experience" that refer to "hallucinations, synesthesia, lucid dreaming, out-of-body and near-death experiences, psi-related (parapsychological) experiences, alien abduction, past-life awareness, unusual healing, and mystical experiences" as belonging to the category of the anomalous.[72]

When Taves states that "whether people consider something anomalous may be highly contextually dependent or it may not," it is not hard to agree. What people actually *know* plays a large role in shaping what people consider anomalous. Thus, the role of background beliefs and accessible frameworks for the interpretation of something as anomalous or not should not be ignored. Our understanding of it is also culture-dependent: "Some

---

70. Taves, *Religious Experience Reconsidered*, 36.
71. Taves, *Religious Experience Reconsidered*, 38.
72. Taves, *Religious Experience Reconsidered*, 39.

experiences, such as spirit possession, may be considered strange or unusual in one culture and not in another."[73]

Similar to *ideals*, "we can consider anomalous things as special, locating them somewhere on a continuum from ordinary to very special, without necessarily considering them so special that they are set apart with taboos against comparison and the like." What also is helpful in Taves's approach here is that she suggests that in discussions about anomalous things, we "can distinguish between anomalous events, places, objects, and experiences that do not suggest the presence of anomalous agents" on the one hand, and anomalous experiences of agency that suggest the presence of an agent on the other hand. The first type of experience displays similarities with ideal things, whereas the second type does not. She claims: "Just as qualities associated with ideal things can be absolutized and set apart, so, too, qualities associated with anomalous things can be reified and set apart." Furthermore, the terms employed for such setting apart are often "mystical" or "spiritual." Such descriptions of events, places, objects, or experiences may signal that the thing in question is ascribed special qualities that make it hard to compare to less special things. "People may use these terms to mark things *as belonging to another realm* or manifesting a different sort of energy or exemplifying a higher aspect of reality that is not just special, but so special that it cannot be compared with more ordinary things."[74]

As Taves points to, events, places, objects, and experiences can be characterized as mystical or spiritual, but this need not imply that they are experiences of an agent. This fact does not rule out, however, that "people may still attribute them to an agent if they believe that there are agents who can and do cause such things to occur." This point leads Taves to distinguish between things that are attributed to the action of an agent (things that people believe to be caused by an agent), and feelings, perceptions, and sensations suggestive of an agent.[75] In both cases, attributions may be at work. It is obvious how it is possible to apply her analysis to the experiences that constitute the backdrop for the claims about God's involvement in Jesus's resurrection.

***

The above considerations have given us an overview of some more theoretical and philosophical topics that are at work in contemporary

---

73. Taves, *Religious Experience Reconsidered*, 39.
74. Taves, *Religious Experience Reconsidered*, 40.
75. Taves, *Religious Experience Reconsidered*, 40–41.

discussions about the resurrection. In the following chapters, we will first present some of the most important (and diverse) approaches that we find in recent New Testament discourse about the resurrection, before we discuss the diverse systematic approaches to the topic. In the last chapter, we develop some more of the theological significance and implications that the topic of resurrection continues to entail.

Part II: The New Testament Discourses on Resurrection

Mapping the Present-Day Terrain

DEBATES ON HOW TO understand the implications of the resurrection claims, about Jesus and in general, have accompanied the church throughout times, and these debates are raised from within as well as from the outside.[1] It seems adequate to say that Rudolf Bultmann's existential and mythological interpretation has paved the way for present-day debates in a special way, whereby the resurrection of Jesus is seen as "Ausdruck der Bedeutsamkeit des Kreuzes."[2] The resurrection is to him a so-called *theologoumenon*. This approach implies that the resurrection of Jesus is itself a mode of *interpretation* of the importance and meaning of his crucifixion, assigning to it abiding significance. Resurrection and crucifixion are woven together in such a way that the first provides nothing but an interpretation of the second. From this follows that Jesus is risen in the act of *proclaiming* his abiding presence.[3] Thus, Bultmann provides a specific interpretation of the resurrection as a sign and integrates it in a distinct process of semiosis. Following in the wake of Bultmann, more recent scholarship has developed various strategies and arguments to come to terms with what the dictum "Jesus has been raised" really amounts to. The following does not aim at sketching a history of contributions, a research history so to say, but to lay out some of the most important arguments and interpretations launched. In

---

1. For a helpful survey, see Lehtipuu, *Debates over the Resurrection of the Dead*.

2. Bultmann, *Neues Testament und Mythologie*, 58. His view on the resurrection is presented on 57–64. His infamous dictum "Christus, der Gekreuzigte und Auferstandene, begegnet uns im Worte der Verkündigung, nirgens anders" is found here.

3. For a critical assessment of Bultmann's interpretation, see for example Fetzer, "Auferstanden ins Kerygma?," 93–110. See also the analysis of Bultmann in the next part of this book.

other words, we provide a typology or a grid which will be a companion and dialogue-partner throughout this book.

Tradition-Critical Considerations: Early is Best

Tradition-critical observations on New Testament texts aim at sifting the sources with regard to date and provenance, thus laying the foundation for a scheme of how things developed or came into being. It is very much about uncovering the *emergence* of this belief. This way of thinking is rooted in a fundamental insight shared by New Testament scholars, namely that there is a gap of time, amounting to some decades between the letters and the gospels. *In casu*, there is a time-span between 1 Corinthians 15, which is the first real engagement in our sources with the issue, and the Easter stories of the gospels. This allows for developments and embellishments, and interpreters seek the oldest version of faith in the resurrection of Jesus. Potentially, a tradition-critical search has a critical and deconstructive force: how we think about this phenomenon ought to be in accordance with the "original" versions of this faith, not the forms it later came to have. Tradition-critical considerations make a starting point for most scholars involved in this issue with a claim to be "biblical" in any sense of that term. We may illustrate such considerations by reference to Gerd Lüdemann, and more recently Andreas Lindemann. According to Lüdemann, as time went on "the traditions of the tomb and appearance were brought increasingly close together, so that the nature of the original appearance becomes almost unrecognizable. However, through Paul, we can gain some idea of the original event."[4] As for Lindemann, a scholar at home in the Bultmann legacy, his arguments help illuminate how tradition-critical reasoning may be used. Key questions are: What does it mean for how we should think about the resurrection that Paul, in citing from what is probably a pre-Pauline "creed," leaves out the empty tomb (1 Cor 15:3–5)? What are the consequences that the empty tomb is absent—and probably also unknown—from the outset?

Moreover, what are the consequences that Paul, when listing those to whom Jesus appeared after his death, includes his own Damascus experience (1 Cor 15:8–9)? His encounter with the Lord was a vision. Should this fact guide the interpretation of the appearances generally? Hence, a tradition-critical approach heaps up questions and paves the way for an adequate understanding of the resurrection of Jesus which takes its point of departure in the earliest evidence.[5]

---

4. Lüdemann, *Resurrection of Jesus*, 171–72.
5. Lindemann, "Resurrection of Jesus," 557–79.

Tradition-critical considerations are a prerequisite for taking on the debate on the resurrection of Jesus. Lindemann demonstrates one way of arguing, and he is by no means alone in urging a dichotomy between the appearance-traditions and the narrative empty tomb-tradition.[6] Likewise, Alan F. Segal argues that "the empty tomb is a Gospel innovation."[7] The fleshly resurrection is characteristic only of the gospels, not of Paul. By implication, there is no consensus in the New Testament on the resurrection of Jesus. In other words, sifting between traditions is urgent, as it provides a critical tool which paves the way for many possible outcomes concerning how the resurrection of Jesus is perceived. Both Lindemann and Segal agree that approaching this faith historically is a category mistake. An issue such as the empty tomb is a historical probability, and it amounts to a rationalism that runs contrary to the true nature of this faith to put it at risk by such probabilities. However, there can be no doubt that their tradition-critical analysis paves the way for *how* they conceive of this faith. In this way, historical analysis and theological concepts are being intertwined—a point we shall see is constantly emerging in the material we discuss in this book.

From this tradition-critical approach, we now turn to hermeneutical models of explanations. The types to be presented here are by no means exhaustive, and overlaps between them do appear. The idea that the resurrection of Jesus is a deliberate deception, like grave-robbery (Matt 27:62–66; cf. John 20:15) or sorcery or tricksters of some kind (Celsus; see Part II, the section Celsus—Gerd Lüdemann's Ancient Like-Mined?), is left out here as such explanations hardly bring anything to the hermeneutical task of coming to terms with the phenomenon, and represent attempts to overcome the semiotic indeterminacy of the texts by ignoring the message they convey. They are simply rejections of the phenomenon. The attempts we present in the following are those we can see as constructive because they present models whereby present-day debates orient themselves.

Psychological Attempts

Psychological explanations come in different fashions, often focussing on some kind of projection, either of guilt or grief. For example, Gerd Lüdemann points to Peter and Paul, two out of the three named persons in the oldest passage about the resurrection of Jesus (1 Cor 15:5, 7–8). Both had

---

6. Smith, *Revisiting the Empty Tomb* likewise traces the development of the Easter faith; more on his book in Part II, The Easter Narratives, sec. Two Independent Traditions?

7. Segal, "Resurrection," 132.

their reasons, albeit very different, to make up for previous sins towards Jesus. They found themselves in a psychological state prone to seek explanations of compensation for their guilt or grief. Peter denied him thrice, even if he showed himself to be the most courageous in advance. Their situation produced wishful thinking and appertaining hallucinations or dreams.[8] Such theories may easily be combined with theories of cognitive dissonance whereby internal psychological consistency is sought for in order to mentally function in the real world. To seek such consistency, projections and imaginations are sometimes necessary. Worth noticing is that psychological explanations, whatever form they take, are prone to focus on the *disciples* rather than Jesus. In other words, the resurrection *of Jesus* becomes something that happened to the *disciples*. This shifting of focus from how the New Testament addresses this, is worthy of notice because it establishes the semiotic field needed for overcoming the indeterminate element in the stories in *their* psychological state. Dicta which in the New Testament and early Christian sources are primarily about Jesus are thus being re-directed and primarily become dicta about the disciples. Applied to Jesus, such dicta and the Easter faith as such are primarily about the impression he made on *them*. A radical re-working of the evidence is going on here, although claims are made to explain how this faith came into being.

Naturally, a true companion of these debates is the issue of relevant *analogies*. Various psychological attempts to explain the belief in Jesus's resurrection are, in fact, ways of defining through analogies what really happened. A special case here may be the suggestion that the appearances of Jesus were equal to apparitions of recently deceased persons. No doubt, such visions can be both vivid and real. Dale C. Allison considers this a relevant analogy and says that "our brains are capable of generating very vivid, realistic and compelling imaginary experiences."[9] This position is very similar to John D. Crossan's claim that human beings are "hard-wired" to have these kinds of experiences.[10] The critical question is nevertheless what it takes to be a *relevant* analogy. About apparitions of recently dead persons, N. T. Wright makes a pertinent comment, namely that if such experiences are so common—and indeed they are—they hardly provide a sufficient reason for the idea that a deceased person is raised from the dead.[11] Furthermore, the New Testament passages in which appearances

---

8. Lüdemann, *Resurrection of Jesus*, 97–100, 173–79.
9. Allison, *Resurrecting Jesus*, 253.
10. Crossan, *Birth of Christianity*, xviii.
11. Wright, *Resurrection of the Son of God*, 690. See also Part III, Contributions to Resurrection Discourse, sec. Appearances: Allison's Contribution.

occur within stories, demonstrate that Jesus did not only make himself *seen* by some people; in the narrative world, he *acted* upon them, through touching, talking, eating, etc. From a narrative perspective at least, analogies that refer to apparitions or visions are hardly sufficiently relevant. Jonathan Z. Smith's distinction between analogies and genealogies is worth considering.[12] Analogies often have an intrinsic influence towards genealogical reasoning; in other words, they are often used to deconstruct, explaining how the phenomenon in question came into being.[13]

Metaphorical Language: Meaning-Oriented Interpretations

In his book *Jesus: A Revolutionary Biography*, John Dominic Crossan has a chapter on Easter with the heading "How Many Years Was Easter Sunday?"[14] Resurrection is, according to Crossan, one possible way of expressing Christian faith: "It is precisely that *continued* experience of the Kingdom of God as strengthened rather than weakened by Jesus' death that is Christian or Easter faith. And that was not the work of one afternoon. Or one year."[15] What we have is, in other words, "not an event, but a process that happened over many years."[16] Crossan does not here refer to the time it took to develop the Easter testimony; in other words, this is not a usual tradition-critical approach. Instead, he refers to the continuous and lasting process of Christ's presence among the community studying the Scriptures and sharing a meal. In his view, this is Easter, properly speaking. Crossan's presentation is inspired by chapter 24 in Luke's Gospel. In effect, Crossan moves in the vicinity of Rudolf Bultmann's reasoning. Crossan makes a distinction between mode and meaning, which is synonymous with literal versus metaphorical, and where the emphasis is on the latter.[17] Mode becomes a means whereby meaning is articulated.

When the New Testament quotes Psalm 110:1, in order to apply it to Jesus being seated at the right hand of God, this is manifestly metaphorical language. Likewise, when this quotation is applied to the resurrection of

12. Smith, *Drudgery Divine*, 47–51, 114, 118.

13. See for example Craffert, "Jesus' Resurrection in Social-Scientific Perspective," 125–51; and his "'I Witnessed the Raising of the Dead,'" 1–28. Craffert refers to experiences of ASC (alternate states of consciousness) in funerary rituals in Africa.

14. Crossan, *Revolutionary Biography*, 159.

15. Crossan, *Revolutionary Biography*, 161.

16. Crossan, *Revolutionary Biography*, 172.

17. Wright and Crossan, "Resurrection," 24.

Jesus—as sometimes happen—it is thereby demonstrated that resurrection is equally valid as a metaphor. What this metaphor conveys is vindication or exaltation rather than a dead body brought back to life. In other words, the resurrection language of Easter is replaced by the language of exaltation. Such runs the logic of a meaning-oriented interpretation. The frequently asked question about what "happened" is therefore considered as misguiding, as it assumes an incident that was observable, to be also noticed by disinterested observers. The adequate question to be asked is rather: what do the resurrection stories *mean*? That question takes us to the insight that Jesus is Lord, and that his disciples *continue* to experience this. Resurrection applies to the disciples and how they are to conduct their lives in the light of Jesus's eschatological life. A key question is if resurrection language is really so flexible. It is a question if not resurrection language in the given historical context is hard-wired to convey in some physical sense that dead comes to life. To this question, we will return later.

"Orthodox" Faith

Within the New Testament guild, N. T. Wright is presently the most fierce and consequent spokesman for a traditional or orthodox perspective on the resurrection of Jesus.[18] He argues that Jesus's resurrection was, and remains without analogy, and that this is part of the very nature of this faith. Belief in the resurrection of Jesus is based on two "historically secure" observations, namely the emptiness of the tomb and the meetings with the risen Jesus. Neither of these pieces of evidence is in themselves, or taken alone, sufficient for concluding that Jesus did rise from the dead. It is *together* that they form a sufficient basis for belief in the resurrection of Jesus. Without these real events, "we cannot account for early Christianity."[19] It is a key argument in Wright's presentation that the theory or explanatory model must account for how and why early Christianity came into being and survived, contrary to movements associated with other religious heroes of the time. Crucial for N. T. Wright's argument is that the language of resurrection is specific and not open to any kind of inference; it cannot be transferred into statements of "spiritual experience" or "exaltation." In the Jewish context in which Christianity gradually came into being, resurrection is about dead bodies coming to life. This language cannot be bent

---

18. N. T. Wright has published on this topic at various occasions; see especially his *The Resurrection of the Son of God*, and also Wright and Crossan, "Resurrection," 16–23, 29–47.

19. Wright, *Resurrection of the Son of God*, 709.

according to the theological notions of present-day interpreters, he claims.[20] Thus, his argumentative strategy relies on the possibility of overcoming the semiotic indeterminacy of the historical basis by declaring that the only way to interpret the empty tomb and the appearances is to interpret them within the then-existing Jewish frame of interpretation. Nevertheless, he then passes too quickly over the fact that this claim is based not only on his abductive reasoning, but it also rests on the abductions of the biblical witnesses. Hence, to say that what happened is "not open to any kind of inference" is, in fact, a misleading way to read the facts at hand. We will discuss Wright further in the systematic part of this book.

---

20. A similar remark is made by Allison, *Resurrecting Jesus*, 243–44.

Neither Witnessed nor Told: An Indescribable Event

CHRISTIAN FAITH IS DEFINED especially by the events of Easter, epitomized in the crucifixion and resurrection of Jesus. As for the crucifixion, the four gospels—in various ways—pass on a story full of details, both regarding persons involved, the time-table, and occasions. The narratives of Black Friday are lengthy, and together they convey minutiae, be they historical or not, regarding the death of Jesus. Such is definitely *not* the case with his resurrection. In the New Testament epistles, the resurrection appears abundantly, but never as a story, albeit narrative elements most likely are assumed (see Part II, section on 1 Corinthians 15). Narratives of the passion are found in the gospels only, and these narratives reach their peak in what happened Easter morning, namely the resurrection. These are the two kinds of texts that comprise the Easter witness of the New Testament.

Mark 16, the first explicit narrative testimony, leaves a big gap or hole when it comes to the resurrection event. It says about the women who arrived at the tomb: "When they looked up, they saw that the stone, which was very large, had already been rolled back" (Mark 16:4). The Greek text does not have the word "already" here; the translators of NRSV introduce it, but it rightly renders the perfect tense of the verb, which demonstrates that the event had taken place *before* they arrived, and *hidden* from their eyes. Jesus had already left the scene. No attempt is made to fill in this gap. Partially, Matthew fills in the gap left by Mark by saying that an earthquake appeared, and an angel descended from heaven and rolled back the stone (Matt 28:2). Although Matthew takes some steps beyond Mark here, nothing is told about Jesus during this event; the focus is on the angel. When the angel addresses the women, the resurrection is already a past event: "He is not here; for he has been raised, as he said. Come, see the place where he lay" (Matt 28:6). The bygone nature of the event is thus clearly stated. Likewise,

Luke says that when the women arrived at the tomb, they found that the stone was rolled away. In other words, the event had taken place, and Luke leaves this gap in his story. Such is also the case in John 20:1. Thus, the gospels unanimously convey a gap concerning what happened at the moment of resurrection. The event itself is opaque and seems to have escaped the curiosity of all canonical gospels. Two obvious, and equally important conclusions can be drawn from this fact: the resurrection is not accessible as an event, and no claim is made that the resurrection had witnesses. It is, therefore, the *belief* in this event with all the *imprints* of this faith that is in focus. Furthermore, this gap or hole is so consistently there in the New Testament, that it must be taken into account when the theology of Jesus's resurrection is considered theologically.

The Gospel of Peter

The so-called *Gospel of Peter* renders a different picture, and thus provides a backdrop against which to see how remarkable the observations mentioned above are. This Gospel was composed later than the canonical gospels, and draws on their narratives, making out of the four of them one harmonious story according to the practice of gospel harmonies, known from for example Tatian's well-known *Diatessarôn*. The *Gospel of Peter* was probably written between 150 and 190 CE.[1] Where the canonical gospels leave a big gap, namely what actually happened when Jesus rose from the dead, the *Gospel of Peter* brings several details. Chap. 12.50 enters the stories found in the canonical gospels, saying that Mary Magdalene, together with her friends, went to the tomb, concerned about the stone, which they eventually found rolled away as they arrived: "they found the tomb had been opened" (13.55). However, *before* embracing this "canonical" picture, the *Gospel of Peter* from 9.34 on relates about events *previous* to the arrival of the women at the tomb:

> 9.34. Now when the morning of the Sabbath dawned a crowd came from Jerusalem and the surrounding region that they might see the tomb which had been sealed. 35. But during the night in which the Lord's day dawned, while the soldiers were guarding two by two according to post, there was a great voice in the sky. 36. And they saw the heavens were being opened, and two men descended from there, having much brightness, and they drew near to the tomb. 37. But that stone which had been

---

1. See Foster, *Gospel of Peter*, 115–74.

placed at the entrance rolled away by itself and made way in part, and the tomb was opened, and both the young men went in.

10.38. Then those soldiers seeing it awoke the centurion and the elders, for they were present also keeping guard. 39. While they were reporting what they had seen, again they saw coming out from the tomb three men, and the two were supporting the one, and a cross following them. 40. And the head of the two reached as far as (*mechri*) heaven, but that of the one being led by them surpassed the heavens (*hyperbainousan tous ouranous*). 41. And they were hearing a voice from the heavens saying, "Have you preached to those who sleep?" 42. And a response was heard from the cross, "Yes."[2]

This version of the *Gospel of Peter* in many ways echo details known from the canonical gospels. Compared to these stories, however, what is told here serves to *enhance* the miraculous character of the event, and thereby also to *authenticate* it. This happens in various ways. First, the sealing of the tomb, mentioned in 8.28 as consisting of seven seals, works this way. The sepulcher was secured, and no humans were able to undo these seals.

Secondly, the two men entering the tomb, and the three coming out, are giants, surpassing the size of normal men. The alteration of the size of the men signifies physical transformation, visible to those present. Inherently, resurrection comes with bodily changes. Bodily metamorphosis is recorded in several resurrection texts, as witnessed to already in the New Testament (John 20:19, 26; Luke 24:16). The longer ending of Mark 16:12 puts it like this: "he appeared in another form (*en hetera morphē*) to two of them, as they were walking into the country."[3] This is most likely a re-working of the Emmaus Road story (Luke 24:13–35); hence, this interprets the appearance of Jesus as bodily and also *transformed*. The size of the men in the *Gospel of Peter* may serve as a spectacular development of this passage, but the fact that the third man, clearly the risen Jesus, surpasses the two angels in size, indicates that more than physical transformation is at stake here.[4] The different size is indicative of *superiority*. We suggest that the relationship between angels and Jesus according to Hebrews 1–2—Jesus is in every respect larger than the angels—is here embodied in bodies differently sized. Possibly also an ontological reference is hinted at here; the angels and Jesus

---

2. Cited from Foster, *Gospel of Peter*, 201–3. In Foster's edition the Greek text is also available.

3. Further references in Foster, *Gospel of Peter*, 422–23.

4. See the discussion in Foster, *Gospel of Peter*, 418–23.

are in their nature differently linked to heaven. While the angels reach "as far as heaven," Jesus surpassed the heavens.[5]

Thirdly, a walking, talking cross is for sure extraordinary, albeit that it is connected to a traditional motif, namely that Jesus preached for those in Hades (1 Pet 3:19; 4:6). These elements bring out "the enormity of the miraculous in these events."[6] Language and motifs at home in theophany narratives come into play here, bringing to mind the baptism story of Jesus where heaven opened (Mark 1:10 parr). Likewise, the radiance emanating from the men takes us to such stories in the biblical tradition.

Another important aspect is the way this event finds *witnesses*; a fact that indeed goes beyond, if not to say against, the canonical gospels. A crowd from Jerusalem saw that the tomb was sealed, and the soldiers are at their post, apparently together with "elders and scribes." From the canonical gospels, the appearance of soldiers is not surprising here, but the presence of members of the Jewish council is innovative. This means that the resurrection, or at least the sealed tomb, was witnessed by Roman soldiers, common people from Jerusalem and Jewish officials; in short, all of Jerusalem is taken to witness this event. The importance this text ascribes to their role as observers of what took place becomes clear from 10.38 where the soldiers, their centurion, and the elders were *awake*. According to Matthew's Gospel, the only story in which guards appear at the tomb, they fell asleep (Matt 28:13). Having the guards saying that they slept, paves the way for the rumor that the disciples stole the body during the night. In the *Gospel of Peter*, they were able to see and observe what happened.[7] Verbs for "seeing" are in the New Testament not used with reference to the resurrection event. This is the only incident where the resurrection is *seen*. When 1 Cor 15:5–8 uses the same verb, it is found in either passive or medium voice (see Part II, section 1 Corinthians 15 "He appeared to Cephas . . . ").

The text then goes on to mention that the soldiers reported to Pilate, one of them saying—in accordance with Mark 15:39—"truly this was God's son." Pilate orders the centurion and his soldiers to keep silent about what they saw. In its narrating the resurrection event, the *Gospel of Peter* is dependent upon the other gospels while being innovative as well. The innovations, of which the most important is that the event as such finds witnesses

---

5. Johnston, *Resurrection of Jesus*, 156–58 gives example from both Jewish and Christian sources about heavenly figures portrayed as giants.

6. Foster, *Gospel of Peter*, 430.

7. It is worth noticing that Julian the emperor, in his critique against the Christians, makes the point that the disciples were at sleep in Gethsemane, thus insinuating that this incident in Jesus's life is without witnesses; see Sandnes, *Early Christian Discourses on Jesus' Prayer*, 166, 79–81. Hence, sleep and being a witness are contrasted.

watching what took place, fill in the gap left open in the canonical gospels. As we will argue later, this gap is deliberate and significant.

Our considerations here run contrary to John Dominic Crossan's evaluation of the *Gospel of Peter* in its relationship to the canonical gospels, and Matthew in particular.[8] According to Crossan, the *Gospel of Peter* in its earliest stratum, i.e., a hypothetical Cross Gospel, is both prior to and independent of the gospels known from the New Testament. The author imitates Old Testament passages, viewed as prophecy, and creates a narrative with little connection to real events. For the resurrection stories, this means that they are "unreliable revisions of an unreliable tradition."[9] We notice, however, that the resurrection stories of the canonical gospels are remarkably free from such Scriptural motifs. As we point this out, we anticipate a view that will be substantiated later.[10]

From the presentation given above, some observations suggest that priority and independence cannot be attributed to the *Gospel of Peter*. Firstly, it is hardly likely that Matthew and the other gospels turned a text with more narrative details that worked apologetically into less pointed texts. That the process took that way is not likely from what we know about the development of traditions and apologies in the Early Church.[11] Expansion towards the apologetic is witnessed in, for example, the *Protoevangelium of James*, written around the time of the *Gospel of Peter*. Charges of the illegitimacy of Jesus's birth, allegedly born of a virgin, are here narratively combatted through the insertion of numerous details. The virginity of Mary as the mother of Jesus—indeed, "against nature," as it says in chap. 19.3—is tried by giving her a test, drinking water that will reveal her sins (chap. 16), and by Salome putting her finger inside her (19.3–20.3), thus echoing Thomas in the Johannine Easter story (John 20:25, 27).[12] Secondly, Jesus proclaiming the gospel in Hades is a dogma which finds support only in sources later than the New Testament, albeit tradition has wrongly attributed this to 1 Pet 3:19.[13] The *Gospel of Peter* here follows a tradition witnessed to in the *Gospel of Nicodemus*, a composite gospel dating from the fourth to

---

8. See Foster, *Gospel of Peter*, 429–30. Crossan's use of the *Gospel of Peter* has found little support among scholars. Crossan's view on the *Gospel of Peter* is an example of how creatively tradition-critical analysis may operate.

9. Quarles, "Gospel of Peter," 119–20 summarizes Crossan's view thusly.

10. See Part II, Towards a New Testament Theology on the Resurrection of Jesus, sec. According to the Scriptures.

11. For a general introduction to how apologetic influenced the mss of the canonical gospels, see Kannaday, *Apologetic Discourse*.

12. See *New Testament Apocrypha Volume One*.

13. See Dalton, *Christ's Proclamation to the Spirits*.

seventh centuries, and also attested in minuscule 614 and some few other manuscripts and Ambrosiaster.[14] The example of the *Protoevangelium of James* demonstrates how apologetic narrative embellishments developed by drawing on previous and more "simple" traditions. It is a similar process we witness in the *Gospel of Peter* with regard to the resurrection.

Why This Detour?

By looking into how the *Gospel of Peter* presents the resurrection event as something observable and witnessed, we realize how different the canonical gospels proceed in this regard. The stories in these gospels pick up when the event has already taken place. No claim is made that this incident was witnessed. Worth noticing in this regard is, for example, the importance Papias, bishop of Hierapolis (late first to early second century) assigned to eyewitnesses and "the living voice" of those who were present during the life and ministry of Jesus (Eusebius, *Hist. eccl.* 3.39.3–4).[15] Papias's emphasis on this is in accordance with the primacy attributed to eyewitnesses in ancient history writing. In his study *Story as History—History as Story*, Samuel Byrskog makes reference to the old dictum of Heraclitus, the well-known pre-Socratic philosopher: "Eyes are surer witnesses than ears."[16] Byrskog considers this dictum representative for the role of witnesses in antiquity. The Greeks were "Augenmenschen," as he puts it with reference to Bruno Snell:[17] "It is important to realize that the notion of the primacy of sight was not restricted to the historians only, but part of the ancient Greek theory of cognition. It was deeply embedded in the socio-cultural setting of the New Testament."[18] Against this backdrop, it is evident that the nonexistence of witnesses with access to the resurrection event must have been seen as a significant obstacle. It was an unfortunate situation left by itself. We see some initial steps towards closing the gap in Matthew's Gospel, and more fully so in the *Gospel of Peter*.

This gap which is *not* filled in by the canonical gospels leaves *fragility* to the claim that Jesus was risen from the dead. The most crucial event in the life of Jesus and the very foundation of the Church took place when

14. This text critical information is found in Nestle-Aland 26th ed., but left out from the 27th ed. on.
15. Bauckham, *Jesus and the Eyewitness Testimony*, 12–38.
16. Byrskog, *Story as History*, 49, 64.
17. Byrskog, *Story as History*, 50.
18. Byrskog, *Story as History*, 65. For his presentation of the ancient material, see 48–65 in particular.

no one was there to watch. The event has no eye-witnesses, no spectators present. For a strictly historical approach, this has a damaging effect: only the *aftermath* of the alleged event is there to be witnessed. Thus, at the very outset of our inquiry into the resurrection of Jesus, we face an *elusiveness* which impacts on a theological approach as well. At the center of Christian faith stands an event that is inaccessible and indescribable. Hence, empirical facts or evidence are clearly not primary terms by which to grasp what Jesus being raised from the dead entails, albeit we will note that the book of Acts gives some weight to this aspect.[19] From the fact of inaccessibility, the theology on Jesus's resurrection develops. Hence, such theologies always carry an element of the resurrection being indeterminable.

---

19. Part II, What Does Belief in the Resurrection of Jesus Do? sec. on the Acts of the Apostles.

What does Belief in the Resurrection of Jesus Do? Pragmatic Contours of New Testament Theology of Resurrection

MANY READERS ARE LIKELY to expect that we would start with Paul's discussion in 1 Corinthians 15, the oldest extant staging of this faith, and then proceed to the Passion stories in which the resurrection of Jesus is told. This would mirror a historical sequence of the available testimonies (cf. on the tradition-critical sifting of the sources above), but this also unwittingly invites a specific reduction of the belief in the resurrection of Jesus, since that approach easily paves the way for two main questions, namely what kind of body the risen Jesus had, and whether the tomb was really empty. In short, the question easily develops into "did this happen or not?" These specific questions, crucial as they are, may pave the way for a narrow apologetic approach, missing out on the broader frameworks with which this faith is at home. In this chapter, we aim at the *entirety* of this belief in the New Testament,[1] and even more so what this faith *did*, or how it *worked*. In other words, a pragmatic perspective, asking what *effects* this belief had, will be taken here. We aim at putting this faith in its proper place according to the New Testament witnesses. This is by no means a denial that diversities and different emphases are found within the New Testament; this will be amply testified when we come to the narrative traditions. The primary aim here is to catch patterns of thoughts rather than the idiosyncrasies of individual writings. We do not aim at a comprehensive survey covering all relevant texts

---

1. Alkier, *Reality of the Resurrection*, 197 likewise points out that there is a danger of reducing the impact of resurrection belief if 1 Corinthians 15 and the empty tomb is one-sidedly in focus. This is not to deny that for example John's First Epistle makes no reference or use of the faith in Jesus's resurrection. There are passages that may indicate such a thought (1 John 2:24, 28; 3:2; 4:2, 15; 5:5, 9). Nonetheless, resurrection cannot be extracted from the letter; it can only be read against such an assumed backdrop.

in the New Testament.[2] Our purpose is to give *sufficient* material, that is, sufficient *to think with* regarding the issue of the present volume. In other words, it is about finding ample evidence to serve as food for thoughts. We will delve into the three main genres found within the New Testament: letters (of Paul), a narrative (the Book of Acts) and an apocalypse (Revelation). As for the first, Romans will be our primary guide, while 1 Corinthians 15 will be addressed on its own later. As the first to put together what the resurrection of Jesus entailed, Paul has been given due emphasis here.

The pragmatic perspective has implications for the selection of texts. For sure, all canonical gospels—in John's Gospel this is made explicit to the readers (e.g., John 12:16)—are *retrospective* in nature, as they present Jesus from the perspective of his being raised. Nevertheless, the gospels will be treated later as providing the Easter narratives, while the Pauline tradition, the Acts of the Apostles and the Book of Revelation, even if some of them may be older than the written gospels, *draw upon* the Easter narrative traditions.

A Colloquium on the Resurrection

It is essential for us that what we conceive of the resurrection of Jesus does justice to relevant passages in the New Testament, and that systematic and hermeneutical considerations develop from there. When we here emphasize what effects the risen Jesus had on those who embraced this faith, we are, of course, dealing with a *textual* construct. Some of the effects worked out did inform how Christian life materialized among early Christians, though, and will hence be addressed towards the end of this chapter. However, before embarking upon the New Testament evidence, it is worth-while pausing, asking how we read these pieces of evidence. To what extent are they coherent, forming a unilateral view on the resurrection of Jesus? Customarily, Christians read the New Testament as a collection of "doctrines." Applied to the topic of this book, that attitude means that the relevant passages are added together and seen to comprise what is the New Testament doctrine on the matter. Our discussion will make it clear that this implies a neglect of the distinct features of the available testimonies. We would now suggest another way of approaching the material on the resurrection. In his *New Testament Theology*, G. B. Caird organizes his presentation according to what he calls the

---

2. For a more comprehensive presentation, see Wright, *Resurrection of the Son of God*, 209–480 and Alkier, *Reality of the Resurrection*, 7–193. However, the two give very much of their related discussions within these pages, and none of them are pragmatic in their approach.

"conference table approach."[3] Caird imagines New Testament writers seated at the same table, engaging each other in a colloquium on theological matters. This model draws on the Apostolic Conference told in Gal 2 and Acts 15. The conference table is, of course, organized and set up by him, or by the interpreter, since the New Testament authors never met in this way. We find this approach especially instructive for our topic, which is about an indescribable event with implications not easily grasped or formulated. Instead of forcing all texts into one narrow, in all aspects coherent discourse, this model will take the richness and distinctiveness of the evidence seriously, and also that we are dealing with a diversity of attempts to come to terms with a conviction with implications that surpassed the imaginable.

---

3. Caird, *New Testament Theology*.

Paul the Apostle: The First to Engage the Issue

IN GENERAL, PAUL IS the first witness to the Christian faith, and this applies to our topic as well. Belief in the resurrection of Jesus is simply ubiquitous in his letters. Written in the fifties, his letters—we here assume a distinction between undisputed letters and letters that developed in a Pauline tradition—are the first extant witnesses to faith in the resurrection of Jesus. Most likely, First Thessalonians is the first extant Pauline letter. Of relevance for our investigation here is the dictum about the faith embraced by his addresses: From the idols they turned to God, "to wait for his Son from heaven, whom he raised from the dead (*egeirein ek tōn nekrōn*)—Jesus, who rescues us from the wrath that is coming" (1 Thess 1:9–10; cf. Rom 10:9). This is the oldest piece of evidence for faith in the resurrection of Jesus. Two observations stand out, the *theocentric* outlook and the present location of the resurrected Jesus. The theocentric perspective is apparent. Resurrection is a divine act, done by "the true and living God," a typical Jewish claim.[1] Hence, resurrection faith is rooted in Jewish faith in the One God. God has placed Jesus in heaven with him, a thought not far from what Paul elsewhere brings out through citing Psalm 110:1. From there, Jesus will return to save them, that is, to provide for them an unending fellowship with him (1 Thess 4:13–18). What Paul here conveys is comfort and encouragement: "Therefore encourage one another with these words" (1 Thess 4:18). "Hope" thus encapsulates what this faith is really about. Hence, the resurrection of Jesus is ingrained in Paul's Jewish concepts of what the true and living God does, and it is formulated with a view to conveying hope and comfort for the believers.

---

1. Feldmeier and Spieckermann, *Der Gott der Lebendigen*, 515–29.

A Divine Act

Paul formulates *the theocentric embeddedness of the resurrection* also in Rom 1:3-4, possibly with reference to a formula handed down to him from tradition: ". . . the gospel of God, which he promised beforehand through his prophets in the holy scriptures, the gospel concerning his Son, who was descended from David according to the flesh and was declared to be Son of God with power according to the spirit of holiness by resurrection from the dead . . . ." We need not address all the exegetical cruces involved here.[2] What matters here, is to notice that the resurrection of Jesus defines what Paul's gospel is about, and that faith in the resurrection is rooted in the Old Testament and in the God of the Fathers. The resurrection of Jesus is a divine act, and hence, intimately associated with God.

This takes us to Romans 4, a context in which Paul addresses the nature of Abraham's faith according to Gen 15:6: "Abraham believed God, and it was reckoned to him as righteousness." As in First Thessalonians, Christian faith is summarized as "hope" (Rom 4:18, cf. 5:2). In Rom 3:30, Paul states, in terms taken from Shema, the Jewish creed, the oneness of God, as the basis for his gospel. Hence, Shema vibrates through the discussion on Abraham's faith in Romans 4. Abraham believes in God "who gives life to the dead and calls into existence the things that do not exist (*ta mē onta hōs onta*)" (v. 17). "Calling into being" echoes Isa 48:13LXX (cf. Ps 33:9) about God's creation of the world. This creed-like dictum is in v. 25 applied to Jesus's resurrection: Christ-followers "believe in him who raised Jesus our Lord from the dead." The parallel with Abraham's faith is obvious and stated.[3] The dictum rendered in v. 17 is also echoed in Rom 11:36 and 1 Cor 8:6 (cf. Col 1:16-17).[4]

Paul formulates himself in analogy with what we find in the iconic martyr-story about Eleazar and the seven brothers in 2 Maccabees 7, and developed further in the more philosophically oriented 4 Maccabees. As one of her sons faced death at the hand of the tyrant, the mother says to the martyr-to-be: "I beg you, my child, to look at the heaven and the earth and see everything that is in them, and recognize that God did not make them out of things that existed (*ouk ex ontōn*). And in the same way, the human race came into being" (2 Macc 7:28). Several observations shed light on Paul's importing of God Creator into Genesis 15 in Romans 4. The

---

2. For a discussion, see for example Dunn, *Romans 1-8*, 11-16.
3. For a discussion on this passage, see Sandnes, "Justification," 147-81.
4. For further references, see Sandnes, "Justification," 170-71. References made here demonstrate that this idea goes hand in hand with the oneness of God; in other words, the Shema and the unique role of God lies at the heart of Paul's reasoning here.

mother of the seven boys does the same: God in whom she puts her trust is God Creator who made "heaven and the earth," a synonym for all creation. God makes things that did not exist, often labeled *creatio ex nihilo*. Furthermore, this is precisely the foundation for her belief in the resurrection: "Accept death, so that in God's mercy I may get you back again (*komisōmai se*)[5] along with your brothers" (2 Macc 7:29, cf. 7:9). The mother speaks again in 2 Macc 7:23: "Therefore the Creator of the world, who shaped the beginning of humankind and devised the origin of all things, will in his mercy give life and breath back to you again (*palin apodidōsin*) . . ." Creation and resurrection form a tandem, wherein the first gives the basis for believing in the second. As we shall see later, this feature is possible to develop on the basis of the reports about Jesus's resurrection, as well. That also goes for the following point:

Worth noticing in this famous chapter is namely that *creatio ex nihilo* comes with the expectations of life being restored to *how it once was*. The adverb *palin* meaning "back," "repetition," or "returning to a position or state" makes that abundantly clear.[6] This adverb is also used in 2 Macc 7:14 expressing the hope of being raised again by God (*palin anastēsesthai hyp autou*); "again" here does not refer to a second resurrection, but to a resurrection that brings back life to how it was previous to death. The third son vividly demonstrates this as he turns towards the tyrant, stretching forth his hands, saying: "I got these from Heaven, and because of his laws I disdain them, and from him I hope to get them back again (*palin komisasthai*)" (2 Macc 7:11). Continuity and restoring life to how it once was are here crucial. Physicality as it once was, prevails. As we will see later, Paul is certainly more bent on transformation.[7] It is, however, important to notice that 2 Maccabees 7 and Paul accommodate resurrection within the same theological universe, in which the power of God Creator is at work.[8] The God of Israel is characterized as "raising the dead" (2 Cor 1:9), almost like an epithet. In accommodating the resurrection of Jesus in this context, Paul treats Jesus's resurrection in analogy with the creation. His resurrection is enrolled in God's actions towards the creation. By raising Jesus from the dead, God shows his abiding solidarity with his creation. This is worth noticing since this embeddedness in the creation and God Creator serves as a reminder that resurrection in a Jewish setting cannot easily dismiss the

---

5. The Greek verb *komizein* means "to get something back" or to "recover"; see BDAG s.v; LSJ s.v.

6. BDAG s.v.

7. See Part II, A Transformed Body or Another Body?

8. For the Jewish indebtedness of the language used by Paul, see Hoffmann, "Auferstehung II/1."

physical aspects involved. Developing from creation theology, resurrection is bound to be more than a metaphor; in some way, physicality is involved, or at least something to be negotiated.

However, in making Abraham's faith a model for the sort of faith that Christ-believers have, Paul conveys that resurrection faith is a matter of hope, future and optimism without the support of "empirical or philosophical proof."[9] The promise given to Abraham was given at an age when the time of begetting children was far gone. Also, Sarah, his wife, had passed the time of motherhood: "In a situation of hopelessness, he put his hope in God who calls into existence what does not exist. This was the only grounds on which the promise of the universal fatherhood could become true. It is this piece of Abraham's biography that lays the foundations for how faith is defined in Romans 4."[10] Again we touch upon the elusiveness or subtlety of this faith, which we have already noted in this study. The nature of Abraham's faith works analogously with the gap we identified in the Easter narratives. Paul in Rom 8:24 voices this kind of "hope" in terms of something "not seen"; in other words, it is not based on a demonstrable fact or argument. It is something requiring patience from which hope is nurtured. Hope in resurrection comes without external support, as it did for Abraham. His faith found affirmation only *afterward*, in his having a son. Stefan Alkier is cited above regarding "empirical and philosophical proof." His statement sums up that Abraham's faith was without any "validation." We do not part ways here, but it is worth noticing that the language of proof and validation is somewhat at odds with the context of Romans 4. At the center of this chapter is not a matter of *proving* the resurrection, but putting one's trust in a *promise*, which in itself carries some precarious aspects vis-à-vis proofs.

A Universal Perspective

As will become clear later in this study, the raising of Jesus from the dead is so much more than the raising of an individual, restoring a poor fellow to life. Raising Jesus from the dead represents the future and accomplishment of *humankind*. Martin Luther formulated this succinctly when he said that Jesus was not raised as a *persona privata*, as a private person, but as a *persona publica*, as a public person. He was raised as *maxima persona*, as a person representing humankind.[11] From this follows that his resurrection is so much more than simply surviving the grave and being found as he was known to

---

9. Alkier, *Reality of the Resurrection*, 49.
10. Sandnes, "Justification," 171–72.
11. See Ringleben, *Wahrhaft Auferstanden*, 42–43.

his disciples prior to his resurrection. In this way, the apostle differs markedly from the expectations found in 2 Maccabees 7 (see above).

Highly relevant is here Rom 5:12–21, because the creation perspective is carried on here. Adam brings to mind human beings as created by God, weak and fallen in sin. Admittedly, the resurrection of Jesus is not mentioned, but the fact that the antithetical analogy between Adam and Christ appears only here *and* in 1 Cor 15:22, 45–49, proves its relevance for the question of resurrection. Throughout Rom 5:12–21 runs the contrast between death (vv. 12, 14, 15, 17, 21) and life (vv. 17, 18, 21), the first imparted by Adam, and the latter conveyed through Christ. They are both, in their respective ways, "progenitorial ancestors."[12] When Paul in the Corinthian passage says that "we will also bear the image (*eikōn*) of the man of heaven," this is an intended analogy to Genesis 1 and Adam's role as a progenitor. This link is further strengthened by his reference in the context to the "man of dust," clearly a reference to Gen 2:7 and 3:17–19. Stripped of these biblical associations and subtexts, what Paul here conveys is that Christ through his death and resurrection initiated a new creation of humankind. This is the substantiation for the *maxima persona* view mentioned above, and this is how Adam and Christ respectively are viewed in Rom 5:12–21.

The Risen Jesus and the Christ-Believer

An argumentative extension of the resurrection is found in Rom 6:1–11, with particular emphasis on vv. 4–8. Paul here construes baptism as analogous to the death and resurrection of Jesus. This serves as an argument to halt critical questions that Paul's teaching paves the way for licentiousness: "Should we continue to sin in order that grace may abound (*pleonasē*?" (Rom 6:1, cf. 3:8). Most likely such questions mirror critical engagement in Rome with what has been conveyed to them about Paul's gospel.[13] Within Paul's text, however, Rom 6:1 picks up on 5:20, where the verb *pleonazein* appears twice in a dictum claiming that grace increases because of sin. Paul's response proceeds from bringing to mind that his addresses are baptized: *ebaptisthēmen* (v. 3). In most early Christian literature this term refers to a *ritual*, the act of baptism. Hence, Paul makes reference here to a *practice* with which his addressees are familiar. Frederick S. Tappenden has demonstrated that baptism here does not work simply as a metaphor but as an embodied practice or ritual.[14] Paul's argument takes into account correlations

---

12. Tappenden, *Resurrection in Paul*, 78.
13. Sandnes, *Paul Perceived*, 104–9.
14. Tappenden, *Resurrection in Paul*, 137–46.

between literary descriptions of resurrection and performative enactments of baptism. Tappenden argues that the ritual took the form of a going down into the water, and then emerging from there, a somatic movement enacting what happened to Jesus in his death and resurrection. Although a generally practiced ritual cannot be assumed, nonetheless, a ritual including "going down and coming up" of the water is well-attested and seems to be assumed in Romans 6. Hermas, *Sim.* 9.16.4 expresses this pointedly: "The seal, then, is the water. They go down (*katabainousi*) then into the water dead, and come up (*anabainousi*) alive."[15] "In this way, Paul exploits in Romans 6 those aspects of the ritual that enable blending with Christ's death and resurrection."[16] Accordingly, both the death and resurrection of Jesus are present here, not only as a metaphor referring to a spiritual reality but as something taking place in the ritual.

The basic structure of Rom 6 correlates with 1 Cor 15:3–4 and can be illustrated in the following way:

Christ	The Baptized
Died	Died with him
Buried	Buried with him
Raised	Walk (*peripatein*) in the newness of life

There is clearly an intended identification between the two being juxtaposed here. The death and resurrection of Jesus is not only a model here but is *enacted* in the life of the believer (cf. 2 Cor 4:10). However, we should not miss that within the correlation Paul consciously makes, a significant shift of time-perspective can be seen. While the two first points of correlation are held in past tense, the resurrection is given a twist.[17] The resurrection is given a double application, first in the present tense (as above), and then in v. 5 in the future tense: "we will be united (*esometha*) with him in a resurrection like his" (cf. v. 8). Paul expresses an eschatological reserve by "relegating the terminology of *anastasis* to the future,"[18] and emphasizes the *ethical* consequences. The "walking" metaphor (*peripatein*) is at home in ethical discourses, to which 1 Thess 4:1, 12; Gal 5:16; 1 Cor 7:17; Rom

---

15. Likewise in Hermas *Mand.* 4.3.1 (*eis hydōr katebēmen*) and *Sim.* 9.16.2 (*di hydatos anabēnai*) to become alive (*zōopoiēthōsin*); see Sandnes, "Seal and Baptism in Early Christianity," 1453–55.

16. Tappenden, *Resurrection in Paul*, 142.

17. Paul's conscious and careful distinction here is not given notice in Col 2:12–13 and 3:1 where it says: "you have been raised (*synēgerthēte*)."

18. Tappenden, *Resurrection in Paul*, 145.

13:13 may serve as examples.[19] The resurrection is present through ethical practices, but it is also to be awaited in full in the future. This is not a contrast between a present metaphorical resurrection and a future literal one, but it refers to two *stages* within the transformation brought about by resurrection. In other words, the bodily transformation is initiated in the lifestyle and is eventually completed in a transformed body. Rather than a metaphorical extension, we should here speak in terms of an anticipated resurrection, which takes its beginning in the somatic interior, heart, mind, and spirit—what Paul labels "our inner nature"[20]—and finds its fulfillment in the bodily resurrection later. Baptism sets Christ-believers on a transformative path which eventually reaches its goal in the bodily transformation, a topic addressed most clearly in 1 Corinthians 15 (see Part II, section A Transformed Body or Another Body?).

Now Paul brings this to bear on the critical voices present among the Romans. The renewal by the Spirit (see below) of the somatic interior enables moral behavior, a fact which Paul's critics have not grasped. In the words of Tappenden: "Just as eschatological resurrection produces a somatic transformation, so too does baptismal resurrection. The former is external, the latter internal."[21] Paul thus conceives of resurrection in terms of *transformation* taking place in two stages, interior and exterior, where the first is present and enables ethical actions, while the latter is impending, yet to take place. The resurrection of Jesus is here a source for Paul's ethical guidance and for his anthropology as well. Hence, eschatology, anthropology, and ethics in Paul's thinking revolve around the resurrection of Jesus.

Paul fleshes in Romans 8 out how his theology at large is informed by the resurrection of Jesus. He picks up on the baptismal theology he assumed in Rom 6:1–11. It is worth quoting Rom 8:9–11 more or less in full here:

> But you are not in the flesh; you are in the Spirit, since the Spirit of God dwells in you . . . But if Christ is in you, though the body is dead because of sin, the spirit is life because of righteousness. If the Spirit of him who raised Jesus from the dead dwells in you, he who raised Jesus from the dead will give life to your mortal bodies also through his Spirit that dwells in you.

This translation is taken from NRSV but differs on one crucial point, namely that *pneuma* in v. 10 is not, like in NRSV, rendered with a capital (Spirit). The point in this verse is precisely the initiated and ongoing interior renewal. The Spirit of God is powerful and raised Jesus from the dead. This Spirit is now

19. See also Finsterbusch, *Die Thora als Lebensweisung für Heidenchristen*, 113–20.
20. See for example 2 Cor 4:16; Rom 7:22; 12:2; cf. Eph 3:16; 4:23.
21. Tappenden, *Resurrection in Paul*, 154.

indwelling in the Christ devotees, forming a somatic link with the risen Jesus, and also warranting life to their mortal bodies. Tappenden has coined a term grasping how Paul locates human existence within a trajectory of transformative embodiment: their earthly and corruptible bodies are "enspirited."[22] Worth noticing is that Paul—very much in line with Romans 6—immediately gives this a practical twist. The fact that the bodies are "enspirited" has implications for how life is conducted now (Rom 8:12–13). It is a matter of being *led* by the indwelling Spirit. From this present resurrection perspective, Paul then turns to the upcoming resurrection: ". . . if children, then heirs, heirs of God and joint heirs with Christ—if, in fact, we suffer with him so that we may also be glorified with him (*syndoxasthōmen*)" (v. 17).

The language of glory has bodily connotations, as is evident from Rom 8:29–30 where resurrection is conceived of as being conformed (*symmorphous*) to the image of the resurrected Christ, and thus to be glorified (*edoxasen*). Then the "enspirited" body is no longer earthly and corruptible. That Paul in this passage envisages a bodily transformation in accordance with the risen Jesus, finds affirmation in Phil 3:21 where Paul puts things in the same terms, but adds explicitly that it is nonetheless a matter of the body: "He will transform (*metaschēmatisei*) the body (*to sōma*) of our humiliation that it may be conformed to the body of his glory (*symmorphon tō sōmati tēs doxēs autou*), by the power that also enables him to make all things subject to himself." This passage echoes the reasoning of Romans 8 where resurrection is conceived of as an ongoing and unfolding process. It is, of course, worth noticing that also in Philippians 3 the context is about "walking" (*peripatein*); in other words, the ethical and the eschatological perspectives are intertwined.

God Has Not Given Up on God's Creation

Especially in Romans, Paul emphasizes that God is trustworthy, a fact which he applies in particular to his promises to Israel. This is conveyed in Rom 3:1–3, and Paul devotes three chapters (chaps. 9–11)—often seen as the climax of the whole letter[23]—to argue this. In a somewhat similar way, Rom 8:18–23 considers resurrection from the perspective of God delivering the entire cosmos, not leaving behind what he has committed himself to. God stands by his creation, and the resurrection of Jesus is not only an

---

22. Tappenden, *Resurrection in Paul*, 155.

23. Many scholars, myself included, stands on the shoulders of Krister Stendahl who claimed that these chapters formed the climax of the entire letter; *Paul Among Jews and Gentiles*, 76–96.

emblem of his faithfulness towards cosmos, but also a *sign* that God has not left the world behind. Worth noticing is the way the resurrection of Jesus here is treated as being *relevant* for the present world. His resurrection works similarly to the Spirit dwelling in the believers as being "a first fruit" (*aparchē*) that will be completed in a transformed creation. Paul here makes a strong claim that the future resurrection is inherently tied up with the creation. It has a direct bearing on the bodies of the Christ devotees. Their bodies will find redemption (*apolytrōsis*), which implies restoration. Likewise, the cosmos will be set free from the bondage to decay (*apo tēs douleias tēs phtoras*) and participate in the glory (*doxa*) which characterizes life and bodies in the time to come. Against this backdrop, it becomes difficult to state that the resurrection belongs only in God's dimension.[24] In this passage the resurrection of Jesus is not a "transcendent happening," but firmly attached to a restoration of God's creation generally. James D. G. Dunn argues that the background of Rom 8:19–22 is Gen 3:17–18. V. 20 on Paul's text paraphrases the words of judgment in Genesis 3: the creation was subjected to futility, not of its own will, but by the will of the one who subjected it. In the Old Testament context, the solidarity of humankind with the rest of creation was conveyed through the wordplay *adam* and *adamah*; man was made from the dust.[25] The resurrection affirms this solidarity and brings it to its fulfillment. Thus, a paradigmatic perspective on the resurrection of Jesus serves Paul's theology more widely, and we realize that much evolve from the way he conceived of the resurrection of Jesus.

---

24. Thus for example Küng, *On Being a Christian*, 350.

25. Dunn, *Theology of Paul*, 100–101.

The Acts of the Apostles

Evidentiary Presence

THE VERY FIRST SENTENCE of the Book of Acts (1:1–2) summarizes the narrative given in Luke's Gospel. This summary mentions what Jesus did and taught until he was "taken up to heaven" (*anelēmphtē*; cf. Luke 24:51). Luke is alone in distinguishing narratively between resurrection and ascension. In Acts, they form two incidents separated by an interim of 40 days (1:3), which is not the case in Luke 24. By implication, Paul's claim to have met the risen Christ in a way comparable to that of other apostles (1 Cor 15:3–8) falls outside of Luke's perspective. In Acts 1:2 the interim is indicated by the participle *enteilamenos* which is to be rendered temporally: "after having instructed" the apostles. However, Luke is not consistent when it comes to the distinction between what in later Church tradition (the Apostolic Creed) has become two separate events. Acts 1:1–2 has a structure, logic and even terminology running in tandem with 1:21–22; the latter passage introduces the ascension and resurrection as synonymous. Furthermore, the recurrent contrast "you killed Jesus, but God raised him," is in Acts 2:33; 3:13–15 and 7:51–56 turned into "you killed Jesus, but God exalted him." Hence, in spite of the narrative distance created in Acts 1, Luke elsewhere considers the exaltation and glory of Jesus to develop from his being raised from the dead. The precise relationship between the two remains somewhat muddled.

Having summarized the narrative of his gospel, Luke immediately mentions that Jesus "showed himself alive" (*parestēsen heauton zōnta*) to the apostles (Acts 1:3). Luke describes this evidentiary, emphasizing the physical presence of Jesus among his disciples. This evidentiary "showing" is presented in terms taken from the language of proof or argument (*tekmērion*). The term refers to demonstrative proofs or convincing arguments and is at home in the ancient rhetorical discourse on issues contested. According to Aristotle, (*tekmērion*) is a "necessary proof" (*Rhet.* 1.2.16–18), and Quintilian says that these kind of proofs—making reference to this particular Greek term—are irrefutable (*signum insolubile*) and beyond dispute; they are "indications from which there is no getting away" (*Inst.* 5.9.3–4). To illustrate this, Quintilian says that a woman who has delivered a child must have had intercourse with a man. This is a non-disputable fact; hence the child is a *tekmērion*. Against this backdrop, Luke's passage comes with a rather strong claim. Indirectly, he conveys that belief in the resurrection was a matter of dispute, and he participated with arguments that, to him, were indisputable facts. Accordingly, the proofs called upon are *empirical* in nature: he appeared (*optanomenos autois*) to them, instructed them and ate with them. In short, they spend time together. This overlaps with Luke 24:13–38 (Emmaus), but differs with regard to duration. According to Acts 1, this took place during "forty days," which is a conventional biblical number for a longer period of time. In other words, Luke does not envisage this as singular visions or appearances, albeit numerous, but as continued *fellowship*, possibly in forms of several visits. Implied is that Jesus were together with them in a corporeal way. This follows naturally from the emphasis on the risen Jesus's embodied existence according to Luke 24:38–43 (see Part II The Easter Narratives, Luke 24, section What kind of Reality?), and thus forms a bridge here. Kevin L. Anderson has demonstrated that Acts 1:3 ("presenting himself alive to them") has a parallel in Peter showing Tabitha, the dead widow, to be alive (*parestēsen zōsan*; Acts 9:41), and works as evidential proof.[1] The way this language works in these two instances makes Acts 1:3 a flashback to the evidentiary role of the physical presence of Jesus in Luke 24:38–43. To this belongs also Acts 17:31, where it says that God has "given *pistis* to all by raising him from the dead." NRSV renders this "assurance," but more is at stake here. The translation "proof" is to be seriously considered, as in Aristotle, *Rhet.* 1.1.3 (1354a) and other relevant ancient texts.[2] In other words, the term works very much like *tekmērion* (above).

According to Acts 2:24–32 and 13:32–38, the Scriptures provide proofs, albeit of another kind. In both passages, different Old Testament texts are taken as prophesying the resurrection of Messiah, but Psalm 15 (LXX) is at the center of these passages.[3] David speaks prophetically that Messiah will not face bodily corruption or decay: "his flesh did not experience corruption." By emphasizing this, Luke's idea about the resurrected body of Jesus is bent on the continuation, since no deterioration took place. Jesus's body

---

1. Anderson, "But God Raised Him from the Dead," 188–90.
2. BGAD s.v. 1C renders *pistis* in this way here.
3. This is discussed at length in Anderson, "But God Raised Him from the Dead," 244–55.

is not subject to decomposition; this is underscored in Acts 2:27, 31; 13:34, 35, 36, 37. In this way, the Scriptures become proof for Luke's emphatic corporeal understanding of the resurrected body, which, however, does not mean that no changes occurred. Kevin L. Anderson combines this, rightly so in our opinion, with the emphasis on physicality in Luke 24, and makes the following comment: "This concern is not explicitly shared by any of the other Evangelists. Paul and Peter, however, mention the incorruption of resurrected bodies."[4] References here are made to 1 Cor 15:42, 50, 54 and 1 Pet 1:4. This reading is unwarranted. No doubt, Luke puts a stronger emphasis on the physical presence of the resurrected than does the other Evangelists, but the reference to Paul and Peter does not work here. As for Peter—with no view on the issue of authorship here—that passage does not speak of the resurrected body. More important to assess is whether the body not subjected to decomposition in Luke, is really the resurrected body as the Pauline references by necessity imply. The body that did not decay is the body of the earthly Jesus, which *continued* in his resurrected body. This is a more likely interpretation of what Luke conveys in these two passages. This means that Luke's use of Ps 15 LXX is not to be paralleled with Paul's statement on the incorruptible body of resurrection, but rather with Paul's dictum that "flesh and blood cannot inherit the kingdom of God" (1 Cor 15:50), a passage to which we will return later. Hence, rather than joining Paul's choir in 1 Corinthians 15, Luke possibly here voices a view on the resurrected body of Christ in which the continuity (the same body) is emphasized.[5]

The Scriptural perspective brings *God* into the picture, stated explicitly in Acts 2:24: "But God raised him up . . ." This is a recurrent and overriding perspective throughout, found most explicitly in the sermons (Acts 3:13, 15; 4:10; 5:30; 17:31). In the Hebrew Bible, God is often mentioned according to his salvific deeds. God is known through what he accomplished for the benefit of Israel and human beings. Thus, God is named after his creation, his election of the Fathers or the rescue from Egypt. In the Book of Acts, God is named after his raising of Jesus from the dead. This is the principal divine deed by which God is known. Accordingly, the resurrection of Jesus is also the primary soteriological event. Salvation and forgiveness of sins are effects of the raising of Jesus (Acts 5:30–31; 10:43; 13:37–38; 26:23); the importance of his death is not equally emphasized.

The latter passage makes the proclamation to the nations a consequence of the resurrection. This is in line with the introductory chapter where the

---

4. Anderson, *"But God Raised Him from the Dead,"* 33.

5. As we will see later, Paul in 2 Cor 5:1 says that the present body will be destroyed (*kataluthê*); see Part II, The Easter Narratives, Luke 24, sec. What Kind of Reality?

empowering effect of the resurrection manifests itself in the power of the Holy Spirit to witness and proclaim to the ends of the earth (Acts 1:8). The apostolic mission narrated is, in fact, giving witness to the resurrection of Jesus (Acts 1:22; 2:32; 3:15; 5:32; 10:39; 13:30–31). The case of Jesus's resurrection, therefore, finds a threefold attestation in Acts; his physical fellowship with the apostles during the forty days, Scriptural evidence and the witness of the apostles. This witness takes place in the proclamation of the gospel to Jews and Gentiles, and is, in fact, the very core of their message, as indicated clearly in Acts 17:18 where Luke renders what Athenian philosophers said: Paul preaches Jesus and the resurrection. In the light of how Acts is introduced as a story *verifying* the resurrection of Jesus, it is natural to see the witness role of the apostles as partially contributing to this aim. Worth noticing is that the women, whose role is to be primary witnesses in Luke 24, fall, more or less, out of the narrative conveyed in Acts.

An Act of Restoration

We have seen the evidentiary aspect in the introduction of Acts, pertaining to the resurrection of Jesus. Another aspect that stands out is the restorative perspective. According to Acts 1:6, the disciples who listened to what Jesus addressed in the forty days following his resurrection, formulated the question: is this the time of restoration for Israel? This question is born out of the resurrection of Jesus and demonstrates what kind of thoughts this insight triggered. This is what Paul according to Acts 28:20 (cf. 26:8, 23) says when he arrives in Rome shackled: ". . . it is for the sake of the hope of Israel that I am bound with this chain." Christine Henriksen Aarflot has in a newly published dissertation demonstrated how Paul in Acts is written into a meta-narrative of God's promises, in which the resurrection of the dead stands out.[6] The Greek verb *apokathistanein*, which appears in Acts 1:6, rendered "restore," is at home in Elijah traditions (Mal 3:22 LXX) and prophetic traditions (Jer 27:19 LXX; 29:6 LXX; Ezek 17:23 LXX) as they appear in, for example, Mark 9:11–12 and Matt 17:11. In these passages, it is about "the restoration of everything," thus indicating the universal and eschatological perspective. Primarily it summarizes what the prophetic visions envisaged in terms of bringing back the earlier good state. This prophetic restoration theology is voiced in Acts 3:21: "Jesus, who must remain in heaven until the time of universal restoration (*apokatastasis pantōn*) that God announced long ago through his holy prophets." The horizon here is not the restoration or salvation of all in an Origenian meaning, but the overall impression of

---

6. Aarflot, *God (in) Acts*, 130–36.

prophetic promises, which is here also called "times of refreshing" (*kairoi anapsyxeōs*; Acts 3:20). Bringing back the original good state is integral to this idea. Hence, Isa 23:17 LXX speaks about restoring things to *eis* to *archaion* ("NETS") and Ezek 16:55 LXX thrice mentions *ap archēs*; both expressions are about a return to how things once were. The idea of the good state is easily extended into a motif associated with the creation as the starting point, i.e., bringing back primordial conditions. In short, resurrection is conceived of as recapitulating creation, as is the case in Mark 10:6parr where *ap archēs* and creation are used synonymously (cf. 2 Pet 3:3–4). Kevin L. Anderson has made a suggestion worth serious consideration, namely that the phrase *kairoi anapsyxeōs*; posits "a resurrectional reference." Thus Acts 1:6 is in line with many other passages in this literature where the hope of Israel is abbreviated into resurrection from the dead. The resurrection of Jesus epitomized this hope and laid the foundation for its fulfillment.[7] Given this is, we notice that creation and resurrection here form a tandem, which in the history of theology has been labeled "recapitulation theology," the coherence and correspondence between the past and the future. The resurrection of Jesus forms the bridge between the two.

---

7. Anderson, *"But God Raised Him from the Dead,"* 226–31 presents the argument at length.

The Book of Revelation

Consolation

THIS LITERATURE ADDRESSES BELIEVERS faced with suffering and trials, by introducing to them Jesus as "the firstborn of the dead, and the ruler of the kings of the earth" (Rev 1:5). Conveyed here is that Christ's resurrection from the dead gives him superiority vis-à-vis the rulers of the world. Furthermore, since he was dead and is now alive, he holds the keys of death and Hades (Rev 1:18, cf. 2:8). The initial vision of Jesus risen from the dead thus forms the hermeneutical key to the situation of the audience.[1] A confrontational perspective comes into play already from the outset. His being raised from the dead is conveyed as a *consolation* since the addressees follow in his footsteps. Chapter 5 gives a throne vision in which Christ figures prominently. He is like a "slaughtered Lamb" (Rev 5:5–6, 9, 12). This becomes "the dominant image for Christ"[2] in this literature.[3] Labeling Christ in this way brings out the sacrificial aspects of his ministry; in other words, his crucifixion is at the center of this image.[4] With regard to our topic, it is worth noticing that the slaughtered Lamb is no other than the risen Christ. His appearance in a throne vision, in the immediate vicinity of God's throne (Rev 5:7, 13; 7:10, 17; 22:1, 3), brings to mind Psalm 109:1–2 LXX.[5] The Apocalypse does not cite Old Testament passages, but it is soaked in the literary world of the Old Testament. In Rev 5:7, the lamb is associated with the right hand of he who is seated on the heavenly throne: "He went and took the scroll from the right hand of the one who was seated on

---

1. Alkier, *Reality of the Resurrection*, 184.
2. Koester, *Revelation and the End of All Things*, 80.
3. See Labahn, "Resurrection of the Followers of the Lamb," 324–26.
4. Hoffmann, *Destroyer and the Lamb*, 117–19.
5. Hoffmann, *Destroyer and the Lamb*, 134–38.

the throne." Thus, the governing image of Christ in Revelation grows out of crucifixion-theology but works within a context of Christ's exaltation in accordance with Psalm 110, the favorite Old Testament passage for Christ's resurrection in the entire New Testament.[6]

From this follow two observations pertaining to the resurrection of Jesus. Crucifixion and resurrection are intimately connected. Due to his resurrection, Christ is now found closely associated with the divine throne and recognized through the accomplishments of his crucifixion. The marks of his crucifixion remain. The book of Revelation conveys a tandem bringing to mind the encounter between Thomas and the risen Jesus in John 20:24–29: the risen Jesus is recognized by his scars. This insight may be formulated in accordance with common theological language: incarnation is not nullified by resurrection; on the contrary, it is perpetuated and remains in the resurrection.

The book of Revelation was introduced with references to Jesus who was dead and now lives, which worked as a backdrop for the consolation given throughout this literature. It is worth noticing that Rev 1:17–18 introduces such a presentation of Jesus with "Do not be afraid," thus making it clear how intimately his fate and the situation of the believers are intertwined in such a way that Jesus's resurrection forms the hermeneutical key to understanding their situation. Furthermore, it is clear that "do not be afraid" is much more than an inner individual feeling; in this writing, there is a *political* dimension to this, unfolded in the judgment against Babylon in chapters 18–20.[7] The resurrection of Jesus gives strength, hope, and courage to face oppressors. The way the resurrection of Jesus is inherently tied up with his Lordship (*kyrios*) brings with it implications challenging to others' claim to be lord.

Confrontational

The combative framework within which the resurrection of Jesus makes sense in this literature finds a germane expression in Revelation 18. As pointed out by Craig R. Koester, "Babylon's downfall in Revelation 18 forms a counterpart to the celebration of Christ's victory in Revelation 4–5."[8] This brings the resurrection of the Lamb to bear upon injustice and the fall of the Roman Empire. Chapter 19 declares that Babylon's fall in the preceding chapter is due to a

---

6. A glance in the Nestle-Aland's 28th ed. (*Loci Citati vel Allegati ex Vetere Testamento*), 854 suffices to see this.

7. Thus also Wright, *Resurrection of the Son of God*, 472.

8. Koester, *Revelation and the End of All Things*, 80.

divine judgment. Injustice is vividly portrayed in how the vision in chap. 18 envisages life in Rome, epitomized in richness, luxury, exploitation of people, even to the point of selling and buying "bodies," an unmistaken reference to slaves (vv. 3, 7, 9–13, 15–17, 19, 20).[9] Hope in the book of Revelation is woven inseparably into the end of injustice and vindication of its victims.[10] The pride of Babylon or Rome, the abundance of cargo, mistreatment of power and people becoming "victims" in this city, are challenged and overcome by the slaughtered and risen Lamb and the hope rising from that faith.[11]

This forms the backdrop against which to read the final vision of this literature, the new heaven and earth in chapters 21–22:5. This vision, inspired by passages like Isa 65:17 and 66:12, takes on a plurality of consolation images from the Hebrew Bible, such as the Paradise, the temple, Jerusalem. In short, it is the visualized presentation of the restoration-theology we noticed at work in Acts 1:6 (see Part II, What Does Belief in the Resurrection *Do*?, section on the Acts of the Apostles, An Act of Restoration.). In a canonical perspective, what is visualized here wraps up the whole Bible and Christian theology of hope. Here, the universal and cosmological dimensions are manifested. The Lamb, slaughtered and risen, is pictured within a framework of visions of a new creation, not against a backdrop of a detached, other-worldly and spiritual background.[12]

The vision of the new world is a *reversal* of conditions. Finding food will not be a problem (Rev 22:3), which contrasts the toil and curse found in Genesis 3. Relevant for the present investigation is that the New Jerusalem is depicted as a bride or a wife in opposition to Babylon, the harlot. The vision is structured according to this contrast. It is a tale of two cities and their inhabitants:

Babylon	The New Jerusalem
Harlot	Holy & bride or wife
Glorified herself	Worship God and the Lamb
A dwelling place for demons	God's presence
Marked with the sign of the Beast (13:16–17; 19:20).	The name of the Lamb on their foreheads

---

9. Koester, *Revelation*, 705–6, 721.
10. See Alkier, *Reality of the Resurrection*, 182–84.
11. Bauckham, *Climax of Prophecy*, 343–78.
12. Thus also Wright, *Resurrection of the Son of God*, 470.

Drunk with the blood of the holy martyrs of Jesus (17:6) Kings and nations drunk from the wine of her fornication (18:3)	The water of life is given as a free gift to drink
Kings and nations flock to her, selling and buying their goods; acquiring wealth for themselves. Luxury (18:3, 9–19)	Nations and kings walk in the light of God, and they bring their goods into the city (21:25–26), but the luxury is not acquired for themselves, but is the adorned bride herself (21:11–21). Healing of the nations is provided (22:2)
Exploitation of people and injustice (18:5, 13, 20, 24, cf. 17:6)	No falsehood or abomination (21:27)
The light of a lamp will shine in you no more (18:23)	No need for light or lamp (21:23), and there will be no night (21:25)
The voice of bridegroom and bride will be heard no more (18:23)	A bride adorned for her husband (21:2.9-14)
Death, mourning, and hunger (18:8)	Deaths will be no more, no mourning, pain and crying (21:4)

Craig R. Koester summarizes this in the following way: "Babylon holds no future for a bride and groom (Rev 18:23), but in New Jerusalem, the redeemed will share in the wedding banquet of the Lamb (Rev 19:7, 9)."[13] Resurrection in this literature means participation in the New Jerusalem. Thus, this final vision is intimately linked with God's judgment on injustice. John Dominic Crossan has in his works on the resurrection of Jesus coined a phrase, namely "God's Great Clean-Up of the earth."[14] The Book of Revelation is possibly the best New Testament example to prove this perspective. Resurrection, both that of the Lamb and the hope of the believers, encourages the readers to certain kinds of action and behavior, laid out in the book itself.[15] Worthy of notice is that this "clean up" acts upon the *earth*, which is not a metaphor. The Book of Revelation brings out the aspect of justice and vindication as a function of resurrection hope, and this applies equally to Christ and his followers. When this perspective is applied to Christ, the implications of his resurrection surpass that of his vindication. This is the case also in the Book of Revelation and implies that this political aspect is not alone. The Gospel of Luke may here serve as an example. The charges that led to the execution of Jesus were mostly political; he was an insurrectionist (Luke 23:2–5). When Jesus in Luke 24 explains his death, the perspective moves far beyond that (e.g., 24:25–27, 46–49).

13. Koester, *Revelation*, 827.
14. Crossan, "Bodily-Resurrection Faith," 182–86.
15. Labahn, "Resurrection of the Followers of the Lamb," 341–42.

Easter Faith Impacts

WE HAVE NOW CARRIED through a paradigmatic perspective on the belief that Jesus was raised from the dead according to some important New Testament genres and appertaining key passages. We announced that the selection of material was made in order to have something "to think with." This chapter so far is a *textual* construct, showing what sense early Christian addressees and readers *ought to* make out of their common faith in the resurrection of Jesus. Only to a limited sense do we know if they actually did so. In two remaining paragraphs of this chapter, we will now draw attention to two observations which take us *beyond* textual constructs, namely to a ritual, the celebration of Sunday, and the biography of some key persons, Peter and Paul. Both matters are changed due to the resurrection of Jesus; hence, these are *real* impacts, as they attest penetrating changes both in ritual practices and in life stories. As such they are demonstrations of *belief* in the resurrection of Jesus.

"The Day of the Lord"

Integral to this pragmatic perspective is the way Christian worship and practices from early on revolved around, not the Sabbath, but "the day of the Lord." Although there is every reason to assume that many Christ-followers, and Jews in particular, continued to organize their piety according to the Sabbath—in line with Paul's injunctions to remain as one were when called (1 Cor 7:17–24)—it is no doubt that the role of "the day of the Lord" epitomized a process towards a separation from the Jewish roots. A key question in the last decades of research into early Christian history is the so-called "Parting of the Ways," how church and synagogue eventually went their separate ways. In the complex and dynamic process towards becoming a distinct group, rituals and practices played a major role.[1]

The oldest witness to the phrase *kyriakē hēmera* is found in Rev 1:10: "I was in the spirit on the Lord's day . . . " The adjective *kyriakos* means "that which belongs to the Lord," as it is found in 1 Cor 11:20 about the Lord's meal (*kyriakon deipnon*). By the turn of the century, it seems that this was about to become a common designation for the day of service and worship for Christ-believers (Did. 14:1; Ignatius, *Magn.* 9:1–2; cf. Origen, *Cels.* 8.22). These passages are instructive as they illustrate how belief in the resurrection of Jesus became entangled in practices that gradually came to foster a distinct identity. They convey that the celebration of "the day of the Lord" was part of the process towards a distinct identity and fellowship. *Didache* gives glimpses of a fellowship where worship practices, such as fasting, prayers, and Eucharist were means of announcing Christian identity vis-à-vis Jewish worship.[2] In this context, the addressees are urged to come together (*synagein*) to worship and share the bread (Did. 14:1). The author quotes from the prophet Malachi to add a scriptural reference to this practice: The Lord is among them as they gather. Ignatius states directly that *kyriakē hēmera* is celebrated as a *replacement* of the Sabbath and the ancient customs (*Magn.* 9:1–2). This change of practice is motivated in both the death and resurrection of Jesus. Origen mentions Passover in his presentation of the "day of the Lord," thus indicating that he is aware of the shift in practices involved here. The passages from Ignatius and Origen are very clear on the connection between this day and the resurrection of Jesus.

Paul urged his Corinthian converts to prepare for the collection to the poor in Jerusalem (Gal 2:10; 2 Cor 8–9), by putting aside savings "on the first day of every week" (1 Cor 16:2): *katà mian sabbatou*, here meaning every first day of the week. The preposition is distributive, thus admonishing a *regular* practice. We learn here that *sabbaton* may mean both the Sabbath, but also a cycle of seven days; hence, week, like in Luke 18:12: "I fast twice a week (*dis tou sabbatou*)." It is worth pondering why Paul instructs them to do this on this *particular* day. The Greek of 1 Cor 16:2 brings to mind the stories about the empty tomb:

---

1. Hurtado, "Earliest Expression," 451–70 summarizes his view expressed in many publications on the issue: "In a number of publications over many years, I have repeatedly emphasized the importance of early Christian devotional practices, particularly as key evidence of the high status of Jesus in early Christian circles" (461). Hurtado does not mention the "day of the Lord" in particular, but it is obvious that it belongs to the "devotional practices"—implied here. See also Hvalvik and Sandnes, "Prayer and Identity Formation," 371–81.

2. See Kvalbein, "Lord's Prayer," 233–66.

Mark 16:1 *diagenomenou tou sabbatou*: This double genitive refers to time, and the verb means "elapse" or "pass."[3] Hence, it can be rendered, "when the Sabbath had come to an end." According to Jewish tradition, this means after sunset, which ended the Sabbath. Thus, *sabbaton* here means Sabbath, but the whole phrase refers to its end.

Matt 28:1 *opsè dè sabbatōn, tē epiphôskoúsē eis mian sabbatōn*: The adverb *opsè* gives the time, referring to the advanced point of the day, usually between sunset and darkness. This introductory phrase is further defined through the dative of time, in which the feminine *mian* supposes a dative *hēmera* to be inferred, thus making it clear that *sabbatōn* here means week; hence, "when the first day of the week was dawning." The plural *sabbatha* is often used when reference is made to the "week."[4]

Luke 24:1 *tē dè mia tōn sabbatōn*: here is a dative of time, meaning on the first day of the week.

John 20:1 *tē dè mia tōn sabbatōn*: echoes the Lukan phrase.

Mark 16:9 *prōi prōtē sabbatou*: In this addition to Mark's Gospel, the adverb *prōi* means early, and the dative gives the day as the first of the week. Here *sabbatou* is used in the singular.

Paul's instruction in 1 Cor 16:2 reflects these stories; they have paved the way for new practices (cf. Acts 20:7).[5] As a Jew, Paul counted the day according to the Sabbath. The fact that he instructs them to put aside money on this *particular* day reserves a special role for this day. When Paul insists on this day it indicates that the day was reserved for the worship, which was in accordance with the core of Christian faith. In other words, already in the fifties, the resurrection of Jesus had a shaping effect on time and worship. However, Paul sees no rivalry with the Sabbath, as does Ignatius later (*Magn.* 9:1-2). It is worth considering if 1 Cor 16:2 assumes familiarity with the empty tomb tradition. Paul in 1 Cor 15:4 connects the third day to *egēgertai*, Jesus being raised. It is worth noticing that "the third day" or the first day of the week in the narrative traditions is associated primarily with the empty tomb; it is only loosely connected with the appearances. This consistent picture is not

---

3. BDAG s.v.

4. See, e.g., Did. 8:1 where it says that the Jews fast on the second and fifth day of the week: *deutera sabbatōn kai pemptē*.

5. See for example Fee, *First Epistle to the Corinthians*, 813–14, which also gives relevant literature.

to be overlooked when Paul's citation in 1 Cor 15:3–5 leaves out the empty tomb and mentions only the appearances. This is a question to which we will return when we address 1 Corinthians 15. Anyway, Paul's instruction in 1 Cor 16:2 is given within the framework of Easter traditions. When we come to Rev 1:10, "the day of the Lord" has become an independent way of speaking about the day of worship for Christ-believers.

The *Gospel of Peter* attests how "the day of the Lord" and the stories about the empty tomb are intertwined in such a way that the first is motivated by the latter. 9.34–35 sets out in terms echoing Matt 28:1 and Mark 16:9 (*prōias dè epiphōskontos tou sabbatou*), and proceeds by mentioning "the night in which the Lord's day (*hē kyriakē*) dawned." In 12.50 this gospel speaks about "the dawn of the Lord's Day (*orthou dè tēs kyriakēs*)"[6] as the time when Mary Magdalene arrived at the tomb. The "liturgical" language that developed from the Easter stories is here inscribed into these stories themselves.[7]

When Justin Martyr describes Christian services or gatherings in Rome (*1 Apol.* 67.3), he affirms the role of this day in Rome in the second century: "And on the day called Sunday (*tē tou hēliou legomenē hēmera*) there is an assembly of those who dwell in cities or the countryside, and the memoirs of the apostles and the writings of the prophets are read, for as long as there is time" (3).[8] This is clarified further in *1 Apol.* 67.8:

> And it is on Sunday that we all make assembly in common, since it is the first day (*prōtē hēmera*), on which God changed darkness and matter and made the world, and Jesus Christ our savior rose from the dead on the same day. For they crucified him on the day before Saturday (*pro tēs Kronikēs*), and on the day after Saturday, which is Sunday (*hēliou hēmera*), having appeared to his apostles . . .

The traditions about Easter and the tomb found empty on the third day are here seen as perpetuating creation, thus affirming observations made earlier in the present chapter. The third day transformed worship practices in a remarkable way, especially seen against the backdrop of Jewish customs. We

---

6. We notice here that this gospel does not say "the first day," but simply mentions the adjective *kyriakē*. This independent use of the adjective is made possible by the fact that it became the technical term for Sunday.

7. See Johnston, *Resurrection of Jesus*, 179–80.

8. This passage does not imply, as most scholars tend to think, that Christians gathered together in *one* place on Sundays. This is highly unlikely due to practical problems. Justin's passage indicates the practice of Christians to meet on Sundays; see Sandnes, *New Family*, 98–99; see also *Justin: Philosopher and Martyr*, 259. The translations given above are taken from there.

notice a process from Paul to whom Sabbath and Sundays were not rivals, to Ignatius, and possibly also Justin where the latter *replaces* the first, whereby exclusiveness is urged, as it was considered a matter of identity. The characteristics of this day for Christians were even noted by an outside observant like Pliny the Younger when he introduced the Christians to Emperor Trajan: he says that they met regularly before dawn on a fixed day (*soliti stato die ante lucem convenire*) (*Ep.* 10.96.7). The Roman governor had observed that Christians' gatherings insisted on a particular day, and he reported this to the Emperor in the year 112 CE.[9]

Transformed Lives

We should not assume that Paul's developed way of making sense of resurrection was commonly shared, albeit he does emphasize that belief in the resurrection of Jesus is a *common* marker of Christian identity (1 Cor 15:11). Neither should we assume that the way he conceives of the Christian life as participating in a resurrection trajectory mirrored the reality in the churches. His letters amply demonstrate shortcomings with regard to lifestyle and disagreements on how to understand what resurrection is really about. Nonetheless, it is essential to observe that faith in the resurrection of Jesus caused dramatic *changes* in the lives of people. Lives of some well-known figures were deeply affected; belief in the resurrection of Jesus rendered their lives altered. In a pragmatic-oriented approach, this effect is worth pondering upon. We start by noting what Reinhard Deichgräber has labeled "conversion terminology" (*Bekehrungsterminologie*),[10] to which belongs for example turning from darkness to life, from blindness to sight, and death to life. This kind of speech is recognizable in the New Testament as well (Col 1:12–14; Acts 26:18: 1 Pet 2:9–10; Luke 15:24; Eph 2:1–3; 4:7–10; 5:8–14). This metaphorical usage gained importance due to the belief that the resurrection of Jesus paved the way also for a general resurrection of the believers. Such language became "flesh" in the stories of many people, among whom we here make reference to Peter and Paul, in particular, the first an insider to the group that accompanied Jesus during his ministry, and the latter an outsider, not to say enemy of the followers of Jesus. Their lives were *lastingly* changed due to what is claimed to be encounters with the risen Jesus, albeit different in mode.

---

9. For a detailed presentation of the Lord's Day, see Bauckham, *Christian World*, 355–84.

10. Deichgräber, *Gotteshymnus und Christushymnus*, 80–87.

The gospels unanimously give Peter a key role during the ministry of Jesus, and he seems to have retained this position also in the Jerusalem church after the resurrection (Gal 1:18; 2:6-9; Acts 2:14). His position in the attestations of the resurrection of Jesus is also undisputed. Paul mentions Christ appearing to Cephas (=Peter) first (1 Cor 15:5). According to Mark 16:7, the women were instructed by the angel to "tell his disciples and Peter." This picks up on Mark 14:28-31 where Peter insisted on his unswerving loyalty. In Luke 24, the rumors about the risen Jesus are rendered in the following way: "The Lord has risen indeed, and he has appeared to Simon!" (v. 34). The Fourth Gospel assigns to him a special role in the Easter traditions, as he is the first to enter the empty tomb (John 20:1-10). Likewise, chapter 21, probably a later addition to the Gospel, pinpoints Peter in a special way as the risen Jesus appears to his disciples (John 21:1-14, 15-23). In spite of the fact that this chapter is written to correct a rumor about "the disciple whom Jesus loved," it is almost throughout a chapter about Peter and the risen Jesus. The decisive role of Peter in the Easter testimonies must be seen against the backdrop of his denial of Jesus, rendered in all the gospels (Mark 14:54, 66-72parr), forming a sharp contrast to his confession earlier (Mark 8:29parr). This is likely more than a textual construct; it was embarrassing both to Peter, a leading figure of the movement, and to the movement handing down these stories.[11] Meeting with the risen Christ served to reconcile and to re-install Peter. There is a gap between the man who wept and broke down as he realized that he had denied Jesus (Mark 14:72parr) and the man who according to Paul is one of the "pillars" of the Jerusalem church. The resurrection of Christ filled in this gap, and "created" the Peter commonly remembered.[12] The New Testament unanimously witnesses to the rehabilitation of Peter due to the risen Christ meeting with him.

Paul's life was also dramatically changed and shaped after his meeting with the risen Christ outside Damascus (Gal 1:15-16; 1 Cor 9:1; 15:8; cf. Acts 9; 22; 26).[13] Paul turned from a persecutor to a follower of Christ, and he embarked on a life-long ministry as an apostle to the Gentiles.[14] Paul re-

11. To Celsus, the betrayal of Judas is presented as something committed by "many disciples" (*Cels.* 2.11-12) and the denial of Peter (*Cels.* 2.45) are demonstrations of the rabble Jesus gathered around himself. This is not only telling about the disciples, but demonstrates also that Jesus was a bad leader: what good commander would be let down by his own soldiers in this way, asks Celsus; see Cook, *Interpretation of the New Testament*, 48-49.

12. See Bockmuehl, *Simon Peter in Scripture and Memory*; as for Peter in the Scriptures, see especially 3-33.

13. There are possibly other references to this event in Paul's letters; for a maximalist reading, see Kim, *Origin of Paul's Gospel*.

14. As for the theological implications of this event for Paul, see Sandnes, *Paul*

views what happened to him in Phil 3:5–11, which is of utmost significance for the perspective of the present study. The change that occurred to him is in vv. 9–11 formulated in terms of the resurrection of Jesus, the power of his resurrection, and Paul's being united with him (*symmorfizesthai*). We recognize this way of speaking from Paul's way of bringing together the resurrection of Christ and the fate of his followers (see Part II, What Does Belief in the Resurrection *Do*?, Paul the Apostle, section The Risen Jesus and the Christ-Believer).

Actually, the verses following upon his resurrection-oriented summary of the Damascus event continues in vv. 12–21, ending up with how God will transform the body, by making it conform to the body of glory of the risen Christ (v. 21). In other words, Paul's life embodies the trajectory of resurrection running through the life of Christ believers, from the present to the future. Paul's Damascus event, which he claims to be Christ appearing to him, will be addressed later in this study.[15] It here suffices to point out that both Peter and Paul embody the transformation that faith in the resurrection of Jesus and meeting with him brought to the disciples. According to James D. G. Dunn, there is "a marked 'before and after' difference in the disciples."[16] He points out that they were "transformed from frightened men cowering indoors 'for fear of the Jews' (John 20:19) to men who could not be intimidated even by the leading Jewish authorities . . ." The adequate explanation for this change is that they really believed in the resurrection of Jesus. At least, so it seems.

Life Changing or Guilt Complex?

Some scholars argue that what we have here labeled the "life-changing" effect of resurrection turns things upside down. It is really to be conceived of the other way around. It is Peter and Paul who had an effect upon the very idea of the resurrection of Jesus. Gerd Lüdemann argues that the appearances and the empty tomb came into being out of hallucinations induced by guilt complexes.[17] In other words, a psychoanalytical approach explains how things came into being, suggesting a direction *opposite* to what is given

---

Perceived, 37–47.

15. See Part II, 1 Corinthians 15, sec. He Appeared to Cephas and . . .

16. Dunn, *Evidence for Jesus*, 59–60.

17. Lüdemann, *Resurrection of Jesus*, 97–100, 173–79; for a related view see also Goulder, "Baseless Fabric of a Vision," 48–61. For an extensive presentation and critique of the psychoanalytical approach of Lüdemann and Goulder and the theory of cognitive dissonance, see Licona, *Resurrection of Jesus*, 479–519; Wright, *Resurrection of the Son of God*, 697–701.

here. Such an approach finds substantiation in theories of cognitive dissonance, as developed for example by Leon Festinger[18] or in psychological studies on the effects that bereavement may have on mourners.[19] Festinger investigated what happened to a group of people who entertained a flying saucers cult in mid-Western America in the 1950s. The group centered on a woman who claimed to receive messages from outer space, culminating in making known to her that a massive flood would engulf America, but that the devotees would be rescued in a flying saucer at a given time and date. When this time had passed, with no flooding and no rescue, the behavior of the group changed, launching themselves into recruiting new members to the fellowship and its belief: "If . . . more and more converts could be found . . . then the dissonance between their belief and the knowledge that the messages had not been correct could be reduced."[20] In other words, mission and outreach were the direct outcomes of cognitive dissonance, bringing to mind the centrality of mission in the New Testament Easter traditions. Although Festinger did not apply this to the development of a Jewish Christian sect's belief in the resurrection, it may well be used in that way.

When Gerd Lüdemann in 2012 looked back and summarized his view on the resurrection, he drew on contemporary psychological research. He refers to examples where mourners claim to have heard or seen the deceased appearing to them. Feelings of guilt often heighten the form such experiences may take: "Here, normal reality controls can break down when the unconscious, unable to bear the loss of a beloved person, creates a pseudo-satisfaction for herself."[21] Judged in this way, Cephas's vision of the risen Christ is a delusion or wishful thinking. There is no reason to question the theories Lüdemann here refers to; they render a phenomenon that is well-known. However, Lüdemann's claim that this approach has an explanatory force vis-à-vis the New Testament evidence of the Easter faith is another matter. Lüdemann seems to think that if psychological explanations are involved, faith in the resurrection of Jesus is bereft of any reality. In principle, it is possible that some of the psychological mechanisms he describes do apply, while something external still occurred the first Easter to the disciples. Lüdemann is overtly genealogical in his position; i.e., his search for analogies serves the aim of explaining how CR came into being, and thus to deconstruct this belief.

18. Festinger, *Theory of Cognitive Dissonance*.
19. In his "Resurrection of Jesus," 554–57, Gerd Lüdemann makes special reference to such experiences.
20. Festinger, *Theory of Cognitive Dissonance*, 259.
21. Lüdemann, "Resurrection of Jesus," 556.

Lüdemann's use of the psychological theories of bereavement is to be assessed both methodically and historically. In other words, the theory itself needs to be assessed vis-à-vis relevant material and also the assumption of what guilt complexes may effect, against a historical backdrop that pertains to the situation at play here. As for the first, the theory developed by Festinger applies to a somewhat limited number of people and cannot be extended to larger groups without further ado. Likewise, bereavement theories address individuals, not effects upon *groups* of people, some of whom had no reason for guilt complexes. According to Lüdemann, the cognitive dissonance of Peter and Paul were indeed infectious, as it gradually came to be shared by others, people who claimed visions of the risen Christ, without any prior reason for a similar feeling of guilt. Here is a leap not accounted for in the presentation of Lüdemann. He concentrates on the case of Peter, and his reason for a guilt complex. In his conclusion, however, he claims that what happened to Peter applies to the disciples *generally*:

> By a bold, if unconscious, leap Peter entered the world of his wishes. As a result, he "saw" Jesus, concluded that he had risen from the dead, and thus made it possible for the other disciples to "see" Jesus in the same way. Hence, the Christian church is to some extent the historical result of the disciples' grief.[22]

The plural "disciples" comes more or less out of the blue here; it does not follow from the theory. The sharing in the vision or hallucination of another, which is here assumed, goes beyond the theories at work here.

When Gerd Lüdemann looks back at his contributions, he adds another aspect, namely that the apocalyptic idea of a general resurrection is applied to an individual, Jesus: "And the transposition was no more than might be expected, because in the company of this single person he (Peter) had already either observed or experienced many things that were expected to happen only at the coming of the new aeon."[23] In other words, in view of his previous experiences with Jesus, Peter understood that his vision or hallucination meant that the new age had dawned. This observation adds some credibility to Lüdemann's view but also parades the *relative* validity of his use of bereavement theories.

From a historical perspective, Peter seems a more likely candidate for guilt complexes than Paul. His special role in the Easter stories has been pointed out above. We need to be cautious, though, not to impose on this historical figure a psychoanalytical grid of our own time. The inner life

---

22. Lüdemann, "Resurrection of Jesus," 557.
23. Lüdemann, "Resurrection of Jesus," 550–51.

of figures appearing in the New Testament is not easily accessed through our post-Easter gospel texts. We are also reminded that within the circle of the disciples there is another figure, Judas, who probably felt betrayed and let down by Jesus—not the other way around—as insinuated by the idea of a guilt complex. Jesus's claim to be Messiah differed markedly from both Judas's and many others' expectations, and guilt is not the only viable reaction to that discrepancy. To cut this short, it is not at all evident that guilt complexes towards Jesus were the only possible reaction. There is also the possibility that a contemporary Jew like Judas, and maybe also Peter, felt betrayed by Jesus.

As for Paul, he represents the Achilles heel for Gerd Lüdemann's thesis. According to Lüdemann, Paul was like Peter, a victim of self-deception. He understands Rom 7:14–25 as referring to Paul's inner conflict prior to the Damascus event.[24] The dissatisfaction that Paul, according to Lüdemann, finds himself in vis-à-vis Judaism, represents an outdated version of Pauline scholarship. Judged by present-day scholarship, Paul's indebtedness to his Jewish faith and tradition is a key to understanding him. For Lüdemann's thesis to work, he has to portray Paul prior to Damascus in a way that runs contrary to the evidence, and also against a commonly held view, namely that Paul was inspired by the ideal embodied in the Phineas traditions evolving from Numbers 25, and manifested in the role of Paul's zeal for the Law, mentioned in Gal 1:14; Phil 3:6 (cf. Acts 22:3).[25] Paul prior to Damascus was not a man of guilt complexes, neither towards Judaism nor towards Jesus and the movement associated with him. The Phineas model points in a somewhat opposite direction. Paul was a man proud of devoting himself to fight fellow Jews whom he found jeopardizing the true worship of the God of the Fathers. In so doing he considered himself in ways similar to John 16:3, as "offering a service to God." In short, Paul prior to Damascus considered himself "as to righteousness under the law, blameless" (Phil 3:6). Furthermore, Lüdemann proceeds from an overtly simple distinction between Paul as a Jew and Paul as a Christian, as though the two are easily kept apart. Lüdemann's portrayal of Paul has been sidetracked by more recent Pauline

---

24. Lüdemann, *Resurrection of Jesus*, 80–84; see also his *Resurrection of Christ*, 166–72.

25. Seland, *Establishment Violence in Philo and Luke* and also his "Saul of Tarsus and Early Zealotism," 449–71. In his *Resurrection of Christ*, 169–70, Lüdemann takes the Phineas tradition into account, but ends up dismissing it for a more depth-psychological perspective. He argues that unless one writes off Paul's change from persecutor to preacher as a miracle (which to Lüdemann is impossible in principle), a psychological interpretation prevails. This indicates that his admittance to the relevance of Phineas is not taken seriously as a historical and theological phenomenon.

studies. It here suffices to mention the many relevant questions raised by the so-called "Paul with Judaism" movement in Pauline studies.[26]

We also need to remind ourselves that the so-called sign prophets, and other prophetic figures mentioned by Josephus—Theudas, the Egyptian, Jesus son of Hananjah, to mention some—with claims not unlike that of Jesus, were slain by the Romans, without giving rise to a movement following in their steps and worshipping them.[27] This means that, even if Lüdemann's theory should apply, it is contingent only, that is to say, it offers no more than a possibility. In the given historical context, it is by no means compelling.

Celsus—Gerd Lüdemann's Ancient Like-Minded?

When Gerd Lüdemann and others explain the resurrection of Jesus as caused by hallucinations, they may appear to stand on the shoulders of ancient critics, Celsus in particular. According to this early and prominent critic, faith in the resurrection came about as a result of the wishful thinking of a "hysterical woman" (see Part II, The Easter Narratives, section Women at the Tomb.) or from some other of her circle of deluders (*allos tōn ek tēs autēs goēteias*) who

> either dreamt in a certain state of mind and through wishful thinking had a hallucination (*phantasiōtheis*) due to some mistaken notion (an experience which has happened to thousands) or, which is more likely, wanted to impress the others by telling this fantastic tale, and so this cock-and-bull story to provide a chance for other beggars. (*Cels.* 2.55/SC132.145.19–416.25)[28]

As pointed out by Horacio E. Lona, Celsus combines a psychological and sociological approach here.[29] As for the first, it is not about guilt complexes, but instead about a confused mind making up things, thus being trapped in one's own delusion. As for the second, a recurrent motif in Celsus's critique

---

26. See, e.g., Nanos and Zetterholm, *Paul within Judaism*.

27. See, e.g., Barnett, "Jewish Sign Prophets," 679–97. Theudas is mentioned in Acts 5:36–37 and the Egyptian in Acts 21:38.

28. According to *Cels.* 3.22 (SC 136.51.9–10), Jesus appeared as a "phantom." This is how Chadwick renders the Greek *skia*, which more accurately means "shadow." Celsus here refers to the shadowy or slippery nature of the appearances of Jesus, portraying them as unreal visions analogous to the phenomenon that those fallen dead may appear to people around the tomb. This is stated with reference to what Plato says; see Lona, *Die "Wahre Lehre" des Kelsos*, 189. According *Cels.* 3.43 (SC 136.104.32–37), Origen holds against Celsus that he accepts the Scriptures when they speak about the death and burial of Christ, but thinks it is a fiction (*plasma*) when it comes to his resurrection.

29. Lona, *Die "Wahre Lehre" des Kelsos*, 162–63.

comes into play here. The Christians are simpletons, easily fooled (*Cels.* 3.44; 3.55).[30] In fact, these two perspectives are intertwined, since the psychological explanation provides a reason for the sociological blame. The two kinds of arguments come together in Celsus calling the Christians *euētheis*, "silly or naïve people" (*Cels.* 3.24/SC 136.56.10–11).

It is worth noticing that Celsus combines these ways of explaining the resurrection belief with a historical phenomenon, namely *sorcery*, which forms a tandem with the notion of delusion (*goēteia*).[31] Celsus portrays the resurrection in a way resonating with ancient sources on how magicians at times deceived simple people and took advantage of them financially. It is difficult to know what precisely he has in mind, but at points, his presentation appears as a blueprint of for example Lucian of Samosata's satirical story about Alexander of Abonuteichos, *Alexander The False Prophet*.[32] Whether Celsus knew Lucian's text or not is a disputed matter, especially since the treatise of the satirist, in fact, is dedicated to his friend "Celsus" (*Alex.* 1).[33] Even Origen is in doubt about the true identity of his opponent (*Cels.* 1.8), and we do not know if the two occurrences of Celsus refer to the same person. Be that as it may, Lucian's piece is well-fitted heuristically, as it fleshes out what Celsus might have in mind. Alexander established a cult based on the appearance of Glycon, a god in a serpent form with a human head. He was the incarnation of this god or Asclepios's false priest, as Lucian sees it. He was trained by the great miracle worker in the ancient world, Apollonius of Tyana (*Alex.* 5). Thus, Lucian refutes and puts on display the falsity of a major miracle worker tradition in the ancient world. Alexander specialized in magic, deceitful tricks, and spells. Selling oracles was a method and becoming rich a purpose (*Alex.* 7–8, 15–19, 23–31). For example, Alexander developed a method to undo the seals of the requests for oracles given to the temple and was thus in a position to give impressive answers, as he knew the questions in advance. Lucian leaves no doubt about how this practice was received: ". . . to those driveling idiots it was miraculous (*terastion*) and almost as good as incredible" (*Alex.* 20). Celsus reasons likewise with regard to the resurrection of Jesus.

30. For more on Celsus's critique, see Sandnes, *Challenge of Homer*, 152–58.

31. For a presentation of Celsus and the New Testament resurrection traditions, see Cook, *Interpretation*, 54–61.

32. A. M. Harmon, LCL Vol 4. Lona, *Die "Wahre Lehre" des Kelsos*, 118–19 also makes reference to this text of Lucian. As for this figure, Lucian's hostile account is the only literary source, but the Glycon cult is attested also in inscriptions and images; see Victor, *Lukian von Samosata*.

33. For a discussion, see Origen, *Contra Celsum*, xxiv–xxvi, and Lona, *Die "Wahre Lehre" des Kelsos*, 28–30. Both are hesitant to identify the two.

It is worth noticing for example that in *Cels.* 2.55 (SC 132.416.23) the resurrection is labeled *terateia*, which echoes *Alex.* 20. In *Cels.* 1.68, Celsus goes into detail to tell how ancient tricksters used stage machinery, displaying expensive banquets, cakes, and fishes that did not really exist at all, and "who make things move as though they were alive" (*hōs zōa kinoúntōn*).[34] This is why Celsus according to *Cels.* 3.50 accused the Christians of attracting people through trickery (*tà epirrētotata*) like sorcerers: "Those who display their trickery in the market-places and go about begging would never enter a gathering of intelligent men . . ."[35] We see here that the label magic also serves a purpose of humiliating Christian belief by disassociating it from rationality and learned men. The "reality" present is only a matter of imagination; it is cheating, as Origen in *Cels.* 2.48–54 unfolds Celsus's approach. These passages provide an explanation for a historical context which according to Celsus enabled resurrection belief. In calling Mary Magdalene "a hysterical woman" and attributing other records of the risen Jesus's appearances to sorcery, Celsus refers to: "those who were deluded by some sorcery (*goēteia*)" (*Cels.* 2.59/SC 132.424.18–23).[36] At first sight, then, present-day psychological theories applied to the belief that Jesus was raised from the dead, may seem to find an ally in Celsus, but this claim is in need of relevant historical and cultural clarifications.

Summary

We have looked into how belief in the resurrection of Jesus is situated in New Testament writings and how it works, thus paving the way for considerations moving *beyond* the biblical texts, but which also are biblically based. What have we found? The investigation has been limited to three main genres: epistles, narrative, and apocalypse. The New Testament is soaked in the belief that Christ was raised from the dead. It is worth noticing how two prominent critics view the situation after having assessed the role of this belief in the New Testament. Michael Goulder puts it like this: "Perhaps the sapient sutlers of the Lord may manage without Jesus' resurrection, or reinterpret it;

---

34. SC 132.266.7–19. Kelhoffer, *Conceptions of "Gospel,"* 289–301 shows how charges of magic and deceptive tricks involving various kinds of manipulations were thrown against heretics by Christians as well.

35. SC 136.118.1–4. This links up with the well-known paragraph in *Cels.* 3.49 where the Christian mission and preaching is ridiculed; see Sandnes, *Challenge of Homer*, 149–58.

36. For the Greek noun *goēteia* as witchcraft, spell, or charm which is deluding, see LSJ s.v.

but it will not, I think, be the same religion."[37] Gerd Lüdemann says that he is now convinced that "disproving the historicity of the resurrection of Jesus willy-nilly annuls the Christian heritage by showing that its ultimate faith claim was based on an error. Consequently, I must reject my 1994 attempt to base Christianity on the historical Jesus."[38] Such assessments rightly take into account the *centrality* of resurrection faith in the New Testament, as well as the claims made there that it was an "event."

Paul, the first to advance the faith in Christ's resurrection, emphasized the *theocentric* nature of the resurrection. God, the source of life, raised Jesus from the dead. God Creator was at the center of this belief. In raising Jesus from the dead, God affirmed himself as God of the living, beyond the point of death. Creation theology is the massive backdrop against which to interpret Paul's theology of Jesus's resurrection. Hence, the resurrection is not set apart from creation but instead understood *within* that perspective and framework. The believer is through baptism united with Jesus's death and resurrection. A trajectory, marked by resurrection, runs through the gamut of Christian life, from the renewal of mind and thought, inclusive of conduct, culminating in a newly transformed body. It makes perfect sense, therefore, that the baptism liturgy, as well as the funeral liturgy of the Norwegian Lutheran Church, are rounded off by reference to 1 Pet 1:3, about "rebirth into a living hope." The life of Christ believers is encircled by resurrection. Hope is, therefore, a key term vis-à-vis Paul's addressees.

The book of Acts turns more *evidentiary* than does Paul. The resurrection of Jesus is framed by a discourse of proofs, empirical and Scriptural in nature. This gives to the resurrection a more physical aspect than in Paul. Nonetheless, the restoration perspective runs somehow parallel with what Paul aims at, although the two formulate themselves in different terms.

Like Paul's "hope," the book of Revelation turns resurrection into a message of consolation. Equally important is that it is also confrontational vis-à-vis powers and rulers, *in casu* Roman tyrannical power. The final vision of the new heaven and earth brings creation motives into play. Intertwined in Old Testament images is the hope extracted from the resurrection of Jesus.

Thus, belief in the resurrection of Jesus permeates the entire New Testament, and it impacted on worship practices and lives of individuals in such a way that both Christian rituals and biographies came to manifest the changing power of this faith. This belief is the substratum underlying all

---

37. Goulder, "Baseless Fabric of a Vision," 59.

38. Lüdemann, "Resurrection of Jesus," 535–36; thus also *Resurrection of Christ*, 11–22.

convictions spelled out. Against that backdrop, it appears as a minimalistic reading when apologists look for evidence, as though it is a topic or an isolated event, and equally so when critics question any historical basis for this faith and still claim its importance. The way this faith is rooted in creation theology is a caveat against one-sided spiritual and metaphorical interpretations. Belief in the resurrection of Jesus, as it appears in the New Testament, makes claims regarding the past, challenges concerning the present, and hopes for the future.

1 Corinthians 15: Resurrection—
Without an Empty Tomb?

HAVING NOW COVERED, ALBEIT a sketch of, relevant passages in general and from a pragmatic perspective, now it is time to turn to more *specific* texts, taken from the double evidence available, an ancient creed and narrative traditions; in other words, the passages about appearance and disappearance (empty tomb). We start with the *oldest* source available. This Pauline chapter invites a tradition critical approach to our topic, as it is the earliest extant treatment of the issue. According to the principle "earlier is best," special attention has been given to this text. We will concentrate on two questions, the absence of the *empty tomb* in what is most likely a pre-Pauline formula or a creed-like statement and the resurrected body. Paul incorporates in his letter a text antedating him with possibly a decade or so.[1] Paul also here addresses the question of what kind of body the resurrected come with (1 Cor 15:35–58) directly. Although this part of the chapter is devoted to the general resurrection, it is, by all means, clear that the resurrection body of Jesus is part of this. There is a mutual relationship between these parts of the chapter, made apparent in v. 22 and v. 44 by the way Christ and Adam are juxtaposed. The resurrection of Jesus and general revivification are bridged by Jesus being conceptualized as the "last" Adam.

Paul's chapter is permeated with questions and answers, a style often labeled diatribe, a rhetorical style associated with instruction and guidance on a given topic. The style may also be occasioned by imaginary or even real interlocutors posing such questions. At points in the text, the latter seems to be the case here, as Paul in 1 Cor 15:12 makes reference to "some" who claim that there is no resurrection. Likewise, Paul's reference to a Corinthian practice of taking baptism for deceased members of the

---

1. Gerhardsson, "Evidence for Christ's Resurrection," 73–91 says that the formula has been put together in the early thirties, a reasonable guess.

Christian fellowship has a ring of being locally relevant. Hence, the first developed affirmation of resurrection faith is simultaneously a witness to the fact that this belief was a matter of debate, even to the extent of being denied. Implied is, therefore, that an apologetic situation is at hand already here. Resurrection has never been easily grasped, and this is attested in the first available possible source, delving into this.

Paul's claim to Christian unity evolving from a common faith in the resurrection of Jesus (1 Cor 15:11), probably owes more to his view than to reality. Relevant Jewish sources, the New Testament, and other early Christian literature vividly attest that different views on resurrection circulated widely. In fact, Paul's chapter is in itself an indirect witness to some plurality which Paul wants to influence.

The first eleven verses of this chapter revolve around an apparently formulaic text, while from v. 12, Paul embarks upon an argument, entering a discourse alive among his Corinthian converts. It is not evident how far the formulaic text extends, where it ends so to say. The brevity style introduced with *hoti* makes it likely that vv. 3–5 represent a transmitted formula, while the rest is additions, at least so in v. 8 where Paul introduces himself, but keeps the formulaic style.[2] It comes clearly through that the formulaic text is conceived as a *summary* of Paul's gospel (vv. 1–2, 11). This observation has important repercussions for the question of the empty tomb (see below). Two conditional sentences, both introduced with *ei* (v. 2), correspond to the several conditions (*ei*) listed in vv. 12–15. This linkage implies that Paul's presentation in vv. 1–11 comes against the backdrop of a situation which he deems as bringing his gospel to a naught. With the *brevity* of this text also follows *sparseness* on information. Worth noticing is that denial of Christ's resurrection is reckoned not a Christological issue, but as testifying against *God* (v. 15). Thus, the theocentric perspective is emphasized, very much in line with observations done in the preceding chapter. The way Paul introduces his errand here echoes what we find in Rom 10:9–13 as well, where also God raising Jesus from the dead is identified as the fundamentals of saving faith. Before delving into the passage, it is worthwhile to contemplate that the passage in question is summarizing key moments in the life of Jesus in a creed-like way. The Old Testament provides examples of similar summaries of God's history with his people (Deut 6:20–24; 26:5–11; Josh 24:2–13). These texts outline larger narratives with the purpose of proclaiming God's presence among them. To be noted is also the identity-forming

---

2. Lüdemann, "Opening Statement," 44–45; Lindemann, "Resurrection of Jesus," exemplifies this nicely.

aspect of such outlines. As for 1 Corinthians 15, there is no doubt about the identity-forming aspect of the resurrection of Jesus.

Tradition: Wording or Substance?

One of the reasons that the passage is commonly seen to have incorporated formulaic sentences, is Paul's explicit reference to tradition here. Verse 1 sees this from the perspective of the addressees; they have received (*parelabete*) this tradition, and v. 2 takes Paul's perspective; he has handed down (*paredōka*) to them tradition (cf. v. 11 which also assumes commonality here). Paul handed down to them this *en prōtois*, which may refer to "at the beginning," "in the first place," or "above all."[3] Any of these renderings give to this tradition a significant role. How this reference to tradition is understood, has a direct bearing upon our main question in this section: what is really included regarding the resurrection of Jesus in the tradition Paul calls upon? The fact that this crucial text makes no mention of the empty tomb is often made use of in ways hardly accounted for: "An important corollary of the analysis is that the appearance tradition originally had nothing to do with stories of the empty tomb." In saying this, Gerd Lüdemann considers 1 Corinthians 15 witnessing that Paul did not know anything about the empty tomb and that he did not need it for his concept of resurrection, and he speaks for many scholars.[4] Lüdemann makes a virtue of the absence of the empty tomb. For sure, there is no *reference* to the tomb being empty here.[5] Nonetheless, the language of tradition and the passing on of tradition and the way this passage summarizes, invite a revisiting of this question. Reaching a conclusion regarding this is not due, however, before a closer look at vv. 3–8 has been undertaken.

At present, we need to point out that Lüdemann's position infers an understanding of tradition which, in our view, amounts to *reductio ad absurdum*, since it implies that the tradition passed on by Paul is *identical* with the very wording found in vv. 3–5. Is it likely that what Paul taught his Corinthian converts is limited to the wording of vv. 3–5? Relevant here is what the dative of instrument *tini logō*, referring to "through which you

---

3. See for example Thiselton, *First Epistle to the Corinthians*, 1186.

4. Lüdemann, "Resurrection of Jesus," 549; see also Lindemann, "Resurrection of Jesus," 574; Crossan, "Bodily-Resurrection Faith," 176–78. For the way this has become a "koinē" in New Testament studies, see also Novakovic, *Resurrection*, 59–61.

5. From a more systematic point of view, it is worth noticing here that this does not mean that an empty tomb is a necessary condition for the belief in resurrection—a point that would make nil the Christian belief in the resurrection of all humanity. For further on this point, see below, on Dalferth, "Volles Grab, Leerer Glaube?," 395–97.

are also being saved," really means. It is a reference to the *wording* found in the quotation (vv. 3–5),[6] which would substantiate a technical and limited reference for the tradition implied here: it is a matter of wording found in the formula. This implies that the very words used in the formulaic passage are at stake here. Anthony Thiselton comments: "Any difficulty dissolves as soon as we recall that *logos* often denotes not simply *word, message*, or *act of speaking* but also *content or* substance *of a declaration, assertion, proposition or other communicative act*."[7] Paul often uses *logos* in precisely this way.[8] Stefan Alkier points out that "[t]he gospel received by Paul and proclaimed by him does not obtain its identity through a formula with fixed wording."[9] This has repercussions on how narrowly one has to define the tradition involved. Alkier presents a critique, pertinent vis-à-vis the common view regarding this passage and the empty tomb. Denying any presence of empty tomb traditions in this text amounts to treating Pauline thinking about passing on tradition as recounting some key "signifiers" only, "as with incantations." In fact, it is like claiming that *logos tou staurou* in 1 Cor 1:18 has no reference beyond the word "cross." No doubt, it refers to the power inherent in Paul's proclamation of the cross of Jesus more widely, and it is expected to include at least some narrative tags. Furthermore, taken together, 1 Cor 15:3–5 provide a narrative substructure of the Jesus story: "The verbs *die—to be buried—raised—appear* are the smallest narrative details that in their sequence reveal the narrative plot of the Jesus-Christ-Story in its Pauline version." Thus, taking into account what is conveyed through "tradition" here paves the way for revisiting the issue of the empty tomb. Maybe the empty tomb is not so absent as often claimed?

"Died for our Sins according to the Scriptures"

This sentence has three components: an aorist referring to a past event, a prepositional phrase indicating for whose benefit Jesus died, and a second prepositional phrase claiming Scriptural basis. Hence, Scripture is called upon in all brevity and generalization, as forming the basis for the soteriology implied here. Commentaries address what texts may be in view here, and Isaiah 53 is probably a primary reference. However, it seems that

---

6. Some scholars take *tini logō* with the introductory verb *gnōrizō*, but the distance between them speaks against this.

7. Thiselton, *First Epistle to the Corinthians*, 1185. The italics and bold are all his.

8. To prove this point, it here suffices to make reference to BDAG s.v.

9. Alkier, *Reality of the Resurrection*, 22–24.

a *general* claim is what is aimed at here;[10] the Scriptures generally provide a basis for what the death of Jesus brought about, very much in line with Luke 24 (see vv. 25–27, 44 in particular). The general reference in Luke 24 is obvious as the risen Jesus states that Moses (the Law), Prophets and the Scriptures—a common denominator for the holy texts as such—unanimously speak about him. It is probable that the formulaic tradition Paul leans on reasons likewise.

"He Was Buried"

In one single word (*etaphē*), this old creed states that Jesus was buried. This single word is crucial as it underscores the *reality* of death. Like any dead man, Jesus was also buried. Equally important, however, is that "buried" also serves as a prelude to what follows, namely Jesus being raised. The rest of this Pauline chapter makes this amply clear; *egeirein* is a verb whose content aims at those who have passed away. Mentioning the burial prepares for the resurrection. From the outset, it is necessary to point out that the formula does not speak about resurrection as such; resurrection is not an isolated or independent topic; it is about the raising of *Jesus* from the dead. The reference to his being buried is a reminder not to turn the text into a general resurrection discourse; it is about the raising of an individual who was buried, thus directing us to a narrative.

John Dominic Crossan has argued that Jesus was *not* buried but left to vultures and dogs to be eaten. According to Roman practice, he was not given a proper burial.[11] John M. G. Barclay rightly points out that "the historicity of the empty tomb story is dependent to a large extent on the historicity of the burial story. It is strange that its defenders have paid so little attention to that matter."[12] Craig A. Evans has given a substantial critical analysis of Crossan's view,[13] and his comments also serve to address the challenge presented by Barclay. Evans argues that a proper burial was regarded as a sacred duty in the Mediterranean world, and especially in the Jewish culture. Several Old Testament texts support this, as does the book of Tobit in particular.[14] This obligation also extended to Jews executed

---

10. Thus, also Thiselton, *First Epistle to the Corinthians*, 1190–91.

11. Crossan, *Who Killed Jesus?*, 160–88; see also Crossan and Reed, *Excavating Jesus*, 230–70.

12. Barclay, "Resurrection," 23.

13. Evans, "Jewish Burial Traditions," 233–48.

14. Evans also makes reference to Josephus; according to *C. Ap.* 2.211, a corpse should not be left unburied, and this applied to enemies as well. In *Bell.* 4.317, it says

by Gentile authorities. Proper burial was mandatory in order to avoid the defilement of the land of Israel. On the basis of available material, Evans concludes that "under normal circumstances (i.e., peacetime) no corpse would remain unburied—neither Jew nor Gentile, neither innocent nor guilty."[15] He considers it unlikely that Romans during peacetime, and at Passover in particular, would ignore a practice so deeply rooted in Jewish religion and culture. Out of sensitivity towards Jewish sentiments, Roman authorities most likely gave Jesus to be buried. A culturally informed reading of "he was buried" therefore implies that the place where Jesus was buried was known. Evans puts it in this way:

> "In my estimation, discussion of the resurrection of Jesus should take into account a known place of burial. Interpretation of the resurrection should take into account, not only Jewish beliefs about resurrection, but Jewish beliefs about death and burial."[16]

In itself, this does not mean that the empty tomb is assumed in the passage under discussion here, but it is nevertheless an important prerequisite for this belief, as the whereabouts of the body of Jesus is *necessary* for stories about the empty tomb to work at all. The empty tomb stories simply require a known place for the burial, and Jews kept track of their dead.

Andreas Lindemann argues that the place of Jesus's burial was unknown; his body could have been buried "anywhere."[17] The absence of the empty tomb in 1 Corinthians 15 is due to the fact that the place of the grave was unknown from the outset. Lindemann pays little attention to the cultural assumptions presented above. As for the place of burial, it seems right to present briefly some key documents regarding this. Eusebius's *Life of Constantine* 3.25–40 and 4.40–47, albeit a polemical text indeed, has in his telling about the tearing down of Hadrian's temple in Jerusalem, preserved a tradition about the place:

> Once upon a time wicked men—or rather, the whole tribe of demons through them—had striven to consign to darkness and oblivion that divine monument to immortality, at which,

---

the ungodliness (*asebeia*) of the Idumaeans was demonstrated in their leaving corpses without burial, "although Jews are so careful about funeral rites that even malefactors who have been sentenced to crucifixion are taken down and buried before sunset." Jacob mourning for his son Joseph, was according to Philo not primarily about his death, but that he did not receive proper burial according to customs (*Jos.* 22–23, 26–27); see also 11QT 64.7–13.

15. Evans, "Jewish Burial Traditions," 239.
16. Evans, "Jewish Burial Traditions," 248.
17. Lindemann, "Resurrection of Jesus," 572–75.

brilliant with light, the angel who has descended from heaven had rolled away the stone of those whose minds were set like stone in their assumption that the Living One was still with the dead, when he announced the good news to the women and removed the stone of disbelief from their minds by the information that one they sought was alive. It was this very cave of the Saviour that some godless and wicked people had planned to make invisible to mankind, thinking in their stupidity that they could in this way hide the truth. Indeed with great expenditure of effort they brought soil from somewhere outside and covered up the whole place, then levelled it, paved it, and so hid the divine cave somewhere down beneath a great quantity of soil. Then as though they had everything finished, above the ground they constructed a terrible and ugly genuine tomb, one for souls, for dead idols, and built a gloomy sanctuary to the impure demon of Aphrodite; then they offered foul sacrifices thereupon defiled polluted altars. They reckoned there was one way alone and no other to bring their desires to realization, and that was to bury the Saviour's cave under such foul pollutions . . . As stage by stage the underground was exposed, at last against all expectations the revered and all-hallowed Testimony (*martyrion*) of the Saviour's resurrection was itself revealed, and the cave, the holy of holies, took on the appearance of a representation of the Saviour's return to life. Thus after its descent into darkness it came forth again to the light, and it enabled those who came as visitors to see plainly the story of the wonders wrought there, testifying by facts louder than any voice of the resurrection of the Saviour. (26.1–3 and 28)[18]

The relative late date of this evidence is, of course, a problem. Two caveats are called for, though. Firstly, the fact that Emperor Hadrian's temple in Jerusalem was built on this site, was seen by Eusebius and Christians as an act of malevolence towards their belief. Be that fair or not, the choice of the site may be indicative that about 130s CE, local tradition pointed this out as the place of Calvary and Jesus's burial.[19] Furthermore, Eusebius mentions visitors; one previous visitor was Melito, bishop of Sardis. In his *On Pascha*, composed about 170 CE, he says that Jesus was killed *en mesē Ierusalēm*, meaning in the middle of the town (72).[20] This piece of evidence militates against the biblical evidence, where it says that Calvary was

---

18. See Eusebius, *Life of Constantine*.

19. See Walker, *Weekend that Changed the World*, 73–103 and Küchler, *Jerusalem*, 433–44 for a relevant archaeological context.

20. See Melito of Sardis, *On Pascha and Fragments*.

situated *outside* the city walls. When Melito visited Jerusalem, the city walls had been moved, and now the site was found *within* the city. Since this tradition refers to inside the walls, which appeared to be contrary to the biblical evidence, it most likely refers to local knowledge, *insisting* on where the place was. There is hardly historical evidence to push the argument further back. What we have presented here is still sufficient to argue that the importance Lindemann attaches to the unknown place, is unwarranted. What we know about Jewish burial practices, paves the way for empty tomb traditions, rather than the other way around.

"He was Raised on the Third Day in Accordance with the Scriptures"

The dictum has three aspects: one verb (*egēgertai*) in passive voice and in perfect tense; it belongs to the *past* although it has repercussions for the present. The passive voice conveys that "he was raised by God." Second, there is a reference to time given in dative, and then a prepositional phrase analogous with v. 3. Stefan Alkier notes that the double references to "in accordance with the Scriptures" together with the *passivum divinum* ("he was raised") make this "speech about God."[21] In other words, this is in line with the very first written statement on the resurrection of Jesus in Paul's epistles, namely 1 Thess 1:9–10: *God* raised Jesus from the dead. The *theocentric* perspective conveyed here through grammar is a way of interpreting the phenomenon at hand. It implies that the resurrection is fused into an already existing belief, and made sense of within that world-view. Thus, the reference to the Scriptures contributes to making the report about the resurrection more stable from a semiotic point of view.

What does "raised" mean here? Four observations are instructive in this regard. "Raised" is to be seen against the backdrop of Jesus being buried. That qualifies this dictum as having to do with being raised from the *dead*. Hence, the sequence of events (dead—buried—raised—seen) is evocative of a bodily resurrection, albeit what that entails more precisely, remains open. This observation is suggestive, while some others are, in our view, rather conclusive. Two other observations draw on the direction taken in the rest of this Pauline chapter. In 1 Cor 15:12–19, it is precisely the meaning of Jesus being raised (*egēgertai*) which is addressed. Paul says that the gospel is nullified if Christ has not been raised. In this context, he mentions those who "deny the resurrection," and he states that resurrection is for

---

21. Alkier, *Reality of the Resurrection*, 24.

those "who have fallen asleep," here a metonymy for death.[22] Most essential is to notice that from v. 35 on, Paul addresses the issue of "how": how are the dead raised (*egeirontai*)? With what kind of bodies do they come? It is, of course, important to notice that *egeirein* here refers to people who are *dead*, thus affirming our observation regarding vv. 12-19. Then *egeirein*, which is also the verb in the dictum of v. 4, is immediately associated with issues related to "body." The third argument will come into play shortly, but already a conclusion is suggested: a purely metaphorical or spiritual interpretation of this dictum is possible only if it is isolated from the *sequence* in which it appears in vv. 3-4, and also from the discussion of "what kind of body" that follows in its wake. To emphasize resurrection as articulating the abiding presence of Jesus is surely in line with Paul's conviction, but fails, nonetheless, to account for the past-ness of this event, as it is presented in this formula. This means that both in the setting presently found, and probably also in its alleged independent setting prior to Paul, a purely metaphorical interpretation whereby resurrection is substituted for "abiding presence or the like," hardly fits the evidence. For sure, Paul speaks about a transformed body (see Part II, 1 Corinthians 15, section A Transformed Body or Another Body?), but the discussion evolves throughout on the issue of *body*. As we will see below, it is precisely the perishable body that is raised according to Paul's discussion later in the chapter.

To many scholars, this line of the formula is about exaltation or vindication. This is stated emphatically by, e.g., Andreas Lindemann who says that "*egēgertai* nicht Widerbelebung, sondern Erhöhung meint."[23] As seen many places in the present study, resurrection and exaltation are intimately associated, for example through the use of Psalm 110:1. But this does not mean that *egeirein* actually means exaltation, as claimed by Lindemann. That is against the lexical evidence (see below). Furthermore, this view does not come to terms with the fact that Paul engages in a discussion on the resurrected body. Dale C. Allison Jr. rightly asks why Jesus's vindication was conceptualized precisely as resurrection, since other options were available.[24] He points to *Jub.* 23.31 about Abraham's burial and death: "And their bones will rest in the earth, and their spirits will increase joy, and they will know that the Lord is an executor of judgment; but he will show mercy to hundreds and thousands, to all who love him." Likewise, Allison Jr. refers to

---

22. See for example 1 Thess 4:13-14; 1 Cor 7:39.

23. See Lindemann, *Der Erste Korintherbrief*, 322. English translation: "*egēgertai* denotes not restoration to life, but exaltation to heaven." See also Lindemann, "Resurrection of Jesus," 562-65; Crossley, "Historical Plausibility," 175.

24. Allison, "Explaining the Resurrection," 127. This is pointed out also by Zeller, "Religionsgeschichtliche Erwägungen zur Auferstehung," 19-20.

Testament of Job 52, where vindication takes the form of the soul being exalted to heaven: "... the soul flew up, embracing it, and mounted the chariot and set off for the east. But his body, prepared for burial was borne to the tomb . . ." The parable about Lazarus and the poor man living next door to him may be perceived along the same lines, as this parable assumes that the poor man was buried and transferred to the bosom of Abraham,[25] there to enjoy the hospitality which was denied him in life. Against that backdrop, there must have been some compelling reason that *resurrection* appears in 1 Corinthians 15. James Ware has convincingly demonstrated that the verb *egeirein* is *not* a slippery term as often assumed, exemplified in Lindemann above.[26] Now the postponed argument indicated above comes into play. This verb is specific "resurrection language."[27] Ware points out that "[i]n no instance within ancient Greek literature does *egeirein* denote the concept of ascension, elevation or assumption. Rather it denotes the action whereby one who is prone, sitting, prostrate or lying down is *restored to a standing position*."[28] According to Ware, the position voiced by Lindemann above is from lexicographical reasons "excluded." In Second Temple Jewish texts, *egeirein* "consistently functions to denote the revivification of the once-dead body laid in the tomb."[29] Likewise, John Granger Cook summarizes his semantic investigation into resurrection terms that "one can conclude that Paul would not have conceived of a resurrection of Jesus unless he believed the tomb was empty."[30] As for the question of Paul's concept of resurrection, it is worth noticing that Ware's statement applies to Second Temple Jewish texts and that "revivification" is not sufficient to grasp the nature of Jesus's resurrection as a *transformed* body.

The resurrection of Jesus took place "on the third day" and in accordance with the Scriptures. This is really the point where the *condensed* character of this passage comes into view; what we have here are *tags* really. From its very inception, the testimony about the resurrection of Jesus has been accompanied by claims that it happened "in accordance with the

---

25. Abraham was a figure of hospitality in Jewish tradition, with reference to Genesis 18. This is seen also in Heb 13:2 where the mentioning of visiting angels is a flashback to precisely that biblical text.

26. See Ware, "Resurrection of Jesus," 490–97 for his analysis of this particular verb.

27. This is, of course, not to deny that the verb in other contexts have a wide currency, ranging from getting up from sleep to resurrection; see Tappenden, *Resurrection in Paul*, 43–86.

28. Ware, "Resurrection of Jesus," 494.

29. Ware, "Resurrection of Jesus," 497.

30. Cook, "Resurrection and Paganism," 56–75, quotation on 56; and "Use of *anistêmi* and *egeirô*," 259–80. See also Cook, *Empty Tomb*, 13–30.

Scripture." This claim is a precursor to the notion that *God* raised him from the dead. Christ-believers were guided to the Scriptures by their conviction that this was an act of God. The two are inextricably linked. There is not much specific material from the Scriptures to call upon here. A special role is assigned to Hos 6:2 ("After two days he will make us healthy; on the third day we will rise up and live before him . . . "; NETS). The Targum to this passage takes "the third day" to refer to the eschatological resurrection of the dead, but it is hard to know if this specific interpretation was in existence already in the forties of the first century CE. From this observation in Targum, Gerd Lüdemann deduces that this is no report of historical narratives, but a theological interpretation.[31] Thus 1 Cor 15:4 reflects not an event or incident, but merely "the context of an eschatological hope." Michael Welker takes "the third day" to refer not primarily to Scripture, but to "dead beyond doubt." Thus "the third day" aims not at theology, namely being in accordance with Scripture, but it works *apologetically*, as a reference to any doubt that Jesus was really dead. There was no hope of recovery.[32]

Birger Gerhardsson takes this piece of information as a reference to the narrative substratum of this formula: "It seems to me, in the end, most probable that this dating in a chronologically arranged text comes from the first appearance of the resurrected Jesus, the one to Peter, or possibly from the discovery of the empty tomb."[33] Clearly, the issue of a narrative substratum works as a shibboleth here, distinguishing a narrative-oriented reading of the passage from a metaphorically oriented one. The third day is in the New Testament exclusively linked to the empty tomb and what took place inside it, never to the appearances. This rather specific use goes beyond what Hos 6:2 speaks about and is suggestive for the question of whether Paul knew the empty tomb tradition.[34] The fact that he mentions only appearances, but still has "on the third day," which is at home in the empty tomb traditions, is worth pondering.

---

31. Lüdemann, "Resurrection of Jesus," 547. According to Lindemann, "Resurrection of Jesus," 559, the special date third day "does not provide any information on what happened in the time between Christ's death and his being raised from the dead by God."

32. Welker, "Wright on Resurrection," 474.

33. Gerhardsson, "Evidence," 83.

34. For a detailed presentation of alternative interpretations, see Novakovic, *Raised From the Dead*, 116–33.

"He appeared to Cephas and . . ."

In Greek, this is given in the word *ōphtē*. This verb is either a passive (was seen) or medium voice (let himself be seen; i.e, appeared); however, the Septuagint style imitated here clearly suggests the latter. The phrase *ōphthēnai tini*, that is the verb in medium voice followed by a dative, introducing to whom the appearance is given, is in the Septuagint at home in theophanies, as it is seen for example in Gen 12:7; 17:1; 18:1.[35] The use of *ōphtē* demonstrates that the formula has been *shaped* according to a theological tradition of God revealing Godself or making Godself seen or known to people. With regard to the death and raising of Jesus, this is evident in the references to the Scriptures; but *ōphtē* implies that the appearances also are in accordance with the Scriptures. Thus, the very first testimony to an engagement with the resurrection of Jesus is *theologically* shaped. Not even this earliest evidence is free from theological embellishments and claims. The appearances of Jesus represent a continuation of God making Godself known to his people in the Old Testament. Hence, it comes as no surprise that Paul in Gal 1:15–16a speaks about his Damascus revelation as given him by *God*, and that Paul shapes it in accordance with Old Testament prophetic vocations.[36] Thus, this verb is in itself an expression of theology rather than a simple reference to mode, or to the how of the appearances.

We have previously in this study noted the so-called "Firstness" of the resurrection as an overwhelming experience which initiated resurrection faith, a phenomenon which was full in itself, immediate and convincing without references beyond itself. Now we see that once this faith is formulated, taken down so to say—be it in terms of theo-centricity or Jesus revealing himself—it comes as an example of "Secondness"—in the belief of those who relate to it ("Thirdness"). 1 Corinthians 15:3–5 may, at first sight, appear as rather "nude," "bare" or unadorned, keeping the necessities only. But here we are easily fooled; the text is "clothed" in significant ways, thus guiding towards "making sense" of what happened. The passage is a response to the "Firstness"—*prior* to this passage—which is being interpreted here, namely the resurrection of Jesus.

---

35. For references, see Eckstein, "Die Wirklichkeit der Auferstehung Jesu," 14–16.

36. Sandnes, *Paul—One of the Prophets?*, 48–70. In 1 Cor 9:1, Paul mentions the Damascus revelation in a different way: "Have I not seen our Lord (*ton kyrion heoraka*)?" In this instance as well, the "Firstness" of his experience becomes "Secondness" by being incorporated in a pattern of justification already in place, namely Easter visions, as they are described in John 20:18: *heoraka ton kyrion* (cf. Luke 24:23).

Worth noticing is the prominence given to Cephas (Peter); then follow the twelve,[37] more than five hundred brothers and sisters at one occasion (Pentecost?), James, all the apostles, and finally to Paul himself. The eminence given to Peter in this pre-Pauline formula is interesting as it antedates the gospels with several decades, a fact which serves as a reminder that narrative traditions which eventually ended up in the gospels, were around already. Furthermore, Paul makes two interesting claims; one is clearly apologetic, and the other is personal. As for the apologetic, the reference to some of the five hundred still being alive serves as an invitation to check out the veracity of the claims that Jesus appeared alive. As for the personal, Paul includes himself in a list of witnesses in which his role was far from obvious (see below). His humility expressed in v. 8 (*ektrōma,* meaning "untimely born" and "the least of the apostles") is no obstacle for claiming to be the last Easter witness. By claiming the position as the last among Easter witnesses, Paul conveys that the appearances of the risen Jesus are of a *special* kind. In Paul's charismatic world-view, where revelations and visions were normal phenomena (Gal 2:2; 2 Cor 12:1; see below), the claim to be the *final* witness implies that something more than visions in general is at play here.

What kind of appearances then? The text is vague on this point, and simply states the fact that Jesus appeared more than once. The only appearance mentioned about which we are justified to infer the addressees' familiarity, is Paul's Damascus revelation. This raises a question: should Paul's case govern the way we think here so that all appearances are visionary like his? As pointed out by James D. G. Dunn, the use of *ōphtē* throughout does not necessarily "specify a uniform mode of appearance."[38] Dunn rightly points out that to Paul, this experience was distinctive and differed from his other visions: "His Damascus road experience was not simply the first of several or many experiences of the same kind."[39] Paul distinguishes between "visions and revelations of the Lord" (2 Cor 12:1), which were still taking place, and his initial experience of seeing the risen Christ (1 Cor 9:1–2; 15.3-11; Gal 1:11–16). The former he regards as private, albeit presented to the fellowship of believers. Through the latter, he embarked on a mission fundamental for the church, a fact of importance for the church.[40] There was a difference in kind between these revelations. This observation paves the way for Paul's claim to be the *last* person to have had Easter

---

37. Codex Beza, F, G, the entire Latin tradition and a marginal Syrian reading has "eleven" here, which makes sense as a more accurate reference here; see this also in the Markan endings.

38. Dunn, *Jesus and the Spirit,* 133.

39. Dunn, *Jesus and the Spirit,* 97–114; quotation on 103.

40. See Sandnes, *Paul—One of the Prophets,* 242–45.

appearances. Hence, Paul's case here is indicative that the appearances mentioned are not dreams or like any other vision, "but as events that happened to certain people once and for all at certain points of time. They are not to be equated with the revelations mentioned in 2 Corinthians 12:1."[41] This is undoubtedly *Paul's* perspective.

We need to remind ourselves that it is in Paul's interest to urge this distinction in order to make him conform with the appearances to the apostles. It simply served his purpose and legitimacy. The Pauline-friendly author of Acts would question that Paul's Damascus experience equaled the appearances to the apostles. Firstly, Paul does not meet the requirements for being an apostle, as Luke formulates it in Acts 1:21–22. Secondly, physicality does not characterize the Damascus revelation in a way equal to how Luke narrates the appearances of Jesus (Luke 24:13–35; 36–49; Acts 10:41–42: ". . . who ate and drank with him after he rose from the dead.") Thirdly, according to Acts 9, Paul had an audition; those with him "saw no one" (v. 7). According to Acts 22, his fellow travelers saw the light but did not hear the voice (v. 9). This is all consistent with Luke's chronology, according to which Jesus appeared to his disciples for a period of forty days only, concluding with his ascension.[42] From all this follows that the single witness about which we have *some* basic information was contested. Paul's claim to have received an Easter appearance is not evident. We should, therefore, be reluctant to use him as the only model for what "he appeared" means in all the instances mentioned.

Are the appearances to be understood in analogy with Mark 6:49 parr where it says that Jesus appeared walking on water, and he was taken to be a ghost (*phantasma*)? This interpretation is, of course, easily combined with psychological theories. But still, there is a need to account for how a ghostly appearance is conceived of as *resurrected*.

Scholars have turned to the phenomenon of *post mortem* apparitions, that is, experiences with deceased persons, to explain what 1 Corinthians 15 is really talking about.[43] In other words, such common experiences may serve to make sense of what is behind the creedal statement in this Pauline passage. Stripping the text from its theological language of divine appearances and resurrection, what remains then is probably a state in which bereaved often find themselves. In times of grief and adversities, the deceased may appear, thus alleviating the situation, albeit grief is not the necessary and only condition for such experiences. Anne Austad has in her recent

---

41. Byrskog, *Story as History*, 226–27.
42. This is pointed out also by Novacovic, *Resurrection*, 63, 147.
43. The most balanced presentation is found in Allison, *Resurrecting Jesus*, 364–75.

1 CORINTHIANS 15: RESURRECTION—WITHOUT AN EMPTY TOMB?

dissertation interviewed in-depth sixteen persons with such experiences, albeit her context is not the question of resurrection.[44] Her study is relevant here as it fleshes out what kind of material and theories may be relevant for understanding Jesus's resurrection according to the classification of post mortem apparitions. Austad's investigation demonstrates that post mortem experiences usually occur spontaneously, but they may last for years. These experiences are undergone mostly alone. Typical for them is sensing presence and signs of presence, such as movements, etc. The experiences keep alive the bonds that were there prior to death. What kind of perceptions are the participants of Austad talking about? The "appearance" of the dead took different forms: voice, perceptions of various kinds, sense of presence, and visions. As for the visions, there were different degrees of clarity. Some saw a shadow which brought to mind the figure of the deceased; others saw a real person, although not quite similar to the dead person—not with distinct features but nevertheless recognizable. Some saw the dead and recognized her/him by the clothes they used to wear, "although they were physically different because they were able to 'show up from nowhere' and 'walk through walls.'"[45] This testimony is interesting as it is phrased in a way reminiscent of the traditions about Jesus's resurrected body. It seems that this participant had visions informed by Christian resurrection beliefs. Austad does not make this comment, but to a biblical scholar, this is rather apparent. This is a reminder that such experience comes with cultural assumptions or within given frameworks.

James G. Crossley has drawn attention to this fact, saying that visions are dictated by a given culture. As he puts it, Bernhard of Lourdes saw the Virgin Mary, not Vishnu.[46] In the culture where the appearance of Jesus took place, one cultural assumption was God's vindication of the righteous sufferer, and also Jesus's sayings during his ministry that he would be raised. Such specific cultural assumptions account, according to Crossley, for how the tradition of the empty tomb came into being through the visions implied. Crossley's point is our argument that Firstness always appears as Secondness: some assumptions or parameters are at play already in the act of formulating what occurred.

Returning to Austad, she says that some participants said that their visions took place "within their head," distinguishable though from their personal memory. There was more to the visions than simply remembrance. The participants felt presence and comfort, but the dead did never leave a message

---

44. Austad, "Passing Away—Passing By."
45. Austad, "Passing Away—Passing By," 148–50.
46. Crossley, "Historical Plausibility," 174–75.

or give instructions to be followed. In order to understand the phenomenon, Austad suggests that such experiences should be understood not as reflecting an inner world, but as representing an imaginal social world.[47]

With regard to analogies to what 1 Corinthians 15 talks about, some observations are germane. The way her interviewees made sense of their experiences varies, but none of them imagined resurrection to be an alternative. Sensing the presence of the departed did not lead to any idea that the dead person had been resuscitated. In other words, it takes more than post mortem experiences to develop the idea that a dead person has returned and is alive again. Such experiences are not sufficient building-blocks for belief in the resurrection. Hence, they are only *partial* analogies; in our view, they do not contribute much to our topic. Worth noticing is also Austad's point that post death experiences are mostly had alone, not in groups or plenary session.[48] This runs contrary to 1 Cor 15:6: "he appeared to more than five hundred brothers and sisters at one time." Finally, the somewhat blurry visions the participants had may have some similarities with Easter appearances, but two differences stand out, although this applies not to 1 Cor 15, but to the narrative traditions. Firstly, the deceased left no message or instruction, a marked difference from the Easter stories in which Jesus urges his disciples to evangelize (see Part II, The Easter Narratives). Secondly, from the observations done by Austad's participants, it is impossible to imagine that the dead showing herself to them would share a meal with them.

No Empty Tomb?

When we raise this question, we return to the issue of what "being raised" really means in this Pauline chapter. What observations have been accumulated so far? We pointed out that the passage's nature of tradition and summary invites a context wider than the precise wording of the passage. This may be illustrated with two of the most important texts in which Paul unmistakably draws on tradition. In 1 Cor 11:23 he renders, in the oldest extant form, the dicta of the Eucharist. He announces this as a tradition, something received and transmitted (*parelabon* and *paredōka*), just like in 1 Cor 15:1–3, at home in a narrative which is only hinted at: "in the night

---

47. The lack of information conveyed to Austad's informants is not evidence for the claim that this never happens: We have learned of others that did in fact get important messages about what to do from deceased who they experienced as present.

48. There are, nevertheless, in other sources, indications of common visionary experiences by several observers. See Part III, Contributions to Resurrection Discourse, sec. Appearance: Allison's Contribution.

1 CORINTHIANS 15: RESURRECTION—WITHOUT AN EMPTY TOMB? 105

he was betrayed." This introduction indicates that Paul was familiar with traditions similar to those about the passion which later came down in the Synoptic Gospels, and also expected his addressees to know them. In 1 Cor 9:14, Paul quotes Jesus tradition ("In the same way, the Lord commanded that those who proclaim the gospel should get their living by it"), which brings to mind Luke 10:7 from Jesus sending and commissioning the disciples on their mission. Many years ago, Björn Fjärstedt made the germane point that 1 Cor 9 is permeated with theme and clusters of theme words from the Jesus tradition, and that v. 14 actually is only like the tip of the iceberg; Paul's familiarity with the Synoptic tradition in these chapters is surprisingly detailed, according to Fjärstedt.[49] Although Fjärstedt's work does not address 1 Cor 15 in particular, it is clear from his investigation that Paul's knowledge of Jesus tradition often comes to expression in tags and indirect references. According to Dale Allison Jr., no one would have been satisfied with the "shorn assertions" in this formula:

> This is no more plausible than arguing that Christians at first said things such as "Jesus went about doing good and healing all who were oppressed by the devil" (Acts 10:38) and only much later enjoyed telling miracle stories about him; or that while Paul and others preached Christ crucified, no supposed particulars about Jesus' martyrdom emerged until decades after the fact, when interest unaccountably set in; or that "he appeared to Cephas" was ever proclaimed without explaining who Cephas was if the audience knew nothing about him.[50]

The sequence: burial—death—raised—appeared is, therefore, suggestive of a narrative substructure in which the empty tomb is likely at home. The way Paul engages corporeality in the rest of the chapter is also worth noticing. Paul's statement regarding the resurrection of Jesus is not detached from the discussions that follow about what resurrection means for the body. On the contrary, the two are intimately connected, so that the latter serves as an instruction for how to read the brevity in style and the sparseness on information in the formula. Together these observations convey that "being raised" implies an embodied state.

In a recent groundbreaking article, James Ware has produced new arguments regarding this much-debated passage.[51] It is necessary to rehearse some of his main arguments. He sets out to answer the following question: did the apostolic preaching accounted in this passage concur with the later

49. Fjärstedt, *Synoptic Tradition*, 65–96, 169–76.
50. Allison, *Resurrecting Jesus*, 235–36; see also 305–6, 314–16.
51. Ware, "Resurrection of Jesus."

narratives found in the gospels on the resurrection of Jesus's crucified body? Or did this account envisage a resurrection which did *not* affect the body? Ware argues that the formula in 1 Corinthians 15 is a summary, a category in which the empty tomb rarely appears. The empty tomb had its proper place in narratives, not in summaries of this kind. References to a vacant tomb are not found in the summaries found in the speeches of Luke-Acts either, even though these summaries were produced by a theological milieu familiar with such narratives. The empty tomb is throughout "assumed, but not creedally expressed."[52] This form-critical observation finds affirmation also in the Old Roman Creed, which eventually developed into the Apostolic Creed: "who was crucified under Pontius Pilate and was buried, and on the third day rose from the dead." If one argues from silence, a comparison between Paul and the gospels suggest that the empty tomb was not a part of the early Easter proclamation.[53] Such a comparison does not take into account the genre nor what it means that Paul presents a summary here.

Ware then argues that Paul's wider discussion in this chapter (see above) is crucial for interpreting the formula. This invites corporeality, as Paul makes explicit that it is the mortal body which is raised, or in other words, the *same* body is transformed: "The evidence of 1 Cor 15:3–5 thus indicates that Paul would understand Jesus' resurrection as the revivification of his crucified and entombed body."[54] Furthermore, Ware investigates the verb *egeirein* around which everything in 1 Corinthians 15 is evolving (see above), arguing that this verb "consistently functions to denote the revivification of the once-dead body laid in the tomb."[55] Ware concludes that the formula presupposes a narrative of which the key verbs found here are indicative, a narrative in line with what is found in the gospels: "The argument that the empty tomb is conspicuous by its absence and thus implies a resurrection event unrelated to the corpse of Jesus is without historical foundation . . . Paul himself understood Jesus' resurrection as involving the revivification of his crucified body."[56] We very much concur with Birger Gerhardsson who sums up his view on the question of 1 Corinthians 15 and the empty tomb in the following way:

---

52. Ware, "Resurrection of Jesus," 481.

53. Lüdemann, *What Really Happened to Jesus?*, 79–80 argues that the empty tomb was added to answer the objection that the disciples had experienced a phantom or a spirit only.

54. Ware, "Resurrection of Jesus," 489.

55. Ware, "Resurrection of Jesus," 497.

56. Ware, "Resurrection of Jesus," 497; see also Gerhardsson, "Evidence for Christ's Resurrection," 89–91.

There are scholars who maintain that the oldest texts about Christ's resurrection consisted of brief formulaic statements and that the real narratives are secondary, all along the line. I think this is a desk concoction lacking an anchor in reality. Elementary psychological considerations tell us that the early Christians could scarcely mention such intriguing events as those taken up in statements about Jesus' death and resurrection without being able to elaborate on them. Listeners must immediately have been moved to wonder and ask questions. Regarding our text there must have existed in support of the different points in the enumeration—the death of Jesus, the burial, the events on the third day, the appearances of the resurrected one to Cephas and the twelve, to James and all the apostles etc.—narratives about how they came about. Our text is, as I have already pointed out, a list rather than a narrative. It cries out for elaboration. A preacher can begin with an outline, but he cannot go on forever repeating mere outlines.[57]

If we keep the narrative appearances tradition out of the scope here, we are left with claims that Jesus made himself seen to various people, probably in various ways as well. Two caveats vis-à-vis Crossley is necessary here (see above). Firstly, although cultural assumptions shape and provide the interpretational framework for visions, Paul's Damascus revelation forms a contrast. He was in no way prepared for what happened to him, and the appearance of Christ turned his life upside down in a way that his assumptions did not account for. This is, of course, not to deny that his making sense of this event, definitely took shape within this world-view.

Due to its brevity and tags, and the sequence between tags, narrative elaborations come very naturally, among which the empty tomb is also assumed. We have made the following observations substantiating that the empty tomb is assumed in this ancient formula. The text is a formulaic summary point beyond its own wording. It tags a broader narrative context. The Greek verb *egeirein* denotes the raising up of people who were dead. This corroborates with Rom 10:7 where the resurrection of Jesus is portrayed through the verb *anagagein*, in which the prefix *ana* indicates an upward movement. The sequence died—buried—raised—appear makes the most sense if a tomb is assumed to be empty. Finally, in a passage where only appearances are mentioned, Paul includes that Jesus was raised on

---

57. Gerhardsson, "Evidence for Christ's Resurrection," 89. A relevant example is how Paul in Gal 1:13–14 assumes his addressees' familiarity with his basic biography, indicated through his introductory "you have heard."

"the third day." In the narrative traditions, this is almost exclusively attached to the empty tomb.[58]

However, all this is not to deny that there are significant differences from the narrative traditions that we do have, all of them in their present form later than the formula. No location for the appearances is made, and the women, so prominent in the narratives, are left unmentioned. We have also noticed that even if "earlier is best," we are at no point without interpretations and shaping. The very first evidence thus comes as a witness of Secondness. In its Firstness, the resurrection is inaccessible even here.

---

58. This is also stated pace Carnley, *Resurrection in Retrospect*, 116–57. The claim that the empty tomb is implicit in 1 Cor 15:3–8 is not based on the question of women witnesses, as Carnley assumes. Our claim resonates with the nature of the text as a condensed formulaic passage, and also with the lexical meaning of *egeirein*.

A Transformed Body or Another Body?

Paul's chapter on the resurrection takes a turn in v. 35 by introducing the question of what kind of body resurrection comes with. Paul now participates in a discourse on the nature of the resurrected body. Worth noting from the outset is that it is a matter of *sōma*, body. This puts some restraint on suggested interpretations, particularly of v. 50: "flesh and blood cannot inherit the kingdom of God" (see below). Interpretations doing away with the body altogether, fail to take this into account. Bodily aspects are inherent to the very question posed. Another thing to be noted from the beginning is the general perspective on resurrection here, which follows upon Paul's emphasis on Christ's resurrection. Hence, the discussion on the resurrection body is simultaneously a discussion on what kind of body the risen Jesus had. That is why this question is relevant to the present study.

Several lines of interpretation have been in vogue regarding this passage, more or less from the ancient church.[1] According to the first, the resurrected body is identified with the earthly, fleshly body raised to life and transformed to be imperishable. Opposed to this are interpretations excluding a literal resurrection of the body. Origen took a mediating position, claiming that Paul envisages a bodily resurrection, but a body consisting of ethereal matter, distinct from the earthly body of flesh. This opinion has found a follow up among recent interpreters. Dale Martin argues that Paul rejects the resurrection of the flesh, and instead speaks of a body consisting of heavenly stuff or matter, "heavenly body composed of *pneuma*."[2] In other words, "Christians will have bodies without flesh, blood, or soul—composed solely of pneumatic substance—light, airy, luminous bodies."[3]

---

1. For these lines of interpretation, see Ware, "Paul's Understanding of the Resurrection," 810–17.
2. Martin, *Corinthian Body*, 120.
3. Martin, *Corinthian Body*, 132.

Troels Engberg-Pedersen stands on the shoulders of Martin, as he claims that Paul's concept is a fusion of Jewish apocalyptic elements and Stoic cosmology, envisioning an ethereally corporeal resurrection body that excludes the reconstitution of the body of flesh. The body is transformed into ethereally material *pneuma*.[4] James Ware succinctly summarizes the hub of Martin and Engberg-Pedersen's view: "Paul's concept of the resurrection envisions an ethereally material body composed not of flesh but of the corporeal substance of *pneuma*."[5] The question is the following: did Paul conceive of resurrection in terms of a liberation from the present body, or in terms of a restoration of the same body?

Verses 36–41 argue by way of analogies before v. 42 (*houtōs*) relates directly to the resurrection body. Paul's analogies, albeit short and pointed, nonetheless make several claims. Strictly speaking not part of the analogies themselves, but serving as a presupposition, is death. Coming to life is dependent upon death. According to Stefan Alkier, Paul mentions death to emphasize both its necessity and radicality: "There is no inherent continuity between the dead body and the newly created body. Paul does not share the Greek conception of a soul that lives on. Death knows no bounds. It devours the whole person."[6] The power of death is surely stated in v. 26 ("the last enemy") and also presupposed in the triumphant vv. 54–57, but this is *not* what Paul aims at in v. 36. The reference to death here works within a horticultural setting, in which death brings forth new life. This is indicated in the prepositional phrase "unless it dies (*ean mē apothanē*)." Furthermore, Alkier's denial of any continuity states how Paul differs from a "soul—body" way of thinking, but fails to notice that within the horticultural setting, the discontinuity between seed and plant is conditioned by a necessary continuation. To say it with Paul: only a seed of wheat becomes wheat! This brings us to the second point made here, namely the *difference* between seed and plant. In other words, what comes up is not what you sow: "you do not sow the body that is to be." Seed and plant are different, although the first becomes the latter. The resurrected body relates to the body of flesh as a flower to its seed. Hence, discontinuity conditioned on continuity is what Paul aims at. After having emphasized this dual reality, Paul's analogies go in another direction, from v. 38 on. Now he points out that there are

---

4. Engberg-Pedersen, *Cosmology and Self*, 8–38. Similarly, Lindemann, *Der Erste Korintherbrief*, 354–67.

5. Ware, "Paul's Understanding of the Resurrection," 816.

6. Alkier, *Reality of the Resurrection*, 26–27. Alkier's one-sided emphasis on discontinuity would leave Paul's argument in 1 Cor 15:29–34 vulnerable, especially with regard to the epicurean-like lifestyle and argument addressed there; see Sandnes, *Belly and Body*, 181–87, 212–15.

different kinds of flesh or bodies. Human beings, animals, birds, fishes—all come with dissimilar bodies and are distinguished by these differences. The distinction between "heavenly bodies" and "earthly bodies"—bodies fit for distinct realities—pave the way for the peculiarity of a "spiritual body" over against a "physical body" worked out in the proceeding.

A crucial passage now is vv. 42–49, epitomizing Paul's notion of the resurrected body, be it Christ's or in general. Vv. 42–44a are organized according to two opposing verbs, "sow" (*speirein*) and "raise" (*egeirein*), which picks up on vv. 36–37 where, however, *egeirein* does not appear, but instead *zōopoiein* ("come to life"; see also v. 45 where the same verb appears). Raising is here a matter of *coming to life* after death. Around these two contrasting verbs are organized a set of opposing pairs:

Sow	Raised (notice that both verbs are used in passive voice)
perishable (*en phtora*)	imperishable (*en aphtarsia*)
in dishonor (*en atimia*)	in glory (*en doxē*)
in weakness (*en astheneia*)	in power (*en dynamei*)
as a physical body (*sōma psychikon*)	as a spiritual body (*sōma pneumatikon*)

Fundamental to this structure is that the subject of the antithetical pairs is *one and the same* on both sides of the contrasts. It is the same body which is both sown and raised, although with new complements. The contrasts occur not in the subject—as assumed by both Martin and Engberg-Pedersen—but in the *predicates* given; that is in verbs and the prepositional phrases or complements. The subject is the present body on both sides of the contrasts. James Ware points out how the overall rhetorical effect of assonance (*speiretai/egeiretai*), asyndeton (no connectors between the paired verbs), repetition and anaphora (the two verbs are each repeated four times in vv. 42–44) "strongly emphasize that the paired verbs have a single subject—the present earthly body of flesh and bones."[7] This lays the foundation for a reading that differs from Martin's and Engberg-Pedersen's reading of this passage. Paul here draws on creation theology voiced in Genesis 1–2 on the human being as weak, formed of earth (vv. 47–48). Thus, the existence of two specific kinds of bodies is given Scriptural proof. Genesis 2:7 on Adam is cited, and Paul adds of his own a second part to this piece of Scripture, formed as an intended parallel and contrast as well:

---

7. See Ware, "Paul's Understanding of Resurrection," 821–24; quotation on 824.

| The first man, | Adam, | became | a living being. |
| The last | Adam, | became | a life-giving spirit. |

The first sentence catches Adam in his progenitor role vis-à-vis humanity, while the second sentence gives Christ a similar role, due to his resurrection. The life-giving spirit is the resurrected Christ. These two figures have given rise to two kinds of bodies, an earthly and a spiritual. This passage is infused with problems when it comes to translation and present-day readers' assumptions. N. T. Wright has aptly commented that "[h]ere the ghost—or perhaps the psyche—of Plato must be chuckling at the quiet triumph achieved in so many English translations."[8] The problem is that "spiritual" to moderns is contradictory to the combination that Paul emphatically makes, namely a body that is spiritual! Moderns conceive of "spiritual" as being in principle incorporeal, a devastating misunderstanding judged by Paul's world view. In 1 Cor 2:14–15, Paul makes a similar distinction, between *psychikos* and *pneumatikos*, and it is here a matter of being able to understand the things of the spirit; substance is not a matter. To a man who is *psychikos*, a term derived from *psychē*, the key word in Gen 2:7 for human beings as created; the spiritual things are out of reach until revealed to him. The created body is according to Gen 2:7 by definition perishable. The natural body, even as a creation by God, is not fit for the world of the resurrection. In the words of Frederick S. Tappenden, spiritual body "denotes a body that is under the rule of the Spirit."[9] He suggests that "enspirited body" is an apt rendering, while the earthly body is "the ensouled body" as spoken of in Genesis 2.

Paul's label "spiritual body" has caused much confusion, primarily so since present-day readers tend to take "spiritual" as the opposite of the corporeal nature of the body. What Paul has in mind is not a body composed of spirit as its substance, but the risen body with flesh and bones, given life by the Spirit of God, in ways similar to how God raised Jesus from the dead according to Rom 8:11: "If the Spirit of him who raised Jesus from the dead dwells in you, he who raised Christ from the dead will give life to your mortal bodies also through his Spirit that dwells in you." The adjective "spiritual" has nothing to do with the body's composition, but with the *source* of its renewal, from the inside first and eventually also with regard to flesh and bones. This brings us to the trajectory of the renewal from interior to exterior, which we have identified in Paul's theology.[10] James Ware makes a pertinent point when he says that if "spiritual body" here refers to a body

---

8. Wright, *Resurrection of the Son of God*, 348; similarly, Tappenden, *Resurrection in Paul*, 115.

9. Tappenden, *Resurrection in Paul*, 117.

10. See Part II, Paul the Apostle, sec. The Risen Jesus and the Christ-Believer.

composed solely of spirit, *sōma psychikon* should be read analogous, namely as a body composed only of soul: "Paul would assert the absence of flesh and bones not only from the risen body but from the present mortal body as well!"[11] Likewise, in 1 Cor 2:14-15 where Paul also works with a contrast between *psychikos* and *pneumatikos*, it makes no sense imagining him to speak about persons composed of soul versus those composed of *pneuma*; substance is not the matter there.

In v. 49, Paul turns to first person plural ("we"), thus applying his argument to his Corinthian audience: "Just as we have borne (*ephoresamen*) the image (*eikona*) of the man of dust, we will also bear (*phoresomen*) the image (*eikona*) of the man of heaven." This "we" is important to notice also with regard to how Paul conceives of the resurrected body: "we" are those to whom both Adam's image and Christ's image apply. There is no replacement of "we," only a fundamental *change* occurring to the same subject "we." The contrast between Adam and Christ continues in this initial summary, and thus brings Gen 1:26-27 on human beings created in "the image (*eikōn*, LXX) of Adam" into the picture. In Rom 3:23, Paul says that human beings as sinners fall short of God's glory—a reference to this biblical passage—and this will be restored in the resurrection. The presence of *doxa* ("glory") in the contrastive list given above is indicative of this notion.

What Paul has said so far, is in vv. 50-54 twice abbreviated in the verb *allagēsometha*: "we will be changed." This is what the argument from v. 35 on has been aiming at. Resurrection is *transformation* of the body; it is metamorphosis. Paul comes out markedly different from what we saw in 2 Maccabees 7, where resurrection was conceived of in terms of returning or giving back the present body. Again, it is of utmost importance to notice the subject involved in vv. 50-54. Paul now leaves behind the contrasts worked out in the preceding section; he concentrates on resurrection or transformation. The transformation he envisions here is equally a change of the perishable body: the subject of the transformation is given as "we," "the dead," or *to thnēton touto* (this mortal body) and *to phtarton* (this perishable body). The change is not a new body, but a restoration of the present body.

In this part of the chapter, Paul introduces another image; however, one which is prepared for in v. 36: nakedness and clothing. The verb *phorein* often refers to wearing clothes, a metaphor spelled out in vv. 53-54 in a contrast which reiterates vv. 42-44 given above:

This perishable body	must *put on (endysasthai)*	imperishability
This mortal body	must *put on (endysē*tai)	immortality.

---

11. Ware, "Paul's Understanding of Resurrection," 833.

Frederick S. Tappenden draws attention to the fact that the metaphor of clothing in this regard is voiced as "one garment (i.e., the heavenly body) being put on over top of another (i.e., the earthly body)."[12] The nakedness of the body, silently brought in already in v. 37, will be clothed in the resurrection. In other words, the image that Paul seeks to convey is not that of a removal of the body or its replacement, but rather an act completing it. This image conveys a point of continuity across the different kinds of bodies. Tappenden here points to 2 Cor 5:1–5, where Paul also speaks of resurrection in terms of nakedness being clothed (see below). Clothing is here a metaphor for the process of eschatological transformation; the enspirited body eventually becomes the spiritual body, thanks to the indwelling spirit or guarantee (*arrabōn*). We discern that resurrection overtones are present in Gal 3:27, namely that baptism is to be "clothed" in Christ, thus forming a bridge to observations done in the section on The Risen Jesus and the Christ-believer (Part II, Paul the Apostle) of this study: resurrection takes its beginning in baptism, starting a trajectory of renewal culminating with the body in the resurrection.

What Kind of Change Then?

We have seen that Paul does *not* think that what is put into the ground in the burial is x, and that what is raised is y. The change implied does something to x, but x is not replaced. In his discussion with Troels Engberg-Pedersen, James Ware addresses Paul's language of change in this chapter.[13] According to both Martin and Engberg-Pedersen, the change is the abandonment of the mortal body, which will exist without the flesh and bones of the present body. Engberg-Pedersen calls upon Aristotle's notion of "change in substance" to explain what Paul has in mind here, implying a specialized use of this term: it denotes the "passing away" of the body and flesh and "the coming-to-be" of the body composed of *pneuma*.[14] Ware argues that Paul's argument finds a much better analogy in Aristotle's other notion of change, namely "change in quality." This applies much better to a concept where the resurrection does not destroy or annul the flesh but enlivens it and enhances it with glorious qualities. Ware is in my view entirely correct when he points out that

---

12. Tappenden, *Resurrection in Paul*, 121–31.
13. Ware, "Paul's Understanding of Resurrection," 827–30.
14. Engberg-Pedersen, "Complete and Incomplete Transformation in Paul," 128.

the contrasts between the present and risen body are located entirely within Paul's verbs and verbal complements. Strikingly, these complements uniformly refer not to the substance of the body but to *qualities*, *states*, or *conditions* of the body, corruption, incorruption, dishonour, glory, weakness, power, mortality, and immortality.[15]

Hence, Ware cites with endorsement Caroline Walker Bynum's pointed dictum about the resurrected body: "enhancement of what is, not metamorphosis into what is not."[16]

Paul Muddling His Case?

We have seen that for Paul, the balance between discontinuity and continuity tips towards the first. Nonetheless, he remains focused on risen embodiment. Post mortem transformation comes with a body. The human body is the location of resurrection.[17] Paul stresses this, and yet he twice manages to shed doubt on his own conclusion. The first passage is found in 2 Cor 5:1, parallel with his clothing imagery; he states that "the earthly tent we live in is destroyed (*kataluthē*)." This is followed up in 2 Cor 5:3, saying that the earthly body "will be taken off (*ekdysamenoi*)." Thus, the image of taking a new garment upon the already existing one, cannot mean to just add one upon the other; or to put it in other words, "the undergarment" is not identical with the earthly body. The source of the resurrected body is not the present earthly body, but it will be brought *from heaven* (2 Cor 5:2); it is yet unseen, but still underway as the "outer nature is wasting away, and our inner nature is being renewed day by day" in a process towards glory (2 Cor 4:16–18). These passages taken in isolation may seem to dismiss the created body from resurrection (see below).

The second passage is 1 Cor 15:50: "flesh and blood cannot inherit the kingdom of God, nor does the imperishable inherit the imperishable."[18] In this dictum, Paul provided critics of bodily resurrection with an argument. It has been a text put to good use for those rejecting the resurrection of the flesh, and for advocates, it was a constant challenge to come to terms

---

15. Ware, "Paul's Understanding of Resurrection," 830–31.
16. Bynum, *Resurrection of the Body*, 8.
17. Tappenden, *Resurrection in Paul*, 229.
18. According to Tertullian, *Res.* 48.1; ANF 3.581, the opponents of the resurrection of the flesh have placed this text "in the front of the battle." Thus saying, Tertullian echoes the crucial role occupied by this Pauline dictum in discourses on resurrection.

with it.[19] The question boils down to what Paul here disqualifies from the kingdom of God. Is it to be taken in line with for example 1 Cor 6:10, where the apostle says that those who commit the sins listed in the list of vices "will not inherit the kingdom of God?" If so, Paul's dictum aims at the sinful nature of human beings, for which he coined the term "flesh." Or is the phrase "flesh and blood" indicative of human beings as created beings, in line with the discussion in the preceding verses? V. 50b picks up on precisely this discussion, suggesting that what Paul denies is that human beings as "en-souled" creations are excluded. Some argue that this dictum should guide the interpretation of the entire passage, paving the way for views in line with Martin and Engberg-Pedersen, thus entailing that Paul militates against Luke's resurrected Christ with a tangible body and eating fish (Luke 24:39).[20] The point in Paul's text is not that the sinful human body has no part in the kingdom of God. "Flesh and blood" together refer to the body as such, or in other words, the body as created, subject to decay. It is the created body that is excluded from the resurrection. This is seen in v. 50b where "flesh and blood" is replaced by "perishable" (*phtora*), which is the body of Adam. This means that the created body has no power or no right vis-à-vis resurrection.

Michael R. Licona helpfully distinguishes between "flesh and blood" as mortal and as a synonym for "physical."[21] He says that it is the first, and not the latter, which is implied when Paul denies those "living" any share in the resurrection. Mortality, and not physicality, is the issue. The first part of the dictum is to be taken together with the second part, which picks up on the issue of the perishable and mortal nature of the created body. This is in line with 1 Cor 2:14–15 (see above), where *psychikos anthrōpos* refers to mere humanity unable to understand the mystery, not to the substance involved. Likewise, 1 Cor 15:50 speaks not about substance, but about human beings as they are naturally. It is wise not to read this dictum in a way that endangers the very argument of this section: annihilation or replacement of the body is not what Paul imagines, but rather its revival, investiture, and transformation. "Paul's affirmation that the present body will be 'changed' thus of necessity implies its continued existence and enhancement."[22] In this quotation of James Ware, we need to emphasize "change." The body participates in the resurrection only by divine intervention. The body is

19. See Lehtipuu, *Debates Over the Resurrection of the Dead*, 91–92, 144–50.

20. See, e.g., Dunn, *Evidence for Jesus*, 74: "What Luke affirms (Jesus' resurrection body was flesh and bones) Paul denies (the resurrection body was *not* composed of flesh and blood)!"

21. Licona, *Resurrection of Jesus*, 417–23.

22. Ware, "Resurrection of Jesus," 487.

given something which is out of reach, namely imperishability (*aphtarsia*) and immortality (*athanasia*) (vv. 53–54).

In the history of modern exegesis, Paul (1 Cor 15) and Luke (chap. 24) are often contrasted, seen as two opposing ways to come to terms with Jesus's resurrection and the resurrected body.[23] We think that it is important, in spite of the differences, not to overlook that even in Luke's Gospel, the body of the risen Jesus has taken on significant bodily changes. G. B. Caird's "conference table" model[24] paves the way for considering Paul and Luke participating in an imagined colloquium of the resurrection of Jesus. Even within Paul, we see that he wrestles with what the resurrected body will be like, taking the risen Jesus as his paradigm. The main texts in which Paul addresses this issue are the following: 1 Cor 6:13; 15:49, 53–54; 2 Cor 3:18; 5:1–10; Rom 8:11, 29; Phil 3:21. From these passages, we gather that this was an issue Paul was trying to make sense of. Furthermore, these passages each have their distinct emphasis. Some observations are sufficient to demonstrate this. In Rom 8:11, resurrection is addressed as a return to life of the mortal bodies (*zōopoiēsei ta thnēta sōmata*), made possible by the Spirit. Similarly in Rom 10:7, Paul says that Jesus was brought up (*anagagein*) from the dead. This phraseology is worth noticing, as it assumes a direction upwards (*ana*)—from where? Most likely, the tomb (see above). Likewise, Rom 8:23 speaks about the "redemption (*apolytrōsis*) of our bodies." The indwelling Spirit is the power by which this is wrought, not the substance of this body. According to 1 Cor 15:53–54 as well, resurrection is happening to mortal bodies (*to thnēton*); the change announced in v. 52, is that mortality is replaced by immortality. These verses summarize the question that introduced Paul's discussion on the resurrected body (v. 35). Also in Phil 3:21, Paul envisages a transformation of the body. Clearly, the present body is not exempt from how Paul conceives of resurrection. In 1 Cor 6:13 a somewhat different issue appears, namely whether the body with *all* its members will take place in the resurrection. According to this passage, the stomach and eating will be left out.[25] While all passages speak of the body being transformed or changed, 2 Cor 5:1–10 adds nuances to this, as we saw above. The imagery of change and transformation includes continuity, or that the mortal body in which Jesus once lived is somehow undergoing restoration. In other words, there is one body, albeit changed and transformed. In 2 Cor 5:1 Paul speaks differently; the emphasis is on the "heavenly body"

---

23. See Part II, The Easter Narratives, sec. Two Independent Traditions?

24. See Part II, What Does Belief in the Resurrection of Jesus Do?, sec. A Colloquium on the Resurrection.

25. A caveat in reading this passage is that Paul here is engaging Corinthian slogans, and his argument is deep into that, to the extent that it is difficult to know when Paul voices his own opinion or that of others.

with which the mortal body will be *replaced* after being *destroyed* (*kataluthē*). This is the passage in which Paul gives most emphasis to the discontinuity.

Although Paul argues extensively and also in detail, taken together, his presentations lack in precision, probably because he did not know, but was searching for an answer through considering what creation and new creation entailed for the body. In lack of precise analogies, it is possible that angelomorphic bodies would come close to what Paul imagines. This being the case, Paul reasons in line with Jesus's statement in Mark 12:25: "For when they rise from the dead, they neither marry nor are given in marriage, but are like angels in heaven." Likewise, Acts 23:6–10 vividly portrays Jewish internal debate on the resurrection. The Sadducees are here introduced as saying: *mè einai anastasin mete aggelon mete pneuma* (v. 8). NRSV renders this "that there is no resurrection, or angel, or spirit," thus assuming three topics implied here. This is affirmed in NRSV's rendering of the rest of the sentence: "but the Pharisees acknowledge all three." However, the Greek text speaks only of two topics (*tà amphotera*), namely angels and spirits. What is implied here are *two* modes of resurrection, either in the form of angels or spirits. The alternatives are appositions, then, to resurrection.[26] Hence, this text attests to a lively discussion on the nature of resurrection in a Jewish setting, naming two main views, spiritual[27] or angelomorphic. Paul uses the term "spiritual" with regard to the transformed bodies, but the way he describes them owes more to an angelic existence.

Compared to the narrative traditions we soon embark upon, Paul emphasizes discontinuity and transformation. He reasons, however, in terms of change, not a replacement of the body, although 2 Cor 5 disturbs this picture. Scholars have wrestled whether this is adequately described as "change of substance" or "change in quality." The first is a replacement, while the latter is more akin to the fact that the changes envisaged here are found in the predicates and the complements applied. Paul tries to make sense of what a *glorious* body is like. An analogy, not mentioned by him though, is the body of angels, which does include *some* aspects of substantial change as well (see Part II, The Easter Narratives, section Conceptualizing Easter or the Resurrected Body).

Summarizing the Formulaic Tradition

We have noticed that Paul in 1 Corinthians 15 leans on past traditions in his presentation of the resurrection of Jesus. The way he intertwines

---

26. Thus also Fitzmyer, *Acts of the Apostles*, 719; Keener, *Acts*, 3291–94.
27. Stated explicitly in *Jub.* 23:30–31.

Jesus's resurrection and general resurrection, may well be his contribution, but anyway, this is the earliest example of Christian discourse on the resurrection. We have argued that the passage about Christ is a condensed summary which tags more extensive narratives, to which also belongs the empty tomb, albeit not mentioned. We have also seen that Paul emphasizes a bodily resurrection, though a *transformed* body. In spite of the brevity of the formulaic passage, it comes clearly through that it has already been through a process of substantiation or justification. The Septuagint style "he appeared" is a claim to divine revelation within a setting where the God of the Jews is active, and the repeated references to "in accordance with the Scriptures," albeit in a very general form, prove this. Thus, this tradition, which takes us back one or two decades before Paul wrote his epistle to the Corinthians, is involved in the process of making sense of Easter. Not even here do we find bare facts.

The Easter Narratives

THE PRECEDING CHAPTER HAS addressed one of two pillars upon which Easter faith rests according to the New Testament, namely the formulaic tradition preserved in 1 Corinthians 15. The present chapter turns to the second pillar, the narrative tradition of which there are several accounts. We start with what is the oldest piece of an Easter narrative.

Mark 16:1–8: A Testimony of a Discovery

With most scholars, we assume that the abrupt ending of Mark in 16:8 is more authentic than the two other endings witnessed to in the mss. Whether the ending best preserved is also the intended ending, is an open question, but instead of speculating here, we will keep to what is best preserved. Admittedly, the ending in v. 8 is unusual for many reasons.[1] The other shorter ending, found in some mss, has no relevance for the present investigation, while vv. 9–20 give an alternative ending, heavily influenced by Luke and John in particular (see below).[2]

In Mark 16:1–8, women are the only figures appearing, except for "the young man" in vv. 5–7, a stereotype for an angel. The disciples appear only

---

1. For an introduction to this question, see Black, *Perspectives on the Ending of Mark*. Recently, Larsen, *Gospels Before the Book*, 115–20, 133 has argued that Mark's Gospel is to be seen as a collection of notes (*hypomnēmata*), not a narrative or a biography. The notes are arranged according to key words and themes. Obviously, this diminishes the oddness of Mark 16:8, which is no claim to bring a story to a close. Larsen's suggestion is intriguing, and the frequent appearance of "and" (*kai*) may at first glance be taken as supportive of his thesis. However, in the passions story, the narrative intention comes clearly through, both in the way the episodes are being connected and the chronology implied.

2. Lunn, *Original Ending of Mark* defends the authenticity of the longer ending, but fails to convince.

indirectly as those to whom the women will convey their message, but this fails to materialize. The role of the women is anticipated in Mark 15:40, in which they from afar see (*theōrousai*) the crucifixion. These women had accompanied Jesus and served him while in Galilee. Among these were Mary Magdalene and Mary, mother of James the younger and of Joses, and Salome. According to Mark 15:47, these women—Salome being now left out—and Mary called the mother of Joses only,[3] "saw" (*etheōroun*) where Jesus was buried. This information paves the way for the empty tomb story in chap. 16, thus reminding us that the burial and the empty tomb make a joint venture in the Easter testimonies.[4]

The women who walked to the tomb were Mary of Magdala, Mary mother of James—now Joses is not mentioned—and Salome. They had bought *aromata* and came, early as the sun was rising, to anoint the body. Vv. 3–4 draw attention to the problem of the stone; it was "very large." This piece of information has much in common with the motif of "the seven seals" in the *Gospel of Peter*,[5] enhancing the miraculous in the event. The size of the stone is given prominence in the text, the women's concern about it, and that they found it removed, all this convey that what goes on here is *beyond* human capability.

Again, the women are those who "see" (*theōrousin*), now the removed stone (v. 4). A textcritical detail deserves some comments. According to the text of Nestle-Aland 28th edition, the women said to themselves (*pros heautas*; v. 3): "who will remove the stone?" Codex Bezae (D) has *heatous* (masculine) here, thus imagining that the women were *not* alone, but came together with some men to the tomb.[6] That this is not a slip of the tongue is seen in how D renders v. 6: here also *autais*, feminine, has become a masculine *autois*. A consistent picture emerges then, with regard to this Codex, namely that the presence of women alone as primary witnesses is reduced by including them in a larger group where also men were included. The role of the women will be addressed later (see Part II, The Easter Narratives, section Women at the Tomb).

According to v. 5, the women again are figures who "see (*eidon*)," now a "young man." This is what the women actually saw; it is how they perceived of the situation. *They* discovered a young man. The reader, however, is gradually introduced to this man as an angelic figure. His clothing is

---

3. Text critical mss adjust this information to fit with Mark 15:40.
4. See Part II, 1 Corinthians 15, sec. "He Was Buried."
5. See Part II, Neither Witnessed nor Told, sec. *The Gospel of Peter*.
6. This information is not given in the Nestle-Aland's 28th edition but is found in Read-Heimerdinger and Rius-Camp, *Gospel Synopsis*.

typical of an angel. At this point, the story is about to turn from discovery to making sense of the discovery. Readers receive information that was not immediate to the women. By their sight, the women are terrified (*exethambēthēsan*). In vv. 6–7 the young man speaks to the women, first urging them not to be afraid: "The crucified has been raised (*ēgerthē*). He is not here." The verbal form here is passive voice, implying a divine act. The risen Jesus has *left* the scene; what is available is only the place where he was laid. The women are invited to "see" (*ide*) this.[7] They are in v. 7 given a mission, namely to tell the disciples and Peter that he will go to Galilee, where "they will see (*opsesthe*) him, as he told them." Worth noticing is that the young man mentions Jesus, not only as crucified but also as coming from Nazareth. The story of the empty tomb is thus not about an idea or notion about the resurrection. Resurrection comes with a name and is connected to a certain *bios*. Thus, the resurrection and the life of Jesus are linked.

Seeing is crucial in this text. Thrice it says that the women saw, namely the stone, the young man, and the place Jesus had left. This emphasis on "seeing" may be seen against the backdrop of Samuel Byrskog's pointing out the ancient world's preference for what is seen: "Autopsy was the essential means to reach back to the past."[8] The emphasis on "watching" here may also serve an apologetic purpose, although that is to some extent undermined by the fact that the witnesses are women (see Part II, The Easter Narratives, section Women at the Tomb), and also the embarrassing reaction of the witnesses, who show themselves victims of their fear. It is, therefore, possible, as does Stefan Alkier, to take their seeing as a manifestation of Mark 4:12: they see and still do not see![9] The emphasis on seeing, therefore, comes with a double message here.

Jesus himself is never seen in this text. No such claim is made. The key figure of the story is not present! His absence conveys his presence though. This is the paradox: the absence of Jesus conveys presence in another way. The last instance of seeing is found in v. 7, which is presented as a citation of Jesus; it has the accusative *auton* as the grammatical object for this act: "there you will see him." In other words, this indicates seeing himself. However, this is future tense and points to something *external* to the text. This will also take place elsewhere, namely in Galilee. Hence, there are *no* appearances in this narrative, albeit it is assumed that this will take place

---

7. Codex D has the imperative *eidete* here.

8. Byrskog, *Story as History*, 64; see Part II, Neither Witnessed nor Told, sec. Why This Detour?

9. Alkier, *Reality of the Resurrection*, 85.

later. Furthermore, the last part of v. 7 brings to mind the ministry of Jesus before Easter. From that perspective, the resurrection is not unexpected but has been announced by Jesus in advance (Mark 14:28).

Verse 8 is really an anticlimax. The women flee from the tomb, frightened and trembling, saying nothing to anybody. In other words, what the young man told them to do, was *not* carried out. Michael Goulder pictures a situation that in his view explains why Mark's Gospel ends like this. There is a *strategy* behind this, namely to cover up that the empty tomb is a Markan invention. Goulder's paraphrase goes like this: "Sooner or later someone will have said to Mark, 'How come we hear this story for the first time thirty years on?' 'Well,' says Mark, 'I suppose the women will have been frightened and kept it to themselves. I only heard it recently myself. You know what women are like.'"[10] In other words, the silence of the women is there to explain why the empty tomb is not heard of before but *introduced* by Mark.[11] Our exegesis of 1 Corinthians 15 runs contrary to this, which is no denial that the abrupt ending of Mark does come with a basket of questions, as the lacuna it represents calls for a further narrative. For example, the Gospel ends with a cognate of the noun *phobos*—Codex Beza and Washingtonianus, the majority of Old Latin witnesses and a Sahidic manuscript assume the noun here—a classical vice according to ancient moral philosophy. Females were, according to current thinking, naturally inclined to this reaction.[12] It is worth perceiving that the first narrative we know about the most fundamental event in Christian identity comes to a close with the presence of one of the cardinal vices in the ancient culture. Brian D. Robinette argues that the sort of reaction of the women (v. 8) shows similarity with the reactions provoked by Jesus's miracles elsewhere in this gospel (e.g., Mark 5:42); hence, amazement is the proper category to him. This may well be the case; nonetheless, the appearance of *phobos* evokes emotions that are out of control, taking the women captive. The term refers to the passions of fear which in Greek moral philosophy were to be mastered.[13]

Summing up this best-preserved ending of Mark, we are struck by the *immediacy* of this passage. One notices the many textual variants, albeit with minor significance if taken as single cases. Taken together though, the

---

10. Goulder, "Explanatory Power," 101. The Norwegian historian Ravnå, *Jesus fra Nasaret*, 241–46 argues likewise. The empty tomb is a Markan invention and Mark 16:8 is an attempt to cover up why no one has heard about this before. No one has heard because it was not told: "For meg er dette den endelige bekreftelsen på at historien om den tomme graven ikke stammer fra gamle tradisjoner, men er diktet opp av Markus selv."

11. Thus also Crossan in Wright and Crossan, "Resurrection," 33.

12. Sandnes, *Early Christian Discourses*, 17–97, 315–24.

13. Robinette, *Grammars of Resurrection*, 91.

number of variants conveys a living text.[14] This in itself serves to bring out the "unfinished" nature of this text. Furthermore, this comes through in the emotional aspects which are so prominent here. The women are overwhelmed, even to the degree that some readers would find embarrassing at least, and the passage is closed by their failure: they do not do as they were instructed to. The Easter message reaches here its dead end; it is simply silenced. The whole passage appears as "raw" and unpolished. It tells about a discovery not yet grasped by those who made it. Thus, the text brings to mind, in a particular way, Peirce's notion of Firstness, to which belongs that it cannot be adequately grasped or described. Firstness comes with surprise and is overwhelming. Feelings of different kinds are a manifestation of Firstness, and they are at home in contexts of discovery. This is not to deny that justification does appear in this story as well, in the ways it is interpreted subsequently (as Secondness). There is no conspicuous use of the Scriptures. Nevertheless, the removal of the stone points to some miraculous intervention. The presence and appearance of the young man bring to mind classical theophany motifs (cf. Mark 9:3), and the reference to Jesus having predicted this, works similarly. Nevertheless, the best-preserved ending brings out more directly than do the other Easter narratives its nature of being a discovery, an experience of Firstness, most clearly witnessed in the emotions and confusion with which this story unfolds. The immediate reaction of the women is to *get out* of the situation.

Mark 16:9–20: The Longer and Secondary Markan Ending

This passage is almost like a textbook example for how later additions seek affirmation and authenticity through making use of preserved traditions, staging them differently, and filling in gaps.[15] The passage may be divided into five sections: vv. 9–11, 12–13, 14, 15–18 and 19–20. Two codices (L and W), as well as the majuscule 083, have clearly found it necessary to form a bridge to the unexpected ending in 16:8. They make a transitory comment, saying that "these things happened after 'for they feared,'" thus clearly picking up on v. 8. These mss thus show themselves to be familiar with the shorter ending, but also demonstrate their uneasiness with it. In the first section of

14. See, e.g., Shepherd, "Narrative Analysis," 77–98; Kannaday, *Apologetic Discourse*, 189–97.

15. Kelhoffer, *Miracle and Mission*, 123–50 on the literary dependence on gospel texts in the longer ending. Larsen, *Gospels Before the Book*, 119–20 has criticized Kelhoffer for considering labelling the alternative endings "forgeries." He argues that Mark's Gospel was unfinished, and, therefore, in need of being brought to a proper end; such attempts have parallels in the ancient world.

this text, the resurrection is mentioned as a participle (*anastas*) introducing the main verb *ephanē* (v. 9): ". . . he appeared first to Mary Magdalene." So, appearances are now introduced to Mark's Easter story, taking place within the narrative. This happened to Mary of Magdala as the first. Christ appearing to Mary alone is taken from John 20 (see above). Verse 10 narrativizes the commission mentioned in v. 7, given in imperative there: "She went out and told those who had been with him . . ." This instruction is not carried out within 16:1-8, but now this happens, at least in part. The disciples are said to be mourning and crying. They were told "he was alive" and that "he had been seen (*etheathē*)" by her. The Easter message has two components here: Christ lives, this is what the empty tomb entails, and he has shown himself to be alive. It is briefly stated that they did not believe: *ēpistēsan* from the verb *apistein*. In Codex D, two versions can be identified; one says that they did not believe her, while the second reading has that they did not believe *him*. This must refer to Jesus himself, paving the way for the accusation of their unbelief and hardheartedness mentioned in v. 14. Thus, there is a tradition that considers their disbelief, not only an expression of how to relate to women's talk but a manifestation of unbelief qualitatively.

Verses 12-13 appear to be an abridged version of Luke 24:13-35, about the two disciples meeting Jesus on their way to Emmaus, albeit specificities are removed. One single sentence catches this Lukan narrative, with emphasis on two aspects. First, it is a story about revelation (*ephanerōthē*) or appearance. The whole scene is conceptualized in accordance with what happened in Luke 24:30-32, namely the moment of recognition. The fact that *ephanerōthē* is followed by a prepositional phrase makes it necessary to translate "he revealed himself, or he appeared." Second, he appeared "in another form (*en hetèra morphē*)." This rendering of the story is worth noting, since it takes us beyond what happened in Luke 24. Nothing there indicates that Jesus appeared to them in another form; on the contrary, he walked with them like any other man, albeit in other parts of this chapter Jesus acts in ways dissimilar to ordinary human bodies. This may, of course, have paved the way for the abridged version in Mark 16:12. At the moment of recognition, he became invisible (*aphantos*) to the two disciples (v. 31). What is at stake here is, therefore, probably that this abridged version draws upon a wider resurrection discourse, in which the form of the resurrection body is under discussion. We have noticed that *morphē* in various combinations appears in Paul's resurrection texts, thus bringing to mind Paul's question in 1 Cor 15:35: with what kind of body (*poiō de sōmati*) do they come?[16]

16. Origen, *Cels.* 6.68 (SC147.3481-350.35) demonstrates how closely connected body and *morphē* are, with regard to how Christ appeared in incarnation and in his transfiguration; resurrection is not mentioned there.

Thus this Markan passage picks up on one of the key issues in resurrection discourse. This phrase brings to mind the discussion between Jesus and the Sadducees regarding the resurrection. Jesus's response is shaped by the question of "form," albeit *morphē* and cognates do not appear: "they are like angels (*hōs aggeloi*) in heaven" (Mark 12:25parr). Luke says that "the children of the resurrection" are *isaggeloi* here (Luke 20:36), meaning "like angels." Becoming "like angels" is an issue of "form" (*morphē*) related to the question of resurrection.[17] We thus conclude that v. 12 is informed by similar discourses. Verse 13 echoes Luke 24:35 where it says that they told the other what happened to them. At the center of their report is the recognition moment, as it is in Mark 16:12 as well. However, the Markan addition brings a moment not found in Luke 24, namely that the others did not believe (*oude episteusan*). The distrust of the disciples is then mentioned twice.

Verse 14 says that Jesus appeared (*ephanerōthē*) to the eleven (cf. Luke 24:9, 33) once they shared a meal. This is probably informed by Luke 24:36–43 and John 20:19, 24–29 where a shared meal is the context for an appearance of the risen Christ (thus also in John 21). However, this Markan scene differs from the others by its emphasis on Jesus *rebuking* the disciples. For sure, some Easter traditions have preserved the memory of the disciples' lack of faith: "Oh, how foolish you are, and how slow of heart to believe all that the prophets have declared" (Luke 24:25; see also Matt 28:17b; John 20:24–29), but the reproach in Mark is more direct, and draws upon similar dicta during the ministry of Jesus. The verb *oneidizein* is never found in the Easter narratives, but it occurs in the gospels when Jesus criticizes people for having turned their back to him: "Then he began to reproach the cities in which most of his deeds of power had been done, because they did not repent" (Matt 11:20). Likewise, the noun *apistia*, "unbelief," never occurs in the Easter narratives, but it does in the ministry of Jesus. This is the response Jesus is faced with in Nazareth (Mark 6:6parr). Matthew 17:20 (cf. Mark 9:28–29) has Jesus speak about "the little faith (*oligopistia*)" of the disciples. In speaking about the stubbornness (*sklērokardia*) of the disciples, manifested in their not believing those who saw Jesus, namely Mary of Magdala and the two disciples, he aligns them with the people of hard hearts in Mark 10:5parr, thus bringing to mind Mark 4:12 (citation of Isa 6:9–10); 6:52; 7:18; 8:16–18, 21 about lack of faith and understanding in the disciples. All this is in Mark 16:14 transferred to and given a bearing upon how they reacted to the testimony of the women and the two disciples.[18] Codex W, and also a Jerome ms, makes a long addition after v. 14, rendering an

---

17. See Lehtipuu, *Debates over the Resurrection of the Dead*, 133–36, 186–89.
18. See also Kelhoffer, *Miracle and Mission*, 95–97.

apology of the disciples. They say that Satan's power was too great for them and ask Jesus to instruct them. Thanks to the speech of Jesus, their stubborn unbelief is turned into a committed mission. Thus, the sudden shift between v. 14 and v. 15 is smoothened.

The section vv. 15–18 marks a sudden shift, from reproach to an assignment to mission, followed by promises that miracles and wonders will accompany them. They will even pick up snakes without being hurt. Old Testament passages like Ps 91:13, a poetic and metaphoric passage, is turned into a narrative, thus bringing to mind how some fellow scholars reason about the resurrection as well. Verse 16 (faith—baptism—salvation) echoes narratives in the book of Acts (16:15, 31, 33; 18:8; cf. 2:38). One is here struck by the contrast between the reproach for lack of faith, and the same disciples being assigned to proclaim precisely faith. The longer ending is rounded off by taking in a Lukan perspective, namely Jesus being taken up to heaven (*anelēmphtē*; vv. 19–20). Thus, Luke's distinction in Acts between resurrection and exaltation informs this ending, and Ps 110:1 is narrativized: "and sat down at the right hand of God." From this position, the risen Christ supervises the mission mentioned in vv. 15–18.

Comparing vv. 1–8 with the longer ending reveals some important shifts. While the resurrection itself is the focus in vv. 1–8, vv. 9–20 focuses on appearances of Jesus and the assignments given by him. The fear, elusiveness, and fragility of vv. 1–8 are in vv. 9–20 replaced by reproach turned into power. The spatial setting is in the first instance indeed local and native, while in the second it is general, broader. Christ is no longer absent, but present in his cosmic heavenly power. And the gospel is proclaimed in all the world; in short, everywhere. The escape of frightened women from the tomb is replaced by victorious proclamation. In Mark 16:15, the proclamation of the gospel is for "the whole creation" (*pasē tē ktisei*). This is an awkward formulation that invites perspectives similar to Romans 8, namely that the renewal brought about by the resurrection of Jesus has implications for the entire creation (vv. 18–22 in particular).

Summing up the longer ending, we notice that many observations which constituted the shorter ending as discovery and as a witness to Firstness, are here reworked and altered. The passage is about what happened afterwards, but this also alters the perspective of the entire scene. The vulnerability that follows from a testimony of Firstness is gone with the emotions that are not mentioned. The failure of the women is made right by having Mary Magdalene—now she is alone, like in John 20—bring the news to the disciples. The absence of Jesus is replaced by his presence through appearances, three of them, in addition to the ascension. Jesus rebuking the disciples for their disbelief serves as a justification, since it becomes an instruction to readers. Reading Mark's Easter narrative from the longer ending leaves it not as a discovery. It becomes a complex testimony of Thirdness, as it is mediation about what this story means to someone. Still, there are no apparent references to the Old Testament, although the continuous dependency on other New Testament texts works likewise. Wayne C. Kannaday has argued that the longer ending is a product of scribal labours, and that the passage at points appears to mirror common charges against Christians found by pagan polemicists.[19] He points to Mary Magdalene, who is introduced as the woman from whom Jesus had cast out seven demons, which serves to refute accusations that she was a "hysterical woman" (see Part II, The Easter Narratives, section Women at the Tomb).[20] The world-wide perspective targets Celsus's view that the Christians did not make any difference in the world. Kannaday also argues that the disbelief of the disciples shows them not to be credulous. We find that this passage has been apologetically influenced, and the examples shown by Kannaday are, at least in principle, possible. However, his understanding of the disbelief of the disciples hardly works apologetically; we tend to think that this is directed inwards, using the disciples as figures in a generally applied admonition to embrace the Easter faith.

Matt 28:1–20: Excessively Present

Matthew's story of the empty tomb picks up on 27:61, where it says that Mary of Magdala and "the other Mary" knew the place, as they were present when Jesus was buried. Together these two women went to see the tomb (*theōrēsai ton taphon*) (v. 1). Verses 2–4 refer to the moment of the resurrection. Matthew is the only canonical gospel conveying *something* about what happened. He does so by shaping these verses in Old Testament theophany language, aimed at narrating God's presence and action. Earthquake and an angel descending from heaven belong within this tradition. The scene bears resemblances to what happened at the transfiguration scene, which likewise was a scene where heaven and earth blended (Matt 17:2). Worth noting is that the transfiguration also implied a change of Jesus himself: "he was transfigured (*metemorphōthē*)." We notice that this verb belongs to the favorites when Paul voices bodily changes caused by resurrection.[21] In other words, Matt 28:2–4 portray a scene within which earthly things are prone to

---

19. Kannaday, *Apologetic Discourse*, 189–97.

20. We are doubtful that Celsus would find this convincing; he would probably find it rather substantiating his view that Mary of Magdala was really a hysterical woman.

21. See also above on the longer Markan ending.

be changed. This appears equally in both transfiguration and resurrection, thus linking the nature of these two events.

While the women according to Mark found the stone rolled away, and thus that the resurrection was already past, Matthew creates the expectation that the women will be able to watch the momentous event. He does so by having them arrive at the tomb *while* an angel is descending from heaven; they watch the stone being rolled away. This expectation is not met, however, as the angel announces that Jesus left the scene even before the stone was removed. The resurrection has taken place, but is now *announced* to them by the angel. Judged by the expectation created in Matthew, this comes as a disappointment. Francis Watson says that the angel appears as a substitute for what the women expected to see, namely Jesus himself.[22] In this way, Matthew portrays the resurrection event in terms similar to what we will find in Luke and John, namely that he passes through closed doors, or here a tomb stone. Those who were present, the guards, were unable to witness. Out of fear when seeing the angel—notice that they do not see Jesus—they were like dead. Hence, witnesses to the event are not there, and what took place remains secluded and inaccessible. The event is there only as a proclamation that looks *back* at what happened.

The body of Jesus which had been there was no longer there: "Come and see . . ." The women are also instructed to tell his disciples that he "was raised from the dead," and that he went ahead to Galilee where they would see him. The future tense in *opsesthe* (v. 7) has Jesus as an object or content; hence, the text envisages an appearance, pointing forward to the scene in Galilee to come in vv. 16–20. In fact, this instruction is never carried out narratively, since the women are interrupted by the risen Jesus in vv. 8–10. The empty tomb is followed by a first appearance to the women in which the resurrected Jesus affirms what the angel had already told them. This meeting with Jesus took place as they left the tomb in order to tell the disciples. Verse 8 gives the reaction of the women. The overwhelming nature of what happened is expressed in a mix of emotions, fear, and joy, and in their running to inform the disciples. This verse speaks from the level of discovery or Firstness. The preceding scenes speak from a justification perspective; theophany language is a way of making sense or interpreting what happened, while the message of the angel makes reference to "what Jesus had said," which is a reference to his pre-Easter instructions.

Literally, they ran into Jesus, who greeted them. At this point the angelophany becomes Christophany. Regarding emotions, Matthew mentions joy in addition to fear; the running (*edramon*) serves to pinpoint the

---

22. Watson, "'He is not here,'" 102–3.

immediacy of the situation. Jesus reiterates the message of the angel that he will meet with the disciples in Galilee. In this emotional moment, a scene resembling some kind of worship (*prosekynēsan autō*; v. 9; cf. v. 17 and 2:11; 26:49) as the women take hold (*ekratēsan*) of Jesus's feet. The mention of the feet here serves a dual purpose; it is a gesture of respect and worship, but also a gesture assuming his *corporeal* presence.

Vv. 11–14 make a narrative interlude, picking up on the guards in Matt 27:62–66. The text renders the planting of a rumor that the disciples stole the body at night while the guards were asleep. Bribery and lies are means of getting this rumor out. This is the second time Jesus is betrayed for money. Clearly, Matthew has included this story for apologetic reasons. The rumor is still around (cf. Matt 27:8), and is referred to as giving the reason why the tomb was found to be empty. It is worth noticing that the rumor agrees that the tomb was empty and that some kind of explanation was needed. It is difficult to imagine how the resurrection of Jesus could be proclaimed in Jerusalem if the tomb found there was demonstrably intact with the body of Jesus. The comment that the rumor is still there takes us to the context of Matthew's composition and is highly indicative that the narrative is formed by this context. Justin Martyr says that the Jewish leaders organized a counter mission, proclaiming that

> a certain godless and lawless sect has been raised by one Jesus of Galilee, a deceiver, whom we crucified, but his disciples stole him by night from the tomb, where he had been laid after being unnailed from the cross, and they deceive men, saying that he is risen from the dead and has ascended into heaven. (*Dial.* 108.2)[23]

For the theological issue of the empty tomb, this rumor is crucial, as it demonstrates that the empty tomb is no evidence; at best it is a *sign*. This scene also demonstrates that the narrative is not only some kind of report, but it assumes alternative stories and is told against them.

The meeting in Galilee takes place in vv. 16–20. The disciples are now eleven, not twelve when they meet at a mountain. No mountain has been mentioned so far in this chapter; it comes out of the blue. Verse 17 assumes a situation of mixed feeling. Veneration and doubt go hand in hand here, and thus continues a motif from v. 8. Verse 18 interprets the resurrection in terms of Jesus having been attributed power and majesty. The Greek *edothe* is *passivum divinum*: God has given him this role. This introduction finds an echo in the longer Markan ending (see Part II, The Easter Narratives,

---

23. The citation is taken from Stanton, "Early Objections to the Resurrection of Jesus," 85. For the Greek text, see Justin Martyr, *Iustini Martyris, Dialogus cum Tryphone*.

section Mark 16:9–20). Different from Mark's shorter ending, mission is here emphasized, a mission involving the world and nations. The perspective is dramatically altered from the scene on which Jesus has hitherto been active during his life and ministry. However, resurrection is not only interpreted in the sense of majesty but also an abiding presence: "I am with you always, to the end of the age."

The Matthean Inclusio: Emmanuel—"I Am with You"

This last dictum of Jesus carries weight within Matthew's story of Jesus in general, and it is particularly apt to illustrate an important point regarding the resurrection as following in the wake of his life and ministry. This dictum, "I am with you," is a flashback to Matt 1:23: "they shall name him Emmanuel." Thus, the risen Jesus affirms the name he carried from his birth on—indeed a symbolic name like a prophetic sign-name (cf. Jes 7:3; 8:1–4; Hos 1–2). This was also the name that characterized him throughout his ministry, manifesting itself in his presence among people, with teaching and healing (Matt 9:36; 10:19, 29–31; 18:20). When the risen Jesus speaks about his presence in exactly these terms, he considers his ministry a prelude to what he will now accomplish *excessively*. The change of scene, from Palestine to world, from Jews to all nations—all this is indicative of a surplus, but still a continuation of his ministry. What resurrection entails can, therefore, not be rightly understood if not seen as a consummation of what Jesus performed during his ministry. The meaning of what happened to Jesus in God raising him from the dead is to be seen in relation to his whole life. We observed this connection also in Mark, where the message of the "young man" at the tomb was about Jesus *from Nazareth*. This is what Matthew also conveys in having Jesus's last word echo the name he was given and the name he put into practice during his ministry. Matthew conveys this also by having Jesus speak of his relationship to the world and the nations in terms taken from his pre-Easter ministry. It is all about becoming disciples (*mathēteúsate*). When Matthew wrote his gospel, this was not a current name for Christ devotees. Here it serves to unite post-Easter devotees with his followers during his life. Resurrection thus perpetuates the past, but in a re-directed way marked by *surplus*, as the nations are now within view. Worth noting is also that the instruction that the mission will pass on to the nations is what Jesus has taught them during his ministry.

Furthermore, Matt 1:23, a Matthean subtext of 28:20, directs us also to the Old Testament, as it is a citation from a prophecy (Isa 7:14, cf. 8:10). This means that the frame of interpretation provided for the resurrection is not only the life of Jesus portrayed in the gospel, but God's larger story with his people, and the promises given by him. The instruction to be given also refers back to what Jesus taught when with his disciples. "Teaching them to obey everything that I have commanded you" is a flashback to Jesus as teacher in this Gospel.[24]

---

24. See Byrskog, *Jesus the Only Teacher*, 291–94.

Luke 24: Recognizing the Risen Jesus

THE STORY OF THE empty tomb (vv. 1–12) picks up on Luke 23:55 about the women who saw the burial. Now they come to the tomb, bringing with them spices. Luke makes no mention of "the third day" in the narrative, but includes it in the predictions alluded to later. Verse 10 mentions names, Mary of Magdala, Johanna, Mary the mother of James "and other women with them." Luke thus gives the picture that numerous women were present. Hence, the majority of the mss, including Codex Alexandrinus, harmonizes this information by adding in v. 1 *kai tines syn autais*. They find the stone rolled away as they enter the tomb, but the body was not there. They were perplexed at this. Two men in dazzling clothes only increase their fear. The men announce to the women that they are seeking the living Jesus among the dead, where he is no longer: "he has risen (*ēgerthē*)" (v. 6). Verses 6–8 are rather similar to both Mark and Matthew in bringing to their mind Jesus's teaching on this while he was with them—in Galilee. Luke, however, echoes more intentionally the predictions found in the Gospel (Luke 9:22, 44–45; 13:32–33; 17:25; 18:31–34; 22:15–38; cf. 24:46).[1] Luke's use of "remembrance" (*mimnēskesthai*; 24:6) paves the way for a more thorough instruction of what it means to "remember" what Jesus said (Luke 22:61; cf. 2:19, 51; 24:32), thus bringing to mind a typical Johannine motif.[2]

Although the women receive no instruction to tell about their experience, they nonetheless do so, and vv. 9–12 address this. They told the eleven and "all the rest." The apostles are mentioned in particular: "But these words seemed to them as idle talk (*lēros*), and they did not believe them" (v. 11). The Greek noun used implies nonsense or humbug.[3] The

---

1. See Anderson, *"But God Raised Him from the Dead,"* 163.
2. In John's Gospel, proper "remembrance" of what Jesus said, is the result of the Spirit's guidance (John 2:22; 12:16; 14:26).
3. BAGD s.v.

apostles here voice contempt in which resounds male pejoratives vis-à-vis women's testimony (see later).[4] Peter runs to the tomb to see for himself (v. 12).[5] Again the running motif conveys the nature of this as an immediate, emotional, and hasty situation. As he looked into the tomb, he saw nothing but the linen clothes. He left the place wondering about this. There is no faith here, only bafflement.

Luke's presentation of the women is somewhat ambiguous. It is conveyed that they implicitly trusted the two men's (read: angels') announcement, at least sufficiently to make them tell the apostles. In this way, they are set against the disbelief of the male apostles. Kevin Anderson makes the point that the women at the tomb bring to mind Elizabeth's and Mary's trust in the angelic messages in Luke 1, while Zechariah disbelieved the words of the angel (Luke 1:20).[6] On the other hand, Luke diminishes the role of the women, as they receive no message from the angels, and their words need male validation.[7] Furthermore, Luke has no appearance to the women. This may be a deliberate minimizing of the testimony of women, but one wonders if the disciples' labeling the women's talk idle, really disqualify the women, and not the men themselves. After all, Luke leaves no doubt that it was the women who got things right here. From v. 13, Luke embarks upon a discourse on the resurrection, revolving around two questions: recognition (vv. 13–35) and then what reality is involved (vv. 36–43). To that, we now turn.

Wrestling with Recognizing Jesus (vv. 13–35)

These are the most extended and detailed appearances found in the Easter narratives, and it is a Lukan idiosyncrasy. The story is clearly influenced by apologetic motives and the issue of Scriptural interpretation. At the center of the narrative is recognition. The first scene (vv. 13–27) is a dialogue between two disciples and the risen Jesus who appears incognito (vv. 15–16): "their eyes were kept from recognizing him." The sudden appearance conveys that Jesus arrives from somewhere else, thus linking up with his disappearance later in this narrative (v. 31) and his sudden presence again in v. 36. One possibility is that v. 51, "he withdrew from them," is analogous, thus implying that Jesus appeared from heaven. His ascension then marks the end of the appearances.

---

4. See Part II, The Easter Narratives, sec. Women at the Tomb.
5. This verse is missing in Codex D and in Old Latin translations.
6. Anderson, *"But God Raised Him from the Dead,"* 162.
7. Novakovic, *Resurrection*, 88.

The NRSV translation of vv. 15–16 ("their eyes were kept from recognizing him") gives the impression that their failure to recognize Jesus was so ordained (*ekratounto*). Hence, Stefan Alkier says that "this shutting of the eyes, effected by God, assumes that Jesus otherwise would have been recognized."[8] Grammaticality (passive voice in *ekratounto*) might indicate so, but the narrative as such instead conveys that recognizing Jesus is beyond the capacity of human beings. The question of agency with regard to the shutting of the eyes becomes less important then. Alkier's point rests upon his view (see below) that Jesus's resurrected body was identical to that of his earthly life, a view we question.

Most of the dialogue is devoted to the two disciples who are astonished that the stranger is unaware of what has happened in Jerusalem. The disciples give him a short account of the Jesus narrative presented in the Gospel, ending in their disappointment: "But we had hoped that he was the one to redeem Israel" (v. 21). Their hopes were shattered; this is echoed in Acts 1:6 as well. In vv. 22–24, the Jerusalem apostles report on the women who visited the tomb and found it empty. They were given a vision, an appearance (*optasia*), not of Christ, however, but of angels announcing that Jesus was alive (*zēn*; v. 23). This piece of information takes us back to vv. 5–6: "you look for the living (*ton zōnta*)." When Easter announces that Jesus is alive, that implies an explicit continuation with Jesus's pre-Easter life. Jesus of pre-Easter has come alive. In some way, the past is, thereby, being continued and extended, although the rest of the story brings into this also significant changes and alterations.

While on their way, The Emmaus disciples tell the stranger that some men, not only Peter, went there, and they affirmed the message of the women. Jesus himself was not in the tomb. Their report picks up on the available facts, on which belief in the resurrection is grounded: absent body, an empty tomb, angelic vision and proclamation that Jesus is alive. These facts, however, do not in themselves cause belief in the resurrection; on the contrary, they convey bewilderment. The message of the angels brings the climax of their confusion. In other words, these facts are not identical to a resurrection, which is a category of interpretation. At this point, Jesus enters the dialogue, instructing them on what has taken place (vv. 25–27).

Not recognizing the risen Jesus was due to failure to read the Scriptures adequately, that is, to read them Christologically. The entire Scripture, Moses and the Prophets, convey clearly that their account is in accordance with God's will laid down there. The resurrection is spoken of in terms of Jesus "entering into his glory." In Acts 3:13, the resurrection is labeled

---

8. Alkier, *Reality of the Resurrection*, 130.

God's glorifying (*edoxasen*) Jesus. Luke seems in this phraseology to unite resurrection and ascension, in a way that does *not* pave the way for v. 51 where the ascension is narrated. This ambiguity in Luke's text (and in Acts) has been noticed earlier.[9] Luke conveys that recognition of the risen Jesus is Scripture-based, but also a *gift*! Worth noting is that Luke 24 speaks of "the opening" of both eyes and Scriptures (vv. 31 and 32), and that the first depends on the latter. This parallelism takes us to Luke's *juxtaposition* of recognizing the risen Jesus and Scripture. Richard B. Hays has presented a fascinating perspective on the dictum that "their eyes were opened" (*autōn de diēnoichthēsan hoi ophthalmoi*; v. 31).[10] Although there is no overt allusion to any Old Testament precursor here, Hays draws the attention to 2 Kings 6, where Elisha finds the city of Dothan surrounded by the hostile army of Aram. Elisha comforts a servant who was with him, saying that "there are more with us than with them" (2 Kgs 6:17), and prays that God may open their eyes to see: "So the Lord opened the eyes (*diēnoixen kyrios toùs ophtalmoùs autou*) of the servant, and he saw; the mountain was full of horses and chariots of fire all around Elisha" (2 Kgs 6:17). Such an echo is, of course, only a possibility here, but it adds depth to the story. The Emmaus disciples are given to see "a fiery new world," disclosing to them a reality hitherto unseen.[11]

The next scene brings the moment of recognition. It happens at the table as a meal is shared (vv. 30–31). The act of breaking the bread links resurrection and earthly ministry. However, at this point in the narrative, Jesus eating is not the issue; it is instead the act of sharing and giving with which the disciples are acquainted. The risen Jesus makes them *recipients* of his gifts, as he used to do. The phrase *edidou autois* ("he gave it to them"), which is also found in Luke 9:16; 22:19 is indicative of the nature of this as a *familiar* act: it is a gift. Once recognized, he disappeared to them: "he vanished from their sight (*aphantos*)" (v.31). The risen Jesus shows himself elusive. He is not immediately recognized: it is clearly not his outward appearance or look-alike that makes them recognize him. It is what he *does* that is familiar to them. Furthermore, his becoming invisible also conveys some kind of bodily transformation. According to Stefan Alkier, Jesus's "resurrected body is outwardly identical to that of his earthly life, but it no longer obeys the bounds of space and time."[12] The first part of this citation is not necessarily

---

9. See Part II, The Acts of the Apostles, sec. Evidentiary Presence.

10. Hays, *Echoes of Scripture*, 241–42.

11. Thus, we can say that here is established not only a different context of discovery that determines the "what-ness" of their experience, but also a context of justification that determines the "why-ness," and thus the context of justification for this experience.

12. Alkier, *Reality of the Resurrection*, 131.

substantiated by the narrative. The outward appearance of Jesus hardly plays any role in the recognition scene. If identical, recognition would have taken place more easily and more immediately. It is, therefore, not surprising that the longer Markan ending in commenting on this particular scene, speaks about Jesus having "another form."

Verse 33 brings into this scene the unexpectedness and hasty impression of what happened this day: "The same hour they got up and returned to Jerusalem . . ." When there, it is conveyed to them by their fellow apostles that the Lord had risen indeed (*ontōs*), and that he had appeared (*ōphtē*) to Simon (v. 34). The Greek adverb emphasizes the statement. Verse 34 echoes 1 Cor 15:5, but finds no narrative substantiation in Luke's Gospel. What Luke related in v. 12 about Peter in this chapter is by no means an appearance.

What Kind of Reality? (Luke 24:36–43)

As the disciples are talking about the incident on the road, Jesus again appears to all of them (vv. 36–43). Now Luke participates in a discussion which Paul also addressed, namely what kind of body the resurrected body is. Echoes of this variegated debate, we have come across also in 2 Macc 7 and Mark 16:12. This Lukan scene conveys suddenness and fear, and it revolves around the question: what kind of figure is this? Is it comparable to a spirit or a ghost? Hence, the issue is no longer recognition only, but the issue of *reality*: was Jesus really raised from the dead? They thought they saw a ghost (*pneuma*); worth noting is that Codex D has *phantasma*. This is the noun used by both Mark and Matthew to describe what they thought they saw as Jesus walked the sea (Mark 6:49; Matt 14:26), clearly a ghost. This noun is often associated with imaginary figures appearing during sleep.[13] At this

---

13. BAGD s.v.; see e.g. Wisd. 17:12–16. This passage is interesting as it provides a context for how these nouns work. *Phantasmata* represent the opposite of rationality, and result in lack of understanding. They occur during sleep, and cause much fear. Daniel A. Smith explores the possibility that Luke 24:36–43 ("are we seeing a *pneuma*?") is directed against Paul, as he voiced the idea of a "spiritual body" in 1 Cor 15:44; see Smith, *Revisiting the Empty Tomb*, 14, 106–11; see also Smith, "Seeing a Pneuma(tic Body)." The two passages are linked through the same Greek term: *pneuma* (noun) and *pneumatikos* (adjective), but that seems also to mark the end of the connection between the two texts. If Smith is right here, Luke is definitely misrepresenting Paul and simplifying his use of *pneuma*. Paul's use of *pneumatikos* in 1 Cor 15:44 is rooted in his theology in a way which the Lukan passage hardly accommodates. It may well be, though, that Luke targets ways of thinking about the resurrected Jesus which are non-physical. Such opinions may have found Paul's text in 1 Cor 15 prone to express their view. But Luke's alleged polemic is no guide to a proper understanding of the Pauline passage.

point in the narrative, the apologetic context or concern comes through. It is easily imagined that this issue mirrors concomitant objections to what really happened in the Easter appearances.

Then Jesus himself gives proof by performing demonstrations. He shows them his hands and feet; thus, they will see that it is him. They will recognize him as a human being, known to them (v. 39). Jesus inviting his disciples to inspect his hands and feet brings to mind John 20:27. *Continuity* is here emphasized in such a way that one wonders if Paul would have agreed. This comes somewhat surprisingly, as they were unable to recognize him when they walked together—obviously seeing then the same feet and hands. While the focus in the Emmaus scene was recognition or *identifying* Jesus, the emphasis now is on recognizing Jesus *as a human being*. The body issue is decisive in this scene. The seeming tension between these two scenes can be explained by different foci. Now Jesus is recognizable in bodily terms, and in such a way that it brings to mind 2 Maccabees 7, although Luke adds to the body qualities that go beyond the body as it once was.

The demonstration involves touching and seeing, thus disproving that they saw a spirit or a ghost: "for a ghost does not have flesh and bones as you see that I have" (v. 39). Verses 40–42 give a related acted proof; Jesus shows his hand and feet. The apostles are not yet fully convinced, out of fear and joy—a mixture of emotions—and Jesus, therefore, asks for something to eat. He was given[14] a piece of broiled fish, "and he took it and ate in their presence." The act of eating is now not demonstrating his *altruism*, but that the risen Jesus is a human being, like the one they had hitherto known and associated with. Hans-Joachim Eckstein says with reference to Luke 24:11, 25, 37, 41, that it was necessary to address the problems related to doubt and unbelief in the confession of the resurrection from the outset.[15] Eckstein makes the point, very much analogous to Matt 28:17 ("some doubted"), that Easter faith was accompanied by doubt and questions from the very beginning. The emotional aspects found in all the empty tomb stories give witness to this also. However, Luke leaves no room for doubt on the question of whether Jesus had been raised bodily or not. His hands, feet, and appetite proved the case. This chapter is then closed by including mission as based upon an accurate and adequate reading of the Scriptures. The risen Jesus points to the promise of the Spirit, thus paving the way for the book of Acts.

Summing up this extended Lukan chapter, we realize that this narrative is framed by a discourse on the resurrection, revolving around two related

---

14. Worth noting is that some mss includes the act of giving here, as Jesus having himself eaten, *gave* also them to eat.

15. Eckstein, "Die Wirklichkeit der Auferstehung Jesu," 3.

issues, namely, how is the risen Jesus recognized, and what kind of reality is at play in the Easter narrative. The first issue is given a double answer: the Scriptures and the table. The Scriptures unanimously convey that what happened to Jesus is in accordance with God's will. This claim brings to mind one of the parables told by Jesus in Luke's Gospel, namely about Lazarus and his wealthy neighbor. Finding himself in Hades, separated from Abraham, he asks God to send Lazarus to his five brothers, "that he may warn them so that they will not also come into this place of torment" (v.28). Abraham's response is telling: "If they do not listen to Moses and the prophets, neither will they be convinced even if someone rises from the dead." Resurrection is not foreign to the Scriptures, but it is a matter of reading them rightly.

One is struck by the ambiguous nature of this claim; the Scriptures are called upon as the hermeneutical key, but no passages are referred to. The claim is not given content; nonetheless, what Luke conveys in this claim is that *God* is at work, bringing to completion the history of salvation. At the table, Jesus shows himself in a familiar act, demonstrating the nature of his ministry in *giving*, his altruism. The second issue is also given a double answer here. Firstly, the hands and feet of Jesus are still the same; they may be touched. Jesus also eats food prepared for him, thus demonstrating that the reality in question is very much in continuity with the past. This is not to deny that Luke also is aware of the new dimensions of the resurrected body.

Luke's narrative is probably the New Testament text that most directly expresses a physical resurrected body, and also invites an empirical examination. This trend is clearly observable in the latter part of Luke 24. The first part of the Emmaus scenes is more complicated, though. Recognition is not primarily empiric, but assumes an adequate Scriptural attitude to the phenomenon, and also that recognition of the risen Jesus is not a matter of examination, but of receiving a gift that is beyond their control. As we saw above, vv. 22–24 state the facts on the ground, but these facts need to be interpreted adequately. This story provides such interpretation, in two interrelated ways. First, Scripture, read with a Christological focus, offers what these facts need to become relevant witnesses to the resurrection, and not something else. Obviously, in themselves, they are not necessarily such witnesses. This process is labeled "opening of the eyes." Secondly, it was while the risen Jesus *gave* them to eat that they recognized him. The moment of receiving became revelatory to them; eventually, they knew who he was. Likewise, this is labeled an act of "opening their eyes." Both Scripture and receiving are necessary to have an adequate understanding of what the "facts" of this story were really about. Thus, this story illustrates the abductive reasoning worked out in Part I, Theoretical Presuppositions, section Abduction and its Relation to Experience of this study. The resurrection of Jesus does not necessarily come with the "facts" upon which it is based, or to put it in another way, resurrection and the "facts" on the ground are not identical. Thus Luke 24 holds a prominent place in the New Testament as it provides hermeneutical keys for coming to terms with resurrection.

John 20(–21): Initiating a New "Dispensation"

In what is possibly the intended ending of John's Gospel (chap. 20), we may narratively distinguish between three major scenes; the first about the discovery of the empty tomb (vv. 1–10), and the other two scenes about appearances, to Mary of Magdala (vv. 11–18) and the disciples and Thomas in particular (vv. 19–29). John tells about one woman only, Mary Magdalene. Early, when still dark, she arrives at the grave and finds that the stone has been removed. The recurrent motif of running in the Easter stories appears here as well; she runs to tell Peter and the "disciple whom Jesus loved." Her message is not about resurrection though; she says that the body has been removed and that its whereabouts are unknown. Mary disappears from the narrative then, only to be picked up again in v. 11 as she stands outside the grave.

Peter and the other disciple *run* to the burial place, the latter being the fastest; thus, John conveys immediacy and hastiness here. He did not enter, but looked inside and saw the linen wrappings lying there. As Peter arrives, he enters and finds that the head cloth and the wrappings were neatly laid aside (v. 7). At this point, the story is remarkable in its details. Just like in Matthew (see above), rumours that the body was stolen by disciples, shape the narrative here. The neatly wrapped clothes prove that this is not a crime scene where grave robbers have been active. Thus, this piece of information may also serve an apologetic purpose, very much like in Luke 24 where the issue of Jesus being a "ghost" was addressed. We thus see that apologetic interests have left traces on the narratives.

The other disciple now looks into the tomb, and "he saw and believed" (v. 9). This is a surprising remark, because elsewhere in the narrative traditions the empty tomb is never presented as sufficient basis for faith. Throughout it is encountering Jesus that brings about faith. In John's Gospel, to see and to believe are often used synonymously (John 2:23; 6:30; 11:40). However, v. 9 adds a retrospective comment, indicating that faith comes about later: "for as yet they did not understand the scripture that he must rise from the dead." This leaves the statement about the other disciple somewhat in the air here. The brief comment in v. 10 strengthens this impression, since it here says that the disciples returned home, a rather everyday piece of information against the backdrop of what this is really about.

This leaves the impression that the level of faith indicated in v. 8 is not a full level of faith, a preliminary faith at best, as in John 2:23 and 6:30. However, there is another way to approach vv. 8–9. Much depends on how the Greek *oudepō* is taken. In most cases, this adverb means "not yet" and refers to something still to happen, as is the case in, e.g., John 7:8,[16] 39. John 19:41 is different, though, in speaking about the tomb in which Jesus was laid: ". . . in which no one had ever (*oudepō*) been laid." In this case, *oudepō* introduces a situation changing the circumstances. Accordingly, it is worth considering that John 20:9 implies that a full understanding of the resurrection in the light of the Scriptures has *up until this point* not been in place. This gives another view on "he saw and believed" in v. 8. It may be objected here that a scriptural reference is hardly so far warranted in the narrative. In the light of the Johannine merging of perspectives throughout his story, this may not necessarily be a problem. Anyway, v. 8 is a riddle and a possible exception confirming what is the rule in the Easter narrative traditions, namely that the empty tomb by itself does not convey faith.

Mary now enters again. She looks into the grave and finds two angels there; they see that she is crying. Mary repeats what she previously said: "They have taken away my Lord, and I do not know where they have laid him" (v. 13). Then Jesus appears to her, but she does not recognize him and mistakes him for the gardener. Hence, for the third time, we hear that she asks for the whereabouts of Jesus's body: "tell me where you have laid him, and I will take him away" (v. 15). Structurally, Mary here occurs in a role similar to the Emmaus disciples who failed to know the stranger walking with them. In their case it was a familiar act that opened their eyes to see his true identity; here it is a familiar word, her name in the Hebrew language.[17] There is an ambiguity here; familiarity is not immediate but is *given* to her by the initiative of Jesus who calls her by her name. Jesus is corporeally present, but still absent to her. It is Jesus who bridges the absence and presence here. This ambiguity is not due to weakness on the part of Mary, nor is there any deficiency in the self-manifestation of Jesus. The ambiguity is precisely how the nature of resurrection is available.[18]

Quite a few mss add that Mary ran towards Jesus to touch (*apsasthai*) him, thus forming a bridge to the notorious difficult v. 17: "Do not hold on to me (*mē mou aptou*), because I have not yet ascended to the Father." Tangibility is clearly not an issue here, as John has Thomas touch Jesus later in the same chapter. Hence, it is rather about *clinging to* Jesus in a way that

---

16. In John 7:8, Papyrus 66 reads *oudepō*.
17. This is pointed out by Novakovic, *Resurrection*, 112.
18. Thus also Robinette, *Grammars of Resurrection*, 4.

is no longer appropriate. According to Sandra M. Schneiders, *mē mou aptou* abbreviates how two people historically relate "in the flesh."[19] Such a relationship has now come to an end. Mary has not yet come to that understanding; she imagines that things will be as they had been. Hence, she addresses Jesus as "*Rabbouni*," a term not at all associated with resurrection, but rather with Jesus's ministry (cf. Mark 10:51). This is a marked difference from what she says in her announcement to the disciples: "I have seen the Lord (*ton kyrion*)" (John 20:18).

The resurrection has introduced a new phase or dispensation in how to relate to Jesus. Reimund Bieringer has presented the history of interpretation of this verse and concludes that the "hour" has now come when "Jesus deflects the attention away from himself in two directions, to the Father and to the 'brothers.'"[20] The new phase which was announced in John 4:23 ("But the hour is coming . . . .") is now in place. Jesus withdraws; hence, Mary cannot hold on to him. The Easter marks a new stage in how she is now to relate to Jesus. Jesus directs her to the brethren: "But go to my brothers . . ." (John 20:17b). Schneiders says that the driving question in John 20 is "where is the Lord?" In other words, how and where is the presence of the risen Lord to be found?[21] Jesus responds in v. 17 with a plural "your Father," which includes a communal aspect here, hinted at already in v. 2: "we do not know where they have laid him." Worth noticing is also that John 20:23 is an echo of a communal tradition about forgiveness of sins (cf. Matt 18:18).

Together with Jesus's remark to Thomas, "Blessed are those who have not seen and yet have come to believe" (John 20:29), this becomes significant. More than any of the other gospels, John is rather explicit on the catechetical purpose of his gospel (20:30–31). In other words, John tells the Jesus story in such a way that it involves future believers, *external* to the story itself.[22] This is stated explicitly in John 17:20: "I ask not only on behalf of these but also on behalf of those who will believe in me through their word." With this in mind, the story of Mary and Thomas conveys the *ecclesial* presence of the risen Jesus for future believers. One is here reminded of Paul's ecclesiological use of the body metaphor, which in 1 Cor 12:12, 27 goes beyond the illustrative and pedagogical use of the metaphor to convey that the resurrected Christ is present in the fellowship of believers.

John seems to think that Jesus ascended to his Father Easter morning immediately after the appearance to Mary, but *before* the appearance to the

---

19. Schneiders, "Touching the Risen Jesus," 171–72.
20. Bieringer, "I am Ascending to my Father," 234.
21. Schneiders, "Touching the Risen Jesus," 163–64.
22. Robinette, *Grammars of Resurrection*, 102–3.

disciples. John operates with a chronology that differs from Luke's in this regard,[23] and also in regard to the coming of the Spirit (see below). This has some repercussion on the question from where Jesus comes when he appears or visits the disciples. John's answer is most likely that he comes "from his Father"; in other words, Jesus is "not still around" to pay them a visit.

After having shown himself to Mary, Jesus appears to his disciples; suddenly he stands in their midst in spite of closed doors. In a way remarkably similar to Luke 24, Jesus shows them his hands and his side, clearly a flashback to John 19:34 where a spear pierced his side. This configures the appearance as a scene of recognition: the risen Jesus carries the marks of crucifixion on his body. John thus conveys a dual perspective on the body of Jesus; closed doors are no obstruction to his appearance, but still, the body is the same, recognizable. Hence, the disciples rejoiced "when they saw the Lord." Jesus responds by commissioning them and giving them the Spirit. This is told in a way reminiscent of key passages in Jewish resurrection discourse, namely Gen 2:7 and Ezek 37:9: God creates life by breathing his Spirit into them (John 20:22). The principal verb in this verse (*enephysēsen*) is found in both Old Testament passages. Furthermore, the fact that the setting of this scene is a garden (see later) strengthens the impression that the resurrection inaugurates a new time with new dimensions. Thus, the mission of the disciples and their equipment to do so is construed in continuation to what has happened to Jesus in his resurrection. Thus, Spirit-endowed mission perpetuates the resurrection of Jesus.

After the appearance to the disciples, follows the scene with Thomas. When the disciples attest to having seen the Lord (*heōrakamen ton kyrion*; v. 25)[24]—just like Mary also said—he says that he cannot believe unless he can see for himself the mark of the nails in his hands and put his finger in these marks and his hand in his side. Here, the crucifixion scene is recalled with details not mentioned in that scene. Eight days later, Jesus appears again while the doors are locked, and now he approaches Thomas in particular. As Thomas is offered to do the test he required, he recognizes Jesus ("My Lord, and my God") and comes to believe. Jesus is verified through the marks of his crucifixion, not unlike the metaphor of "slaughtered Lamb" in the Book of Revelation. In a way typical of John's Gospel, Jesus now utters himself with a view to Christ believers figuring outside the story, both in time and place: "Blessed are those who have not seen and yet come to believe" (v. 29).

With most scholars we consider John 21 to be an appendix added later, very much in the same way as what happened to another independent text,

---

23. Luke is in this question alone in the New Testament.
24. Cf. 1 Cor 9:1.

namely John 7:53—8:11. Jesus appears to his disciples: *ephanerōsen heauton* (John 21:1). This phraseology is interesting as it demonstrates that the Easter appearances have a *theological* dimension; they are not only visions but *revelations*, in which Jesus makes himself seen.[25] This is not a historical statement about what happened, but a category aimed at interpreting what happened. Revelation is the adequate category or label to put on them, as a revelation conveys insight which is new to the recipients, and also that this insight is not internal to them; it is *given* to them.

A recurrent motif in the appearances comes into play here as well, namely the difficulties in recognizing the risen Jesus, stated openly in v. 4. How recognition takes place here, is more undefined. The beloved disciple comes to understand this (v. 7: "It is the Lord") due to Jesus' command which initiates a wondrous fish catch. The full recognition takes place in a meal setting where Jesus again *gives* them to eat, although the sharing of a meal—it is not stated here that Jesus eats—here is confirming the recognition which was already there in the heart of the disciples. It is by receiving what Jesus gives to them, that he is fully recognized. When this story makes the comment that this was "the third time" Jesus appeared to the disciples after his being raised from the dead, this raises some interesting questions. Against the backdrop of John's Gospel, this is true when "disciples" is taken to refer to the group of disciples, which would include a male perspective here. One cannot avoid wondering why the appearance to Mary, the first told in the Gospel, and the appearance that triggered the rest of the Easter story in this Gospel is left out. What we see here is probably a disregard of Mary's appearance in this later addition.[26] This paves the way for the role of women in the Easter stories (see Part II, The Easter Narratives, section Women at the Tomb).

Narrating Creation Renewed

In telling about Easter, John draws on language evocative of God's creation of humankind according to Gen 2:7. In other words, imageries of creation are at work in his narrative. Carlos Raúl Sosa Siliezar has argued that Jesus's act in John 20:22 highlights his close association with God in his role of "bringing forth life."[27] This means that the resurrection of Jesus is placed within a setting that brings to mind creation. God's creation provides parameters

---

25. The revelatory aspect in the verb *phaneroun* in John's Gospel is clear from passages such as 2:11; 7:4; 9:3.

26. Thus also Novakovic, *Resurrection*, 117.

27. Siliezar, *Creation Imagery*, 153–73.

for grasping the implications of this event. The women came to the tomb and found it empty early in the morning, while it was still dark (*skotias eti ousēs*; 20:1 cf. v. 19). This piece of information is found in John's Gospel only, albeit Matt 28:1 (*epiphōskousē*) refers to dawn. Separating darkness and light marked according to Gen 2:7 the beginning (*en archē*) of God's creation, a fact which John's prologue picks up on (John 1:1–5). Darkness and night occupy an important role in John's symbolic world (3:1, 19–21; 8:12; 9:4; 11:9; 13:30). The resurrection of Jesus taking place at the moment of transition from darkness to light is, therefore, ripe with connotations, among which the power to bring forth life, as in the Creation, is prominent.

Furthermore, these observations shed light on another Johannine idiosyncrasy, namely that Jesus was buried in a garden (*kēpos*; 19:41). Hence, Mary also takes the risen Jesus to be the gardener (*kēpouros*; 20:15). The story about Eden, the Paradise Garden, in Genesis 2 does not use this term, but Terje Stordalen has demonstrated the symbolic potential and value in the "garden" as something which draws on wider references: "Apparently, gardens were conceived as locations where life forces manifest themselves . . . In biblical Yahwism its context would be belief in YHWH as the ultimate creator."[28] Worth noticing is for example that gardens are important in the salvation images provided by Isaiah (58:11; 61:11), and that in Ezek 36:35, *kēpos* refers to Eden. In the LXX, the phrase *kēpos tryphēs* ("garden of delight") shows how an explicit Eden reference (Hebrew: *gan eden*) takes on a full symbolic dimension.[29]

If we keep together John 20:22, the moment of transition from darkness to light, and the garden, a rather clear image appears: the resurrection of Jesus is to be seen as fulfilment and continuation of God's creation. The allusion to Gen 2:7 in John 20:22 is prone to identify also other elements in John's Easter narrative with the Eden tradition. We notice that John 4:34 and 5:36 speaks about Jesus's ministry in a way echoing Gen 2:2–3 (*synetelesen . . . tà ergata autou*), which further strengthens the impression that Jesus's ministry is conceived of in creation motifs, and that the resurrection marks the peak of this.[30]

---

28. Stordalen, *Echoes of Eden*, 182.
29. See Stordalen, *Echoes of Eden*, 317–19, 324–27.
30. I owe thanks to my colleague Ole Jakob Filtvedt for having drawn my attention to this aspect of the Johannine Easter narrative.

Women at the Tomb

Before summarizing the Easter narrative traditions, we delve into one particular issue, namely the role of women in these stories. Women are mentioned as the first witnesses to the Easter occasions, the event itself being exempt, in *all* canonical gospels. In spite of their primacy, their witness is ambiguous, as it is met with disbelief or with male confirmation. This dual picture is worth noticing since it indicates that the tradition of the empty tomb, not necessarily the resurrection as such, hits historical bedrock.

The role that the narrative tradition gives to the women belongs to the core of these diverse traditions. We noticed that the witnesses of the women were negotiated in various ways, even disregarded and downplayed. Having looked into the various pro et contra arguments, Lidija Novakovic concludes that it is impossible to confirm Jesus's resurrection historically and that it is a matter of higher or lower probability. She points out, however, that "[t]he potential embarrassment that the story of the women's testimony could have caused bolsters its claim to historicity."[31] This is the reason why we offer this issue special attention here. Against the backdrop of how women in general, and women's testimony in particular, were viewed in the culture, it is remarkable that the Easter stories consistently include women as those who witnessed the empty tomb.

Already with Plato, we find that an old wife's tale (*mythos . . . graos*) is not to be trusted but is met with despise (*kataphronein*) (*Gorg.* 527A). It is worth noticing that 1 Tim 4:7 speaks similarly about "old wives' tales (*graōdeis mythous*)" in a context about the raising of children and youngsters. Marianne Bjelland Kartzow has demonstrated how the figure of "old wives' tales" in the Pastoral Epistles is used to discredit opponents.[32] This Pauline tradition thus echoes the current assessment of wives' talk as suited, not for trust, but for lullabies; in short for infants (Plato, *Leg.* 10.887D). When Tatian describes his conversion to Christian faith, he says that he was diverted from the false myths told in his childhood (*Orat.* 30.1). His familiarity with classical Greek mythology, he considers as coming from his upbringing.[33] The Pastoral Paul and Tatian stand on the shoulders of a long-standing tradition. Likewise, Musonius Felix mentions key stories from Greek story-telling as old wives' tales (*aniles fabulas*), at home in children's upbringing:

---

31. Novakovic, *Resurrection*, 134; similarly Allison, *Resurrecting Jesus*, 326–31.
32. Kartzow, *Gossip and Gender*. As for 1 Tim 4:7, see in particular 137–39; 194–95.
33. See Sandnes, *Challenge of Homer*, 87–92.

> Our ancestors were so ready to believe in fictions (*in mendaciis fides fuit*), that they accepted on trust all kinds of wild and monstrous marvels and miracles; Scylla with serpent coils, a hybrid Chimaera, Centaurs half-horse, half-man, or any other fiction of folk-lore fell upon willing ears. Why recall old wives' tales of human beings changed into birds, or into trees and flowers. (20:3–4)[34]

Cicero speaks of "womanish superstition (*superstitio muliebris*)," manifesting itself in strong and uncontrollable emotions in situations of dire grief (*Tusc.* 3.29.72). *Anus delira* (bugbears) represents falsity which philosophers turn away from. In his *Nat. Deor.* 3.5.12–13, he discusses what to believe about the gods; in this context appears *fabellae aniles*, "old women's tales," which is a case of superstition.[35] In short, the lack of trustworthiness of women's tales is a *cultural stereotype*, and it comes with contempt. It is something fit for infants only. A passage from Josephus is illuminating. In a context addressing the administration of justice, he also raises the question of witnesses and testimonies. He cites Deut 19:15 about the need for sufficient evidence for a verdict, which is the presence of two or three witnesses, and he comments upon that text:

> Put no trust in a single witness, but let there be three or at least two, whose evidence shall be accredited by their past lives. From women let no evidence (*martyria*) be accepted, because the levity (*kouphotēta*) and temerity (*thrasos*)[36] of their sex; neither let slaves be witnesses because of the baseness of their soul, since whether from cupidity (*kerdos*) or fear (*phobos*) it is like that they will not attest the truth. (*Ant.* 4.219)[37]

Josephus here enters a halakhic discourse whereby the implications of the Scriptural dictum are negotiated and clarified.[38] His attentiveness to defining the characteristics of a trustworthy witness comes into view, not only in the fact that he adds to what the Scripture here actually says, but also in the way he renders the passage itself. He makes an addition, found neither in the Hebrew text nor in the Septuagint: the witnesses are to be judged by

---

34. Cf. Philostratus, *Vit. Apoll.* 1.16.2. For further references on the stereotype of old women's tales, see Frenschkowski, "Antike kritische und skeptische Stimmen," 287–89.

35. Thus also in *Nat. Deor.* 2.28.70 and 3.39.92; see also Quintillian, Inst. 1.8.19 (*anilibus fabulis*).

36. The fear of the women in the Easter stories would probably serve to substantiate Josephus's point here.

37. Quoted from LCL. See also Byrskog, *Story as History*, 74 on how Josephus here embraces a widely attested tradition in a Jewish context.

38. See Feldman, *Judean Antiquities*, 411–12.

their past lives. Here an ethical standard enters the jurisdiction, which is beyond what is stated in the relevant Scripture passage. A passage in Josephus's biography sheds some light on this. Commenting upon a quarrel he had with John of Gischala, he addresses the embassy from Jerusalem: "had my case against John been tried and had I produced some two or three excellent men as witnesses (*martyras kaloùs kagathoùs*) to my behaviour, it is evident that you would have been compelled, after the inquiries into their character (*bious*), to acquit me of the charges brought against me" (*Life* 256).[39] The setting is clearly forensic or judicial. In the Greek text, "men" are not mentioned explicitly, but describing them as excellent men leaves no room for doubt: what is required are *men* of high standing in the society. To ancient readers, precisely the presence of men loomed large here. These Greek terms form a tandem which points to "gentlemen,"[40] or more precisely, people with key positions or standings in the society as benefactors or nobilities.[41] The Greek tandem *kaloi kai agathoi* simply denotes nobilities or benefactors in the society.[42] The lifestyle of the witnesses is also given prominence here. Their *lifestyle* cannot be isolated from their *gender* and *social position*. In these key words, essential expectations of a worthy witness are given. It is not hard to imagine how Josephus would evaluate the testimonies of the women regarding the empty tomb; both gender and social standing disqualify them, and with them the trustworthiness of the stories. Worth noticing is that the Greek word *kouphotēs*, used by Josephus in *Ant.* 4.219, frequently occurs when Celsus, the pagan who targeted Christian faith on philosophical terms ca. 170 CE, gives his view on the credulity of the Christians vis-à-vis both miracles and resurrection.[43]

From Origen's refutation of Celsus, we know that this cultural stereotype was taken advantage of with regard to the resurrection of Jesus. Celsus's work is lost, but Origen's procedure has preserved large parts of his work *Alēthēs Logos* (*True Doctrine*) by citing extensively from it. Such a passage is found in *Cels.* 2.55 (SC 132.414.16–416.25) about the Christian claim that Jesus was raised from the dead. Celsus says:

---

39. Quoted from LCL.

40. This is the rendering of this by Mason, *Life of Josephus*, 117, but in present-day English this is probably too conventional and misses the social standing which is involved.

41. See Mason, *Life of Josephus*, 22 which rightly speaks of the aristocratic sense of this tandem in Greek literature.

42. Winter, *Seek the Welfare of the City*, 11–23.

43. Sandnes, "Ancient Debates on Jesus as Miracle Worker."

But who saw this? A hysterical female (*gynē paroistros*),⁴⁴ as you say, and perhaps some other one of those who were deluded by the same sorcery, who either dreamt in a certain state of mind and through wishful thinking has a hallucination due to some mistaken notion (an experience which has happened to thousands), or which is more likely, wanted to impress the others by telling this fantastic tale, and so this cock-and-bull story to provide a chance for other beggars.⁴⁵

Origen's response in *Cels.* 2.59–60 identifies "the hysterical woman" with Mary Magdalene. According to Celsus, *she* was the instigator of the story of Jesus's resurrection. Celsus considers Mary Magdalene's role in the resurrection story to represent the climax of emotionally motivated falsity, a fact which aligns her with his version of a movement guided by people with no education and status in society. Celsus sees a clear correspondence between the nature of the witness and the movement claiming her testimony: the one is born out of the other.⁴⁶ Worth noticing is that according to both *Cels.* 2.55 and 2.59 (SC 132.424.20), Celsus introduces his label "hysterical woman" with a comment, namely "as you say," thus claiming that he is in accordance with the biblical tradition here. Origen points out that no such thing is ever stated (*Cels.* 2.60), but Mark 16:9 about Mary's former demon-possessions, may be a candidate here. Origen makes the point that Celsus invented the "hysterical" part here to overcome the problem that Jesus appeared to Mary during the day, while dreams and visions usually take place at night. Interestingly, and in many ways confirming the cultural stereotype at work in the Easter narrative traditions, Origen says about Celsus's *True Doctrine* that "what old woman lulling a child to sleep would not be ashamed to say such thing as he does" in his book (*Cels.* 6.74; SC 147.364.17–20). In *Cels.* 5.20 (SC 147.62.12–13), Origen throws back on his opponent that *his* cultural stories are far "worse": "And if one may jeer at anyone for believing in paltry stories fit for old women, it is more appropriate in their case than in ours."

The remains of the work commonly called *Apocriticus* has preserved the most detailed critique against Christianity from Antiquity, written during the time of Valens (364–78).⁴⁷ Macarius of Magnesia's *Response or the Only Begotten to the Greeks concerning Questions and Answers in the*

---

44. *The Brill Dictionary of Ancient Greek*, s.v.

45. Quoted according to Origen, *Contra Celsum*. Greek text in Borret, *Origène Contre Celse Tome 1*; see also *Cels.* 2.60 (SC 132.424.1–427.23).

46. Sandnes, *Challenge of Homer*, 149–58.

47. See *Macarios de Magnesie*, 57–65.

Gospel[48] presents itself as a contest (*agōn*) between the Christian author Macarius[49] and his opponent, as clearly seen in, e.g., the Narrative Prologue to Book 3.1–2(51):

> This is the third contest which our much admired opponent prepared for us, after bringing a notable assembly of auditors. This, dear Theosthenes, we now unfold to your incomparable wisdom, relating to the best of our power the propositions which were the results of this reflection. When we had found a quiet spot, we spent a great deal of the day in discussion (*dialegomenoi*). He began to roll down upon us the loftiness of his Attic oratory, so that the mighty throng of onlookers almost felt themselves joining in the contest, as they saw the terror of his wrath, which was meant to scare us away. Then as though he were descending on us at a run from some hill, he threw us into consternation by troubling us with the force of his tongue.[50]

One of the contests was about resurrection, and it is no surprise that the role of the women in the Easter testimonies figures prominently here. An important objection is based upon whom the risen Jesus appeared to (*Apocriticus* 2.25.1).[51] He did not appear to Pilate, nor to king Herod, nor to the high-priest; in short, he did not appear to people "worthy of credit, and more particularly among Romans both in the Senate and among the people." In other words, Jesus did not appear to nobilities who are considered the best witnesses. This accusation is introduced as something which is talked of "everywhere" (*pantachou*); clearly an exaggeration, but still indicative of a stereotype at work in many critiques against Christian belief. We are here reminded of our observations regarding the *Gospel of Peter* in which the resurrection as such was publicly witnessed by people of all different status in society.[52] That Gospel addressed objections of the type witnessed to later in *Apocriticus*. According to the latter, an objection sounded like the following:

---

48. Goulet's edition (Tome II) has replaced Blondel-Fouchardt from 1876. A partial translation in English is available in *The Apocriticus of Macarios Magnes*. Crafer's text is available on the internet.

49. As for the identity of the author, see the discussion in Sheehy, *Arguments of Apocriticus*. In accordance with Crafer, Sheehy raises doubt about Macarius being a bishop of Magnesia around 400 CE, known by this name.

50. Crafer's translation with some alterations. I agree with Sheehy, *Arguments of Apocriticus*, 42 that the present dialogue is most likely fictitious, due to the fact that there is no real development in it. The objector never replies, so there is really no exchange here. In this way it differs markedly from Justin's encounter with Tryphon.

51. In Crafer's translation this is chap. 14.

52. See Part II, Neither Witnesses nor Told, sec. *The Gospel of Peter*.

> But he appeared to Mary Magdalene, a coarse (*gynaiki chydaia*) woman who came from some wretched little village, and had once been possessed by seven demons, and with her another utterly obscure Mary, who was herself a peasant woman, and a few other people who were not at all well known. (2.25.2)

Social contempt is clearly a subtext here. Not only does the fundamental claim of Christian faith fail to meet the primacy of witnesses who watched the event, but even the empty tomb, with a claim to witnesses, rests upon private visions and on women. Furthermore, the contrast between public and private, which is at work here, juxtaposes a distinction between male and female, in which public and male versus private and female form two separated tandems. When, for example, Minucius Felix, *Oct.* 8.4 says that Christians are "speechless in public, but gabble away (*garrula*) in corners," this is closely attached to the fact that the Christian fellowship attracted the unskilled and women. It is worth noticing that Jerome's *Epistle* 53 (PL 22.544–45) mentions the tandem women and idle talk (*garrula anus*). This terminological correspondence suggests that this stereotype is at work also in the objection in *Octavius*'s contrast between public and private.[53] The appearances stories in the New Testament are seen as representing the tandem private and female, which does not lend much credibility. The objection is responded to in 2.30.1–13 (Crafer chap. 19). What most ancients found to throw doubt on the Easter stories, is here turned upside down:

> But He made himself manifest to women who were not able to give help, nor to persuade anyone about Resurrection. Then he appeared to the disciples who were also themselves without power, and largely obscure because of their poverty. This He did fittingly and well, that the story of Resurrection might not be heralded by the help of the power of the world's rulers, but that it might be strengthened and confirmed through men who were inferior and made no show in their life according to the flesh, so that the proclamation might not be a human thing, but a divine. (2.30.12–13)[54]

Macarius makes a theological argument out of the social fact thrown against the resurrection stories. Actually, Macarius anticipates how many present-day interpreters view the role of the women in these stories. The fact that their testimony was prone to foster doubt and ridicule indicates that their

---

53. See MacDonald, *Early Christian Women*, 30–41; Sandnes, "*Ekklêsia* at Corinth," 248–65.

54. See also Part II, Towards a New Testament Theology on the Resurrection of Jesus, sec. What Does the Empty Tomb and the Appearances Convey?

presence in these stories represented a firmly established piece of tradition. Their presence in the very fundamental claim of Christian belief was a problem, and no secondary tradition is likely to have added to the complexity of the gospels by inventing their role as those who found the tomb empty. This lends credibility to the authenticity of this tradition; in other words, these *stories* have preserved very old pieces of tradition. In principle, the *event* as such is not affected by this, since the women witnessed the empty tomb only, not what had caused the tomb to be empty. In other words, one of the cornerstones for belief in the resurrection of Jesus according to the New Testament, the empty tomb, is not without historical substantiation. As pointed out regularly, this is not the same as the resurrection, which is an interpretation of the empty tomb.

We have seen that the role occupied by women in the Easter stories was taken advantage of by pagan critics. However, it is worth noticing that similar sentiments loom large also within these stories themselves. According to Luke 24:11, the disciples—all males—did not believe the women who found the empty tomb. They considered it "empty talk (*lēros*)," a term conveying male superiority.[55]

Contrary to the event itself, which is untold, its immediate aftermath is unfolded—with varying details though—and here the canonical stories convey not triumph and joy on the part of those present. On the contrary, what is told renders a picture of women and of disciples who are frightened (Mark 16:8), who are in doubt (Matt 28:8, 10, 17), who don't understand what is going on. The constant running is a fascinating witness to the confusion. This was clearly beyond, not to say against, their expectations, and the untold event invited other optional explanations; the body was stolen (Matt 28:13) or removed by a gardener (John 20:13, 15). The credulity often claimed on the part of these people,[56] is not what these stories convey; it is instead vice versa. Rather than being a projection of their own situation, they acted hesitantly and even in denial. The fact that such a foundational story evolved from women is from a historical-cultural perspective, an embarrassing fact which calls for a positive assessment regarding historical questions involved, the empty tomb in particular.[57]

---

55. Kartzow, *Gossip and Gender*, 169–71. Kartzow mentions Rhoda in Acts 12:13–16 as a similar example.

56. See for example Crossan, "Appendix," 185. In Crossan's argument credulity becomes a slogan serving his argument. For a balanced presentation of the complexity in the ancient world, ranging from naivety to critique with regard to miracles, see Frenschkowski, "Antike kritische und skeptische Stimmen."

57. Ravnå, *Jesus fra Nasaret*, 245 comments that this argument misses the target since the empty tomb is not used as an evidence in the New Testament for the

Two Independent Traditions?

An intriguing expose of the early history of Easter has been suggested by Daniel A. Smith, very much in line with the common view that Easter faith is founded on two pillars, the empty tomb and the appearances. He argues that there existed two independent traditions which gradually merged into what has become the Easter stories, consisting of empty tomb and appearances.[58] The labels put on these two convictions are the disappearance tradition (empty tomb and the absence of Jesus) and the appearance tradition (Jesus is here). These two convictions circulated separately and did not originally form the one belief that Jesus had risen from the dead. Smith argues that the process of bringing the two together under the one umbrella "the resurrection of Jesus," can be studied through how the New Testament evidence presents itself: "Only gradually and incrementally did the empty tomb stories become stories about the risen Jesus appearing at the tomb."[59] The advanced point of this process is observed in John's Gospel in which the first appearance, to Mary Magdalene, takes place at the very spot, just outside the tomb.[60] In this way, the empty tomb is included—almost as a proof—for the resurrection in a way unprecedented in the New Testament. Mark's Gospel foresees an appearance outside the narrative story time (Mark 16:7); not even in the longer Markan ending are the two narratively connected in a way similar to John's Gospel. In Matthew 28, the appearance takes place in Galilee, and in Luke 24, the first appearance takes place on the road to Damascus and only later in Jerusalem, but not adjacent to the empty tomb. In other words, both spatially and temporally the appearances are removed from the empty tomb. In our view, Smith is right in his

---

resurrection of Jesus. It is, he says, the appearances that have such a role. For sure, the appearances are primary to the empty tomb for the emergence of resurrection faith, but the empty tomb stories serve as a prequel to the appearance stories. Since this is not the case in Mark's Gospel, Ravnå's argument works only with Mark, and even within that passage, v. 7 envisages an appearance to take place later. In Mark's Gospel, the women are not witnesses; hence, according to Ravnå's view, Mark makes up a story where women figure prominently, precisely because their *failure* to witness is what matters. They were doomed to fail, due to their sex. In Matthew, Luke, John, and the longer Markan ending, women and appearances are connected in a way which Ravnå does not come to terms with. What we see here, however, is that the testimony of women is being negotiated, which precisely proves Ravnå wrong: the women and the appearance tradition were a problem. Furthermore, Ravnå's argument hinges on the assumption that 1 Corinthians 15 does not have the empty tomb in view, a point we have contested due to the fact that the passage *summarizes* events.

58. Smith, *Revisiting the Empty Tomb*, 2–5, 22–25, 178–82.
59. Smith, *Revisiting the Empty Tomb*, 2.
60. Smith, *Revisiting the Empty Tomb*, 181–82.

observation regarding John's Gospel vis-à-vis the other Easter narratives. We question, however, the way he urges independence of the two convictions. Our reasons for doing so are the following. On a general basis, we are hesitant about tracing developments taking place over such a short period of time. More particularly we question Smith's position that the silence about the empty tomb in 1 Corinthians 15 is equal to Paul's unfamiliarity with that tradition.[61] With John Granger Cook, and in line with our previous observations pertaining to this,[62] we hold the position that ". . . Paul could not have conceived of a resurrection of Jesus unless he believed the tomb was empty."[63] Granted Paul's knowledge of this tradition, the starting point for Smith's tracing of a development becomes blurry. Furthermore, Smith argues that Mark 16:1–8 represents the disappearance tradition. Smith is, of course, aware that v. 7 does mention the appearance of Jesus to take place outside the narrative in Galilee; hence, he makes reference to an alleged pre-Markan story in which the appearance was likely not mentioned.[64] Such a story is envisaged in Q 13:35 "You will not see me." This runs contrary to Paul and is, according to Smith, at home in ascensions/assumption stories in the Bible. It is not at all clear to us that this Q-text resembles the empty tomb narratives, and less so that it envisages resurrection as an assumption. From Smith's tradition critical analysis follows that resurrection and assumption are synonymous.[65] This was the culturally defined way for an author of the first century to narrate about what happened to an empty tomb. The empty tomb, or the missing body, is thus a sign that God has taken Jesus to Himself, in analogy with an apotheosis. Smith finds this warranted by for example Phil 2:8–10, where ascension replaces resurrection. Smith's theory of development can be presented thusly:

Appearance tradition	Disappearance tradition
Q, especially 13:34–35[66]	Paul
Pre-Markan narrative to 16:1–8	
Assumption	Resurrection

Mark, Matthew, Luke, and John gradually combine these two to form a coherent Easter story in which the appearance follows naturally about

---

61. Smith, *Revisiting the Empty Tomb*, 40–45.
62. See Part II, 1 Corinthians 15, sec. No Empty Tomb?
63. Cook, "Resurrection and Paganism," 56.
64. Smith, *Revisiting the Empty Tomb*, 76–78.
65. Smith, *Revisiting the Empty Tomb*, 90, 97–98.
66. Found now in Matt 23:39 and Luke 13:35.

the empty tomb. Smith is right in stating that the way The New Testament speaks about resurrection at times takes the shape of ascension or assumption, but he is wrong in saying that "Mark narrated Jesus' resurrection as an assumption."[67] The use of *ēgerthē* in Mark 16:6 invites images of the return to life.[68] Finally, the fact that Luke, one of Q's witnesses, features different ways of narrating the story (return to life and assumption)[69] indicates that the two should not be seen as competing models. This is, of course, not to deny the differences between the tomb stories. We are dealing with stories having distinct features.

Summarizing Narrative Easter

All the Easter narratives are attempts to come to terms with the Firstness of experiences, those of the empty tomb and Jesus appearing alive to some women first and then to disciples. These narratives are *responses* to these experiences, making sense of their baffling nature. These experiences occurred as signs which overwhelmed them, but which still were indefinite to them. This becomes evident in the narrative traditions by the fact that other and more likely explanations of the empty tomb are voiced, and also the fact that Jesus was *not* recognized immediately. His immediacy was that of a stranger. This is the Firstness that these stories are making sense of. They do this by drawing on Old Testament patterns, albeit not in detail, thus conveying that the faith that was grounded in the God of Israel and the texts giving witness to that belief, provided the context within which these experiences could find their relevant interpretation. Mark's Gospel has kept more of the indefinite and baffling nature of the event (*discovery*), although initial steps towards *justification* are taken. Other gospels render more elaborate versions in which justification becomes more dominant. They respond to experiences done in this world; whether all the details conferred in these stories are historically accurate, is another matter, and indeed less likely.

We have seen that the narrative traditions have two foci, the empty tomb, and the appearances. As for the relationship between these foci, the stories told convey that the discovery of the empty tomb was an overwhelming fact, stirring emotions and much running to and fro. The empty tomb as such did not convey faith in resurrection; it had other possible explanations. In the words of Lidjia Novakovic: "the discovery of the empty tomb could

---

67. Smith, *Revisiting the Empty Tomb*, 90.

68. See Part II, 1 Corinthians 15, sec. "He was Raised on the Third Day in Accordance with the Scriptures."

69. Luke 24.

have meant many things, but the least likely among them would have been the idea that Jesus has been raised from the dead."[70] The empty tomb brings a *confusion* which only an interpreting angel, or even more so, the appearances of Jesus could do away with. It is the appearances that bring recognition, and they verify that the risen Jesus is still the same, albeit also not immediately recognized and having a trans-physical body.[71] Mark's story is here an exception as there is no appearance, only an angelophany. The discrepancies between the Easter narratives are considerable, and at times even contradictory. This applies to location (Galilee or Jerusalem), the persons involved (which women and how many), the number of the angels (one or two) and the content of their message, the stone (was it removed or not), how many times did Jesus appear, the order of events etc. These discrepancies were noticed in the early Church as well, as demonstrated by Eusebius, *Gospel Problems and Solutions* 10.147–84.[72] It is not possible to put together these stories, like pieces of a jigsaw, into a continuous, harmonious, and chronologically structured narrative.

In the stories of the empty tomb, there is more discoveries than justification; that is, fear, joy, running, wondering, and doubt are more prominent than apologetics and Old Testament references, albeit there are claims to be in accordance with the Scriptures and apologetics is not absent. Running

---

70. Novakovic, *Resurrection*, 81. Allison, *Resurrecting Jesus*, 299–337 gives a comprehensive presentation of arguments pro et con regarding the historical basis for the empty tomb. He concludes that there is "a decent case for it (my addition: the empty tomb), and there is a respectable case against it" (331). For a fuller treatment of arguments pro et contra the empty tomb and the appearances, see Dunn, *Evidence for Jesus*, 53–77; Barclay, "Resurrection," 20–26; Novakovic, *Resurrection*, 127–60. Licona, *Resurrection of Jesus* is in a special way devoted to the historical dimensions involved. More than 600 pages are here used to argue that the resurrection of Jesus is the best explanation of the many historical issues. Licona's book is very helpful in addressing a number of questions and letting different voices be heard. His conclusions are throughout on the conservative side of the debate.

71. Novakovic, *Resurrection*, 114 uses this term to describe the dual nature with which Jesus appears in these texts.

72. Eusebius, *Gospel Problems and Solutions*, 287–95. The style of this writing, preserved not in complete, brings to mind Philo's work on Genesis (*Quaestiones et Solutiones in Genesin*) and Exodus (*Quaestiones et Solutiones in Exodum*), found in Loeb Classical Literature. This is a well-established genre in ancient "zetetic" literature, which means discourses on the literary nature of classical texts, focused particularly on seeming discrepancies. For more on this genre, see Niehoff, *Jewish Exegesis and Homeric Scholarship*, 38–57, 177–85. It is worth noticing that these discrepancies identified in the Easter narratives rather early were addressed in ways similar to contemporary literary approaches.

conveys immediacy, even if there is doubt to embrace Kenneth Bailey's intriguing interpretation of this as a shameful activity.[73]

Within these easily demonstrative diversities is found a stable *core* of a story, conveying that some women came to see the tomb early morning the first day of the week and found the tomb empty.[74] The absence of Jesus is announced by angels claiming that he has risen. Our concern in this book is not primarily with the historical question of what really happened. The primary focus has been to make sense of the multiple voices conveyed in the New Testament, to which also belongs to account for the diversities involved. We have assumed, however, that the Easter narratives throughout their diversities convey an *event*, which theologians have to account for.

Hole and Surplus

For those bent on the historical aspects of the resurrection of Jesus, it is worth noticing the fact that the New Testament evidence altogether leaves the moment of Jesus's resurrection by itself, untouched so to say. It finds no witnesses, no one watched and observed it. None of the gospels even tells about it. A narrow historical and apologetic approach to the resurrection of Jesus may run the risk of filling this narrative gap. This risk is equally there in reductionist attempts to explain what *really* happened, be it hallucinations, apparitions of dead, or complexes of guilt and grief. The gap is maintained so consistently that it must be reckoned as part of the message conveyed by the Easter narratives; it is simply integral to how Easter is conceived of. Here is a room *reserved* for God, unsatisfying as that may be to historians (and theologians). What took place is inaccessible; it is made accessible only through its being *announced*. Thus, the narratives pave the way for a certain reluctance and reticence towards any attempt to "prove" or "disprove" the resurrection. This means that the normal historical procedure, by making reference to immanence, analogies, and causality—to mention the legacy of Ernst Troeltsch—hardly comes to terms with all aspects involved.

Francis Watson has intriguingly asked the question if it is "theologically preferable to ask whether the gospel narratives can be read as an appropriate testimony to the raising of Jesus precisely *in* their fragmentariness, and not *in spite of* it."[75] The fragmentary nature is attested in what is possibly the original ending of Mark's Gospel, in the diversities found in the narratives, in the surrogate role (for Christ) of angels, and in the hole left in the story as

---

73. Bailey, *Poet and Peasant*, 181–82.
74. Dunn, *Jesus Remembered*, 829–31, 858–62 also speaks of a "stable core."
75. Watson, "'He is not here,'" 99.

nothing is told about the moment of the resurrection. As we noticed above, especially Matthew tells the story of the empty tomb in a way that creates an expectation that the event itself will be told, as the stone is still in place when the women arrive. In a way, the hole grows bigger in the mind of the reader as this expectation is not met. This enhances the impression that the event is shrouded in secrecy and silence. The fragmentary nature of the gospels' resurrection tradition is unanimous and may be seen "not as subverting its own authority, but as essential to the peculiar nature of its testimony."[76] There is thus a hole or a gap which any attempt to come to terms with the resurrection of Jesus must account for. *What precisely happened in Jesus's resurrection, the New Testament authors refrain from telling, because they did not know.* They had to rely on abductions. Efforts to close this hole or gap, be it by historical evidence or by declaring it a metaphor only, are beyond the Easter narrative traditions. The narrative traditions convey a dual and paradoxical picture of absence and presence. In Mark's Gospel, there is only absence, while presence is announced. It is worth noticing how this develops in the other narratives. The announced presence becomes presence manifested, and even with an outlook to the mission and to the world. The paradox of absence and presence thus becomes excess and surplus, as it now also includes people and places outside the narratives themselves.

This *widening* of the perspective is worthy of notice. The presence of the risen Jesus continues his earthly ministry but in an excessive way. Hence, in Matthew's Gospel, his last dictum to the disciples brings to mind the symbolic name he carried throughout his ministry. The surplus that characterizes Easter faith is vividly demonstrated in John 21 about the wondrous fish catch. The fishing nets were not able to hold the catch and they tore. Thus, excessiveness and surplus are narratively demonstrated. Precisely in the hole left untouched in the empty tomb stories, and in their discrepancies, we witness, not primarily historical problems, but narratives filled with excess and surplus in the mode of telling. At times this leaves tensions, even within one single author. When relating the discovery of the empty tomb, Luke—like the other gospels—faithfully leaves the hole or the vent untouched. However, in Acts 1 the style is evidentiary, accommodating the risen Jesus within a framework of necessary proofs. While the event itself is without evidence, justification perspectives are at work in Matthew (rumours), Luke (Jesus eats), and John (grave robbery, touching) as well, albeit more modest.

---

76. Watson, "'He is not here,'" 101.

Conceptualizing Easter or the Resurrected Body

In previous chapters, we have addressed attempts at finding relevant analogies to the appearances stories in for example psychological experiences related to death, bereavement, hallucinations, or Marian apparitions. Common to all such attempts is that analogies are found and that they demonstrate similarities, sufficient to shed *some* light on the phenomenon told in the gospels. We have pointed out that analogies very often become keys to explaining resurrection belief genealogically. However, if the resurrection of Jesus is seen as a "saturated phenomenon," it defies our attempts to relate fully to ordinary experiences or analogies. In the words of Brian D. Robinette, as a saturated phenomenon, "Jesus' resurrection is the condition of its own possibility."[77] Contemporary analogies need to take into account that many Jews expected the resurrection of the righteous at the end of the times, "not a resurrection of a single individual in the midst of history."[78] Attempts to explain the phenomenon we are dealing with in terms of projections or failed wishes, need to take into account this relevant historical context.

Lidjia Novakovic has rightly pointed out that the question of analogies should, therefore, be about *conceptualizing* the phenomenon. This means not to search for analogies able to explain what kind of event the appearances really were (genealogy), but rather to investigate in what language a phenomenon hitherto unknown was portrayed—in what context of interpretation can it be placed? In other words, what kind of language was found appropriate? In seeking to answer that question, analogies are mandatory. The key notion here is the revelatory language of *ōphthē*: "he was seen," as it is used in a Septuagint context.[79] Jesus's appearances are never presented as dreams or visions, the only exception being Luke's presentation of Paul's Damascus experience. Novakovic demonstrates the use of this Greek verb in stories where angels appear in human figures, or where men are appearing disguised as angels,[80] thus bringing to mind how the Easter narratives waver between "men"—their number is not fixed—and angels present at the tomb. The men visiting Abraham in Genesis 18 come as men; they have their feet washed, and they eat (cf. Gen 19:1–11; Judges 6:11–24).[81] It is worth noticing that in Gen 19:1, the men are called

---

77. Robinette, *Grammars of Resurrection*, 114.
78. Novakovic, *Resurrection*, 144.
79. See Part II, 1 Corinthians 15, sec. "He Appeared to Cephas and . . . "
80. Novakovic, *Resurrection*, 146–49.

81. Philo unfolds this iconic text on hospitality in *Abr.* 114–118. To him, the fact angels were eating was, due to their divine nature, problematic. Hence, he says that they gave the *appearance* of eating and drinking. Likewise, in Josephus, *Ant.* 1.196–198 the

angels (*aggeloi*), which is also the reason why Heb 13:2 speaks about hospitality—for which Genesis 18 is the primary model text in the Bible—as entertaining angels. Recognition is important in these stories. Human appearance, human attributes displayed by an angel, and the failure of the protagonist to recognize the angels, represent common motifs in a number of contemporary texts. Hence, resurrection is often depicted as becoming like an angel in relevant Jewish stories, which happens in the New Testament as well (Mark 12:18–27; Matt 22:23–33; Luke 20:27–39; Acts 23:8).[82] Jake O'Connell has pointed to similar material in ancient Jewish texts, 2 Baruch 49–51 in particular. This text renders an explicit discussion of what the resurrected body will look like.[83] The alternatives are to have its present form or being changed. The text takes a middle way, envisaging that the present form will remain temporarily; transformation will take place gradually. The transformation that will take place is portrayed as angelic in nature. It is appropriate to quote Novakovic on this:

> While this suggestion does not resolve the question of whether Jesus' appearances were subjective or objective, it nonetheless moves the debate to the first-century world that shaped the earliest perceptions of Jesus' resurrected body and supplied the imageries to express it in linguistic terms.[84]

We have noticed in our sources a growing interest in the body of the risen Jesus. While Mark's original ending showed no interest in this issue, this changes vividly as the women in Matthew take hold of his feet, Jesus showing his feet and hands and eating with the disciples in Luke's Gospel, and carrying the marks of his crucifixion, nails and spear, on his body according to John. Here, a meal is also involved, although it is not specified that Jesus took part in it; he was primarily *giving* them to eat. In various ways, Matthew, Luke, and John render narratives in which the body that disappeared from the tomb, and the one that was laid in it was, in fact, the same body. New Testament scholars, bent on identifying developing traditions, naturally see here an emergence

---

same biblical passage is rendered. The angels gave Abraham the impression that they ate, but they did not. In these passages, "Docetism" is in play with regard to angels.

82. 1 Cor 6:2–3 makes a parallel statement about the believers and the angels; they will both "judge the world" (cf. Matt 19:28). This chapter is permeated by motifs at home in discourses on the resurrection. The idiom "inheriting the Kingdom of God" (vv. 9–10) brings to mind 1 Cor 15:50, and v. 11 echoes Rom 8:30. It therefore comes as no surprise that in vv. 13–14, resurrection is mentioned directly. An inference from these observations is that Paul here conveys, albeit indirectly, that the resurrected body has its closest analogy in the angels.

83. O'Connell, "Jesus' Resurrection and Collective Hallucinations," 93–97, 102–3.

84. Novakovic, *Resurrection*, 149.

gradually driven by apologetic needs. This is also most likely the case. Some caution is necessary, though, due to the fact that the latest text, the more extended Markan ending does not show much interest in the body; the only remark is that he appeared "in another form." This remark seems less interested in the continuity between the crucified and the risen Jesus than what we find especially in Luke and John (also in the Book of Revelation). This destabilizes a smooth development from no interest to an ever-increasing interest in what kind of body the risen Jesus came with.

Towards a New Testament Theology on the Resurrection of Jesus

THE AIM OF THIS chapter is not to summarize the findings in this part of the study, albeit it draws upon them. We now bring together our findings by pondering theologically upon them. The paragraphs treated indicate major issues that have been involved and which grow out of the preceding discussions, and which will also find a follow up in the next part of this book.

Not so Credulous After All

An often repeated assumption is that people in antiquity were credulous, believing almost anything. Accordingly, belief in the resurrection of Jesus has one of its fundamental prerequisites in the naivete and uncritical attitude of contemporary people. Marco Frenschkowski has demonstrated that already in antiquity, credulity and miracles were being discussed; the picture was, indeed, a complex one, ranging from naivete to a critical attitude.[1] Two caveats follow naturally from these observations. Firstly, sweeping generalizations are to be avoided. Secondly, the issue of credulity is *not* a modern category to be imposed on antiquity; it was a matter of debate already then. Ancients knew the power of death and its irrevocable nature; in many ways, they were closer on these realities than many moderns are.

According to Celsus, God cannot in any way act contrary to nature (*parà physin*) (*Cels.* 5.14).[2] Hence, Celsus turned against the biblical dictum that "anything is possible to God," found in Mark 10:27parr. According to Celsus, Christians took refuge in this idea when they were under pressure

---

1. Frenschkowski, "Antike kritische und skeptische Stimmen"; see also Sandnes, "Ancient Debates on Jesus as Miracle Worker."

2. SC 147.48.12–50.25. Origen addresses this issue also in *Cels.* 3.70.

for lack of arguments.³ This opened the gate for all kinds of credulity. Celsus states this in a context where resurrection is debated, and in particular the raising of what he labels a "rotted body." It is worth noticing that the resurrection belief to Celsus was a result of sorcery, manifested in dreams, wishful thinking, and hallucinations, or in the wish to impress others.⁴ Origen shows his understanding for some of the arguments of his opponent here.⁵ For our concern, it is worth noticing that these provide a *contemporary setting* for the question of credulity.⁶

In distinguishing between a *discovery* and a *justification* aspect, we have been able to see how the Easter stories, and here Mark's Gospel stands out, are marked by how the women were overwhelmed, terror-stricken and doubtful. Neither the empty tomb nor encountering the living Jesus was what they expected or even hoped for. We have seen how emotions of disappointment loom large in the Easter narratives. The immediacy, emotions, and doubt witness to this as a story of discovery indebted to Firstness. The Easter narratives unanimously convey that the resurrection of Jesus ran *contrary* to their expectations. It was not a projection of their own belief; instead, they needed to learn Jesus *anew*.

Part of this picture is also that the New Testament evidence for the resurrection of Jesus is both sufficiently uniform to be found within the canon, and also sufficiently different to warrant that from the plurality of this evidence developed contrastive theologies of resurrection. Paul's dictum in 1 Cor 15:50 ("flesh and blood cannot inherit the kingdom of God, nor does the perishable inherit the imperishable") in particular, and Jesus's dictum to the Sadducees ("For when they rise from the dead, they neither marry nor are given in marriage, but are like angels in heaven"; Mark 12:25 and parallels), paved the way for spiritualizing interpretations of resurrection,

---

3. See for example Justin Martyr, *1 Apol.* 19; Tertullian, *Res.* 57; ANF 3.589–90.

4. Andresen, *Logos und Mythos*, 46–51 points out that there is a tension in Celsus. On the one hand, Celsus denies this with reference to what is contrary to nature, and nonetheless, he says with reference to Asclepius that "a great multitude of men, both Greeks and barbarians, confess that they have often seen and still do see not just a phantom, but Asclepius himself healing men and doing good and predicting the future" (*Cels.* 3.24; SC 136.56.1–5). Origen draws the attention of his readers to this apparent tension.

5. Reemts, *Vernunftgemässer Glaube*, 157–58.

6. Endsjø, "Immortal Bodies," 417–36 argues that the resurrection of Jesus was not impossible to imagine for a Greek mind, since he had been dead for such a *short* time. This allowed for the possibility to restore a body not yet decomposed. Hence, in Greek thinking, resurrection was seen as *bodily continuation*; the body had to be raised *as it was*. This was, of course, impossible with a general resurrection applied to people who had been dead for a long time, and whose decomposed body had ceased to exist in any form other than dust. In other words, Jesus's resurrection was more imaginable than a general resurrection.

both of Jesus and in general. On the other hand, the gospel narratives, with Luke's physical description of Jesus in Luke 24 in particular, paved the way for corporeal interpretations. Although the aftermath should not direct our interpretation of the relevant passages, it is still a reminder that there is a *potential* within the New Testament for contrastive developments. While Paul emphasizes discontinuity between the earthly body and the Spirit-animated body, the gospel narratives seem to have their primary aim in establishing the continuity between the two, albeit Jesus also there appears with a body having other qualities. The emphasis on identity may have been caused by needs to counter docetic-like approaches to the resurrection of Jesus. Lidija Novakovic makes reference to Ignatius, *Smyrn.* 2–3, in which the incarnation is presented in what is clearly anti-docetic sentences:[7]

> For he suffered all these things for our sake; and he truly (*alēthōs*) suffered, just as he also truly (*alēthōs*) raised himself—not as some unbelievers say, that he suffered only in appearance (*dokein*). They are the ones who are only in appearance; and it will happen to them just as they think, since they are without bodies, like the daimons. For I know and believe that he was in the flesh (*en sarki*) even after the resurrection. And when he came to those who were with Peter, he said to them: "Reach out, touch me and see that I am not a bodiless daimon (*ouk eimi daimonion asōmaton*)." And immediately they touched him and believed, having been intermixed with his flesh and spirit. For this reason, they also despised death. And after his resurrection, he ate and drank with them as a fleshly being (*sarkikos*), even though he was spiritually united with the Father.[8]

This passage may be relevant for understanding why physicality is so much stressed in the narrative tradition. Some comments are in place here. The polemic context is obvious as opponents are even mentioned, and the conflict revolves around the physicality of Jesus: was it real or not? Ignatius's use of the term *daimon* is confusing to a modern reader. It does not necessarily refer to demons or evil spirits, although that may be the case in the first instance with regard to the opponents. However, when Ignatius renders Luke 24:39, that Jesus was not a bodiless *daimon*, the term takes on the meaning of a "being" more generally. Furthermore, it is interesting to see that Ignatius twice makes use of *sarx* with regard to the resurrection of Jesus, which,

---

7. Novakovic, *Resurrection*, 124–25.
8. Quoted from Ehrman, *Apostolic Fathers*.

judging from 1 Cor 15:50, runs contrary to Paul. With regard to terminology, the two certainly differed.[9]

The diversity uncovered here is worth noticing in discussions on credulity. Things were, indeed, rather complicated. If we had delved deeper into the aftermath of the New Testament, we would find disparate discourses which throw doubts on sweeping generalizations about credulity.[10] The lively debates which can be traced to the New Testament are not signs of a simple-minded credulous environment in general.

An Abductively Interpreted Reality

This study has not established the authenticity of the historical testimonies available in the New Testament texts, be they appearances or narratives—if at all possible—nor have we argued against attempts to do so. The commitment to history mirrors a fundamental trace in Christian belief; it includes the present world and the bodies inhabiting it. However, a careful reader will have picked up that we accept the fundamental trustworthiness of a core of events told in the New Testament, while still believing that we are talking about an event that cannot be established as an empirical fact. From a historical point of view, something precarious and unwarranted looms large in the Easter belief. Relevant texts show discrepancies, and even inconsistencies, thus parading the impossibility to organize one harmonious story, and also the fragility when it comes to historical "evidence." Most likely, we are looking at developing traditions already in the New Testament. Taking into account the discrepancies which are there, the question of the exactness of these stories is entirely opposite. All of them *cannot* have it right. Embellishments and apologetic purposes have expanded on a core.

This study moves between historical, literary, and theological perspectives on Jesus's resurrection. Although we tend to be positive towards the core of the traditions, found within the discrepancies of the testimonies, we do not think that sufficient proof or convincing historical arguments can be produced to affirm the ground on which belief in the resurrection of Jesus may rest. However, together with literary observations on how this faith work within the New Testament, observations pertaining to history come into play in this study primarily as paving the way for how we theologically

---

9. This should, however, not be exaggerated. John 1:14 likewise uses *sarx* in a way which Paul does not very often, albeit Rom 1:3 is an exception. This observation does not mean that Paul denied incarnation.

10. According to Athenagoras, faith in the resurrection caused doubt and dispute also "among those who accept our basic assumptions" (*Res.* 1.5).

can make sense of the resurrection. In that way, both affirmative and critical observations with regard to history point towards a framework within which theological assessments may work. In this regard, even historical elusiveness may be a virtue, and guiding us to the *otherness* of the Easter event. The discrepancies may, of course, be seen as illustrations of the deficit or weakness in the Easter narratives. Observing the differences between the stories, paves the way for many who judge them fictitious. The discrepancies are given and *cannot* be harmonized. It is, however, worth considering that testimonies usually come with differences and even contradictions. In itself, this is by no means indicative of historical unreliability. As we now have these narratives, they witness to a living tradition. The discrepancies may be seen not primarily as a historical problem, but as examples of the excess which is characteristic of the Easter message. Easter faith in the New Testament assumes some concepts and given frameworks, but the narratives demonstrate beyond any doubt the difficulties those involved had in coping with what happened to them. Faith in the resurrection of Jesus was in no way constituted by their concepts and pre-given interpretative frameworks; it rather comes like a response to their being overwhelmed. Thus, the whole enterprise of Easter is accompanied, not by confirmation of concepts or projections, but by surplus, change, and otherness. Watertight concepts and language regarding the resurrection of Jesus are not to be expected, as it represents a future hitherto unknown. To formulate this properly is the challenge of Easter faith, and was so already when the relevant New Testament passages came into being.

Our purpose in the presentation of relevant texts has been more constructive than defensive; the main task has been to provide material "to think with" for theologians interested in reflecting on this tenet of Christian faith. Nonetheless, we have throughout spoken about resurrection in terms of "event." Already here protesting voices will be heard. The resurrection of Jesus is not without references to history, but it cannot be secured on an external ground or by empirical facts. By labeling it a "saturated phenomenon,"[11] it is in some sense groundless; it is not conditioned by anything else. Although we have consistently been involved with tradition critical considerations ("early is best"), this approach, possibly dearest to New Testament scholars, has not been primary. Approaching the phenomenon at hand as a "saturated phenomenon" invites us, not primarily to seek how belief in the resurrection of Jesus developed, but with a perspective "in front of the text," to approach it as a *given*, "allowing it to propose a

---

11. See Part III, sec. "Resurrection as a Saturated Phenomenon." Schweitzer, "Jesus' Resurrection as a Saturated Phenomenon," 501–15.

world we might inhabit."[12] As worked out by Brian D. Robinette, the New Testament testimony speaks about the resurrection of Jesus in terms *both* of "historical" *and* "more-than-historical."[13] It took place in our world, within our history, and still, it cannot be plotted just as one event among other events in history. The resurrection narratives are permeated by paradoxes: seeing and not seeing, recognizing and not recognizing, presence and absence, familiarity and alterity or strangeness, continuity and discontinuity. The simultaneity of these things has left marks so penetrating on these stories that they are not adequately dealt with as deficits or as historical problems. They are pathways to the *nature* of the event itself. Robinette calls this the "both-and structure" of these narratives,[14] which mirrors the futility in putting down in fixed terms what the resurrection body implies. In other words, the narratives are marked not only by the presence of a fundamental "hole," a leap in the narrative which conveys absence, but also when presence is conveyed, it is described paradoxically. Robinette calls this "textual analogies (or 'traces')" of the Easter event."[15] The Hole, the ambiguities, and fragments have a *revelatory* effect on the nature of the event and the body that was involved. Thus Jesus's resurrection, albeit an event which is part of our history, cannot be regarded merely as one among other historical events. It is another kind of event as well. The title of this paragraph—an abductively interpreted reality—gives three words which are hermeneutical keys to understanding the resurrection of Jesus. The relevant passages and the Easter narratives, in particular, respond to historical experiences without necessary being historically accurate in all details. Resurrection is an inference from experiences that are not the resurrection itself, but which are attached to the assumptions and claims about it.

This is how the New Testament addresses this, and, still, the assumption is that if the resurrection of Jesus has no historical basis whatsoever, it also makes less sense to consider it from a hermeneutical perspective . We thus agree with Gerd Lüdemann who argues that bereft of any historical bedrock, faith in the resurrection of Jesus, not to say Christian faith in general, is an error. While in his 1994 edition of his book, Lüdemann still considered the historical Jesus as a ground for faith,[16] he is more critical in his 2004 edition, arguing that since Jesus did not rise from the dead, "we

---

12. Robinette, *Grammars of Resurrection*, 76.
13. Robinette, *Grammars of Resurrection*, 40–42.
14. Robinette, *Grammars of Resurrection*, 103–6; see also 25–26, 64–66.
15. Robinette, *Grammars of Resurrection*, 26, 65.
16. Lüdemann, *Resurrection of Jesus*, 180–84.

cannot be Christians any longer."[17] This leads us to consider what it entails when the resurrection of Jesus is labeled an *eschatological* event. Can this label allow us to ignore or detach the claim about the resurrection from history without reserve?

An Eschatological Event—Narratively Hardbound

Our investigation has demonstrated that the resurrection of Jesus is an eschatological event. Surely, what is meant by "eschatological" is negotiable, but from within a relevant setting, this refers to an incident which in some way launches the climax or the end of the history of this world. In our presentation, this is most clearly seen in the role attributed to Jesus's resurrection as anticipating the general resurrection. We noticed in 1 Corinthians 15 that the two were weaved together; they were practically inseparable. This marks the resurrection of Jesus off from the instances in which he raised people fallen dead. Lazarus was doomed to pass away later; this was not the case with Jesus. With reference to the uniqueness of Jesus's resurrection, many scholars withdraw this event from history and the world in which we live. According to Hans Küng, "the resurrection of Jesus was not an event in time and space."[18] The event belongs to the new world, and, hence, takes place in a new world, out of reach, so to say. Such dicta are numerous among scholars, and they tend to betray the "both-and" structure mentioned above (more below).

This way of thinking may be illustrated with the view that an empty tomb is not necessary for the resurrection faith since the resurrection marks a totally unprecedented and new event. It marks the new creation where God creates not only anew but also out of nothing. Peter Lampe asks if it would matter at all if traces of Jesus's DNA were found in an ossuarium, or his legs in a mass tomb.[19] Point of departure is the finding of an ossuarium in Jerusalem, allegedly from the family tomb of Jesus.[20] Although Peter Lampe with most scholars dismisses this claim on historical grounds, it still raises an adequate theological question: what if the ossuarium of Jesus, containing his bones *were* found, would that in any way affect Christian faith? Lampe answers: "Gott ist in seinem Neuschaffen des gestorbenene Menschen, so

---

17. Lüdemann, *Resurrection of Christ*, 189–208.
18. Küng, *On Being a Christian*, 350–51.
19. Lampe, "Jesu DNS-Spuren," 72–76.
20. See for example Magness, *Stone and Dung*, 145–80; Gibson, *Final Days of Jesus*, 175–87.

glauben viele Christen, nicht auf Moleküle des alten Körpers angewiesen."[21] Applied to the resurrection of Jesus, its eschatological nature distances Jesus from the body laid in the tomb. God provides him with a *new* body, which is also *another* body. This logic may find substantiation in the fact that faith in the resurrection in its Jewish and Christian version appeals to God as Creator, as stated in for example Matt 3:9: "God is able from these stones to raise up (*egeirai*) children of Abraham." The use here of the most common verb for resurrection (*egeirein*) in the New Testament is telling. Lampe substantiates this further with reference to 1 Cor 15:50: "flesh and blood cannot inherit the kingdom of God." This passage became in early Christian discourse on the resurrection a textbook example for those who found a physical resurrection hard to accept. Lampe is, therefore, in his view on this Pauline passage in line with a widely attested tradition, but the prerequisite for that interpretation is that the verse is *isolated* from its Pauline context.[22] We think Lampe might have a better case with 2 Cor 5:1–10 taken by itself.

Gerd Lüdemann argues that Jesus cannot have risen from the dead if his tomb was not found empty. Hence, all depends on the importance of the empty tomb. This logic, which runs contrary to Peter Lampe, has been vehemently denied also by Andreas Lindemann, who says that "it is irrelevant whether or not Jesus' tomb was actually empty as proof for this. Faith is not based on or put at risk by historical probabilities." A full tomb is simply of "no consequences for the faith in Christ's resurrection."[23] This is so since the resurrection of Jesus is merely an expression of faith, not a statement concerning history. To illustrate this view, it has become a commonplace to say that if a surveillance camera—hypothetically, of course—had been set up outside the tomb, the resurrection would *not* have left any imprints on the camera. The "event" belongs in another dimension, the argument goes. The way Lindemann here in principle detaches theology from history marks him a theologian different from us who write the present book. However, even if we insist on the resurrection faith as based in events that took place in common human history, this is not to be seen as a warrant for a mere uncritical or positivist approach. Hence, we have already indicated that, e.g., the camera illustration is probably not very helpful, since it takes for granted that what the camera would have shown would have been immediately understood as

---

21. Lampe, "Jesu DNS-Spuren," 75.

22. See Part II, A Transformed Body or Another Body?

23. Lindemann, "Resurrection of Jesus," 578–79. Lindemann's position is informed not only by emphasising the eschatological nature of Easter; he draws heavily on a tradition-critical approach whereby Paul's not mentioning the empty tomb is crucial. Furthermore, a Bultmannian legacy of existential emphasis is voiced here. Cf. also the reflections provided by Ingolf Dalferth, referred to in the next part of this book.

resurrection and ignores the necessary abductive inference connected to the context of interpretation, but also related to its potentially diverse contexts of justification. The problem is that since resurrection is an interpretative category, it would hardly have appeared on the camera or the film. Resurrection is coming to terms with some historical experiences (empty tomb and appearances), and does not manifest itself as an ordinary event, but as making sense of events. It might be more relevant to consider the camera—for hermeneutical reasons only—with regard to the appearances of Jesus. As they are presented, particularly in Luke 24 and John 20, they convey a rather physical appearance; hence, apt to be "recorded" by the anachronistic camera. However, we have seen that recognizing the risen Jesus is something given; it is not immediate and not made available to all. This makes the camera analogy rather ambivalent also in the case where we would find it helpful. Accordingly, the camera illustration is more confusing than helpful; it is too simple to grasp how "resurrection" comes into being.

Narratively—that is from within the Gospel stories themselves—as well as theologically, the empty tomb conveys a question that the appearances answer. However, the empty tomb carries in itself a message as well, as it is crucial for grasping the nature of the resurrection. With Lindemann's view, one has to ask if it matters that it was *Jesus of Nazareth* and not Herod the Great who was raised. John Austin Baker once made this point,[24] which is worth pondering. The resurrection of Jesus comes with a binding, or it is hardbound, at home in a specific *narrative that builds on historical circumstances that took place in the history of which all humans are part*. It cannot be switched to any other narrative or deemed to be only a metaphor or independent from the narrative in which it is found. The resurrection of Jesus becomes what it means through the fact that it happened to *him*. His ministry is perpetuated through his resurrection. This is clearly voiced in Acts 10:38–40, where Jesus's ministry is summarized as "doing good and healing all who were oppressed by the devil." Verse 40 emphasized that it was *this Jesus* (*touton*) who was raised on the third day. It is indeed not another Jesus that is raised; his earthly ministry now finds fulfillment. This finds affirmation in Rev 21:4 where the new heaven and earth imply the wiping away of tears, and the ceasing of mourning, crying and pain, a poetic way of describing Jesus's altruistic ministry told in the gospels. Thus, the famous dictum that the gospels are passion stories with extended introductions (Martin Kähler) may be rephrased: *The gospels are stories serving to identify who the risen Jesus is.*

---

24. Baker, *Foolishness of God*, 278.

By cutting the understanding of the resurrection loose from the stories about Jesus, inclusive of the empty tomb, the resurrection is isolated from the story to which it forms the climax. Recognition, so essential in the developing Easter traditions, becomes meaningless in Lindemann's interpretation; recognizing is inherently tied up with a narrative and with relationships, including a present vis-à-vis the past, not with theological principles, how right they may still be. Removing the resurrection of Jesus from history is tantamount to removing it from the world as we know it. The eschatological nature of the event can be emphasized in such a way that the resurrection of Jesus escapes this world. It seems a good idea to keep in mind incarnation when we wrestle with grasping the nature of Easter faith.

Most scholars would consider the ascension an example of a metaphor translated into narrative. In other words, Jesus seated at the right hand of God in heaven (Psalm 110) is *not* to be taken in a literal sense. This finds substantiation in the fact that Luke—and also the more extended Markan ending—is the only New Testament writer turning this idea into an independent narrative. Furthermore, even within Luke-Acts, two different chronologies frame this story. According to Luke 24, the ascension takes place on the day of the resurrection, while Acts 1 assumes a time interval of forty days. Advocates of a metaphorical understanding whereby the resurrection is substituted for abiding presence or the like, rightly point out that since Psalm 110 elsewhere in the New Testament is intimately associated with precisely the resurrection, it cannot be metaphorical in the one and not in the other. Hence, a metaphorical or poetic piece, an important one at that, is already part of the resurrection message in the New Testament. Why not, then, declare the whole idea a metaphor, a story that conveys Jesus's abiding presence or his being alive with God in some sense, and not an event? James D.G. Dunn addresses the question of metaphor and says that "we can hardly avoid drawing on the category of 'metaphor' to characterize the concept 'resurrection.'" He does so with reference to Paul Ricoeur's dictum that the power of a metaphor is the power to "describe a reality inaccessible to direct description." That dictum fits the notion of a "saturated phenomenon" nicely. Dunn goes on to say that attempts to translate "resurrection" into something more "literal," such as Christ's abiding presence, the significance of his message, his impact on the disciples, etc., is not to translate it, but to abandon it. We concur with Dunn on this. It is precisely this kind of metaphorical interpretation that our considerations question. Such interpretations fill in the gap or hole in the Easter narratives and thus empty this faith by expressing it in other terms.[25]

25. Dunn, *Jesus Remembered*, 878–79.

The genre of the resurrection of Jesus is *narrative*. As for the gospels, this is obvious. We have argued that this applies to Paul as well. The formulaic tradition voiced in 1 Corinthians 15 has a narrative substructure. Hence, faith in the resurrection of Jesus is firmly based in a narrative setting and belongs within a narrative plot. This has significant repercussions for the question of metaphor. Obviously, the narratives at several places make use of metaphors, but these are not intimately tied up with the narrative plot of the larger story in the same way as the empty tomb. In short, the narrative setting, the genre, and plot within which this belief is at home are not supportive of considering faith in the resurrection of Jesus a metaphor for something else. The narrative binding of the New Testament evidence on the resurrection of Jesus is directive for how the New Testament makes sense of this belief. If we take Andreas Lindemann and others seriously here, there is no salvation *history* left, only salvation images. The resurrection of Jesus has narrative integrity, which is directive for how this aspect of Christian belief is to be unfolded.

A one-sided emphasis on the eschatological nature of the resurrection, in fact, leaves in doubt whether the category "event" at all is applicable. It becomes problematic to consider the resurrection as something that happened to *Jesus*, not only to his disciples. Scholars who emphasize psychological factors often end up arguing that Jesus did not need Easter; Peter and the disciples did. Resurrection is then primarily something that happened to the disciples. The word "happen" by its very nature locates the resurrection in time and space. Eschatology often becomes a vehicle by which the resurrection of Jesus is removed from our world. For sure, the crucifixion is rooted in history in a way that cannot be claimed with regard to the resurrection. This is easily demonstrated with reference to how different the passion stories and the empty tomb stories are with regard to details; this applies to *when* things happened, *where* they happened, the number of *details* mentioned, etc. Nevertheless, the two are inextricably connected also, as it was the crucified Jesus who was raised. We noticed that Luke and John, in particular, were bent on conveying precisely this connection. This ties the resurrection in with the incarnation, as we saw Ignatius worked it out in his *Epistle to the Smyrneans* (see above). We now need to consider more clearly theological implications of the empty tomb.

What Does the Empty Tomb and the Appearances Convey?

The post-resurrection appearances seem to have been decisive for the emergence of belief in Jesus being raised from the dead. Hans Küng rightly says:

"But there should be agreement on the fact that the empty tomb alone even in the light of the stories *cannot provide any proof of the resurrection* or justify any hope of the resurrection."[26] The empty tomb is ambiguous and open to misinterpretations. Speaking theologically, it serves as a *sign*, nothing more. The message of the empty tomb taken by itself is only "He is not here."[27] Resurrection faith is indeed more than the *absence* of Jesus, although the absence paves the way for his *presence* in a new mode. However, when Hans Küng states that the women who visited the tomb were not led to faith by the empty tomb and that the empty tomb instead led them to fear and terror, his approach ignores the sequence of the stories in which the empty tomb is *followed* by appearances, albeit not in Mark's Gospel. The backdrop of the women's fear as well as their faith is, of course, this wider narrative setting of the empty tomb. To exclude that aspect from their coming to believe is artificial. It is only when taken *together* with this that the empty tomb conveys this message. This gives to the narratives of the empty tomb a *secondary* character in how the Easter testimony emerged. For many scholars, this observation forms a tandem with the fact that no empty tomb is mentioned in the formulaic traditions, thus paving the way for the conclusion that "these two traditions developed independently of each other."[28] In the light of the exegesis presented of the formulaic tradition in the present study, we are reluctant regarding this conclusion. As for now, we want to point out that although the empty tomb is secondary to the appearances, this should not distract from the theology conveyed by the tomb found empty. The empty tomb taken by itself means nothing but disappearance; hence, it is no proof at all. On the other hand, without the disappearance of the body of Jesus, "the early Christian proclamations would have taken a substantially different form."[29]

Therefore, the empty tomb still paves the way for an adequate understanding of resurrection. It is now time to work out what meaning the discovery of the empty tomb carries. The first thing to point out is the "hole" in all the Easter narratives. The moment of the resurrection, or the event itself, is inaccessible; it is beyond "what human eyes witnessed "(cf. 1 Cor 2:9). To use Francis Watson's words, the resurrection "is unobservable and shrouded

---

26. Küng, *On Being a Christian*, 365. His italics.

27. When we embarked upon writing this book, we considered initially to have the title "He is not here." We now realize that this dictum from the Easter narratives is inadequate to express what Easter faith is about. Easter faith is primarily about meeting the risen Lord, not viewing an empty tomb.

28. For example, Novakovic, *Resurrection*, 151–52; see also Part II, The Easter Narratives, sec. Two Independent Traditions?

29. Robinette, *Grammars of Resurrection*, 119.

in mystery."³⁰ Not only is the evidence fragmentary; it also directs to the fact that divine actions may take a different form than human actions do. Hence, the nature of the testimony is not prone to formulate precise dogmatic formulations. Astonishment, amazement, and wonder rather than clear-cut dogmatic dicta characterize Easter faith. This is in line with the notion of a saturated phenomenon, as such phenomena invite a plethora of interpretations. Saturated phenomena generate different interpretations due to the fact that they exceed human capacity to grasp their nature adequately. Secondly, the empty tomb conveys that Jesus is *vindicated*. God is the hidden figure in raising Jesus from the dead. This is stated very often in the Book of Acts (2:32, 36; 3:15; 4:10; 13:26–31; 10:39–40), with emphasis on this as an act of God of the fathers. This idea is important throughout the New Testament. Narratively, it is significant that the resurrection follows upon the crucifixion and the burial, since that chronology serves both to identify Jesus and also to emphasize his vindication: "Während die Erscheinungen hinsichtlich der Leiblichkeit also eine *Differenz* implizieren, markiert das leere Grab als 'Leerstelle' die Kontinuität zwischen der Leiblichkeit des vorösterlichen und des österlichen Jesus."³¹ Brian D. Robinette frequently speaks of the risen Jesus as "the risen victim." This formulation gives to the resurrection a narrative context, whereby God has overturned the verdict against Jesus. An aspect of *reversal* is involved: in the book of Acts this is often found in the notion "you did this, but God has done this!"³² The empty tomb brings this out. An aspect of this continuity between Jesus's ministry and his resurrection is also that the empty tomb serves to identify the resurrected as Jesus, and not somebody else. The identification of Jesus in the appearances is endangered by a tomb wherein still lies Jesus's body.

Thirdly, the body is the indispensable vehicle of Jesus's risen life, as Francis Watson puts it.³³ For sure, this argument does not require an empty tomb, as an entirely new creation (*creatio ex nihilo*) may imply a body as well. Nonetheless, the "enfleshment" of the resurrection comes to a full meaning if this is seen as perpetuating the incarnation. A tomb wherein the dead body of Jesus still rests is a poor expression of that. In other words, the empty tomb is not necessary, but still conveys what the resurrection is really about: "Die Betonung einer *creatio ex nihilo* als eines voraussetzunglosen Schaffens aus Freiheit droht den zentralen Bezug zu Gottes eigener Geschichte mit Jesus in diesem Schöpfungsgeschehen zu übersehen: Die

---

30. Watson, "'He is not here,'" 106.
31. Thomas, "'Er ist nicht hier,'" 192–93.
32. Robinette, *Grammars of Resurrection*, 189–90.
33. Watson, "'He is not here,'" 106.

Schöpfung am Ostermorgen ist ein Handeln an der Person, am Geschick und an der Geschichte Jesus von Nazareth voraus."[34] The empty tomb is a sign that the new creation really is God trusting himself to his old creation, conveying that new creation is not *another* creation. The empty tomb conveys this in a way that the appearances leave more open. This leads us to look at the appearances.

For sure, the appearances also bridge the risen and crucified Jesus, and their primary aim is *recognition*, especially so in the Easter narratives. The very idea of recognition is, of course, prone to form a bridge to the pre-Easter life of Jesus, as re-cognition by its very nature bring together present and past. For sure, this aspect is certainly there. However, things get more complicated. Recognition usually takes place by means of face, gestures, voice, and other bodily marks. This is hardly so with Jesus. Although he carries the marks of crucifixion in John's Gospel, he is not recognized by such external things. It is through what he says and does that he is recognized, and that does not happen immediately. Hence, the appearances bring as much discontinuity as continuity. Furthermore, the appearances are *limited* to insiders, be they the women or disciples. N. T. Wright questions this, pointing to Paul, Thomas, and James, all people of doubt, and some even inimical, to whom Jesus appeared.[35] Nevertheless, this is not really convincing, since all these figures, also Paul the persecutor, are known from an insider perspective only. The fact that Christ appeared only to his own—spelled out in Acts 10:40–41 (God "allowed him to appear not to all people but to us who were chosen by God as witnesses")—is an Achilles heel to apologetically oriented believers. It can hardly be denied that as Jesus's resurrection appears in the New Testament, it is *reserved* for disciples. Moreover, if there was no empty tomb, this fact would have made difficult, or even compromised, the possibility for identifying Jesus as the content of what appeared to the disciples.

Celsus and others took advantage of this fact, as they noticed that Jesus did not appear to people of note or worth.[36] The impression of the critics was that the resurrection of Jesus was something reserved for those who believed already. Was it accessible only for believers' eyes? The context of Celsus and also the critic in Macarius Magnes's *Apocriticus* is clearly a discussion of "evidence" and persuasive arguments. According to Acts 10:40–41, the appearances are to be seen in another context, namely that of a *gift*; hence, it literally says "God *gave (edōken)* him to be seen." It is through

---

34. Thomas, "'Er ist nicht hier,'" 198.
35. Wright, *Resurrection*, 704.
36. See Part II, The Easter Narratives, sec. Women at the Tomb and Part II, Towards a New Testament Theology on the Resurrection of Jesus, sec. What Does the Empty Tomb and the Appearances Convey?

faith that the phenomenon of Jesus's resurrection is meaningfully perceived. Just like in the "hole" of the Easter narratives, so also with the appearances, the relevant New Testament sources are not bound up with evidence and the rhetoric of persuasion as is much later Christian tradition, especially those apologetically motivated. The answer given in Macarius Magnes's *Apocriticus* is worth pondering (*Apocriticus*, 2.30.1–13).[37] In answering a stereotypical charge against the resurrection of Jesus, namely that he did not show himself to people of worth and power, such as Pilate, Herod, or the Romans, Macarius says the following:

> Nor did He approach men of repute (*tois axiologois*) of the company of Romans, that there might not seem to be need of human support and co-operation for the confirmation of the story of the Resurrection. But he made himself manifest (*emphanizei*) to women who were not able to give help, nor to persuade (*peisai*) anyone about the Resurrection. Then he appeared to the disciples who were themselves without power and largely obscure because of their poverty. This He did fittingly and well, that the story of the Resurrection might not be heralded by the help of the power of the world's rulers, but that it might be strengthened and confirmed through men who were inferior and made no show in their life according to the flesh, so that the proclamation might not be a human thing, but a divine. (2.30.12–13)[38]

Macarius Magnes's response is, of course, informed by the accusations, and is clearly apologetically shaped. However, it is worth observing that his strategy is a turning of the tables; theology paves the way for the argument. The theology at play is not primarily about evidence, but about the *nature* of God and his actions. Jesus appeared only to those with whom he had shared his ministry, not just to anybody. Macarius thus makes a virtue out of the fact that Jesus did not appear to nobilities. To him it would amount to forcing people to believe. Most likely, the critics would consider Macarius Magnes's response a "hide and seek game," wherein attempts are made to evade history. From the viewpoint of the New Testament Easter narratives, however, such critique is tantamount to close the hole or gap in them and to deny the *paradoxes* found there.

---

37. In Crafer's translation this is chap. 19.

38. Crafer's translation. For a French translation, see Goulet. See Part II, The Easter Narratives, sec. The Women at the Tomb.

Why Insisting on Resurrection?

Resurrection and ascension are intimately connected; with the exception of Luke (Luke 24 and Acts 1, cf. 13:31), they refer in the New Testament to the same event, namely the resurrection as Jesus's enthronement according to Psalm 110.[39] Jesus sitting at the right-hand side of God is metaphorical, as God's right hand in the Old Testament is a phrase designating God as Ruler, Judge, or making reference to God's power. To some interpreters, the resurrection portrays narratively Jesus being translated to heaven in accordance with, e.g., Enoch. Although the two "events" are intimately connected, it is important to notice that they are not identical. The ascension evolving around Psalm 110 conveys an independent or insulated message or image. The resurrection, however, finds it meaning as culminating a narrative in which death and burial are prequels. The idea of ascension does not by necessity include passion and death. Contemporary Judaism had different kinds of language and imageries available to express eschatological hope, and the resurrection of a single individual prior to the general resurrection was certainly not among them. The New Testament envisages that this issue was negotiated (Mark 12:18–27; Acts 23:6–10). These passages, and also 1 Cor 15:12; 2 Tim 2:18 hint at various opinions being around. Against this backdrop, it is worth noticing that the resurrection language becomes so pervasive and dominant in the New Testament. It was by no means an inevitable choice.[40]

So why does the New Testament insist on the language of resurrection if translation to heaven was equally valid? The reason is that resurrection, in a way different from ascension, picks up on the *narrative* aspect. Both the ascension and vindication language carry aspects important for understanding the resurrection of Jesus, but only the resurrection language makes full sense of its role within a passion story, inclusive of death and burial. What prompted this particular claim to Jesus's *post mortem* existence was the conviction that something had happened "on the ground."[41] The disappearance of Jesus's body in combination with his appearances paved the way for this particular mode of speaking. The expression "on the ground" has historical implications here, like the empty tomb. In the words of Brian D. Robinette, "it is extremely difficult to imagine the circumstances under which the earliest

---

39. Traditionally, Hebrews has been seen as ignoring the resurrection of Jesus; for an extensive presentation of this topic, critical of the consensus, see Moffitt, *Atonement and the Logic of Resurrection*.

40. Thus also Dunn, *Jesus Remembered*, 866–70, 874–78; Allison, *Resurrecting Jesus*, 324–26.

41. See Robinette, *Grammars of Resurrection*, 86–88, 117–18.

Christians would have risked affirming Jesus' 'resurrection' if the events on the ground did not conspire together to urge them to do so."[42] Why early Christianity so clearly prioritized the resurrection language is, therefore, a question with *historical* implications. The resurrection language is far most dominant in the New Testament, and it is not to be absorbed into ascension or the like. From the historical context relevant here, this language carries with it issues such as death, life, and body.

This study has so far argued that an empty tomb, as well as appearances of deceased people, are not in themselves extra-ordinary phenomena, albeit they do not belong to daily routines. What is unique is that these phenomena were interpreted as resurrection. This is probably the most demanding interpretation chosen, and the *insistence* is worth pondering upon. What resources came to their use when early Christians interpreted the two phenomena in question as signs of resurrection? Taken together, the New Testament witnesses that the interpretative category resurrection depends on several aspects, among which the most important are the following. From Jesus's ministry and teaching, predictions regarding his vindication and resurrection were available, albeit in their present form these passages are retrospectively shaped. Furthermore, Jesus's ministry conveyed an eschatological awareness; the time for God to bring to fulfillment the prophecies and promises has dawned. Naturally, this paved the way for belief in the resurrection. Among the Scriptural traditions that accommodated these prophecies and promises were also texts that came to be understood in Second Temple Judaism as resurrection texts, albeit they speak about a general resurrection, not that of an individual. These Scriptural passages, as well as other relevant contemporary texts, paved the way for the notion of resurrection. They portrayed God as Creator who called forth from life non-existent. Finally, among the appearance traditions are found passages in which Jesus's presence is corporeal; he is touched and embraced, and he even participates in meals. These resources did come to use when faced with the experiences of the empty tomb and the appearances of Jesus. By themselves, these resources were in no way sufficient to bring into being the notion of an individual being raised to new life by God. In spite of the insistence on the resurrection, this faith did not arise easily. Something happened "on the ground" to trigger it.

---

42. Robinette, *Grammars of Resurrection*, 88.

According to the Scriptures

Donald H. Juel has dubbed the role of Scriptural evidence in the New Testament "the primary mode of theological reflection,"[43] and this applies to our topic as well. According to Paul, Christ was "raised on the third day in accordance with the Scriptures." Scripture here works almost like a tag. The risen Jesus instructed his disciples on this particular issue. He "opened their minds to understand the Scriptures" (Luke 24:45–46; see also vv. 25–27). At the center of this understanding is that the Scriptures foresaw the resurrection of Jesus. In Luke 24, the failure to recognize the risen Jesus is juxtaposed with failure to understand the Scriptures. In other words, the two form a tandem. On the other hand, the stories about the empty tomb are remarkably free from Scripture citations and allusions, very much in contrast to the passion stories. Hence, there is a *claim* to Scriptural (Old Testament) evidence for understanding the resurrection of Jesus, but such evidence is indeed sparse, especially if we by that ask for *what texts* are underpinning or explaining this claim.[44] This dual impression, claims to Scriptural justification and simultaneous lack of references, calls for some considerations.

The distinction between a context of discovery and a context of justification proves helpful in organizing how the Scriptures shaped the stories about the empty tomb. Given frequent and vigorous references to "in accordance with Scriptures" and the claims that what happened fulfills God's will, we would expect these stories to thrive from Old Testament texts. This is, however, not the case. Both in Paul and in the Easter narratives we are hard-pressed to locate Scriptural allusions and texts. Lidija Novakovic has demonstrated that references to the Scriptures are indeed rare in the canonical gospels' Easter narratives, although not entirely absent. She mentions Ezek 37:12; Isa 26:19; Dan 12:2; and Genesis 2–3.[45] Compared to the hard-wired claim to be "in accordance with Scriptures," this list of references is nothing less than strikingly poor, albeit some other texts may be alluded to. Novakovic comments: "On the whole, however, it is difficult to deny that the resurrection narratives are told with a minimum of scriptural resonances."[46] In comparison with the passion stories, this becomes a significant fact. What we do find, however, is that some thematic blocks or motifs appear, such as the sign of Jonah, theophany patterns, the three-day

---

43. Juel, *Messianic Exegesis*, 8.

44. Pointed out also by Wright and Crossan, "Resurrection," 21 and Craig, "Wright and Crossan," 145.

45. Novakovic, *Raised From the Dead*, 196; for a somewhat longer list, see 219 (Gen 2:7; 2 Sam 7:12–16; Ps 2:7; 8:7; 16:8–11; 86:2; 110:1; 132:10; Isa 45:23; 55:3).

46. Novakovic, *Raised From the Dead*, 196.

motif, creation and Adam motifs. One is left with the impression that the discrepancy between claims like "according to the Scriptures" and actual references, left the witness about resurrection somewhat vulnerable. Thus, the context of *justification* is built into how this testimony is expressed, but in a way that does not suggest that apologetic aims were dominant, or that the stories simply are a result of the reading of the Old Testament. For sure, apologetics is at work, noticed already in the formulaic passage in 1 Corinthians, but the New Testament evidence taken together is not predetermined by the need for apologetics. This is one aspect among others; the more important was the need to make sense of overwhelming and baffling experiences. The dual situation—consistent claims to Scriptural substantiation and simultaneously a minimum of texts—mirrors a situation of discovery in the process of finding justification.

As Novakovic rightly points out, none of the Old Testament passages which are given a bearing on the question of resurrection in the New Testament express resurrection hope in their original setting. This is not to deny that some of them include imagery that proved conducive to the development of this hope in Second Temple Judaism.[47] In the role they are given to play in the Easter testimonies, these texts and motifs appear with clarity and a claim *attributed* to them, rather than coming from them. In the Easter narratives, we have identified elements of both discovery and justification, and references to the Scriptures are prominent with regard to the latter, albeit often as tags or motifs, rather than text references.

At the end of the day, it seems that faith in God as Creator and God of life is the real Scriptural basis for this claim. It is a claim to divine intervention and vindication, and the Scriptures serve to identify this divine act as belonging with what the God of Israel accomplished. The scant biblical substantiation for the resurrection of Jesus is worth noticing since it implies that, although the interpretation of this grows out of theology, the empty tomb and the recognition of the deceased Jesus in apparitions were unprecedented and something that came inadvertently upon them. Hence, it is *not* a phenomenon deduced from Scripture, like prophecy turned into history. A concept like "historicized prophecy" requires another presence of Scriptural material to be an option worth considering.

James G. Crossley considers the Easter stories as no more than vivid examples of "creative storytelling in Judaism."[48] He claims that all the gospel narratives make sense within the context of such practice. Crossley's textbook example is, of course, Matt 27:52–53 about dead promenading

---

47. Novakovic, *Raised From the Dead*, 219.
48. Crossley, "Historical Plausibility," 178–82.

around Jerusalem, being watched by many, all caused by the dramatic death of Jesus. Likewise, in the assessment of Dale C. Allison Jr., this story "may communicate theology; it does not preserve history."[49] The imagery of the opening of graves brings to mind Ezek 37:12 and the hope for a general resurrection (Isa 26:19; Dan 12:2)—all these passages have left their marks on this Matthean text—demonstrating that Jesus's death (sic!) has inaugurated the hope for a *general* resurrection in the future. Charles L. Quarles argues that this passage nicely fits Matthew's Gospel in both style and content.[50] This, however, has no bearing on the question of how *literal* the passage is to be taken. Furthermore, how decisive its structure is, hardly applies to the question if it is a historical narrative or poetry, since *mimesis*, mimicking ancient venerated texts, was an important aspect of literary activities generally in antiquity.[51]

Two points need to be made here in relation to the abovementioned approaches. Firstly, the Matthean passage is apocalyptic in its content; this is not surprising since the issue of general resurrection is at home in apocalypticism. We know that symbolism and images were characteristic to this genre—the Book of Revelation is the textbook example—with no claim to be taken literally. Second, Matt 27:52–53 is *not* attached to the resurrection, but to the crucifixion story and the death of Jesus. This means that although the text indicates that Christians created texts aimed at illustrating theology, this has no direct bearing on the resurrection story. Furthermore, although the passage in question is not taken literally, no one would use this text to declare the story about Jesus's crucifixion and death as poetry in general. In other words, the presence of a symbolic passage is not directive for the passion story as such. It should be even less so for the resurrection story since it is not attached to that story.

There is no doubt that early Christianity had the narrative capacity and training to invent such stories, aimed at illustrating theology rather than rendering events. When Mark's Gospel introduces Jesus' ministry with the notion that he was together with wild animals in the desert—a piece of information found only here (Mark 1:12–13)—this brings to mind the eschatological harmony in nature envisaged in poetic and metaphoric language in Isa 11:1–10,[52] and it raises historical questions as well as questions

---

49. Allison, "Explaining the Resurrection," 127; thus also Licona, *Resurrection*, 548–53.
50. Quarles, "Matthew 27:51–53," 271–86.
51. See, e.g., the contributions in MacDonald, *Mimesis and Intertextuality*.
52. See Bauckham, "Jesus and the Wild Animals," 3–21.

regarding intentionality. Are the Easter narratives to be understood along the same lines? This question picks up on the nub of Crossley's view.

References to full-blown stories can be made as well, like the narratives of the so-called magi from the East and the flight to Egypt (Matt 2). These are found in Matthew only—likewise Mark 1:12–13 is idiosyncratic—and they are soaked in Old Testament passages. Two caveats are in place, though. Firstly, Matthew's Easter story depends on Mark's Gospel, and there the story of the dead having a walk in Jerusalem is not found; this is a Matthean idiosyncrasy. An observation pertaining to Matthew alone cannot without further ado be applied to Mark's Gospel. We may well be speaking of a particular Matthean embellishment. Admittedly, the relevant passage in Matthew 27 raises the nagging issue of what kind of story the next chapter in Matthew tells. If the story in chap. 27 is meant to be metaphorical, conveying that the hoped-for general resurrection is anticipated, Matthew is running the risk of muddling his case for the resurrection in chap. 28. The second caveat takes as its point of departure the missing Old Testament intertextual background in the empty tomb story, and this also applies to that of Matthew 28. Albeit, traditional theophany patterns are discernable in the text, no citation is found. This strikes us as somewhat different from Matt 2 in which the stories are organized according to citations from the Scriptures. The passage in Matt 27:52–53 is, therefore, to be considered an example of theological story-telling, not aiming at describing what really happened. However, the text is no paradigm for how the Easter stories are to be understood. A caveat is to be mentioned here though, as this text is not without any connection to the Easter story, as it says that the saints entered Jerusalem "after the resurrection."[53] This piece of information possibly conveys that Jesus was really the firstborn of the dead (cf. Col 1:18; Acts 26:23; Rom 8:9; Rev 1:5). Regardless of how present-day readers look upon Matt 27:52–53, Matthew's "after his resurrection" indicates that this author took both Jesus's resurrection *and* that of the saints literally.

In Theophilus of Antioch's *Ad Autolycum*, composed late 3rd century, we have an interesting example regarding the Scriptures and the resurrection. He presents himself in this way: "I too did not believe that resurrection would take place, but now that I have considered these matters I believe" (*Autol.* 1.14).[54] His former disbelief he shared with most Greeks: "But you do not believe that the dead are raised" (*Autol.* 8, cf. 1.13). How did Theophilus, according to his own testimony, come to believe in the resurrection? In *Autol.* 3.2 he states the Greek ideal that "writers ought to have been

---

53. Allison, *Constructing Jesus*, 452–53.
54. See Theophilus of Antioch, *Ad Autolycum*.

eye-witnesses (*autoptas*) of the events about which they make affirmations or else they should have learned about them accurately from those who witnessed them. Those who write down uncertain statements (*adēla*) are, so to speak, striking in the air." Theophilus makes no claim that he has access to eyewitnesses, but the Scriptures worked similarly. His embracing faith in resurrection was reaped from reading the Scriptures (*Autol.* 1.14). The predictions found there offered sufficient proof (*apdeixis*)[55] of the events; there was described how the events would take place. The correspondence between predictions and event proved trustworthy. He reasons from within a "proof from prophecy" model. However, Theophilus fails to demonstrate this claimed correspondence by means of biblical texts. Instead, he turns to a number of other "proofs," speaking of *tekmērion* and *apodeixis*) for the resurrection (*Autol.* 1.13, cf. 2.14). Among these are the changes between days and nights, between the seasons, seeds and fruits and the moon; they all die and rise again. *Life* as we know it witnesses to the reality of the resurrection, as a body falling sick loses flesh and regains it at the recovery. What unites all these events, is that they are "works of God." To Theophilus, this is Scriptural evidence, because all these examples speak about God as Creator: "he created you, bringing you from non-existence to existence (*epoiēsen se ex ouk ontos eis to einai*) . . . Then do you not believe the God who made you can later make you over again" (*Autol.* 1.8). This description of resurrection is informed by how he elsewhere presents God's creation: "he made everything out of the non-existent (*ex ouk ontōn tà panta epoiēsen*)" (*Autol.* 2.10, cf. 2.13), paving the way for Theophilus to speak about resurrection in 2.14. Theophilus claims exactness (*Autol.* 2.9) between prophecy and the events of resurrection, and yet, he ends up arguing from creation. There is a fundamental incongruity in his presentation at this point. In what appears to be his personal way to embrace Christian faith in the resurrection (*Autol.* 1.14), he confuses what comes second with what comes first. In other words, justification is presented here as what came first to him. In spite of his claim, we think that the incongruity demonstrates that he came to believe from other reasons and that the Scriptural evidence *justified* this.

Negotiating Creation

Taking Paul in Romans as the point of departure, resurrection is the fulfillment of creation, realized in history and revealing history's ultimate future as well, "proleptically inaugurating its climax while revealing its original

---

55. See Part II, The Acts of the Apostles, sec. Evidentiary Presence.

purpose."⁵⁶ Hence, resurrection discourse by its very nature will always develop into talks about creation, to which the body also belongs. Christ believers are captured within a trajectory of transformation, eventually in a body transformed, which is *creatio ex vetere*, a new creation out of what already is. Body is inherently a part of God's creation. This is what prompted the critique of a philosopher like Celsus (*Cels.* 5:14).⁵⁷ He finds this belief in a corporeal resurrection disgusting, calling it the "hope of worms": "For what sort of human soul would have any further desire for a body that has rotted." The body (*sarx*) is "full of things not even nice to mention; God would neither desire nor be able to make it everlasting contrary to reason." His main point is not that God could not raise people from the dead. Even granted that "anything is possible with God," Celsus still asks if this is *desirable*, consonant with nature, and most importantly, is it consistent with God's character? Celsus has a concern for keeping God undefiled from things of the body. Resurrection was to him, as stated by Brian D. Robinette, "a category mistake,"⁵⁸ a confusion of realities which were distinct, God and human bodies. Celsus holds against Christian belief that it is about raising from the dead "the same body" (*Cels.* 2.57;⁵⁹ 5.14;⁶⁰ 5.23;⁶¹ 8.49⁶²). The Christians were to him "bound to the body" (*tō sōmati syntetēkosin; Cels.* 8.49).⁶³ Celsus seems not to have understood the implications of resurrection as a transformation of the body, especially as Paul puts it.

Origen's response in *Cels.* 5.14, therefore, draws heavily on Paul's distinction between seed and plant, between what is sown and what comes up. By all means, his intention is to take Paul's idea of a transformed body seriously. Due to his philosophical assumptions, he must have felt it uneasy to be accused of being "bound to the body." Hence, he betrays Paul's creation-oriented thinking when he says: "We maintain that the soul, and especially the rational soul, is more precious than any body, since the soul contains that which is 'after the image of the Creator' whereas this is in no sense true of the body" (*Cels.*

---

56. Robinette, *Grammars of Resurrection*, 21.
57. SC 147.48–50.
58. Robinette, *Grammars of Resurrection*, 123.
59. SC 132.420.3–4.
60. SC 147.48.10–12. A body that has rotted (*diaphteirein*) cannot return to its original state. This sums up pretty much how Celsus considered faith in resurrection.
61. SC 147.68.1–4.
62. SC 150.280.2–3.
63. SC 150.280.6.

8.49).⁶⁴ Paul's concern for the renewal of creation, as it is found in for example Rom 8, comes to naught in this dictum of Origen.

Although the New Testament gives witness to a *transformed* body, the body is still constitutive of identity. Creation theology embraces both the incarnation and resurrection of Jesus. Hence, creation, anthropology, and eschatology are deeply informed by the resurrection of Jesus. We have also seen that ethics, especially as worked out by Paul, is putting resurrection into practice.

To bring out the bodily nature of New Testament resurrection faith, N. T. Wright speaks of the "transphysicality" of the risen Jesus.⁶⁵ This term aims at bringing out both the continuity and newness in the resurrected body. Thus, this term seems well-fitted to balance the picture. However, Michael Welker has criticized Wright for not coming to terms with the *sophisticated* way in which the New Testament speaks about the resurrection. This is not to be understood in terms of resuscitation, which Wright's phrases "alive again" and "robustly physical" may be taken to indicate. The Easter narratives do not portray resurrection as "a physical reanimation of the pre-Easter Jesus."⁶⁶ The appearances are not Jesus coming to live again, picking up where he left his disciples before Easter. He is *not* recognized through his face, movements, gestures, voice, etc. Resurrection implies newness and otherness; "a new form of life and existence appears," as Welker puts it. Nowhere in the New Testament is the resurrection rendered like: "it is good to have you back again." Easter faith is not about perpetuating the present in all aspects.⁶⁷ There is always something elusive and altered in the Easter testimonies. The appearances are more like *visits* than Jesus continuing what he and the disciples had together before Easter. Even Acts 1:3–4 does not consider the period of forty days as a continuous fellowship in analogy with his ministry; the forty days are instead a period of time within which he regularly visited (read: appeared to) them.

Already in the New Testament, and also in the early Church, resurrection belief revolves around the body in one way or other. The way body is high on the agenda here epitomizes how deeply rooted this faith is in creation, and thereby also in anthropology, eschatology, ethics, and soteriology.

64. SC 150.282.24–27.
65. Wright, *Resurrection of the Son of God*, 477; see also 616–17, 678–79.
66. Welker, "Wright on the Resurrection," 470.
67. Although we find that Peter Carnley in his recent book tends to downplay the bodily aspects involved, we nevertheless agree that the "meetings" with the resurrected "are spoken of as though they were in principle not unlike the historical meeting of David Livingstone and H, M. Stanley in Africa on 10. November 1871." Carnley, *Resurrection in Retrospect*, 7. Carnley stats this pace N. T. Wright.

Being conformed with Christ is a process initiated through baptism, and which eventually finds its consummation in a transformed body in analogy with Christ's resurrected body. Christ's resurrection sets the standard for the full purpose of what God did in creation. Western theological tradition has revolved around issues such as death, cross, reconciliation. Eastern tradition included more consistently an ontological aspect as well: the transformation of human beings into what Christ is. The bridge here is the resurrection of Jesus. In a way bringing to mind John 20:17 ("But go to my brothers . . ."), Paul's ecclesiological metaphor likewise draws on the abiding presence of the risen Jesus among his followers.

The All-Pervasive Resurrection

As the resurrection of Jesus come into play in the New Testament, it is by no means sufficient to hold it for "true," but then to give this belief no effect on other parts of Christian faith, theology, and practice. This kind of reductionism often emerges in apologetics. We are not talking about a topic, an image, or a standpoint; belief in the resurrection of Jesus is pervasive and omnipresent, forming the foundation for why and how Jesus was remembered, and for what Christian faith, ethics, and hope are really about. The pre-Easter ministry of Jesus is also told from this perspective. In other words, resurrection is not only a stage in the story about Jesus; it is the point of view that made it worth remembering, and also why and how it was remembered. From this follows that resurrection not only has far-reaching implications on both theology and history, but even forms the condition on which Christian faith comes into being and is upheld. It provides parameters of hope and future for what it means to reason and act in a Christian way. This also means that the resurrection of Jesus belongs to "the Christian web of belief"[68] and that it finds its sense within this belief only. "Resurrection" is, therefore, a category of interpretation. It is a claim based on historical experiences, the empty tomb, and the appearances of Jesus.

We have seen that as a saturated phenomenon, the resurrection of Jesus invites a plethora of interpretations, and is accordingly open to various elucidations. A watershed regarding the interpretations available has proven to be whether the resurrection of Jesus is something that happened to *him* or to his *disciples*. This is a distinguishing mark in the debate, as the two respectively pave the way for fundamentally different approaches to the phenomenon. The present study has argued that it is not sufficient—judged by the New Testament evidence—to say that Jesus was *experienced* after his death, claiming

---

68. Thus Allison, *Resurrecting Jesus*, 341.

that this is what resurrection means. The resurrection happened to *Jesus* first. Even though resurrection is an interpretative category, it presupposes that there is a story to be told about *the resurrected one*.

The Resurrected Body: Admitting and Grappling with Vagueness

When Paul in 1 Cor 15:35 raises the question of the nature of the resurrected body, he puts his finger on one of the key issues in resurrection faith, both at his own time and in the present. Belief in the resurrection of the body comes with a bunch of unsolved questions, and the history of solving them reveals that too much precision often proves damaging and ridiculing to the very belief it serves to unfold. It is worth reminding ourselves that the passages raising the question "what kind of body then?" are by necessity *explorative* in nature.

Paul raises that question with regard to the general resurrection, but the context, culminating in the dictum that Christ has been raised from the dead as "the first fruits of those who have died" (vv. 20–23), leaves no doubt that his discussion applies equally to Christ. All Easter traditions found in the New Testament, be they Pauline or narratives, assume bodily changes, be that put in terms of transformation, his not being easily and immediately recognized; his sudden coming and going; his traversing closed doors, etc. The best way to reason about the balance between continuity and change is probably to keep them together in a somewhat *vague and nebulous* way. This is in accordance with the elusive and subtle nature of the Easter evidence found in the New Testament. From an indescribable event follows an indescribable body.

The following will make a virtue of the *imprecise* by asking some unresolved questions to which Christian theology on the resurrection does not have satisfying answers. The questions can be abridged in the following: how bodily need the resurrected body be in order to be identified as an embodied life? Out of this grow a number of issues, of which two appear most prominently: What is a perfect body? How much of the old body is necessary to restore it? Although both questions apply to both Jesus and the general resurrection, they were addressed in the early Church with particular reference to the latter. The reason is, of course, that the body of Jesus had hardly decomposed before it was raised.

The aim here is not to answer these questions. Honestly, we don't know; for now, it is worth pondering that some sense of vagueness remains even within a firm belief in the resurrection, be it that of Jesus or the general. While Paul in 1 Cor 6:13—if we believe that this is Paul and not slogans of opponents—says that stomach and food have no share in the resurrection, Jesus eats according to Luke 24:42–43. Likewise, he has hands and feet to show the disciples and for them to touch (Luke 24:39–40; Matt 28:9; John 20:24–27). The wounds of the crucifixion remained, as John, in particular, makes evident.

Matt 5:29–30 speaks about entering the Kingdom of God with bodily limbs. The vision of renewal according to Rev 21:1–4 includes the elimination of all imperfections. Naturally, therefore, Tertullian and Augustin envisage that resurrection will provide a perfect body; it is the original unblemished state that is restored (Tertullian, *Res.* 57).[69] But the body of Jesus had scars from his crucifixion, according to John's Gospel. Tertullian wrestles with the question of why all limbs are to be raised if their use is superfluous, like with the genitals (cf. Mark 12:18–27parr on the Sadducees). To this belongs, of course, the question of resurrection and gender: is Gal 3:28 to be applied to the resurrected body? For Tertullian, it is vital that the flesh with all its components remains, albeit some of their functions will cease since the idea of a just judgment demands this: sins were committed in the flesh and with the limbs (Tertullian, *Res.* 60–61).[70] This view is fundamental to Athenagoras, and forms the basis for his argument that the resurrection will bring back the body as it once was: the same men must rise again" (Athenagoras, *Res.* 25.3). Augustin makes reference to the dictum of Jesus that "not a hair of your head will perish" (Matt 10:30; Luke 12:7),[71] and the resurrected body is perfect in the sense that it has the age of thirty, the age of Jesus, which he considers a sign for the blooming age (Augustine, *Civ.* 22.15, 19–20). In his *De Civitate Dei* Book 22,[72] Augustine has put together and addresses numerous of the issues mentioned here. Clearly, Augustine is not the first to do so. Pseudo-Justin's treatise *On the Resurrection* does the same, albeit less detailed (ANF 1.294–99).

Amos Yong has asked such questions in a fascinating way from the perspectives of a disability identity.[73] He points out that ideas of the perfect body have repercussions on how body issues are addressed in the present. A theology of resurrection abbreviated in "normal at last" will influence people with disabilities in the present. In addition to this ethical point, Yong also raises the issue of recognition. He makes reference to a girl asking her

69. ANF 3.589–90.
70. ANF 3.591–93.
71. Thus also Tertullian, *Res.* 35; ANF 3.570–71.
72. See the edition in Loeb Classical Literature.
73. Yong, *Theology and Down Syndrome*, 259–92.

parents: "'Will I be retarded when I get to heaven?' The parents answered that she would not. There would be no sickness, no pain. Everyone would be perfect. To this, she responded, 'But how will you know me then?'"[74] The simple, but still very relevant question this raises implies that resurrection often is understood narrowly in individual terms and with reference to bodily conditions; what about the *relational* and communal aspects?

The other issue that received attention in the early Church was resurrection and the chain of consumption, an issue with no relevance for Jesus's resurrection. A stereotype in this discourse was the case when a seaman fell from his boat and was devoured by a fish, which eventually was taken by another fish (Tertullian, *Res.* 32;[75] Athenagoras, *Res.* 3[76]). We now reach a point where the precision sought, in fact, undermines the very idea of resurrection as something that cannot be fully grasped.

Why have we briefly summarized the discourse on the resurrected body, in which the general resurrection is dominant? The body of the resurrected Jesus was a paradigm for how a general resurrection was conceived of, and, therefore, there is a going forth and back between these two issues. We see already in the New Testament that Jesus's risen body was a mysterious phenomenon. Historians, theologians, and Christian apologists are all, in different ways and with various purposes, bent on making this enigma understood. We are no exception in this intellectual endeavour. If we take seriously that the resurrection of Jesus is a saturated phenomenon, this "event precedes any recognition thereof." [77] Living with this faith can never suspend balance between presence and absence, and accordingly, neither between sense and vagueness.

---

74. Yong, *Theology and Down Syndrome*, 259.
75. See ANF 3.567–68.
76. For Athenagoras, see ANF 2.150–51 and Athenagoras, *De Ressurectione*.
77. Robinette, *Grammars of Resurrection*, 113.

Part III: Resurrection Faith

Contributions to Resurrection Discourse: Presentation and Analysis

A FUNDAMENTAL POINT OF departure for the discussion is that Jesus's resurrection appears as unexpected and unconditioned by any present circumstances. There are simply no conditions that we can identify in ordinary human knowledge that provide opportunities for it. This unconditional character is reflected in the fact that the New Testament never says anything about *how* the resurrection took place, or *what* really happened. The statements only say *that* it happened, or report of what happened *after* the event. The event is never reported as such. Moreover, there are no identifiable agents bringing it about, no one who has to do something in order for it to happen. The resurrection is a mere event, but we do not know, and we probably *cannot* determine fully what it really is. From a theological point of view, we can take the elusive and indefinite character of resurrection as a token of its character of gift: a real gift is unconditionally given, but when given, it is providing us with a new point of orientation that we nevertheless are not able to grasp fully or exhaustively.

The presumably unconditional character of the resurrection also suggests that it expresses what seems to be a *surplus* over against what are the present conditions of the world. The notion of surplus allows us to see it as something that expressed an excess compared to what can be determined from experience. This excess is in some ways anticipated in how the gifts of life are expressing themselves as surplus in Jesus's life before Easter, but in the resurrection, this excess is more radical as compared to the feeding miracles. The continuation between before and after Easter implies a *reconfiguration* of the very manifestation of the life of Jesus, as he is not present in the same way as before, according to the reports about his resurrection. As we shall emphasize in the following, we hold that it is crucial to maintain the relationship between the pre-Easter ministry of Jesus and the resurrection in order to establish the significance of the latter. There is nevertheless something more to say about Jesus after his resurrection: a surplus, a difference is at hand, *although we have no possibility of saying exactly what is changed, or what the difference is, and what and how exactly he is present and presenting himself in this new way.* This lack of possibilities for pinning down and exhaustively determining the newness in the resurrection expresses the excessive surplus this reality reveals compared to the one in which we now live. Moreover, it underscores the gift-character of Jesus's resurrection-presence as something that cannot be possessed—it is something that has to be given over and over again—it remains a gift in giving, something still to come, not yet fully to be understood.[1] The elusiveness indicated in the textual witnesses to the resurrection is an indication of this ungraspable character of the resurrection.

From a theological point of view, belief in the resurrection maintains that God is still at work in the world as the power of life and the Creator ex nihilo, and that this world is not to be conceived as if murder and death have the last word. This interpretation does not imply that death has *no* word, *no* impact, and that resurrection is a consolation which lets us ignore the horrors of death or a way for those believing in it to have their narcissistic dreams about eternal life fulfilled. But as a point of orientation, resurrection opens a new perspective of the world: the world has a future that is not determined finally by death. Hence, the existential dimension of the resurrection is that it allows us to be liberated from the closed horizon which death imposes on us in such a way that this horizon appears as the only and final one. Instead, by stating "Resurrection!", there is a witness to something more, something other than what is present. The radical otherness of resurrection also implies that it is not just a continuation of the best of the present—it signals something *different*. No matter how we understand it, the New Testament witness sees the resurrection of Jesus as something more than resuscitation. It is a reversal of the powers of death so that these powers are no longer in control. Moreover, the resurrection means that Christ is alive and that he will never die again (unlike those New Testament reports that he resuscitated).

What do we believe when we believe that Jesus was raised from the dead? This question cannot be separated entirely from another question, namely: why do we believe that Jesus was raised from the dead? It is important to recognize both these questions, both in their distinctive difference from each other, and the way they are interconnected. The historical

---

1. This is a point of view that has important implications for how to evaluate attempts to "secure" the historicity of the resurrection of Christ.

and the theological questions are interconnected, and it would not only be a mistake to separate them from each other—it would also be futile to think that it is possible to do so.

Resurrection as a Saturated Phenomenon? Jean-Luc Marion on the Emmaus story

The previous part closed with pointing to the vagueness in the stories about the resurrection. Another way to understand this would be to consider the topic as one that cannot be captured easily in already established categories of interpretation. In our discussion of Alkier in the Introduction in Part I, we noted that he uses the notion of *an overwhelming phenomenon* when he addresses the reality of the resurrection. In the present section, we want to develop this point further by taking up Jean-Luc Marion's notion of the *saturated phenomenon,* which has been used already in our reflections on the texts, and see how Marion develops it in his interpretation of the Emmaus story. This approach may then provide us with a suitable entry to the diversity of understandings of the resurrection present in contemporary systematic approaches to the resurrection.

Marion speaks of saturated phenomena or phenomena of excess. These phenomena present themselves by intuitional excess or saturation.[2] They require the subject to relate to the phenomenal world in a different way than the one given by the ordinary phenomenological reduction, where we try to understand something on the basis of the already known or as mere objects to an observer. Hence, he points in the direction of the immediacy that we also saw that Alkier was oriented towards. In the article "The Banality of Saturation," he writes: "Now, the entire question of the saturated phenomenon concerns solely and specifically the possibility that certain phenomena do not manifest themselves in the mode of objects and yet still do manifest themselves. The difficulty is to describe what would manifest itself without our being able to constitute (or synthesize) it as an object (by a concept or an intentionality adequate to its intuition)."[3] In other words: how can we understand something when we have no established presuppositions for doing so, based on our previously established frameworks of understanding?

2. A more extensive description of Marion's understanding of saturated phenomena can be found in Marion, *In Excess*. For an extensive study of Marion's intepretation of the resurrection against the backdrop of his phenomenology, see also Johnstone, "Resurrection in Phenomenology," 23–39. The following analysis of Marion is a reworking of main elements in Henriksen, *Desire, Gift and Recognition*, 344–50.

3. In this and the following, we build on the introduction in Gschwandtner, *Degrees of Givenness.*

Marion's definition of saturated phenomena implies that although they give "too much," although these phenomena present our intuition with abundant data, our intention is nevertheless insufficient and fails or falls short when it comes to determining their signification: "Because it shows itself only inasmuch as it gives itself, the phenomenon appears to the extent that it arises, ascends, arrives, comes forward, imposes itself, is accomplished factically and bursts forth—in short, it presses urgently on the gaze more than the gaze presses toward it. The gaze receives its impression from the phenomenon before any attempt at constituting it."[4] The excess that saturated phenomena contain or present us with implies that they "defy our attempt to analyze them as deriving from a clear cause. Saturated phenomena undo all our usual categories of experience."[5] Thus, in Marion's view, they are not constituted by our consciousness, but the opposite happens: they constitute consciousness, and create a specific effect in us and present us with something that we relate to as witnesses.

Against this backdrop, we can analyze a small article where Marion deliberates on the possibilities of grasping the resurrection.[6] He develops his argument in opposition to an understanding of faith that sees faith as compensation for lack of clarity and faulty intuition. Such an understanding of faith makes it possible to believe what we cannot otherwise hold as true. Instead of seeing faith as a compensation for what can be established by intuition, Marion suggests that "we should believe not in order to recapture a lack in intuition, but rather to confront its excess in relation to a deficiency of statements and a dearth of concepts."[7] This approach, as one can see, allows for us to understand the resurrection first and foremost as a conceptual and epistemological impossibility. The resurrection presents us with an intuition that is so excessive that it cannot be expressed or developed by means of our ordinary epistemic tools.

Marion presents the two men on the road to Emmaus as examples of what is at stake when he sees the resurrection as an epistemic challenge which points in the direction of the above-mentioned saturated phenomena. Instead of seeing the story about these men as something remote from the reality in which we participate, he formulates the similarity between them and us with relation to what happened at Easter thus:

> Like us, it is thus not the intuition of facts that they lack, but rather the intelligence (the concepts), as do we, today: well do

---

4. Marion, *Being Given*, 159.
5. Gschwandtner, *Degrees of Givenness*, 6.
6. Marion, "'They Recognized Him,'" 145–52.
7. Marion, "'They Recognized Him,'" 146.

they know, as do we, with scientific certainty, that Jesus died, and that one does not come back from the dead; we can deplore this fact, especially in this case, but in the end that's how it is; we must stay reasonable and not lose our heads. They stick by this evidence no less than do we, to the point of no longer envisaging that the question might even be worth discussing.[8]

By talking about his death without understanding, the disciples are also kept from recognizing Jesus when he enters their company and speaks with them. Marion holds that this lack of recognition was not due to any lack in their perception or intuitions. The reason for their lack of recognition is due to their lack of *imagination*: they cannot even imagine that it is him.[9] All their preconceptions and ways of understanding what has happened are saturated with the conception of the impossibility of the resurrection and imply that they "see" the resurrection as exactly that: as the impossible. Hence, the story is about *the travelers' lack of recognition*. Or, as Marion says aptly: the events "leave them petrified within a matrix of irrefutable prejudices."[10] The presence of the resurrected presents them with a phenomenon and with a situation in which they are given intuitions that their concepts are unable to catch. There is no obvious context of interpretation for what they experience, and hence, what presents itself goes beyond their *immediate* grasp.

Marion uses the notion of intuition here, and with good reasons: intuitions are *given us* and are, as he says, phenomena of excess or surplus, i.e., they contain more than can be contained in concepts, and they are also passively constituted, while conceptually based understanding demands an active effort of cognition and re-cognition. What the disciples on the way to Emmaus lack, however, is an understanding of the events that took place, even the event of the resurrection, which they have heard reported, but not comprehended. Marion writes: "Why do they not understand? Because they do not recompose the significations from the starting point of the Passion as a revelation of the charity of God, and thus also of the Resurrection as the fulfillment of this very charity."[11] Marion consequently argues that the lack of recognition is due to a lack of concepts by which they can make sense of their intuitions. There is no lack in *revelation*, but only in the travelers' (i.e., our) ability to deal with the intuitions that revelation gives rise to. In this way,

---

8. Marion, "'They Recognized Him,'" 147.

9. Marion, "'They Recognized Him,'" 147.

10. Marion, "'They Recognized Him,'" 147. A critical discussion of Marion's position here can be found in Mackinlay, "'Eyes Wide Shut.'"

11. Marion, Marion, "'They Recognized Him,'" 148.

Marion describes how the solution to the tension between the pre-established concepts and the actual intuition is given with the teaching of Christ, which gradually—by means of the scriptures—allows for a different reading of the reality in which they find themselves, or—with our words—for a different interpretation of the reality they experience. "By allowing themselves to be taught by Christ, they finally experience that the concept, at last, matches the intuition."[12] By being open to receive this teaching,

> they ask to receive his *logos*, his interpretation of what has happened in the intuition and which they have nevertheless neither seen, nor caught, nor understood. They, at last, ask him *his* meaning, *his* concept, *his* interpretation of the public, yet unintelligible to spectators, intuition of Easter.[13]

Marion points to something of great importance here, not only for the interpretation of the story in Luke, but even more so concerning the conditions of resurrection faith: this faith cannot be the result of any deduction based in present conceptions but must—as the event itself—be conceived as a gift. As he construes what takes place among the disciples on the way to Emmaus, all that happens in order to change their perspective is a gift. They are given the intuition with which they cannot cope, they are given by Christ the concept that finally makes them realize the significance of the events and recognize Jesus; he becomes visible to them by including them in a meal that manifests community, and where he (again) shares the gifts of God with them. Moreover, this gift allows them to see their place in the world differently, and to orient themselves anew. The stranger, who, as long as he is not recognized as Jesus remains an Other, allows them to see and perceive the story differently. The difference is manifested because they cannot fit what he says into an already anticipated pattern of sameness. Their openness to the difference is made possible by the way the stranger appears to them.

This means that the capability to understand the resurrection as resurrection is something that itself must be given and/or revealed. We have previously described this from the point of view of abduction. Because abduction is not only based on established conceptions but adds something new to what was hitherto the case, it can aptly be considered *a gift to intuition* that reveals reality in new ways, and subsequently provides new opportunities for thinking about it. Thus, revelation is not abstract, but concrete and personal, and a chance for recognizing both oneself and God.

---

12. Marion, "'They Recognized Him,'" 149.
13. Marion, "'They Recognized Him,'" 150.

We can add to this point that the text itself suggests that the ability to receive this revelation of the resurrected Christ as a gift is conditioned by how his appearance can be linked back to previous stories about sharing meals with him. Thus, the opportunities for recognizing and relating to the revealed one as the resurrected Jesus are offered by incorporating this experience into the previous experiences they have with Jesus. It is the experiences of Jesus prior to his death that is the possibility not only for recognizing him, but also for attributing a specific significance to the experience of him as present at hand. The resurrected is identifiable only if he can be recognized in what he does (sharing a meal) as the one who did so also previously. Hence, the experiences of the resurrected are always an experience of features that were present in Jesus's earlier practice. These experiences are those which condition the abductive inference that identifies Jesus as resurrected.

Hence, the need for an abduction also points to the lack of immediate access to the phenomenon of resurrection. To employ "resurrection" as an interpretative category requires an interpretative context of discovery. Marion actually points to how difficult it is to establish some kind of objective status that allows for the resurrection to appear—and even more to appear as an event in the history of God with God's people. The interpretation of the Scriptures that Jesus reportedly offers to the men traveling to Emmaus in order to explain what has happened is only one among many possible approaches to the event. It is, however, the only one that has proved solid enough to persist through history—at least among those understandings of this event that did not render it impossible in the sense of being *rejectable*. In this sense, the recognition that Jesus himself opens up to is also a recognition of what is at stake in this history.

From Marion's point of view, it becomes clear that resurrection can *only* be understood from the point of view of faith—or as we would argue, from the point of view of an abduction in which you put your trust and engagement. This does not mean that resurrection cannot take place outside of faith, but it means that resurrection as a phenomenon cannot appear as a phenomenon without faith. Faith is what makes us *see* what is at stake:

> What we lack in order to believe is quite simply one with what we lack in order to see. Faith does not compensate, either here or anywhere else, for a defect of visibility: on the contrary, it allows reception of the intelligence of the phenomenon and the strength to bear the glare of its brilliance. Faith does not manage the deficit of evidence—it alone renders the gaze apt

to see the excess of the pre-eminent saturated phenomenon, the Revelation.[14]

The problem that emerges from this way of understanding the phenomenological conditions for grasping the resurrection is linked to the fact that this can be read as faith being requisite for the content of faith. However, at this point, we are well served by considering how the very language that we share also allows us to shape perspectives and points of orientation that indicate different possibilities of understanding. Despite the fact that you need a specific faith in order to understand the resurrection as something that God made happen, you can nevertheless contemplate that possibility already by listening to, and being provided with, a particular understanding that someone else shares with you and offers you. You may share a context of discovery with the other. By entertaining such a possibility, you can either come to the conclusion that you understand the resurrection as a resurrection, or you can conclude that there is something here that you are not able to assess as significant, or that it is something that you do not see as a phenomenon altogether. But when you believe, you believe in something that is there, something that is not constituted by your concepts but *given to you in intuitions and concepts as a gift, an event presenting itself.*

Seeing the revelation implied in the post-resurrection events as *saturated phenomena*, as Marion does, allows for these phenomena to be richer than what can be conceptually articulated, but without having to take recourse to apophatic mysticism. Instead, it allows for several different and explorative ways of understanding the revelatory event in question. We can illustrate this by providing two different ways of understanding the elusiveness of Jesus at the end of the Emmaus story.

Marion sees the disappearance of Jesus as an indication that the issue is not, from now on, to see Jesus, but to *show him*, "to make it so that all receive the significations that allow them to see that which the intuition offers, without rendering it manifest again."[15] Furthermore, he claims that such a saturated phenomenon cannot be touched, nor even contemplated in this world, which does not have the space to contain the significations that could have been written.[16] He does not, however, in the context of the article develop

---

14. Marion, "'They Recognized Him,'" 150. For a different, but still in many ways parallel account of the same, cf. Coakley, "'Not with the Eye Only.'" Coakley also points to how the language of the resurrection destabilizes and subverts common forms of understanding the world and opens a whole new way of "picturing" the world.

15. Marion, "'They Recognized Him,'" 151.

16. Marion, "'They Recognized Him,'" 152; with reference to John 21:25.

this point further, but the last point underscores the point that this is a phenomenon that allows for a multitude of interpretations.

"A theology of the risen Jesus will always be, to a greater or lesser degree, a negative theology, obliged to confess its conceptual and imaginative poverty—as is any theology which takes seriously the truth that God is not a determinate object in the world," writes R. Williams.[17] If we accept this consideration, then the elusiveness of Jesus after Easter not only underscores his presence in the world as an unconditional event (as an instance of Firstness in the Peircean sense, or a saturated phenomenon), but furthermore, it also suggests that Jesus cannot be possessed by or taken captive by the forces of this world. His resurrection existence as an instance of Firstness means that his presence in the world as an ultimate object cannot be adequately represented in the world or seen as conditioned by something else we know or have control over. If that was the case, the resurrection itself would be a case of Secondness. Nevertheless, the presence of Jesus is represented—in its absence—by the community of believers who by the belief in his resurrection by God not only keep the memory of him present, but also, by keeping this memory present, keep the future that his life and resurrection promised open to faith and future experience in their witness.[18] Thus, the resurrection transforms the lives of those who believe in it—and creates a specific mode of Thirdness, as Peirce understands it.

On "Miracles"

Before we enter the discussion of some prominent studies of different aspects in the contemporary scholarship on the resurrection, we need to consider some elements in the contemporary discussion of so-called "miracles." The reason is obvious: the resurrection is by many considered to be a miraculous event, and if it falls under such a category, the category itself needs to be clarified. Then we will also be able to see why some may have reasons for claiming the possibility for miracles, whereas others may find reasons for rejecting them. As we shall see, much depends on the definition.

---

17. Williams, *Resurrection*, 84.

18. This is not so only for present believers, but for the first ones as well. As Williams, *Resurrection*, 20 says, "The preaching of Jesus crucified and raised occurs in a specific human context in which Jesus and his death are available in the public memory. This man and his way of living and dying, this man rather than any other, is exalted, approved and vindicated."

It is David Hume that to a large extent has set the agenda for the modern understanding and rejection of miracles.[19] In the section on miracles in *Enquiry Concerning Human Understanding* (1748), he defines a miracle as an event that is contrary to natural law.[20] However, as Wolfhart Pannenberg has pointed out, "This is a self-defeating notion of a miracle, of course, because the logic of the concept of natural law requires that there be no exceptions—otherwise the pretended law in question would turn out not to be truly a law of nature. The concept of miracle as a violation of natural law subverts the very concept of law and in effect exposes the futility of the assertion of miracles."[21] A weaker understanding of the natural law, implying that it points merely to statistical probabilities, would not be subject to the same criticism, though.

However, Pannenberg himself claims that the understanding of the miraculous in Christian theology is not based on the violation of natural law, but "refers to extraordinary events that function as 'signs' of God's sovereign power." Augustine held, accordingly, that "Whatever is unusual, is a miracle," and emphasized explicitly "that events of that type do not occur contrary to the nature of things." If something appears as contrary to their nature, for Augustine it is because of our *limited knowledge* of the "course of nature."[22]

Pannenberg argues in favor of the Augustinian understanding of miracle over against the later development which resulted in an experiential concept of nature rather than the theological concept of nature as constituted by God's creative action. This latter view implies that miracles came to be understood as *contra naturam*. The concept of nature and of the order of nature became based on human experience. Consequently, a miracle was considered a violation of the laws of nature.[23]

Instead of accepting this later development of the concept, Pannenberg sees the Augustinian, theological understanding of miracle as more apt. He argues that "Theology should avoid purely objective concepts of miracles as

19. For a thorough analysis of Hume's position, in its historical context and with a critical evaluation of its inconsistencies, see Schulz, "Das Ende Des Common Sense," 1–38.

20. Hume's understanding of miracles is sharply contested in Earman, *Hume's Abject Failure*, and defended in, e.g., Fogelin, *Defense of Hume on Miracles*. On the contemporary discussion of Hume's notion of miracles, see the contribution in Wahlberg, *Revelation as Testimony*, 182–85.

21. Pannenberg, "Concept of Miracle," 759.

22. Pannenberg, "Concept of Miracle," 760. Italics added.

23. Cf. Pannenberg, "Concept of Miracle," 760. A more extensive overview of how miracles have been considered in theological scholarship can be found in Alkier and Moffitt, "Miracles Revisited," 315–37.

occurring *praeter naturam* or *contra naturam* and return to Augustine's idea of miracle as related to the subjectivity of our human experience of nature, especially to the limitations of our knowledge."[24]

The advantage of the Augustinian concept of miracle is that it is related to what and how humans experience something as unusual and exceptional in contrast to the accustomed patterns of events. Thus, it fits well with what Taves understands as conditions for the anomalous, as described in the previous section. The actual contingency of some events is the *objective* basis for such experience. Pannenberg points to the rather uncontroversial fact that "Unusual events really happen. Sometimes they are very unusual, including unusual effects produced by human persons."[25] Furthermore, he also points to how

> miracles are ambivalent, and that is one reason that the Bible warns against asking for signs as legitimation. It does not belong to the nature of a miracle that it is an action of God, although God does work the greatest miracles. A miracle is just an unusual event or action, and religious interpretation identifies it as an act of God. It is at this point that faith enters the picture. To those who believe in God the Creator, the world is full of miracles.[26]

At this point, Pannenberg makes some reflections that are relevant against the backdrop of our previous presentation of semiotic theory. He refers to Schleiermacher, who said that miracle is the religious name for an event. This means that all that happens is interpreted as a sign, or as having some kind of significance. Pannenberg goes on, writing:

> The religious mind takes nothing as simply a matter of fact. It is aware of the contingency of every single event and experiences everything that happens as a manifestation of the contingency of the world of creation, especially the gift of each new day. Human beings are not always aware of the extent to which our life depends on contingencies, because in our everyday life we tend to take for granted that the world, the order of nature, is going on as usual. Once in a while, however, contingencies occur that make people aware of the basic contingency that permeates all reality. Such an unusual occurrence may be experienced as a "miracle," and religious persons will take it as an act of God, a

---

24. Pannenberg, "Concept of Miracle," 760.
25. Pannenberg, "Concept of Miracle," 761.
26. Pannenberg, "Concept of Miracle," 761.

"sign" of the continuing activity of the Creator in creation and perhaps of new things to come.[27]

As is apparent from these reflections, one of the crucial elements in Pannenberg's understanding of miracles is the notion of *contingency*. Contingencies make it possible to see that events which are considered as miraculous are not opposed to the order of nature or to the concept of natural law. He sees natural laws as describing the "repetitive patterns in the sequence of events, and the emergence of such patterns and, therefore, of the order of nature by natural law is not self-evident but a miracle indeed, basic as it is for the emergence and existence of all complex creatures."[28]

All regularities described by formulas of natural law are based on events that can be described as initially contingent. Pannenberg speaks about the "contingent substructure of the processes" that leads to the formulation of laws. Hence, he can also suggest that it is possible that unusual occurrences follow patterns of law that we do not know. Accordingly, there may be events or phenomena that we at present are unable to explain, which "may be explainable in the future, when a more comprehensive understanding of natural processes emerges."[29] He furthermore applies this line of reasoning directly to the resurrection:

> Even the resurrection of Jesus, the central miracle of the Christian faith, need not defy such explanation in principle, although at present it certainly does. If the Christian hope for a future resurrection of the dead is fulfilled sometime in the future, the resurrection of Jesus will no longer be completely exceptional, although its occurrence in the midst of history will still remain particular.[30]

There are, in addition to the line of reasoning based on contingency and law, here also one more element that is worth considering: the fact that Pannenberg does not see the resurrection as an eschatological event that is separate from other events of history, but is instead based on what is potentially the same conditions for events as one can expect for other events, including the future resurrection of humankind.

Hence, Pannenberg's understanding of the miraculous carves out a space for the possibility of the resurrection to happen without abolishing the notion of natural law or seeing this event as one that violates the laws

27. Pannenberg, "Concept of Miracle," 761.
28. Pannenberg, "Concept of Miracle," 761.
29. Pannenberg, "Concept of Miracle," 761–62.
30. Pannenberg, "Concept of Miracle," 762.

of nature. Instead, our lack of comprehension of this is not only pointing to the limitation of our own understanding by or through our intuitions (as in Marion), or towards it as something anomalous (as in Taves, see Part I). Instead, it

> only requires us to admit that we do not know everything about how the processes of nature work. Therefore, there can be unusual events, some of which, though uncommon, are explainable on the basis of our present knowledge of natural law, and some of which are not but may be understood better in the future. In any event, the awareness of the limitations of our knowledge may keep us from denying on principle the possibility of unusual events, even if they are extremely unusual. That their occurrence is "against all custom and (former) experience" is no sufficient reason, as Hume thought, to deny their possibility on principle; that would be a form of dogmatism and not consonant with the empirical attitude of science.[31]

Another and entirely different contribution to the notion of miracles that has relations to the pragmatist position, is found in Heiko Schulz. He makes a critical observation in his careful analysis of different dimensions of the New Testament writings. He argues that we do not find there any hints about what he calls the *causal account of miracles,* i.e., a concern with explaining what happens from a causal point of view. He does not see this as a surprise, though, as "the obsession with causality as a paradigm of natural laws and correspondingly, the concept of miracle as a violation of the latter, does not proliferate prior to the Enlightenment-period."[32] He sees the most important element for those who experienced the miracles surrounding Jesus in the suspension of the uniformity of their ordinary experience. When something extraordinary happens and interrupts the regular and ordinary, it is seen as a testimony to the presence of "some divine and/or numinous, but in any case, strictly transhuman, power." From this perspective, it is, according to him, possible to see the biblical notion of a miracle as something that can also be defined philosophically as "divine or numinous acts perceived as such."[33] As we shall see soon, this notion of a miracle does not address Hume's notion at all, but has still some implications for the assessment of the veracity of an event considered as miraculous.

There are some other points that Schulz makes that are important in order to reflect on the various dimensions of a miracle from the point of

---

31. Pannenberg, "Concept of Miracle," 762.
32. Schulz, "Concept of Miracle," 362.
33. Schulz, "Concept of Miracle," 362.

view of experience, as well. First, he holds that there is a substantial gap that needs to be bridged in order to make some experiences count as religiously relevant and as miraculous in the sense of being a divine act. He writes:

> It is obviously one thing to perceive someone apparently resuscitating a deceased person; it is quite another to believe—let alone: rightly to believe—this to be a miracle; and yet another to believe (and rightly so) that as such it was and had to be done by a god-man.[34]

Against this backdrop, from the point of view of a *first-person-perspective*, three aspects are uncontroversial with regard to what is considered a miracle: "(a) Peter has indubitably *experienced* something (= experiential aspect); (b) Peter has indubitably experienced *something* (= referential aspect); and (c) Peter has indubitably experienced something *as something*— namely: as somebody (here: a God-man) resuscitating a deceased person and thereby performing a miracle (= symbolic aspect)."[35] What remains as controversial, though, is the above-mentioned *veridical* aspect: is what Peter has experienced really a miracle? In order to establish an answer to that question, one would have to leave the first-person-perspective. In line with what we have presented earlier, we can say that one would have to go from the position that saw what happened within the context of discovery and transfer the reflections to a context of justification.

Furthermore, and second, we can compare the above epistemic considerations with those implied when one is confronted with an *indirect* claim (that someone else makes) about a miracle. Then the epistemic question takes on a different form, and one must ask if the witness of an allegedly divinely performed miracle is credible. Accordingly, "the account of the witness may appear dubitable not only in terms of what happened but also in terms of something to have happened at all!" Schulz holds that this situation is precisely our situation unless we have ourselves directly been experiencing something as miraculous.[36] This is also the situation from which we consider the witnesses who speak about the resurrection of Jesus. To apply the above-mentioned distinction again: unless we have ourselves first-hand experiences that allow us to see these within a context of discovery that can make sense of what happens to us, we are, almost by necessity, considering reports of such events from a context of justification.

---

34. Schulz, "Concept of Miracle," 368.
35. Schulz, "Concept of Miracle," 368.
36. Schulz, "Concept of Miracle," 369.

If one understands a miracle as Schulz does, however, there is, according to him, only one option possible when it comes to considering the possibilities about miracles: "either an event lends itself to being conceived of as possible, or we are talking about a miracle. *Tertium non datur.*"[37] This understanding is different from Pannenberg's, which does not presuppose such a strict divide between miracles as originating in God's actions, and what is possible on more generic terms.

For Schulz, a miracle must be—and must be conceivable as—an extraordinary event. Thus, he seems to be able to follow Pannenberg's notion of miracles as instances of contingency. Accordingly, miracles are not necessarily extraordinary "in the sense of a causal irregularity qua violation of a law of nature, but definitely as an astonishing, wondrous or awe-inspiring event, which indicates that it exceeds any human cognitive and practical capacity, and as such prompts the idea of a divine purpose and/or cause." It is against this backdrop he can claim that "either what we are talking about is to be conceived of as humanly possible—or we are talking about miracles."[38] *Tertium non datur.*

Schulz's notion of a miracle thus implies an idea about a divine purpose or cause. Hence, we can say that he moves further than does Pannenberg in defining miracles as instances in which God is at work. This is an ontological determination which feeds into what Schulz develops as a more profound *theological* concept of miracle, against which backdrop he also sees the following implications:

> Hence, the more we might gain apologetically (by making the respective event appear probable or at least possible), the more we are about to lose conceptually (namely by betraying the ideality or true nature of miracles) and vice versa. However, if that holds true, then every Christian (and every religious person, for that matter) must be a supernaturalist—nota bene: as long as he or she wants to cling to a belief in miracles.[39]

We can here define a "supernaturalist" as someone open to God as the one who acts and need not put anything more into that category for our argumentative purposes. The effect, though, of Schulz's definition of a miracle, is that he reserves this for a category of that which does not seem possible or probable from the point of view of other things we know, and sees such events as the result of divine will or agency. Hence, miracles continue to be, in his view, something that is improbable within the context of our established

---

37. Schulz, "Concept of Miracle," 369.
38. Schulz, "Concept of Miracle," 359.
39. Schulz, "Concept of Miracle," 369.

reservoir of knowledge (or our encyclopedia, to use Alkier's notion, see Part I), but which also is referred to as originating in God. For Schulz, there is no non-theological definition of a miracle.

As a conclusion to our presentation of these different positions, we can first of all observe that neither Hume, Augustine, Pannenberg, or Schulz disputes that a miracle must, from both an epistemic and ontological point of view, be something extraordinary. The main question is to what extent one is willing to admit to there *actually* being something that can be conceived as extraordinary. Even the Humean position does not rule that out in principle. However, we see a difference between Pannenberg and Schulz in how Pannenberg argues for the possibility of seeing contingent events as instances of the extraordinary or the miraculous, and thereby establishes "miracle" as a generic category which need not be supported by a theological assumption about some *specific act of God,* whereas Schulz sees such apologetic moves as emptying the notion of miracles of its ideal content as something that happens due to God's will and interference. The latter element he holds to be of importance for the notion of a miracle. However, this approach seems to limit God's work to specific events, and thus, it needs further qualification. Such qualification can be developed by seeing miracles as composites of nature and grace, as we shall see in a later chapter in this part. Then, the miraculous or extraordinary is not something that is *contra naturam,* but rather a specific and graceful way of nature to be fulfilled or accomplished beyond what can be expected on the basis of our established knowledge.

***

The discussion of "miracles" in this chapter is based on the intention to clarify some of the main lines of argumentation that present themselves when we approach the notion of "resurrection" based in that discourse. However, given our previous discussions on semiotics and saturated phenomena, we want to point out the fact that the discourse about resurrection as a "miracle" is based on the premise that it is possible to determine it as an event with a specific character. When we, instead, have argued that resurrection is as an interpretative category based on abductive inference, we signalize a certain distance to such a robust categorization. The actual experiences that led to resurrection belief do not present themselves as miraculous, although they can be categorized as extraordinary and unusual, as Ann Taves describes experiences "deemed religious." That point notwithstanding, the theological elaborations and the stories that grow out of these experiences do not describe the actual experiences with the resurrected as miraculous—instead, the New Testament authors are at pains in describing these experiences as not being experiences of a ghost. Therefore, we argue that it is of the utmost importance to try to avoid giving too much attention to the question about the miraculous character of the resurrection. Instead, we should try to see in what way the New Testament reports experiences that a) can be identified as different from other experiences that could be seen as analogous to those that gave rise to the abductive interpretation of the resurrection. Moreover, b) see how these reports provide us with a basis for understanding the contemporary significance of the full Jesus story, which would somehow be different unless it was possible to identify Jesus as the resurrected.

Engaging Key Voices

THE RESURRECTION IS A much-discussed topic in modern theology. We have already suggested the reason why: it is not something that is consonant with human experience. Hence, different approaches to the texts are, as we have already suggested, necessary, be it in terms of hermeneutical, theological, or other means. In the following, we discuss some of the contributions in the past decades. The discussion is conducted with two aims in mind: a) to present the different concerns and foci of the authors in question, and b) to show how their contributions can be interpreted in light of the theoretical approaches we have delineated in the previous chapter. The chapter will therefore not only be a presentation of existing positions that have contributed to the discussion but will also have an accumulative character, in which we develop essential points for further consideration in the subsequent sections.

Rudolf Bultmann

It is possible to see Rudolf Bultmann's understanding of resurrection against the backdrop of his understanding of miracles, since his elaborations on this topic display central elements in his theological conception of reality. Furthermore, the resurrection can potentially be seen to fall under the category of what he considers a miracle, although he does not explicitly relate it to that category himself.

Bultmann discusses the topic of miracles along similar lines as those we have encountered already. He sees miracles (or wonders/German: Wunders, as he prefers to call them) as defined by two features: they are the result of God's action, and not the result of natural causes or human volition, and they are events that must be described as *contra naturam*, i.e., as contrary to the regularities of natural events.[1]

Bultmann rejects the idea of miracles as something contrary to the regularities of nature. There can be no competition between God's actions, on the one hand, and the events of nature on the other hand. Such an idea is untenable and must be discarded.[2]

Bultmann argues furthermore that miracles are not a specific Christian notion, and refers to their ambiguous character. Such events can be for good or for bad. Once one recognizes this, one has given up on the notion that all wonders are the result of God's action. He holds that Christian faith has no interest in miracles as such, but is concerned with them to the extent that they can be understood as *God's action*. This action is linked to how God has meaning for one's own personal existence. Accordingly, belief in God and in wonders are, in this perspective, two sides of the same coin.[3] In order to interpret this position, we need to consider the following elements:

Bultmann's concern for understanding God is as someone that cannot be objectified, but who is only accessible in the *modus* of our existence. This concern becomes apparent when he defines the world not primarily by means of the notion of (the regularities of) nature, but as the reality in which we live. The notion of God and God's action are primarily oriented towards the human existence, and towards the realization that it is without God, according to Bultmann. Hence, we cannot see or find God there. Futhermore, the wonder, as God's action, is not objectively accessible, but hidden, non-objectified, and not related to what we can observe in the world.[4] Thus, Bultmann defines God's action as something that does not take place in the world of common experience—and hence, it cannot ground faith or provide it with any warrants. This, of course, have profound consequences for how he considers resurrection, as well. It is not something that takes place in the world of human experience. The following quote illustrates his point:

> Es gibt also nur ein Wunder: das der Offenbarung. Das aber bedeutet: Offenbarung der Gnade Gottes für den Gottlosen, Vergebung. Aber streng verstanden als Ereignis, nicht als eine Idee von Vergebung, ein Gedanke von der Gnade Gottes als zum Wesen Gottes gehörig, sondern als Gottes Tat.[5]

---

1. See Bultmann, "Zur Frage des Wunders," 214.
2. Bultmann, "Zur Frage des Wunders," 216.
3. Cf. Bultmann, "Zur Frage des Wunders," 219.
4. Bultmann, "Zur Frage des Wunders," 219.
5. Bultmann, "Zur Frage des Wunders," 221.

Faith is required for the recognition of the revelation, and revelation is the only wonder for Bultmann. Revelation is, accordingly, realized only because of a shift in human existence and its orientation. To try to see revelation or wonder as something that is under human control, or not the result of God's own action, is to remain in a sinful state.[6] Accordingly, we can reinterpret Bultmann's position on resurrection as a wonder as one in which the main emphasis is on how revelation as an instance of Firstness not only appears as unconditioned, but also how the elements of Secondness that other authors discuss extensively (AJ/VJ and ET) are rendered as irrelevant for theological reasons. What counts is what they imply with regard to understanding God as active.

Bultmann's hermeneutics is, as is well known, close to the Heideggerian understanding of human existence. Implied in Heidegger are certain pragmatic elements, i.e., elements that underscore how what primarily matters is what things mean for us and for our practices and our existence, and not "objective facts" that we can relate to in a more distanced fashion. If we take Heidegger's position as a clue to interpret Bultmann from a more pragmatic angle, there are two elements that present themselves as relevant with regard to the understanding of the resurrection. First, that it is dependent on a specific, non-necessary interpretation with abductive character, and second, that this interpretation has a pragmatic effect with regard to how those who make it conduct their lives. With these elements in mind, consider the following quote:

> Das Handeln Gottes ist nicht sichtbar, für einen Beweis nicht erreichbar; die Heilstatsachen können nicht demonstriert werden, der Geist, mit dem die Gläubigen beschenkt werden, kann nicht objektiv betrachtet werden; halten wir fest, dass wir von dem allen nur reden können, wenn es uns um unsere eigene Existenz geht. Dann kann gesagt werden: Glauben ist ein neues Verständnis der persönlichen Existenz. Anders ausgedrückt: Gottes Handeln verleiht uns ein neues Verständnis unserer selbst.[7]

In this quote, if we consider the event of the resurrection as God's action, we can agree with Bultmann that this is not possible to reach or to prove in any way. Nevertheless, if we do understand the resurrection thus, it has profound consequences for our lives, or, to say it with Bultmann, for our

---

6. Cf. Bultmann, "Jesus Christus und die Mythologie," 173: "Das Handeln Gottes ist jedem Auge verborgen ausser dem Auge des Glaubens. Nur die sogenannten natürlichen, weltlichen Ereignisse sind für jedermann sichtbar und dem Beweis zugängig. In ihnen aber findet Gottes verborgenes Handeln statt." See also 180.

7. Bultmann, "Jesus Christus und die Mythologie," 181.

existence. It reshapes and reorients our attitude towards ourselves and the world. However, we can also agree with Bultmann that the actual action of God in the events that take place with Jesus is not possible to observe directly. All instances of Secondness that is (abductively) interpreted as God's actions are not necessary, not something that can be demonstrated beyond questioning. Hence, it is also possible to agree with Bultmann when he writes the following:

> Wir können diese Behauptung paradox nennen; denn was Gott in Jesus Christus getan hat, ist nicht eine geschichtliche Tatsache, die geschichtlich bewiesen werden kann. Der objektive Historiker als solcher kann nicht sehen, dass eine geschichtliche Person, Jesus von Nazareth, das ewige Wort, der Logos, ist. Aber ausgereichet die mythologische Beschreibung Jesu Christi im Neuen Testament macht es klar, dass wir Person und Werk Jesu Christi auf eine Weise sehen müssen, die nicht in die Kategorien passt, durch die der objektive Historiker die Weltgeschichte versteht, wenn anders Person und Werk Christi als die göttliche Heilstat verstanden werden müssen. Das ist ein echtes Paradoxon. Jesus ist eine menschliche geschichtliche Person aus Nazareth in Galiläa. Sein Werk und sein Schicksal geschehen in der Weltgeschichte und fallen als solche unter die Untersuchung des Historikers, der sie als Teil des fortlaufenden Geschichtsfadens verstehen kann. Dennoch kann solche isolierte geschichtliche Untersuchung dessen nicht innewerden, was Gott in Christus getan hat, nämlich des eschatologischen Ereignisses.[8]

Nevertheless, there are issues to discuss in relation to Bultmann's position as stated here. First of all, he defines as eschatological that which happens in the life of Jesus as the result of God's action. What he does *not* affirm, though, is that these eschatological events take place in history and are rooted in history. Hence, he establishes a split between the world of human experience as the realm in which all humans participate, and the eschatological existence of faith that is only accessible in faith. It is against this backdrop that he also places the resurrection as something that does not belong to human history, and instead sees it as an eschatological event that is no more than a specific way to interpret the cross of Christ. Hence, the resurrection is for him only the result of a decision for a specific *interpretation* of other events—it is not itself considered an *event*. However, according to him, if it is not understood as an eschatological event, we fall back into what Bultmann calls mythology,

---

8. Bultmann, "Jesus Christus und die Mythologie," 185.

i.e., ways of describing events that make what happens objects of understanding, and something under human (sinful) control.

Although Bultmann's position exhibits specific elements that can be analyzed by the tools we have presented in the introductory chapter, he nevertheless develops a specific theological conception for the interpretation of New Testament texts that makes it hard to assess these with regard to what the *events* they portray can be said to have of theological significance. Historical events are, in his view, not theologically significant as anything but the spark for existential decisions that must leave the historical "behind" in order to serve a theological function that cannot be discredited as objectifying. Hence, for Bultmann, the de-mythologizing of texts is a necessary condition for his existential interpretation of the same texts. De-mythologizing implies that the texts can and must be interpreted as something else than reliable accounts of what has taken place in history. Their actual function must be identified as something different: as the proclamation of the Gospel of forgiveness, that can only be responded to in the faith that does not base itself on uncertain, controversial, or discussable historical events. As a consequence, Bultmann's position is one that would make the discussion about the historical basis, conditions, and context of *resurrection* faith unnecessary or superfluous. The reason is simple: it is only in the Word of God, or in the proclamation of the Gospel, that it is possible to identify the resurrection. Klaus Kienzler summarizes it thus:

> Der gekreuzigte und auferstandene Christus ist ausschließlich im Wort der Verkündigung präsent. Dieses Wort, das Kerygma, ist für Bultmann die einzige, nicht hinterfragbare Positivität des Offenbarungsgeschehens. Das Wort von der Einheit von Kreuz und Auferstehung ist Postulat des Wortes Gottes selbst, das jedem Verstehen zuvorkommt. Dieses Wort Gottes ist für die eschatologische Einheit der beiden Heilsereignisse in einem solchen Maß konstitutiv, daß das Kerygma zum Geschehen von Kreuz und Auferstehung mit hinzugehört. Mit anderen Worten: das im Osterereignis entsprungene Wort der Verkündigung gehört selbst zum eschatologischen Geschehen. Zum einen gründet das Wort der Verkündigung im Ostergeschehen, zum anderen wird das Ostergeschehen selbst so worthaft, daß Bultmann davon spricht, Christus sei ins Kerygma auferstanden.[9]

As becomes evident from Kienzler's analysis, Bultmann's juxtaposition of *kerygma* and history places the resurrection indubitably at the side of the

---

9. Kienzler, *Logik Der Auferstehung*, 61.

kerygma, and thereby, it is no longer necessary to consider it as an event that is part of human history independent of this *kerygma*.[10]

Wolfhart Pannenberg[11]

Pannenberg's position on the resurrection of Jesus can be seen as a reaction to that of Bultmann and dialectical theology. Pannenberg is critical of both demythologizing and of the existential interpretation, but he also affirms that there is an eschatological dimension to the resurrection that cannot be ignored, and which calls for both exploration and interpretation. However, his framework for doing so is totally different from Bultmann's.[12]

Similar to Bultmann, though, Pannenberg also presupposes a specific theological position with regard to how he understands historical events. However, where Bultmann separates *kerygma* and history, Pannenberg seeks to unite the two, insisting that history cannot be separated from its interpretation. Pannenberg sees the possibility for such a unity in his concept of "universal history," which is the frame within which all events find their meaning and significance, and which is the place where God is at work. Unlike Bultmann, Pannenberg holds that this history is accessible not only for those who believe in God: instead, he underscores how all humans share the realm of history. It is, however, God who is the principle of unity for this history. Of course, we cannot know yet what is the outcome of history, but the central role that Jesus's resurrection takes on in Pannenberg comes to service here: *In the resurrection, the end of history is already anticipated.*[13]

Against this backdrop, the understanding of universal history for Pannenberg allows him to consider particular events. Therefore, he can also consider in detail the historical evidence for the resurrection, understood as a historical event within the framework of universal history. It is notable

---

10. Cf. Carnley, *Structure of Resurrection Belief*, 13: "Rudolf Bultmann [holds] that the Easter faith of the disciples is primarily a subjective response to the Easter kerygma with no clearly objective content. In this case the resurrection is not to be spoken of or described as an event of the objective order. It can only be spoken of in the most equivocal sense as the event in which the disciples came to faith in response to the address of the raised Christ who is said to be 'present to the believer' in so far as his address is heard in the church's ministry of proclamation. It is not to be talked about as an objective occurrence by employing one's discursive reason, but the living Word of the raised Christ is to be responded to in an individual decision of will."

11. A good and updated summary of Pannenberg's position on the resurrection can be found in Wenz, *Introduction to Wolfhart Pannenberg's Systematic Theology*, 152–55.

12. Pannenberg discusses Bultmann's position critically in several places, but see especially his discussion in "Hermeneutic and Universal History."

13. See Pannenberg, "Die Auferstehung Jesu," 207–25.

that he thus places the event of the resurrection (because he is convinced that it is a historical event) within the parameters of the shared history of humankind. He sees the traditions related to ET and the VJ as independent strands of tradition. None of them is considered legendary. A critical and careful consideration of these strands and their possible alternative explanations points in the direction of the resurrection as the most probable explanation for the emergence of the Christian church.

Thus, Pannenberg's understanding of the resurrection is intimately connected to his understanding of history and of God. He cannot accept that belief in the resurrection is merely statements of what he calls anthropological convictions, i.e., statements about how one understands one's own existence, as is the case in Bultmann. Furthermore, as many have pointed to, his development of the implications and the plausibility of the resurrection of Jesus is mediated not only by the eschatological convictions of his own times but also by the fact that "the phenomenology of the human being, in general, reveals that he or she projects existence beyond death."[14]

Pannenberg is highly critical toward excluding God from the public understanding of reality. Such an exclusion, as he sees it, eliminates the possibility of the resurrection of a dead person *a priori*.[15] However, as he sees it, this exclusion relies on prejudice that has consequences for how one considers the textual evidence of the Easter tradition. He writes: "The negative judgment on the bodily resurrection of Jesus as having occurred in historical fact is *not a result* of the historical-critical examination of the Biblical Easter tradition, *but a postulate* that precedes any such examination."[16]

How does Pannenberg himself understand the event of the resurrection? He seems to admit that there are different ways to understand it, although he is also very clear on how it is *not* to be understood:

> If we talk about "resurrection" in terms of a metaphor for some sort of spiritual encounter with dead persons, or with their image, after their death, it is a very different matter from talk about a bodily resurrection of a person, though the idea of body itself is open to a range of different interpretations. In one sense, bodily resurrection can be taken to mean the revivification of a corpse as we have it in John 11:43ff. It can also mean, however, the transformation of the dead body into a different form of bodily life, and this seems to be indicated in many places in Paul's letters. It can also mean, finally, that the spirit of

---

14. Thus Macquarrie, *Jesus Christ in Modern Thought*, 326.
15. See Pannenberg, "History and the Reality of the Resurrection," 64.
16. Pannenberg, "History and the Reality of the Resurrection," 64.

the dead is invested with a different body, and there arise different opinions on the extent to which this new body is related to the former one.[17]

As we can see from this quote, Pannenberg lists different ways to understand the resurrection, among which he instantly rejects those who would see Jesus's resurrection as analogous to encounters with dead persons. In light of how such appearances have been reported,[18] it is striking that he rejects this interpretation without any argument, and also that he lists the other options (resuscitation, transformation, and re-incarnation of spirit in a new and different body) without any further mentioning of them.

Paul's report of his own visionary encounter with Jesus is often assumed to be similar to the appearances in visionary experiences to Peter, and "on that basis it could be conjectured that the reality of Christ that was perceived in those early experiences was of a spiritual nature without any necessary connection with the dead body of the crucified Jesus."[19] However, Pannenberg does not consider this to be the best solution, given the other elements in Paul's writings that describe this event. He claims that it is clear that Paul's understanding "of resurrection and of the new life issuing from the raising of the dead was connected with some idea of bodily existence though with a different kind of such existence."[20] Moreover, Paul also emphasizes the parallel between Jesus's resurrection and the resurrection that is implied in the Christian hope for all of humanity.

However, Pannenberg seems here to rely on what Paul writes, and hence, about how he understands these phenomena, but he does not move beyond this into the reality of what is actually taking place or how it can be verified beyond the textual evidence. E.g., it is not clear how what Paul called the "spiritual body" of Christ is related to the present bodily reality of human life (flesh).[21] Paul speaks of how "our present earthly life will be 'transformed' into the new imperishable life that has become manifest first in Jesus' resurrection," and thus, he suggests a continuity from the old life to the new one, "a continuity that consists in the process of transformation itself." However, Paul also speaks about the replacement of the old body with a new. He concludes:

---

17. Pannenberg, "History and the Reality of the Resurrection," 66.
18. See for these Allison, as referred to in sec. Appearances below.
19. Pannenberg, "History and the Reality of the Resurrection," 67.
20. Pannenberg, "History and the Reality of the Resurrection," 67.
21. This topic is discussed further below in light of M. Welker's criticism of N. T. Wright's position on the resurrection. See Part II, 1 Corinthians 15, sec. A Transformed Body or Another Body?

Paul, then, does not seem to have sensed an important difference or even contradiction between the idea of one form of body replacing the other and the idea of a transformation of the present body into another form of life. But taken by itself, the idea of replacement is different from transformation. It would allow for the mortal body to decay in the tomb while another one will be provided by the creator God in the future.[22]

Hence, we see in Pannenberg a willingness to nuance the possible ways to interpret the appearances of Jesus and to ground these appearances in experiential conditions. However, as becomes clear instantly, this raises questions with regard to continuity, transformation, and/or replacement. Nevertheless, *the body* is at the center of all this. This center is not without significance since it is by means of being a living body that humans are humans. This needs to be underscored in the case of Jesus and in the case of the rest of humanity alike: God is, in the resurrection, not making anyone into anything else than a human being. The emphasis on bodily resurrection can, therefore, be seen as the necessary condition for both being human and for being recognized as a human (and not as a ghost or some spiritual being). Bodily resurrection is therefore also an affirmation of humanity.

Unless one stresses the point about bodily resurrection in the interpretation of Jesus's resurrection, Jesus could have been understood to have taken on a new, "'spiritual' form of existence that would have nothing to do with his former body decaying in his tomb."[23] According to Pannenberg, this interpretation of the bodily resurrection "would render it possible to conceive of Jesus' resurrection and of the one the Christian believers look forward to in strictly parallel terms." However, there are elements in the historical evidence that makes such a close parallel between Jesus's resurrection and the future resurrection of humankind more complicated: the story about the empty tomb, which it is not probable to assume in a similar manner with humankind as with Jesus.[24] This point notwithstanding, the VJ interpreted as Jesus resurrected seems to be made more plausible by the ET, as it is the connection between VJ and ET in the claim about the resurrection that makes it possible to state continuity with regard to the body and thereby maintain the identity of Jesus before and after Easter.

Against the backdrop of what was said above about the prejudices that determine historical research, Pannenberg holds that the story about the empty tomb needs to be taken more seriously than has been often the case.

---

22. Pannenberg, "History and the Reality of the Resurrection," 68.
23. Pannenberg, "History and the Reality of the Resurrection," 68.
24. Pannenberg, "History and the Reality of the Resurrection," 68.

He also holds that "there is a general historical consideration suggesting the historicity of the empty tomb."[25] He goes on: "It seems inconceivable, under such circumstances, to imagine the situation of the earliest Christian proclamation of Jesus' resurrection at Jerusalem, the place of Jesus' crucifixion, without assuming that all parties knew that his tomb was empty."[26]

At this point, Pannenberg is careful about the limits of the argumentative power of the observation of the empty tomb. It never provided the decisive evidence of Jesus's resurrection. However, without the empty tomb, the Christian proclamation of Jesus's resurrection at Jerusalem of all places would have been in serious trouble, because it could have been easily falsified by just pointing to the place where Jesus had been buried. Accordingly, Pannenberg seems to hold that the empty tomb was, at least, a *necessary condition* for the claim about Jesus as resurrected (CR).

Exactly this premise has been addressed critically by Ingolf Dalferth. He holds that the confession of the resurrection is not something that seeks to explain or offer reasons for the empty tomb; it is the other way around: the empty tomb is among the reasons why there is a confession of the resurrection. This also means that there could be other reasons why the tomb was empty: one does *not* have to assume a resurrection in order to explain that fact.[27]

Moreover, Dalferth asks if the empty tomb is the only possibility from a *theological* (and not a historical) point of view for assuming the resurrection of Jesus.[28] He interprets Pannenberg as if he thinks that is the case.[29] But as Dalferth himself approaches this problem from a distinctively theological point of view, he first points to how it was never the case that Christians confess that Jesus did come back to *this life* in a sense that meant that his body was resuscitated. The point is that Jesus was raised by God and lives with God. Furthermore, only when the identity of Jesus was linked to his earthly body would it be inconsistent to speak of resurrection and a tomb in which there still was a body in the process of corruption.[30] But the Christian faith does not imply that: Christians assume that their bodies will be subject to decay and that this will have no impact on their resurrection. So also in the case of Jesus, if Jesus died a death like ours. If it was impossible that Jesus's body was still in the tomb despite his resurrection, then it

---

25. Pannenberg, "History and the Reality of the Resurrection," 69.
26. Pannenberg, "History and the Reality of the Resurrection," 69.
27. Dalferth, "Volles Grab, Leerer Glaube?," 395.
28. Dalferth, "Volles Grab, Leerer Glaube?," 395.
29. Dalferth, "Volles Grab, Leerer Glaube?," 396.
30. Dalferth, "Volles Grab, Leerer Glaube?," 396.

would be much harder to argue that we can expect a future resurrection like Jesus'. "Wäre die Verwesung seines Leibes ein hinreichender Grund, Gott an seiner Auferweckung zu hindern, dann wäre das auch bei uns so; und ist die Verwesung unseres Leibes kein hinreichender Grund, Gott an unserer Auferweckung zu hindern, dann gilt das erst recht für Jesus."[31]

It is important to note that Dalferth does not argue against the historical possibility that the tomb could have been empty. What he intends, is to show that it is not necessary to assume the ET in order to maintain the Christian faith in the resurrection. The point is that the topic of continuation of personal identity cannot rely on an identity with the dead body, be it for Jesus or for others. He argues that from a theological point of view, such identity must be seen as constituted by an act of God, and not by the history that our body undergoes.[32] As we shall see later, this is a mode of reasoning that may fit well with our suggestion about seeing the resurrection as the result of the graceful agency of God in order to fulfill human nature.

Dalferth's conclusion is therefore that it is not *necessary* for Easter that the tomb was empty. For the witnesses to the appearances (AJ), even if the grave was full, they would still have two contradicting experiences: Jesus was dead—Jesus appeared to them as alive. The fact that the tomb was occupied would have contributed to the first of these experiences, whereas it would make the second even more provocative.[33]

On his part, Pannenberg argues that it is necessary to show "that the Jewish community of that time in history could conceive of a resurrection from the dead without being concerned with what happens to the dead body" if the message about the resurrection should appear as plausible in the given context. "It must be judged extremely implausible that the Christian congregation at Jerusalem proclaimed Jesus' resurrection while his body was resting in his tomb."[34]

Nevertheless, writes Pannenberg, "Given the fact that the issue of the empty tomb is at best of secondary importance in the overall question of the resurrection of Jesus, because the basis for the Christian proclamation of the risen Christ is provided by his appearances to those who in consequence of that experience became his apostles, the heat of the debate about the empty

---

31. Dalferth, "Volles Grab, Leerer Glaube?," 397.

32. Dalferth, "Volles Grab, Leerer Glaube?," 398. In our view, though, this cannot mean that our life-story is irrelevant or neglected when it comes to its role for the constitution of our identity. See below, on the discussion of resurrection, illness, and disability. We take Dalferth's point to be that the identity of the human in the resurrection nevertheless is something that would not be without the initial act of God.

33. Dalferth, "Volles Grab, Leerer Glaube?," 399–400.

34. Pannenberg, "History and the Reality of the Resurrection," 70.

tomb and the particular bias of criticism against that story is astonishing."[35] Here, he seems to downplay the role of the ET for the CR, because he sees the CR as rooted primarily in the visions. However, that does not mean that the ET is without significance for how the resurrection life of Jesus, as well as his followers, is understood. The ET significantly reduces the possibilities of spiritualizing interpretations of the Christian Easter message. Instead, one needs to consider it as based on some form of transformation of the old life into something new. However, at this stage there appears to be a difference, nevertheless, between Jesus and his followers: it is only in the case of Jesus, however, that the two conceptions [spiritual vs. transformative event] present a clear alternative, because of the short time between his death and resurrection.[36] In order to say what happens with the rest of humanity, Pannenberg becomes speculative in a way that moves far beyond what there are resources for in the writings of the New Testament.

In the case of the Christians whose bodies decayed in their graves and whose earthly lives are preserved only in the eternal memory of God, the issue is different. There, the transformation occurs through the participation of whatever is remembered of our earthly lives in the life of God's eternal life, and when a new life of their own is given to them, it will be something entirely new. Hence, in any event, there is a lack of analogy at this point between the content of the Christian hope and the resurrection of Jesus, supposing it is to be understood as related to his empty tomb.[37]

Pannenberg supplies these considerations with a further reflection in which he seems to admit to the abductive character in the inference from the observations to the claim about the resurrection. He says: "How that event occurred was not observed by anybody then, according to the Biblical tradition, and it certainly surpasses our imagination at present." Then, he adds, notably, "But this cannot provide a sufficient reason for objecting to its historicity."[38]

Finally, Pannenberg connects the above reflections to what we presented initially as his understanding of history. Moreover, what he says can also be seen in relation to Schulz's considerations about miracles as something that must be seen as events caused by God. He writes:

> Accepting the affirmation of Jesus' resurrection as an event in history on the one hand, and the role of historical reason on the other, can go together, if the concept of history allows a place for

---

35. Pannenberg, "History and the Reality of the Resurrection," 70.
36. Pannenberg, "History and the Reality of the Resurrection," 70.
37. Pannenberg, "History and the Reality of the Resurrection," 71.
38. Pannenberg, "History and the Reality of the Resurrection," 71.

God in the reality of historical processes. God's power can bring about what exceeds the limitations of our human knowledge at a given time. Still this does not mean that affirmations on past events should be accepted without historical examination.[39]

In other words: the acceptance of the CR is not excluding the possibility of a critical examination of the biblical sources. We shall see how this critical scrutiny comes to expression in the following four theologians that have considered the evidence for the resurrection and its implications. Furthermore, this also means that the "otherness of the eschatological reality of the resurrection" does not exclude the resurrection of Jesus from being a *historical* fact.[40]

Peter Carnley

Anglican theologian Peter Carnley stirred considerable debate when he published a book on the resurrection some decades ago. In his study, Carnley argues that the resurrection is the center of the Christian faith in Jesus and that it is primary to other elements, like the doctrine on the incarnation. Accordingly, he argues that the resurrection is "more than the final episode and climax of the story" and therefore fundamental for the Church, its worship, and its theology as well. He points especially to how the resurrection makes it possible to perceive the contemporary presence of the raised Christ. "Resurrection theology is, in turn, the foundation of all theology in the sense that secondary affirmations of belief are drawn from it concerning Christ's messianic role and divine status. Eventually, this leads on to incarnational talk of God's sending of his Son into the world," he argues.[41] Hence, the resurrection has both logical and temporal priority over "incarnation talk" and in the evolution of faith, because it "marks the historical beginning

---

39. Pannenberg, "History and the Reality of the Resurrection," 71.

40. See Pannenberg, *Systematic Theology*, 2:361: "Theological interest in the assertion of the historicity of the resurrection of Jesus, as of his incarnation, depends on the fact that the overcoming of death by the new eschatological life has actually taken place in this world and history of ours." Along similar lines, Pannenberg also rejects a theological argumentation that objects to the possibility that the resurrection could be a historical event, since the resurrection manifests the beginning of a new aeon. Such an argument, Pannenberg claims, makes it impossible to see the resurrection as a historical event of this world at all and implies that "there is no justification for affirming Jesus' resurrection as an event that really happened, if it is not to be affirmed as a historical event as such." See *Jesus—God and Man*, 96.

41. Carnley, *Structure of Resurrection Belief*, 8.

of the telling of the Christian story."[42] He quotes Walter Künneth who claims that "the Resurrection is the primal datum of theology."[43]

Carnley rightly points to the importance of the *doctrine* of the resurrection (and hence, not only to the historical dimension) for a Christian understanding of other matters, including Christ's person.[44] However, his emphasis on the importance of doctrine does not imply that he leaves the historical questions out of sight: "Indeed, it was primitive resurrection faith which initiated the various attempts of the early Church to express its understanding of the uniqueness of Jesus' person. What had happened to Jesus, what God had done to and for him and, indeed, for the world, preceded talk of who he was and how it was that the divine was united to the human in him."[45] Carnley furthermore points to how it was more central for the early church's understanding of Jesus that he had been resurrected than it was to develop a Christological account about his incarnation.[46]

As one can see from the above, Carnley is concerned with how one articulates and understands the resurrection within the church context. He therefore also warns against approaches to the resurrection that "resort to such a wholly abstract and altogether too complicated understanding of the Easter experience as to remove it from the comprehension of those who comprise the majority of the community of faith."[47] The resurrection must be possible to articulate in ordinary language and in relation to ordinary perception, "without generating an esoteric vocabulary of highly technical terms or defining the Easter experience in such a rarefied way as to deny access to it to all but those acquainted with the most up-to-date existentialist theory."[48] In order to meet these challenges, he points to three interrelated elements that determine his own approach:

From a methodological point of view, Carnley holds that it is insufficient, although not totally unhelpful, to only address the different biblical authors way of redacting their stories about the resurrection. "We need to

---

42. Carnley, *Structure of Resurrection Belief*, 8–9.
43. Carnley, *Structure of Resurrection Belief*, 9.
44. Carnley, *Structure of Resurrection Belief*, 5–6.
45. Carnley, *Structure of Resurrection Belief*, 6.
46. Carnley, *Structure of Resurrection Belief*, 6.
47. Carnley, *Structure of Resurrection Belief*, 22.
48. Carnley, *Structure of Resurrection Belief*, 22. The criticism implied here is most likely directed against Bultmann. However, it could also be read as a warning against employing the theoretical framework we have presented in the previous chapter when one addresses the resurrection in the context of preaching and doctrine: The theories above are for philosophical use only, and not to be part of the ecclesially employed vocabulary about the resurrection.

try to penetrate behind the redactional *ikonastasis* upon which these doctrinally didactic images are hung to grasp the structure of the experience of Easter faith itself. We may attempt this by seeking to uncover the more primitive experience behind the developed redactional presentations in a history-of-traditions study of the narratives."[49]

Carnley also finds it important to "recognize the limitations of the critical historical method normally used in the exegetical work of redactional criticism." By stating that, he opts for a position in which he is open to the fact that the Easter event may elude what a redactional-critical study of the narratives can contribute, "precisely because the Easter reality is not amenable to treatment purely by the scientific methods of historical research of the kind that such a study necessarily relies upon." Furthermore, "It may be that the reality of the raised Christ must be approached with additional conceptual tools and from a different perspective or set of perspectives." Thereby, he not only acknowledges the need for a variety of approaches to the resurrection, but he also underscores what we have identified as the relative indeterminacy of the event, or what Marion would claim when calling the resurrection a saturated phenomenon: "This is because the multidimensional richness of the Easter event, its uniqueness and transcendence, will simply not permit it to be handled with critical-historical methods alone. Indeed, as critical-historical research spreads its net around the raised Christ to capture and 'have' him, he, passing through the midst of it all, will 'go his way.'"[50] He thereby also points to the ambiguity of the event, since on the one hand, "the resurrection appears as a historical event which invites treatment with normal tools of critical-historical research; from another it appears as an other-wordly [sic!] event, defiantly awesome and inscrutable."[51]

Accordingly, it becomes quite clear that Carnley presupposes, at least for the sake of argument, that Jesus did, in fact, rise from the dead. We need to take note of this presupposition, as some of what he writes can be taken to imply otherwise. However, it is also clear that Carnley does not consider the resurrection to be only a historical event: there is something at stake in this case that eludes the grasp of historical investigation. Therefore, he also finds that "attempts to handle the resurrection purely as a historical event are destined to appear pathetically inadequate; the raised Jesus, precisely because he is raised, is no longer available for handling simply by the normal

---

49. Carnley, *Structure of Resurrection Belief*, 23.
50. Carnley, *Structure of Resurrection Belief*, 23–24.
51. Carnley, *Structure of Resurrection Belief*, 24.

methods of historical and scientific enquiry appropriate to the understanding of historical and natural occurrences of this world."[52]

Carnley is not alone in recognizing the insufficiency of a mere historical approach. It is striking that most of the authors we discuss in this chapter argue for a combination of systematic, hermeneutic, and historical perspectives (especially Bultmann, Pannenberg, and Allison). How they articulate these additional perspectives are nevertheless varying to a large degree. Carnley himself articulates the additional dimension based on a presupposition of the "eschatological uniqueness" of the event, which implies that "we must begin to speak theologically and not just historically."[53]

What Carnley points to here is notable: he holds that theological language opens up dimensions with regard to the resurrection that is not possible by a mere historical approach. His concern for how the resurrection affects the continuing life of the church in worship and mission means that he sees the need for "various images and models of the resurrection; "each with its own method of approach and, of course, each with its own limitations."[54] It is the combination of the different approaches that are of importance here since none of them can do the job alone. "By trying to hold various models together we shall see that each goes some way towards reducing the Easter mystery to a measure of comprehension by illuminating a different aspect of it, whilst the Easter reality transcends them all."[55]

Finally, Carnley points to the task of systematic theology in articulating Christ's living presence with his people. It is by means of the systematic approach that one can see how "faith in principle has access to an object of present experience from the point of view of those of us who live in the temporal framework of history. This means that the structure of our experience of faith and what is both presupposed and implied by our claims to know the presence of Christ is not an irrelevant theological datum."[56] Hence, the contemporary relevance and implications of resurrection faith are part of what needs to be explicated in order to understand what it means and how it affects the present believer's mode of being in the world, thus addressing the pragmatic implications of the resurrection implicitly. Carnley therefore also warns against a mere past-centered apologetics for the historicity of the resurrection.[57]

52. Carnley, *Structure of Resurrection Belief*, 25.
53. Carnley, *Structure of Resurrection Belief*, 25.
54. Carnley, *Structure of Resurrection Belief*, 25.
55. Carnley, *Structure of Resurrection Belief*, 26.
56. Carnley, *Structure of Resurrection Belief*, 26.
57. Carnley, *Structure of Resurrection Belief*, 27.

Against the backdrop of the here reported concerns, Carnley then enters into a critical analysis of different contributions to the topic of the resurrection in past decades. We cannot go into all his analyses here, but there are some notable elements that are of specific relevance to our overall argument.

Carnley addresses with good reason how "theological defenders of the Easter faith have, at least until very recently, done their work in the belief that they possessed a reasonably clear idea of what it was they were defending." Despite the recognition of the mysterious dimensions of this event, which presumably go beyond human capacities of understanding, the contention they have defended was that the resurrection of Jesus was a historical event which had actually occurred in the past, at a particular point in time and at a given place.[58] It is based on this presupposition that the modern discussion about the veracity of the CR has developed: "Whilst the theologian took up the challenge to explain and defend the propriety and reasonableness of the Church's resurrection belief in the face of the sceptic's doubt and criticism, both theologian and sceptic were agreed that they were arguing about the occurrence or otherwise of a historical event which could be pinned down both temporally and geographically, just like any other historical event." The issue at stake is then simply to be put thus: did the resurrection of Jesus actually happen?[59] It is within this context that we can see the contributions from Pannenberg, Wright, and Allison we discuss in the present volume, whereas there have also been developments in modern theology that have tried to develop other approaches that do not rely so much on the historical issues, such as Bultmann and Barth. Carnley addresses challenges in both these camps.

With regard to the historical approach, Carnley distinguishes, as we do, between the three different components of the faith in the resurrection: CR, ET, and VJ. With regard to ET, he critically discusses some of Pannenberg's historical arguments for it, especially where he bases his argument on the empty tomb story as a *sine qua non* for the success of the early proclamation. This argument presupposes that the ability of early Christians to assent to the truth of the Easter proclamation depended precisely on the inability of their Jewish opponents to produce the grave with the body of Jesus still in it. In other words, the historicity of the empty tomb is not said to be given credence because the disciples could not originally have believed without it, or because they could not have even conceived of the resurrection of Jesus without it, but because they could not have continued to believe without it.[60]

---

58. Carnley, *Structure of Resurrection Belief*, 32.
59. Carnley, *Structure of Resurrection Belief*, 32–33.
60. Carnley, *Structure of Resurrection Belief*, 54.

Why is ET central in this context, then? Because it would be easy to silence the CR and those who were committed to it by producing Jesus's body. Pannenberg thus argues that "it is not so much that the historicity of the empty tomb is logically necessary to the primitive Christian conception of the resurrection, but that it is practically necessary for the continued assent to the validity of Easter claims." Here, he relies on Paul Althaus's claim that the resurrection kerygma could not have been maintained in Jerusalem "if the emptiness of the tomb had not been established as a fact for all concerned."[61]

Carnley sees three problems with this line of reasoning:

a. The arguments rely "on the presupposition that the early proclamation cannot be conceived, except anachronistically, without implicit acceptance of the empty tomb."

b. It furthermore "relies on the additional pre-supposition that the proclamation of the Easter message in Jerusalem 'not long after Jesus' death' was in fact soon enough after his death to allow for the possibility of finding and positively identifying a tomb as the one in which Jesus' body had been placed. It would also have had to be soon enough to allow for the positive identification of a body as certainly that of the dead Jesus."

c. However, "Even if the content of the early proclamation was of such a kind that the production of the body in the tomb would have been an ultimately devastating factor, the success of the early proclamation may possibly have been guaranteed by the fact that, by the time the Easter message got from Galilee to Jerusalem, the exact location of the tomb could not be traced."

d. Finally, "The gospel assurance that the women noted the place of burial may well represent an apologetic answer to the Jewish charge that they had perhaps gone to the wrong tomb, rather than a factual report of their original observant attention to detail and tenacious memory."[62]

We shall see below when we discuss N. T. Wright that he is of a different opinion than is Carnley with regard to these matters. Carnley himself draws the careful conclusion from the above list of reasons that the arguments that defend the historicity of the ET because it was the *sine qua non*

---

61. Carnley, *Structure of Resurrection Belief*, 54. The quote from Althaus is taken from Carnley.

62. Carnley, *Structure of Resurrection Belief*, 55.

for the truthful proclamation of the Easter kerygma, fall short of proof.⁶³ He questions the argumentative structure of Pannenberg's approach since he seems to rely on arguments that focus on the necessary conditions for the successful proclamation of the Easter Gospel. "None of these arguments, however, is capable of dismissing the alternative possibility that the story was generated by faith for a kerygmatic, apologetic, or perhaps even liturgical reason."⁶⁴

On the other hand, Carnley emphasizes more strongly than does Pannenberg the arguments in favor of the primitiveness and essential historicity of the empty tomb tradition that depends on the "undisputed fact that women rather than men feature in it as witnesses." Women were not qualified to supply reliable testimony, and accordingly, any invented story, whether for kerygmatic, apologetic, or liturgical purposes "would have furnished the scene at the tomb with male witnesses whose testimony would have been held to be beyond dispute." This is an argument that Pannenberg does not consider.⁶⁵

So, what can be concluded from the ET experiences, if they took place? Carnley argues that the capacity that these experiences with regard to warrant an inference like "Jesus must have been raised from the dead is, to say the least, somewhat problematic. In other words, the inference from 'what was seen' to the conclusion that Jesus must have been raised from the dead does not follow with logical necessity."⁶⁶ This is hardly surprising, given the relative indeterminacy of this at the level of Secondness, and the fact that in the realm of experiences, nothing can be said to happen with logical necessity. Hence, Carnley here seems to overstate his case. When pointing to the ambiguity of the evidence, he claims that it has to be overcome at two levels,

---

63. Carnley, *Structure of Resurrection Belief*, 55.

64. Carnley, *Structure of Resurrection Belief*, 58.

65. Carnley, *Structure of Resurrection Belief*, 59. Cf. also 141: "It is very pertinent to observe at this point that Paul may have omitted mention of women in his list of primitive witnesses to the resurrection in 1 Cor. 15, precisely because he understood the concept of kerygma in the sense of a bearing witness to what happened that is of a kind with that belonging in a law court, where women were denied the ability to give evidence. The exclusion of women from the list of witnesses would mean that Paul did, after all, understand the primitive kerygma as testimony. It is the proffer of evidence to be considered and assessed, and the proclamation (cf. 1 Cor. 15:11 and *kēryssetai* in v. 12) of the resurrection is proclamation in the sense of bearing witness to an event whose occurrence is to be inferred from the evidence of testimony." See the discussion of 1 Cor 15 above in Part II.

66. Carnley, *Structure of Resurrection Belief*, 61. "Even if the historicity of the story of the arrival of the women at an empty tomb were to be conceded, as it was in later Jewish polemic, it is possible to explain it in a variety of other ways, which is precisely why the Jews are able comfortably to remain Jews to this day!"

which both seem to fit with how we have discussed the semiotic character of the resurrection earlier:

> First, the ambiguity of the evidence concerning the bare occurrence of the event of finding the tomb empty has to be overcome. We cannot assume the historicity of the tradition [. . .]; Pannenberg's own attempts to prove it do not succeed. Second, once the bare historicity of the emptiness of the tomb is said to be secured, the ambiguity of its meaning has still to be overcome so that it is interpreted as evidence of nothing else except the resurrection. The best we can do is conclude that the assertion of the resurrection of Jesus is one possible interpretation of the available evidence. *The story is a sign*, which alerts us to the possibility that Jesus was raised.[67]

Carnley's careful considerations and conclusions concerning ET are therefore articulated in a way that keeps the field open for a diversity of different approaches. Whereas he, on the one hand, holds that "there is insufficient evidence to deny categorically that the tomb was found empty," he also holds that the evidence is insufficient "to prove beyond all doubt that it was found empty." Moreover, and fully in accordance with our previous line of reasoning, we cannot prove beyond doubt "that the emptiness of the tomb can have resulted only from the raising of Jesus by God."[68] Nevertheless, the story of the empty tomb continues "to raise the possibility of the resurrection in our minds and offer itself for our puzzlement."[69] This is due to the last point he identifies; that the story is a sign in need of interpretation.

Turning then to the appearances (VJ) and their role in the overall argument, Carnley makes a careful analysis in which he not so much addresses the question about the character of these appearances as their framework of interpretation and the way Pannenberg argues on the basis of this framework. Carnley holds that there is a fundamental confusion in Pannenberg's theology. It comes to the fore in the way he develops the argument for the historicity of the resurrection. As we have seen, his understanding of universal history as the interpretative context for everything that happens means that he is critical towards notions about a unique redemptive history known through faith. Universal history, in which also the resurrection takes place, is accessible through the exercise of reason and the use of the historical method. Essential for the thrust of Carnley's criticism here is that

---

67. Carnley, *Structure of Resurrection Belief*, 61. My italics.
68. Carnley, *Structure of Resurrection Belief*, 61.
69. Carnley, *Structure of Resurrection Belief*, 62.

Pannenberg insists that historical knowledge is logically prior to faith as trust. However, it is here that the problem arises, according to Carnley:

> Yet, for all his emphasis both on the fact that faith cannot make certain what the historical evidence is itself unable to establish, and on the impartial nature of the historical judgement upon which faith is based, Pannenberg admits that the resurrection of Jesus is not even highly probable, unless one first believes in "the resurrection of the dead" in general and in principle. With this prior belief in the general resurrection of the dead, the historical evidence becomes confirmatory and satisfactory in the specific case of the resurrection of Jesus.[70]

In his criticism of Pannenberg, Carnley seems to overstate Pannenberg's position in the direction of him intending to offer a final proof for the resurrection. However, as he himself writes, Pannenberg's claim is that the resurrection of Jesus *may be* historically demonstrated (our emphasis). The important thing in his argument, as we read him, is that Pannenberg thereby places the question about the resurrection within the frame of human history, and does not declare it as some inaccessible eschatological event. However, such an approach does not preclude that the evidence is somewhat ambiguous and inconclusive, but instead must be seen to imply that point. When Pannenberg then points to how the evidence at hand "only led to resurrection faith for those who entertained a prior apocalyptic belief in the future general resurrection of the dead," this is not, as Carnley holds, a point where Pannenberg attempts to "'prove' the historicity of the resurrection of Jesus by considering the Easter tradition of empty tomb and appearances in the light of the eschatological hope of a general resurrection of the dead."[71] Instead, it is what he (Pannenberg) points to as the accessible context of interpretation that offers plausibility for this interpretation of the events. We, therefore, consider Carnley's criticism of Pannenberg for somewhat overstated, when he writes that

> Despite his methodological commitment to approaching the resurrection as a historical event via the methods of critical historical research, he in the final analysis admits that it must be understood as an eschatological event, to be apprehended by being placed in the context of eschatology in the specific form of apocalyptic expectation. Instead of faith (trust) and dogma being based squarely upon knowledge arrived at by reason, the resurrection is placed in the context of eschatological faith. This

---

70. Carnley, *Structure of Resurrection Belief*, 91–92.
71. Carnley, *Structure of Resurrection Belief*, 91–92.

entails that the facts of history are approached from a particular perspective and the partiality of faith in God.[72]

Furthermore, when Carnley argues that Pannenberg holds that, in order to believe in the resurrection of Jesus, we must accept the broad contours of what Jesus himself accepted, this seems to be an exaggeration as well. It is also not in accordance with how Pannenberg throughout his theology underscores the controversial character that belief in God entails. Hence, to claim that "the apocalyptic belief in the End, the general resurrection of the dead, and final Judgement" is what is concomitant with the belief in the resurrection, because it was due to the pre-understanding which comprised these elements "that the early Christians interpreted their experience of the appearances as the 'resurrection' of Jesus,"[73] is to go too far.

Carnley seems nevertheless to be right when he points to how belief in the resurrection requires some kind of prior faith in a specific framework of interpretation, although this needs not be fully developed and/or articulated beforehand. It does not, however, mean that one has to believe in the resurrection in order for it to be a resurrection, but it is *what* you believe with regard to the interpretative context for ET and VJ that determines *how* these elements can be seen as a basis for the CR. Thus, faith is needed prior to affirmation of the resurrection. When Carnley discusses these matters, he, therefore, argues that "the resurrection is hardly the historical foundation of faith; it is a further extension of a pre-existing faith."[74] This claim seems apt, but it does not necessarily imply that the conclusion is given with the premises contained in the framework of the interpretation. Carnley thus seems to overlook the abductive character in the inference, which makes it more problematic to state that "the argument is from faith to faith and is thus circular."[75] What seems apt, though, is to maintain that the belief in the resurrection rests on a prior established belief in God, and that without such belief in God (and more specifically: the God that Jesus proclaimed) there would be fewer chances for making the abductive inference that Jesus was resurrected by God.

The most important critical point in Carnley's criticism of how Pannenberg deals with the instances of the VJ, is that Pannenberg seems to be "arguing that the appearances could not be interpreted in any other way, given the early Christians' prior belief in the general resurrection of the dead." If he is right in this, it follows that contemporary believers must entertain a

---

72. Carnley, *Structure of Resurrection Belief*, 92.
73. Carnley, *Structure of Resurrection Belief*, 92.
74. Carnley, *Structure of Resurrection Belief*, 92–93.
75. Carnley, *Structure of Resurrection Belief*, 93.

prior belief of a similar kind, based on the apocalyptic hope of a future restoration to life. Carnley concludes that, "Clearly, this seems to call for some general kind of faith as a presupposition of resurrection belief."[76] But that it is a necessity for contemporary believers is not apparent: it is, e.g., possible to see the VJ as something that is in analogy with other similar visions,[77] and still maintain a belief in the resurrection that is based on the ET. However, we also need to underscore that the actual presence of belief in a general resurrection at the time of Jesus is not something that makes the interpretation of the ET/AJ easier: also Jesus's contemporaries knew that dead do not live again, and they, as well, had no obvious experiential context to interpret what happened, as we saw in Marion in the previous chapter.

Hence, although Pannenberg commends the evidence of the resurrection to reason, his line of reasoning nevertheless displays the need for a context of interpretation, in his case provided by faith and dogma. Carnley sees this as a circular argument, and to some extent that is right. However, the circularity involved here differs from cases where one believes that the resurrection cannot take place and interprets the evidence accordingly. As long as we operate within the context of abductive reasoning, such types of circularity seem to be, if not unavoidable, at least something that may occur.

The main question necessary to answer in order to solve this problem is if the faith assumptions operate in the context of discovery or in the context of justification. At this point, neither Pannenberg nor Carnley seems totally clear, although Carnley seems to presuppose that Pannenberg operates within the context of justification. We would argue for the other option: when someone believes that the resurrection is an instance of the apocalyptic faith, this faith provides the context of discovery. However, to justify that this is a likely interpretation, one has to move to the context of justification, in which historical reasoning also has its valid use.

Carnley concludes the treatment of Pannenberg's argument for the resurrection by highlighting the importance as well as the ambivalence related to viewing it as a historical event which resembles any other historical event of the natural order. Although the first experiences that led to the conviction that Jesus had been raised from the dead and exalted to heaven, were experiences in space and time, there are other elements that are not so easy to place within such parameters. The resurrection of Jesus also involves "a transformation and glorification of his body, appropriate to its new eschatological mode of existence," and this is not similar to any other event of history. In the latter case, the category of "historical event" is of

---

76. Carnley, *Structure of Resurrection Belief*, 93.
77. For such an approach, see Allison, *Resurrecting Jesus*, discussed below.

limited use. Carnley draws two conclusions from this: a) "the historicity of the resurrection cannot be proved in the way that any other event might in principle be proved to have occurred," and b) "we cannot even understand exactly what the resurrection was if we seek to deal with it only in terms of the category of 'historical event.'"[78]

The problems connected to the establishment of historical warrants for the resurrection faith led the two main representatives of dialectical theology, Rudolf Bultmann and Karl Barth, to develop alternative lines of reasoning, in which the attempts to ground this faith in history appeared as *theologically* problematic. Carnley discusses their positions as an alternative to the historical line of reasoning represented by Pannenberg. Thus, he aims to show two things: First, that it is necessary to go beyond the line of historical reasoning in order to ease out the theological significance of the resurrection, and second, to show that such historical grounding is nevertheless necessary, also from a theological point of view.

Carnley describes Barth's position as one in which there is no appeal to historical reasoning. On the other hand, the methodological presuppositions which are shared by Barth and Bultmann make it almost impossible for them to resolve the impasse that has developed between them. Instead of appealing to the concept of mystery in the theological approach to the resurrection, Carnley says that "Barth came to accept a somewhat naive and uncritical, one might almost say crudely realist, portrayal of the appearances in material, bodily terms." However, there is no line of historical reasoning for this approach, either. Instead, there is a kind of naïve reading of the scriptures here:

> His only defense is that the Word is not quite equivalent to a surface reading of the words, but lies "behind" them and that the Holy Spirit's task is to illuminate the meaning so that the believer comes to a right understanding of them. That Easter involved an objective appearance of Jesus is asserted by Barth because this is what rings out from scripture as he hears it, with the illuminating help of the Holy Spirit.[79]

For both Barth and Bultmann, their theological decisions seem to be based in other elements than historical research—and thus, there seems to be even more reason for criticizing them for letting faith ground faith than is the case in Pannenberg. That "Easter involved an objective appearance of Jesus is asserted by Barth because this is what rings out from scripture as he hears it, with the illuminating help of the Holy Spirit." As for Bultmann, he holds

---

78. Carnley, *Structure of Resurrection Belief*, 94.
79. Carnley, *Structure of Resurrection Belief*, 127–28.

that the kerygma calls for decision and that the Holy Spirit moves to faith—
"but nothing rings out from scripture about an object of faith over against
him. He just hears a call to obedience."[80]

Thus, Barth and Bultmann base their positions more on a dogmatic understanding of how the Scriptures work as the Word of God. The relevance of historical investigation for the understanding of the resurrection is sidelined, although within different theological frameworks. Despite his affirmation of the need for at theological explication of the resurrection, Carnley is therefore quite critical to how they handle the issue. This is so since they, unlike him, do not see the need for elaborating the topic (resurrection) in a way that combines historical and theological reasoning. He writes:

> Certainly, pending the illumination of the Holy Spirit, and without a historical analysis of the Easter traditions, we are left somewhat in the dark as to what it was that led the disciples to begin the Easter proclamation. Barth and Bultmann cannot really tell us, for even as men of faith, they have to admit that it remains mysterious: only the Holy Spirit can illuminate us. How can we know that the truth as we perceive it bears the authorization of the Holy Spirit? To argue that the word is self-authenticating does not explain anything for the assurance that we shall know the truth as truth when it comes to us rings a little hollow when two theologians claim that what is heard as the alleged self-authenticating revelation in their own case, is entirely different.[81]

Accordingly, Carnley points to how these positions, despite their difference, nevertheless seem to end up with arbitrary results, theologically speaking. It is, therefore, no surprise that he questions their point of entry to the discussion about the resurrection. Although he recognizes that it may be appropriate to address the soteriological content of the resurrection based on faith, he nevertheless questions the "systemic exclusion of critical-historical enquiry in favor of a freestanding, independent faith, as a response to grace and which is alleged to be inimical to critical-historical

---

80. Carnley, *Structure of Resurrection Belief*, 128.

81. Carnley, *Structure of Resurrection Belief*, 128. "Bultmann rejects all attempts at description on the ground that objectifying discourse is in principle illegitimate. Even primitive talk about an object of faith is myth, to be demythologized rather than historically analysed in quest of the most primitive kernel. But Barth also refuses to use historiographical techniques to sift through the early witness in order to separate what seems to be the earliest and most reliable account of what happened from later developments of the tradition. Somehow he thinks the Holy Spirit can bypass this sifting so that each individual believer 'gets the intended message' as to the general nature of the event." Carnley, *Structure of Resurrection Belief*, 130.

investigation." Moreover, he asks if "it is equally inappropriate to use the methods of critical-historical research on the traditions to try to determine what the primitive Easter experience was claimed to be?"[82]

It is worth noting here that the fundamental presupposition for Carnley's critique of Barth and Bultmann rests on the assumption that there is some kind of historical core, or some type of foundational experience, on which the CR is based. Against this backdrop, it makes sense that he claims the necessity for a logical distinction of what the resurrection experience was like, as "distinct from the questions of whether it was God who caused it and what it achieved for man's salvation."[83]

Carnley's line of reasoning here, and his concomitant critique of Barth and Bultmann, then lays the groundwork for an analytic approach that accepts that, on the one hand, "the scientific historian cannot without faith enter upon an answer to these latter two questions." However, on the other hand, "it is not equally clear that faith is a prerequisite in order to understand the claims of the early Christians and to try to interpret what they were talking about."[84] In other words: the texts cannot simply be accepted in faith and taken at face value if one wants to be able to "reach back to the nature of the original Easter experience and the first understandings of the object experienced." Carnley holds such critical investigation of the texts "not only valid but essential," and thereby he positions himself over against Barth and Bultmann, for whom such criticism seems irrelevant for resurrection faith.[85]

At this point, we can see clearly how the line of abductive reasoning from the experiences of ET and VJ to the CR fits with Carnley's way of thinking. The historian can, at best, say something about the likeliness of the two first components, but the last one is one that adds to and goes beyond secular reasoning. Hence, he accepts that "the secular historian cannot explain the divine cause or the salvific repercussions of the resurrection in terms of theological categories, and may not be able to prove its occurrence," but this is not the same as a rejection of the historian's qualifications for offering "a descriptive analysis of the primitive witness in his attempt to come to the clearest possible understanding of the nature of the early experience."[86]

Carnley, therefore, holds that the CR is grounded in experiences that took place in human history and that this historical dimension cannot and

---

82. Carnley, *Structure of Resurrection Belief*, 129.
83. Carnley, *Structure of Resurrection Belief*, 129.
84. Carnley, *Structure of Resurrection Belief*, 129.
85. Carnley, *Structure of Resurrection Belief*, 129.
86. Carnley, *Structure of Resurrection Belief*, 130.

should not be excluded on theological grounds. If this is not possible, we are not able to say anything about the nature of these experiences. Accordingly, he lists a range of different theological judgments that nevertheless require historical criticism:

a. to prove that it was alleged to be an event having a particular nature;
b. to prove that it was constituted by alleged experiences of one specific kind rather than another;
c. to prove the occurrence of the event;
d. to prove that it was an event that was caused by God;
e. to prove that it was an event having soteriological repercussions.[87]

With this list, Carnley contributes to the analytical transparency that is necessary if we are to combine theological and historical reasoning about the resurrection. In the list above, one would not expect a secular historian, on the basis of the available evidence, to have success with (d) and (e). The reason is apparent: according to him, to establish answers to these elements would presuppose faith. (In our view, however, one could ask instead if it would not be just as adequate to say that one could test different hypotheses in order to explore which one would provide the most coherent interpretation.)

In the case of (c), Carnley holds that the evidence is not sufficient to prove the occurrence of the resurrection. This does not, however, imply that he rejects its possibility. But he argues that the fragmentary and inconclusive nature of the evidence, as well as the fact that men normally do not rise, calls for this conclusion of insufficiency. Hence, he is less convinced by the historical evidence than, e.g., N. T. Wright, G. Habermas, and W. Pannenberg are. Furthermore, he adds to this point that "even before we seek to establish the truth or otherwise of the claim that it occurred, we are logically obliged to know what 'it' was and it is here that the methods of the historian may not be either in principle illegitimate or entirely inadequate. It is not self-evident that the historian can in principle have no success in relation to (a) and (b)." Thus, the findings of the historian are relevant when one seeks "to provide answers to questions concerning the nature of the original Easter experiences."[88]

The consequence of this line of reasoning, which Carnley openly admits, is that resurrection faith needs to acknowledge that it rests on an insecure foundation, historically speaking. A theological approach that ignores

---

87. Carnley, *Structure of Resurrection Belief*, 131.
88. Carnley, *Structure of Resurrection Belief*, 131.

this fact ends up in a type of arbitrary subjectivism. However, this also has the effect that faith in the resurrection requires an abductive decision that goes beyond the historical, but without leaving it behind. Another way to state this point is to say that even though faith rests on abductive reasoning, it is necessary that there exist some premises for this abduction unless its result is going to be a simple assumption out of thin air, inseparable from mere wishful thinking. Faith as abductively developed needs some premises unless it is to be blind or arbitrary.

The commitment of faith, therefore, cannot ignore the historical evidence, but it also cannot base itself merely on it. Belief in the resurrection has to ground itself on something more: not only on the acceptance of the witnesses but on the fact that this event somehow makes sense of the whole story that the New Testament tells. Therefore, it is not surprising that also those who emphasize the historical evidence as important for resurrection faith (like Pannenberg), must point to the eschatological character of the event in order to commend assent to it. The abductive inference that accepts this character implies that the theological meaning of the historical events requires *faith*. Nevertheless, Carnley rejects the position "that historical enquiry, therefore, has no place whatsoever in the structure of resurrection belief. Even if the evidence, as we have seen, is insufficient of itself to prove the occurrence of the resurrection, the historical assessment of it may nevertheless raise the possibility of the 'resurrection of Jesus' in some sense of the term 'resurrection.'"[89]

We leave Carnley's study at this point. There are three important things that we can take away from his analysis: a) He points to the ambiguity of the historical evidence for providing us with a firm conclusion with regard to the CR claim, but nevertheless also argues that it is not excluded by this evidence. b) He insists on the need for a combination of historical and theological reasoning if we are to understand what the resurrection is all about. c) He is open about the fact that it is necessary to establish some kind of clear notion about *what we are talking about when we speak about the resurrection if such talk is to have any meaning.*

N. T. Wright

N. T. Wright's monumental *The Resurrection of the Son of God* presents and discusses most of the material that is relevant for a historical consideration of the resurrection. This book is also one in which it becomes clear how the decisions of the interpreter about which contexts of interpretation are

---

89. Carnley, *Structure of Resurrection Belief*, 144.

suitable shape the approach to the resurrection. Against this backdrop, it is worth noting that Wright investigates several ancient contexts for the claim about the resurrection of Jesus. Accordingly, themes treated in the chapters "Life beyond death in ancient paganism," "Death and beyond in the Old Testament," and "Hope beyond death in Post-Biblical Judaism" provide elaborations of different background beliefs that can shed potential light on the understanding of what took place with regard to how the resurrection of Jesus of Nazareth was interpreted. Some of this variation in approaches can be seen as the result of the relative semiotic indeterminacy of the instances of Secondness (visions, empty grave) since these make it so difficult to determine what the adequate interpretative horizon of these elements can be (in case such determination is possible at all). Thus, both the historical and the theological framework for interpretation are not a given.

From a systematic point of view, we need to say from the outset that there is something insufficient in an investigation that focuses on what people have believed in a different context and under different circumstances. There are two questions that then easily fall under the table: *why* they believed what they did—and: are these beliefs something that we can still identify reasons for upholding in the present world? It should be noted, though, that Wright does address these questions to some extent in the last sections of his book, which are the parts on which we will focus our attention.

In other words: there must be a common horizon of experiences that can make it possible to understand why they believed what they did in the ancient world, and make plausible to what extent these are reasons that can still be identified as accessible by us; i.e., as reasons and warrants that can make sense of experiences today.

Exactly here, the resurrection presents us with difficulty because of its presumably unique character. But precisely what this uniqueness consists in, we cannot decide unless we have determined its hermeneutical horizon.

Wright refers to ancient and modern examples of visions of dead humans (as he says: plenty of them), but he infers from this simply that these are visions that indicate that these persons are dead, not that they were alive when they appeared.[90] Hence, he seems to dismiss this as actual examples for the interpretation of the resurrection faith. As we shall see in the next section, this dismissal is challenged by Dale C. Allison Jr.

The main thrust of Wright's argument, from the point of view of systematic theology, is the following: Wright distinguishes between *necessary* and *sufficient conditions* for the belief in the resurrection. A necessary

---

90. Wright, *Resurrection of the Son of God*, 691.

condition is something that has to be the case for the conclusion to follow, whereas a sufficient condition is something that will with necessity bring about the conclusion.[91] He is thereby able to ask to what extent the empty tomb and the appearances of Jesus can be seen as *sufficient* conditions for the rise of early Christian belief; and what should be seen as *necessary* conditions for this faith. Wright's conclusion is that "the combination of the empty tomb and the appearances constitute, with qualifications, a sufficient condition for the rise of the early Christian belief." Furthermore, "with more substantial qualifications, they also constitute a necessary condition."[92] The qualifications he makes are important because they imply that he is not presenting any arguments that are in themselves necessary (like a mathematical proof). He nevertheless argues that when everything is taken into consideration, the conclusion of his argument goes "well beyond historical possibility to high probability."[93] He brings this distinction into play when he considers the following seven elements that need consideration with regard to the conditions for the resurrection:

Wright holds, firstly, that his historical investigation makes clear that "the early Christian beliefs were conceived and formulated within the context of second-Temple Judaism." Accordingly, he sees these beliefs as something that "makes sense as a mutation from within one well-known position on the Jewish spectrum," despite the fact that there are no other positions similar to the one that can be identified as the result of this "mutation." However, he notes that the early Christians themselves point "to the strange stories at the end of the four canonical gospels" when they are asked why they believe what they do. "The tomb was empty, they say (being careful to let us know that it was certainly the tomb in which the dead Jesus of Nazareth had earlier been buried), and they saw him alive, talked with him, and ate and drank with him."[94] What is notable in this point, is that Wright here implicitly argues that it is not the context of second-Temple Judaism that provides the most basic arguments for the belief—the belief is based on the *events*, whereas the interpretative resources for the events are found by the believers in that specific context. From an analytical point of view, that is important to take note of, although in practice, it may be impossible for the first believers to separate their experiences from the interpretative resources that make sense of them.

---

91. Cf. Wright, *Resurrection of the Son of God*, 733.
92. Wright, *Resurrection of the Son of God*, 734.
93. Wright, *Resurrection of the Son of God*, 734.
94. Wright, *Resurrection of the Son of God*, 734.

Wright furthermore, and secondly, argues that "Neither the empty tomb by itself, however, nor the appearances by themselves, could have generated the early Christian belief."[95] Hence, he considers what we have so far called ET and AJ/VJ from the point of view of the distinction between necessary and sufficient conditions, and holds that neither of these, taken in isolation, can be said to contribute anything sufficient to warrant the CR. An empty tomb would in itself have proved nothing for neither Jews nor pagans, and its appearance would also not be seen as a confirmation of the resurrection since not even the disciples seem to have expected it. "The empty tomb is by itself insufficient to account for the subsequent evidence."[96]

AJ/VJ, or "Meetings" with Jesus, as Wright calls them, could also "by themselves have been interpreted in a variety of ways." With regard to this phenomenon, Wright points, rightly, to how widespread the visions and appearances of recently dead people are. Accordingly, he recognizes that "such 'seeings,' even such 'meetings,' occur and that people have known about them throughout recorded history, there should be no question."[97] He nevertheless seems to downplay the frequency of such meetings, without offering any argument for why.[98] He also points to how such meetings normally do not involve physical contact, or the dead person eating and drinking. However, even if such meetings "involve seeing, touching, or even eating and drinking with the recently dead person," if these were meetings with someone possible to identify as Jesus, "they could not possibly, by themselves, have given rise to the belief that Jesus had been raised from the dead. They are a thoroughly insufficient condition for the early Christian belief."[99] He goes on:

> The more "normal" these "visions" were, the less chance there is
> that anyone, no matter how cognitively dissonant they may have

---

95. Wright, *Resurrection of the Son of God*, 734.

96. Wright, *Resurrection of the Son of God*, 735. Wright discusses a possible counterexample to this approach by referring to John 20:8, where it is not the empty tomb, but the grave-clothes that are seen as a sign of what had happened. As he interprets these details, the conclusion he draws is not compromised: "an empty tomb, by itself, could not have functioned as a sufficient condition of early Christian belief in Jesus' resurrection." Wright, *Resurrection of the Son of God*, 735.

97. Wright, *Resurrection of the Son of God*, 736.

98. Wright quickly dismisses Riley, *Resurrection Reconsidered*, but is not looking thoroughly into other disciplines and materials that seem to suggest that at least 40 percent of modern-day humans have had such experiences, sometimes also including touch and physical contact, which he seems to pass by too quickly. For a more favorable approach to these phenomena and their relevance for the assessment of the AJ/VJ, see the sec. on Allison, below.

99. Wright, *Resurrection of the Son of God*, 737.

been feeling, would have said what nobody had ever said about such a dead person before, that they had been raised from the dead. Indeed, such visions meant precisely, as people in the ancient and modern worlds have discovered, that the person was dead, not that they were alive. Even if several such experiences had occurred, if the tomb was still occupied by the dead body they would have said to themselves, after the experiences had ceased, "We have seen exceedingly strange visions, but he is still dead and buried. Our experiences were, after all, no different from the ones we have heard about in the old stories and poems."[100]

It is evident from this line of argument that Wright is aware of these phenomena, but that he considers their occurrences as something that would provide a context of interpretation of the VJ that would make these "normal." However, if we take into consideration the context of interpretation that he pointed to in the previous point, then it would not be totally irrelevant to think of Jesus as resurrected, given the many occurrences of him after his death, and the fact that some of these also seemed to involve touching and eating and drinking. Combined with the experience of the ET, it does not seem impossible that the many AJ/VJs could in themselves lead to the inference that Jesus had been resurrected. This case is made even stronger if we consider the counter-argument to Wright's position that can be developed on the basis of Paul's vision of Jesus. Wright holds that it is highly likely that Paul knew at least that the followers of Jesus claimed that his tomb was empty.[101] This provides his own visions of Jesus with an interpretative context "where at least the report of an empty tomb may be assumed."[102]

So far, then, Wright's line of reasoning suggests that it is the *combination* of the ET and VJ that makes the belief in the resurrection possible: "There seems to be a constant sense that 'appearances' by themselves have to be backed up with evidence that what was seen was a substantial body such as must have left an empty tomb behind it."[103] Thus, the combination is what makes the case, since "neither an empty tomb nor visual 'appearances'—however we categorize them—would be sufficient to generate the early Christian beliefs."[104] When seen in isolation, neither one of the VJs nor the ET is sufficient to account for the belief in the resurrection. It is when the two work together that it is possible to determine them as conditions for

---

100. Wright, *Resurrection of the Son of God*, 737.
101. Cf. Part II, 1 Corinthians 15, sec. No Empty Tomb?
102. Wright, *Resurrection of the Son of God*, 737.
103. Wright, *Resurrection of the Son of God*, 738.
104. Wright, *Resurrection of the Son of God*, 738.

the belief in it. "The point of the empty tomb stories always was that Jesus was alive again; the point of the appearance stories always was that the Jesus who was appearing was in bodily continuity with the corpse that had occupied the tomb. Neither, without the other, makes the sense that the early Christians believed they made."[105]

Against the backdrop of the previous points, Wright' third point rightly suggests the fact that "putting two insufficient conditions together, of course, guarantees nothing."[106] He argues that it nevertheless happens to be the case that two insufficient conditions, when put together, can produce a sufficient one. The VJ and ET in combination provide this possibility, he says. "From everything we know both of the second-Temple context and of the beliefs of the disciples about Jesus and his mission, we can be confident that if they discovered on the one hand that his tomb was empty, and found on the other hand that, for a while, they kept meeting him in ways which gave every appearance that he was dead no longer, but actually alive, the belief we have studied throughout the first two centuries of Christianity would certainly emerge."[107]

This is not an obvious and indisputable conclusion, though, as Wright himself points to. Not everyone did believe, despite the appearances and reports. Thus, to say that VJ and ET in combination "constitute a sufficient condition for the rise of the early Christian belief"[108] seems to be a long shot. Wright admits to this problem and modifies the claim in order to strengthen the claim: VJ and ET would be sufficient, he holds, for second-Temple Jews who had followed Jesus and were hoping he would turn out to be Israel's Messiah. Wright nevertheless argues that the fact that some did not believe is no argument against the fact that others found the VJ and ET a sufficient condition for them to believe in the resurrection.[109]

Before we proceed to the next point in Wright's line of reasoning, it is necessary to point out that a considerable part of his argument hinges on the beliefs of second-Temple Jews, although the resurrection belief is said to be a "mutation" of these, already existing, beliefs. Thus, the context which provides the interpretative context for the events VJ and ET is not so far brought into question—it is only admitted that it is one of several options. We note this point here, and will return to it later, as it shall turn

---

105. Wright, *Resurrection of the Son of God*, 738.
106. Wright, *Resurrection of the Son of God*, 738.
107. Wright, *Resurrection of the Son of God*, 739.
108. Wright, *Resurrection of the Son of God*, 739.
109. Wright, *Resurrection of the Son of God*, 740.

out to be very crucial for Wright's overall assessment of the arguments for the resurrection of Jesus.

Proceeding from the claim that the ET and VJ are, at least for some, a *sufficient* condition for the rise of the early Christian belief, Wright then, fourthly, asks if they are also a *necessary* condition. The procedure for determining if this is the case is to ask and consider if there are other conditions that could have produced the same belief. If that should turn out to be the case, what has hitherto been established by Wright as sufficient conditions would nevertheless not be possible to define as necessary conditions for resurrection belief.

At this point, our previous considerations about the range of contexts of interpretation come into play once more. Wright himself points to how "It will always be possible for ingenious historians to propose yet more variations on the theme of how the early Christian belief could have arisen, and taken the shape it did, without either an empty tomb or appearances of Jesus."[110] He goes on by addressing different topics that have bearings on this argument and can provide reasons for limiting the possible scopes of interpretation.

The first topic he addresses is the meaning of "resurrection." The point that in its cultural context, "resurrection" meant embodiment, is closely linked to the fact that historians with different attitudes towards the resurrection consider that the tomb must have been empty (in other words, that it is a necessary condition for the subsequent phenomena) in order to speak of it. Wright, therefore, concludes that "whatever else had happened, if the body of Jesus of Nazareth had remained in the tomb there would have been no early Christian belief of the sort we have discovered." Wright "therefore regard the empty tomb as a necessary condition (though by itself, as we have seen, an insufficient one) for the rise of the very specific early Christian belief."[111]

According to a similar line of reasoning, Wright argues that the appearances of Jesus are necessary conditions of the early Christian belief. They are a "necessary supplement to the discovery of the empty tomb; they provide the extra element which turns the first insufficient condition (the empty tomb) into a sufficient one."[112] Thus, it is the combination of ET and AJ/VJ that makes these sufficient as well as necessary conditions. The appearances of Jesus are therefore necessary for the belief in his resurrection.

---

110. Wright, *Resurrection of the Son of God*, 740.

111. Wright, *Resurrection of the Son of God*, 741. Cf. the discussion in the sec. on Pannenberg above, where Dalferth problematizes the underlying assumptions of this position.

112. Wright, *Resurrection of the Son of God*, 741.

Wright adds one more element to this line of reasoning, which relates to how the resurrection seems to imply some kind of transformation. Transformation implies not only continuity, but also changes, so that Jesus is seen not only as embodied but also as someone "whose body has unprecedented, indeed hitherto unimagined, properties."[113] He holds that it is "impossible to explain these pictures as fictional projections from early Christian theology." The best explanation at hand for these accounts is "that it was the appearances of Jesus that precipitated this transformation in the understanding of resurrection." Therefore, the language of "resurrection" is only possible to understand against the assumption that "early Christians believed they had clear evidence, against all their own and everyone else's expectations, both of continuity between the Jesus who died and the Jesus who was now alive and of a transformation in his mode of embodiment. Appearances of this living Jesus would have provided such evidence. Nothing else could have done."[114] Hence, Wright concludes,

> that the combination of empty tomb and appearances of the living Jesus forms a set of circumstances which is itself both *necessary* and *sufficient* for the rise of early Christian belief. Without these phenomena, we cannot explain why this belief came into existence, and took the shape it did. With them, we can explain it exactly and precisely. The other explanations sometimes offered for the emergence of the belief do not possess the same explanatory power.[115]

In order to substantiate these conclusions, Wright then, as a fifth element in his argumentation, enters into a lengthy discussion about alternative explanations of the belief in the resurrection. By doing so, he tries to move the discussion from a more open-ended approach that asks whether ET and VJ are "simply *one* thing that might have caused early Christian belief to arise, or is it the only thing that could possibly have done so?"[116] His conclusion to this discussion, for which we need not go into detail, is that the alternative approaches cannot account for the emergence of the belief in the resurrection—on historical grounds.[117]

---

113. Wright, *Resurrection of the Son of God*, 742. What this means, is nevertheless unclear.
114. Wright, *Resurrection of the Son of God*, 742.
115. Wright, *Resurrection of the Son of God*, 742.
116. Wright, *Resurrection of the Son of God*, 743.
117. We have briefly touched upon some of these alternatives in the previous sections of the present book.

Given the historical evidence, Wright, therefore, in his sixth point, concludes that it is "highly probable that Jesus' tomb was indeed empty on the third day after his execution, and that the disciples did indeed encounter him giving every appearance of being well and truly alive." Furthermore, "The empty tomb and the 'meetings' with Jesus, when combined, present us with not only a sufficient condition for the rise of early Christian belief, but also, it seems, a necessary one. Nothing else historians have been able to come up with has the power to explain the phenomena before us."[118]

There is one point in Wright's argument that is especially important to highlight for the present discussion: he holds that the order of faith and the warrants and explanations for it must be placed in a specific sequence: "The early Christians did not invent the empty tomb and the 'meetings' or 'sightings' of the risen Jesus in order to explain a faith they already had. They developed that faith because of the occurrence, and convergence, of these two phenomena."[119] Thus, given the kind of proof that historians normally accept, the case Wright makes for what generated early Christian belief "is as watertight as one is likely to find," he holds.[120]

The seventh and final step in Wright's line of reasoning opens to considerations that go beyond historical argument. It is constituted by the question about how it is possible to explain the two facts, the empty tomb and the "meetings"?

At this point, we need to introduce the distinction made earlier between the context of discovery and context of justification. As we saw, this distinction was employed by Peirce in order to explain in what contexts abductive reasoning is functioning. We have seen that Wright's line of

---

118. Wright, *Resurrection of the Son of God*, 752. One could ask, though, if this is not to stretch the argument too far: It is totally possible to consider the resurrection faith as an instance of coincidences. a) Jesus did appear, as others have done, after his death, in a mode that also was perceived as embodied (which is not unheard of in other contexts), and b) the tomb was empty, without there being any accessible explanation for this among the disciples. In the combination of the two, the resurrection faith emerged among them. This belief could be seen as both enabled by, and confirmed by, the context of second-Temple belief, as Wright emphasizes. The argument here suggested is not sufficient to represent an explanation of all the facts in need of such, though, but it can nevertheless make problematic the claim by Wright that there are no alternative routes for a historian to travel. Hence, necessity with regard to explanation is weakened. He remains entitled to comment, though, that "Almost nothing is ever ruled out absolutely; history, after all, is mostly the study of the unusual and unrepeatable. What we are after is high probability; and this is to be attained by examining all the possibilities, all the suggestions, and asking how well they explain the phenomena." Wright, *Resurrection of the Son of God*, 752–53.

119. Wright, *Resurrection of the Son of God*, 753.

120. Wright, *Resurrection of the Son of God*, 753.

argument so far has led to the abductive inference that the resurrection is the best accessible explanation of ET and VJ. Hence, he seems to see the CR as belonging in the context of justification of the beliefs, whereas the first Christians used the resurrection as the element that constituted the discovery of what had taken place. Accordingly, Wright's own argument bears witness to how the complex issues that are related to CR have moved from the original context where it was used as an interpretative concept for specific experiences, to a concept that presumably has the power to justify itself as the best possible explanation of what took place.

Against this backdrop, we can assess the overall conclusions of Wright's argument, which ends with the conclusion that nothing else explains ET and VJ "as thoroughly and satisfyingly as the bodily resurrection of Jesus."[121] The abductive inference he makes is therefore well stated in the following claim: "If Jesus was raised, with (as the early Christians in their different ways affirmed) a 'transphysical' body, both the same and yet in some mysterious way transformed, the two key pieces of evidence, the empty tomb and the 'meetings', are *explained*."[122]

A good deal of weight lies here on what Wright means by *explained*. One way to put it is to say that a resurrection is the most likely assumption about what happened. However, as long as the variable "resurrection" is not itself accessible or defined in a precise manner, one can ask if the abductive inference amounts to anything like an explanation in the strict sense, where one establishes and is able to demonstrate either a relation of origin, or of causation between *explanans* and *explanandum*. Wright's own admission of the fact that there is no strict proof here points in a similar direction, but is complicated by the fact that he also sees this as "watertight," as we saw in the quote above.[123]

There is more to say here with regard to the inferences that Wright points to as analogies: both in archeological and juridical inference, there are analogies that make a case likely, and which turns out to be confirmed by different types of corroborating evidence. In the case of the resurrection, though, there is no similar corroborating evidence: the reported instances of the ET and VJ are the only elements we have to rely on in order to make the CR. Furthermore, as Wright admits, "What we do not know—not

---

121. Wright, *Resurrection of the Son of God*, 757.
122. Wright, *Resurrection of the Son of God*, 757.
123. We therefore concur with Allison, *Resurrecting Jesus*, 347, when he comments that Wright's "apologetical moves really amount to evidence that demands the verdict he so relentlessly summons us to return. His argument, which puts more faith in historical reason than I can summon, does not and cannot raze all the arguments of those of a different view."

because we inhabit a modern scientific worldview, but because at this point all human history tells the same story—is that someone who is well and truly dead can become well and truly alive again."[124] Against this backdrop, we can formulate in a precise manner what the resurrection entails with regard to the relation between knowledge and belief: We know that dead people do not ordinarily rise from the dead. We also know that some believers claim that Jesus did. When Christians believe, they therefore believe in the reliability of the inferences that have caused the first believers to believe what they did. Accordingly, Wright can be read as defining the content of Christian faith when he writes: "The fact that dead people do not ordinarily rise is itself part of early Christian belief, not an objection to it. The early Christians insisted that what had happened to Jesus was precisely something new; was, indeed, the start of a whole new mode of existence, a new creation. The fact that Jesus' resurrection was, and remains, without analogy is not an objection to the early Christian claim. It is part of the claim itself."[125]

However, at this point we need to address the way Wright formulates the content of the resurrection belief: how is it possible to combine the two statements about Jesus coming to life *again* and the claim about his transformation. One of those who has addressed this topic critically is Michael Welker: Welker sees Wright's affirmation of the "still physical body" of Jesus as problematic with regard to the continuity and the transformation that is necessarily involved in the resurrection. His criticism seems to suggest that when Wright emphasizes the continuity in the way he does, his understanding of the resurrection comes close to resuscitation or reanimation. Accordingly, Welker also finds it problematic to speak of Jesus as "being alive again."[126]

Welker himself interprets the empty tomb as a withdrawal of the body of Jesus, in a way that does not do away with the ambiguities and the doubts that surround these stories.[127] This also has consequences for the disciples' ability to recognize him: "The pre-Easter body of Jesus Christ is withdrawn! For they all speak of the immense difficulty of the disciples to reidentify and recognize the resurrected Jesus. And this could not have been a problem if he had been 'thoroughly alive again'"[128]

---

124. Wright, *Resurrection of the Son of God*, 757.
125. Wright, *Resurrection of the Son of God*, 758.
126. Welker, "Wright on the Resurrection," 474.
127. Welker, "Wright on the Resurrection," 467–68.
128. Welker, "Wright on the Resurrection," 468. Cf. Part II, 1 Corinthians 15, sec. A Transformed Body or Another Body.

Similar to what we have repeatedly underscored above, the reports about Jesus's resurrection reports do not point to empirical experiences. The texts instead seem to stress the variety of appearances, the drawing away—to the point of disappearance at the moment of recognition. Thereby, "and by generally emphasizing the aspects of not seeing, not knowing, not daring to ask and doubt, these texts work constantly and in an extremely powerful way against the impression that here we have to deal with a mere reanimation," Welker holds.[129]

Against Wright's physical and literal interpretation, Welker holds that the resurrection cannot "mean that his biological body is 'alive again,' but rather his entire life which was borne by the biological and mental-spiritual body, but which now seeks and finds a new body for those and in those who witness to him, a new body to be the bearer of his earthly, historical existence." This is only understandable against the backdrop of "the connection between the life of the resurrected Christ and that of the pre-Easter, historical Jesus."[130]

Although Welker here insists on bringing the spiritual dimension more strongly than Wright seems to do, Wright as well here moves beyond the mere historical towards metaphysical questions: he holds that approaches that deal with the resurrection in terms of whether one accepts miracles or is open to the "supernatural" are misguided. He argues that the lack of analogies to Jesus's resurrection cannot be subsumed under such categories. Instead, he claims that what is at stake here is something else: "the direct question of death and life, of the world of space, time and matter and its relation to whatever being there may be for whom the word 'god,' or even 'God,' might be appropriate. Here there is, of course, no neutrality. Any who pretend to it are merely showing that they have not understood the question."[131] He develops this point in explicit criticism against post-Enlightenment historians, who "rule out, a priori, certain types of answer to questions that remain naggingly insistent."[132] Moreover, he sees the claim about the resurrection (CR) as a "socially, culturally and politically explosive force" that challenges "the holding apart of the mental and spiritual on the one hand from the social, cultural and political on the other." Accordingly, "To address the final historical question is to face, within the worldview model, not only questions of belief but also of praxis, story and symbol."[133] Thus, he reiterates a point we have

129. Welker, "Wright on the Resurrection," 470.
130. Welker, "Wright on the Resurrection," 471.
131. Wright, *Resurrection of the Son of God*, 758–59.
132. Wright, *Resurrection of the Son of God*, 759.
133. Wright, *Resurrection of the Son of God*, 760.

already made above: resurrection makes sense only when it is articulated as a belief in the God that Jesus proclaimed.

Without making it explicit in a comprehensive way, Wright here opens up to the pragmatic implications of resurrection belief, in a way that resonates with what we have suggested previously. He admits that resurrection faith is "self-involving." It has implications for the one who believes in it. The person who makes the statement about Jesus as risen "is committed to living in this different world, this newly envisioned universe of discourse, imagination and action" to which the resurrection opens.[134] For the one who believes it, it is life-changing, whereas the opposite is not the case: for the one who does not believe, the denial of such belief need not be crucial to his or her life and practice. This situation seems to lead to an impasse since it seems to involve a position on which there can be identified no neutral or common ground for the believer and the non-believer. Wright, however, counters this problem by using the story about Thomas in John 20 as a model:

> In the story, Jesus welcomes him and invites him to do what he wants, even though there is still a gentle rebuke in store. Neither circle, it seems, is closed. There is enough evidence to lure skeptics forward, even if they still have lessons to learn about how we know things as well as about what there is to be known. And the faith which, in its most mature form, might be happy to go forwards without either touch or sight, is after all a belief and trust not simply in otherworldly realities, but (for John of all people!) in the Word made flesh, which can be heard, seen and handled. The idea that faith must never have anything to do with history, so popular in certain circles for many years, is long overdue a decent burial.[135]

Wright seems, in this quote, to come close to Pannenberg, who also insists that historical realities are what faith is based upon, even when these are in principle unrepeatable. Thus, the CR rests on a historical challenge to other explanations and other worldviews. "Precisely because at this point we are faced with worldview-level issues, there is no neutral ground," and accordingly, to say that "'Jesus of Nazareth was bodily raised from the dead' is not only a self-involving statement; it is a self-committing statement, going beyond a reordering of one's private world into various levels of commitment to work out the implications."[136]

---

134. Wright, *Resurrection of the Son of God*, 760.
135. Wright, *Resurrection of the Son of God*, 762.
136. Wright, *Resurrection of the Son of God*, 763.

When it comes to the theological considerations that Wright makes on the basis of his considerations so far, we will return to those in the final chapter of this part of the book.[137]

Dale C. Allison Jr.

In his book on the resurrection, Dale Allison lists seven options for how to interpret the CR. They are as follows:

1. The orthodox interpretation as described here, predominantly in the analyses of Pannenberg and Wright: Jesus was raised bodily from the dead.
2. The CR rests on a misinterpretation of the events—e.g., the body could have been stolen, or Jesus was not really dead.
3. The CR is based on hallucinations.
4. The CR rests on deliberate deception by the disciples/authors of the Gospels.
5. The CR is based on genuine visions.
6. The CR is based on the belief in God's vindication of Jesus.
7. The CR can be explained as a combination of a rapid disintegration of the body plus visions.[138]

Allison's own treatment of the material ends up with an assessment that is close to the orthodox position. We will not here go into all of his critical discussion of the other alternatives. The primary emphasis will be on the reasons he offers for his own position. Emphasis will, therefore, be on where he stands out from the other writers treated so far. In that regard, it is especially notable that he is more open to some of the evidence having parallels in known experiences from other contexts. Thus, he contributes to an approach that allows for seeing some analogies between the ET and VJ, in a way that makes the experiential basis for the abductive inferences that constitutes CR less unique.

---

137. "There remains one final question, which is closely intertwined with the directly historical one. The early Christians declared that because Jesus had been raised from the dead he was 'son of god'. What did they mean by this? What light does this shed both on the historical question and on its meaning and results today?" For a critical discussion of Wright, see Welker, "Wright on the Resurrection," 458–75.

138. Allison, *Resurrecting Jesus*, 199–213 discusses these different options.

Allison first claims that the teaching of Jesus would be empty without the resurrection. Then his death would be a testimony to the failure of his message. He, therefore, suggests that although it might have been the case that a few of Jesus's closest followers would have continued to hope for his vindication, "a wider public would not have gone along." For this, Allison also offers parallel examples of failure.[139] He concludes this line of reasoning thus: "Without proclamation of the resurrection, probably only a few would have summoned the inner resources to reckon Jesus anything other than a false prophet, and so his cause might eventually have been lost to oblivion."[140]

To this first point, Allison adds a second, personal reason: if the resurrection happened, it would mean that "the Creator is not as indifferent and distant as appears to me." Accordingly, the resurrection would be a testimony to "an intervening God who, at least for a bit, cares more about making a point than keeping the so-called laws of nature" and "comes out of hiding for a moment to break the monotony of death and to do something truly wonderful, like happy endings, and this would be a very happy ending indeed."[141] He nevertheless adds to this remark that whom God have resurrected is a point of relevance here. God did not raise a random individual, but "precisely Jesus of Nazareth." Thereby, Allison adopts, on a personal basis, the more generic theological point that implies that in the resurrection, God endorses Jesus's character, and the values incarnate in him. He quotes John Austin Baker in order to make this point:

> The nature of existence is such that the only credible God is one whose values are those exemplified in Jesus. If Herod the Great had risen from the dead, this would not have been tolerable to reason as a testimony to God. For a God who ratified monstrosity might explain the evil in the world; he could never satisfy us as a source of goodness. But the God who ratifies the values incarnate in Jesus . . . can be seen as having a good purpose which gives meaning to the evil in the world.[142]

---

139. Allison, *Resurrecting Jesus*, 214. Accordingly, Allison sees the resurrection as the only possibility that could validate Jesus's teachings: "Unlike the wisdom sayings of Proverbs, Jesus' sometimes otherworldly, sometimes ascetical, often eschatological, often counterintuitive teachings—"Love your enemies," do not be "angry," "do not divorce and remarry"—are not self-validating. On the contrary, they are at every turn debatable." Allison, *Resurrecting Jesus*, 215.

140. Allison, *Resurrecting Jesus*, 214.

141. Allison, *Resurrecting Jesus*, 215–16.

142. Allison, *Resurrecting Jesus*, 216. The quote is from Baker, *Foolishness of God*, 278.

A further point of theological—as well as pragmatic!—relevance, is that to "believe in the non-metaphorical resurrection of Jesus is that this makes a compelling statement for the goodness of creation and so against *contemptus mundi*."[143] Thus, the affirmation of the resurrection is also a way in which one can counter those elements in the Christian tradition that "has too often denigrated the physical through an unbalanced Platonism." The resurrection is therefore also a recognition of the positive character of human embodiment and shows us a God who is caring for flesh and blood, of which there are no reasons to be ashamed.[144] This has profound consequences for the positive manner in which humans are called to affirm and enjoy the embodied character of their own existence.

The final initial reason Allison has for treating the idea of the resurrection sympathetically, is that the literal resurrection of Jesus "entails his surviving death; and hope for a life after this one is, despite all of modernity's objections to it, very near the center of my own faith."[145] To believe in a good God is hard to do if one "simultaneously disbelieve in a life beyond this one."[146] Thus, he can also see the emergence in early Judaism of a robust faith in an afterlife of rewards and punishments "as a way of maintaining belief in God's goodness and justice despite the agonies and unfairness of this world, a way of maintaining 'that even a mortal life of disprivilege can have meaning and value.'"[147]

There is a profoundly theological element in this line of argumentation that is worth noting since it implies that the idea about the resurrection has an impact on how we understand God. "God cannot be thought good in any authentic sense of that word if the world as it is, this desert in which so many briefly live, suffer, die, and are forgotten, is the alpha and the omega, the beginning and the end."[148] The resurrection is a testimony to the fact that God is as Jesus believed: profoundly good.

---

143. Allison, *Resurrecting Jesus*, 216.

144. Cf. Allison, *Resurrecting Jesus*, 217.

145. Allison, *Resurrecting Jesus*, 217.

146. Allison, *Resurrecting Jesus*, 217.

147. Allison, *Resurrecting Jesus*, 218. "The heartbreaks and horrors and injustices of this age cannot be squared with the doctrine of a consoling Providence unless all is not as it seems to be, unless there is something more than death and extinction." Allison, *Resurrecting Jesus*, 218.

148. Allison, *Resurrecting Jesus*, 218.

Appearances: Allison's Contribution

Against the backdrop of the theologically guided premises for affirming the resurrection referred above, there is especially one element in Allison's contribution that interests us, and which is not discussed to the same extent in the contributions of, e.g., Pannenberg or Wright, although they seem to be aware of this issue. The question is to what extent it is likely to consider what we have called VJ (or better, AJ: Appearances of Jesus) as without analogy. Much of what Allison presents on this topic seems to contradict the claim that these instances of VJ/AJ are unique and without real analogy.

Allison points to the fact that there are "many firsthand accounts of several people seeing at once the apparition of a person recently deceased." Given that appearances sometimes are considered as the result of hallucinations and only something that happens to individuals, such accounts seem to be more in consonance with the biblical witness. Similarly, he refers to the "innumerable accounts of various people seeing an apparition over an extended period of time."[149] From this, he infers that "the literature on visions of the dead is full of parallels to the stories we find in the Gospels," and he is, unlike other theologians, interested in finding out what it can mean—from a theological point of view.[150]

Allison is well aware of the fact that references to such experiences are not fashionable in scholarly circles.[151] He nevertheless holds that it is necessary to remain loyal to "the realities of human experience" and the

---

149. Allison, *Resurrecting Jesus*, 270. Another scholarly work that points to such events is Wiebe, *Visions of Jesus*.

150. This approach has not been appreciated by all contemporary scholars. Alkier, e.g., writes: "As in all analogical models, it is robbed of its absolutely unique specificity. The resurrected Crucified One turns into a dead man who makes contact with the living, like millions and millions of other dead men and women before and after him as well. It is precisely Allison's openness to other realities, as a historian of the New Testament thinking in terms of analogies—which rightly warns against cultural prejudices—that overlooks the eschatological uniqueness of and impossibility of analogy to the resurrection of the crucified Jesus of Nazareth and the cosmological dynamic bound up with it. By means of Allison's well-intended analogical approach, the Crucified One becomes a dead man among other dead men and women and the event of the resurrection thus loses its cosmological meaning and its soteriological power." Alkier, *Reality of the Resurrection*, 231.

151. Allison, *Resurrecting Jesus*, 271. "Putative encounters with the newly departed are, if not exactly everyday events, rather far-flung. The circumstance is often overlooked because, given our current cultural prejudices, many are discouraged from sharing their seemingly paranormal or mystical experiences, including seeming encounters with the dead—a circumstance that allows popular and uninformed stereotypes about so-called 'ghosts' to persist. People do not want to be stigmatized, to have others think them shackled to superstition." Allison, *Resurrecting Jesus*, 271.

studies from various parts of the world that "indicate that perceived contact with the dead is, however we interpret it, a regular part of cross-cultural experience."[152] He also recounts personal experiences and experiences of others to conclude that "we are indubitably dealing with a phenomenon about which generalizations can be made, regardless of the etiology one advances."[153] He also acknowledges that the gospels know about these analogies and that they try to refute them by referring to Jesus as eating, speaking, being touched—all of which would indicate that it was not a *ghost* that the disciples experienced.[154]

Allison nevertheless does not believe that these potential analogies are able to fully account for the content of the early Christian traditions and parallel experiences in other contexts. He even suggests that these analogies may produce a situation of *ignotum per ignotius* with regard to these traditions. Hence, he holds that it is not necessarily the case that "if only we knew enough about apparitions of the dead in general, we would necessarily know enough about the appearances of Jesus in particular." Nevertheless, such potential parallels should not be ignored. He writes:

> [J]ust as later Christic visions should not be ignored by New Testament scholars, and just as the parallels between the resurrection stories and certain Greco-Roman legends assuredly have their place to play in discussions of Christian origins, so too do we need to learn what we can from the study of apparitions of the dead. The differences or points of contrast between such apparitions and the New Testament data can, in any case, be taken to prove too much.[155]

Against this backdrop, we need to ask: why may such parallels mistakenly prove too much? At this point, Allison makes a reflection that refers back to one of the underlying premises of the hermeneutical approach to the resurrection that we try to develop: the context in which such an occurrence takes place is of utmost importance for the determination of its significance. As he writes: "Context begets meaning."[156] Therefore, the experiences of such appearances may prove to have distinctively different pragmatic consequences. In some cases they may have none at all, whereas in others, they may be life-changing: "the reappearance of a messianic figure whose followers are living within an eschatological scenario that features the resurrection

---

152. Allison, *Resurrecting Jesus*, 271.
153. Allison, *Resurrecting Jesus*, 277.
154. Allison, *Resurrecting Jesus*, 278.
155. Allison, *Resurrecting Jesus*, 284.
156. Allison, *Resurrecting Jesus*, 284.

of the dead" may perceive such experiences as totally different from those who experience appearances of their departed in a more secular context.[157] The interpretative context, therefore, plays a role.

This consideration can be taken one step further. Allison finds such parallel appearances heuristically profitable in an approach to the resurrection that is open to methodological pluralism. Such pluralism is "attempting to sort and then explain the data to the best of our abilities from different points of view and within different interpretive frameworks." Accordingly, "no one method or set of comparative materials will give us all the answers we seek. We strive rather to learn what we can from each method or set, in the knowledge that each may help us with some part of the picture we are trying to piece together." From this he draws two related conclusions: First, he does not want to *explain* "the appearances of Jesus in terms of typical appearances of the dead," but he nevertheless holds that the potential parallels allow us to ask "what light a wider human phenomenon might shed on some of the issues surrounding the resurrection traditions."[158] Hence, although we have limited knowledge and understanding of apparitions, what we do know may help us to assess some of the other scholarly positions on these matters. He not only counters Crossan's position[159] but also problematizes Pannenberg's claim that "the appearances reported in the Gospels, which are not mentioned by Paul, have such a strongly legendary character that one can scarcely find a historical kernel of their own in them."[160] Allison holds that what we know of such appearances from elsewhere might imply the need for some second thoughts on the matter: "The unexpected appearance and disappearance of Jesus, for instance, and the brevity of the speeches are par for the appearitional course. It is also credible that encounters with the risen Jesus, like some apparitions, produced doubt as well as belief, and likewise plausible that the earthly setting for the canonical stories is not a fiction, for apparitions are typically terrestrial."[161]

As a conclusion to his considerations of the AJ/VJ reports, Allison, therefore, argues in favor of their historical core, and accordingly, for the

---

157. Allison, *Resurrecting Jesus*, 284.

158. Allison, *Resurrecting Jesus*, 285.

159. Allison, *Resurrecting Jesus*, 285. Allison therefore also rejects Crossan's assessment that the New Testament resurrection narratives are events that do not look like visionary accounts we know from elsewhere. Allison's own work refers to many parallels of which we have knowledge, and they resemble those we find in the Gospels. Cf. Allison, *Resurrecting Jesus*, 285.

160. Allison, *Resurrecting Jesus*, 285. The quote is from Pannenberg, *Jesus—God and Man*, 89.

161. Allison, *Resurrecting Jesus*, 286.

likeliness of them being authentic. Hence, they should not be "explained away," but seen in the light of what we know from elsewhere. He writes:

> Despite their myriad disagreements with each other and their late and legendary features, the appearance stories in the canonical Gospels, if reckoned akin to other apparitional accounts, may on account of that kinship be considered not wholly imaginary but instead reminiscent in certain particulars of the original experiences—although delineating those particulars is an uncertain business. Such a conclusion would be consistent with my claim, made earlier, that old appearance narratives probably lie behind 1 Cor 15:3-8.[162]

There remains one important element that needs further consideration, though: How are we to understand the embodied appearances of Jesus? Is it possible to find parallels to these as well, in other experiential contexts? Furthermore, if there are indeed parallels, what is the unique theological significance, if any, of Jesus appearing?

Embodied and Transformed: Experiential Analogies/Parallels

We have seen in the previous part of this book that there are texts in the New Testament that present Jesus after Easter as speaking, eating, preparing food, and possible to touch. All of these instances suggest that the AJs that are reported are about him as existing in space and time, and as materialized and embodied. Allison comments on modern biblical scholarship that considers the texts that report on such matters as late and apologetic and argues that at closer scrutiny its critical approach does not hold. His arguments for an alternative position are what will occupy us in this section.

Allison employs two different contexts of interpretation in order to counter these modern views: First, he points to how both Jewish and Christian texts depict *angels* in ways similar to how Jesus is depicted—as possible to handle, as eating and drinking, etc. Allison, therefore, concludes: "Such stories mean that, apart from the express denial in Luke 24:39, the risen Jesus, in the traditions that have come down to us, does nothing to distinguish himself clearly from the angels."[163] Moreover, and second, "Just as the seemingly solid nature of the risen Jesus clearly fails to distinguish him from the incorporeal angels, so too, interestingly enough,

---

162. Allison, *Resurrecting Jesus*, 288.
163. Allison, *Resurrecting Jesus*, 289–90. Cf. Part II, The Easter Narratives, sec. Conceptualizing Easter or the Resurrected Body.

it does not set him apart from many apparitions."[164] When people speak of visions or appearances of deceased others, these apparitions are usually not described as ghosts, since they commonly appear to be just like real human beings. What is more characteristic is their unexpected or odd arrival, sudden disappearance, or the identification with a deceased individual that gives them away: "Time and time again people not only hear and see apparitions: they even touch them."[165]

Thus, the contents of the VJ/AJ seem to be determined not only by the fact that these experiences have things in common with other experiences in other times and places (the more universal dimension), but also by the way in which these stories are linked to the specific features of the Jesus story in its cultural context (the distinctive or singular features).[166] Hence, the evolution of the Jesus tradition "matches a pattern, a process of memorialization, commonly found in bereavement"; but as Allison holds, "remembering Jesus was not just a normal psychological reflex to his death: it was also a theological necessity occasioned by the resurrection."[167]

Allison does something noteworthy in his approach: he maintains all the way through that the meaning of the resurrection must be seen in relation to the whole Jesus story. It is within the context of that story that it finds its meaning and significance. "Those who proclaimed the resurrection were saying nothing unless they were remembering who Jesus was before he died, and those who heard their proclamation could not have understood it unless they too remembered the man or were informed about him."[168] It was as a historical being with a specific history that Jesus was remembered and against which backdrop his resurrection could attain the meaning it has for those who were backing the claim about his resurrection (CR) as well. Thereby, Allison implicitly argues that the meaning of the resurrection can only be accessed fully by paying attention to the whole life and ministry of Jesus. Previously in this study we have, likewise, pointed out the narrative binding of the resurrection of Jesus; it is

---

164. Allison, *Resurrecting Jesus*, 290.

165. Allison, *Resurrecting Jesus*, 290.

166. I have elsewhere argued that this combination of the universal and the particular is what should be seen as the constitutive elements of the Christian religion and done so against theological positions that want to maintain the uniqueness of Christianity without paying sufficient attention to how it is based on patterns, experiences, and practices that are found elsewhere, as well. See Henriksen, *Christianity as Distinct Practices*.

167. Allison, *Resurrecting Jesus*, 375.

168. Allison, *Resurrecting Jesus*, 375.

part of a narrative and finds its meaning through this particular story.[169] The analogies to the AJ/VJ are insufficient to convey the full religious or theological significance of what it means that *Jesus* had been resurrected. Hence, although it is possible to speak of other appearances as analogous to those who are reported about Jesus, and which somehow (although unexplainable) seem to belong to what happens in the created world, in Jesus something is happening that allows for other abductive inferences than "ghosts"—due to the very history of which Jesus is part. This is what makes the Christian belief in the resurrection something else than a belief in ghosts. Christians believe in Jesus the resurrected, and not in an ungraspable or fluid ghost with no significance for life and hope.

This point also allows Allison to formulate some critique of Wright's understanding of the resurrection. He holds that the way Wright has developed his argument does not make it clear that different opinions about the pre-Easter Jesus should make any difference when it comes to the assessment of the meaning of the resurrection.[170] He underscores the valid point that judgment about the resurrection cannot be isolated from one's worldview. Given this point, how one argues for (or against) the resurrection "equally cannot be isolated from one's estimation of the pre-Easter Jesus—and yet Wright, who would no doubt agree, executes his argument with this fact in the background rather than the foreground."[171] Hence, we can conclude that even though possible analogies to VJ/AJ may be likely, and even support the basis for the abductive inference that leads to the CR, the full semiotic capacity of the CR is only possible to develop against the backdrop of an understanding of Jesus's life and the God to whom he gave witness.

---

169. Part II, Towards a New Testament Theology on the Resurrection of Jesus, sec. An Eschatological Event—Narratively Hardbound.

170. Allison, *Resurrecting Jesus*, 349.

171. Allison, *Resurrecting Jesus*, 350. Allison refers to Graham Stanton in his development of this point: "Early objections to the resurrection hardly ever seem to have been made in isolation from negative assessments of the teaching and the actions of Jesus. Opponents and followers alike saw that claims about the resurrection of Jesus raised the same issues as his actions and his teaching: for opponents, the whole story was riddled with trickery and deceit; for followers, the story was God's story." Allison, *Resurrecting Jesus*, 349–50. The quote from Stanton is from Stanton's article in Barton et al., *Resurrection*.

Part IV: Concluding Reflections

Resurrection from History to Theology

THE PREVIOUS CHAPTERS HAVE helped us to identify and offer reasons for three interrelated elements that seem necessary in order to develop a nuanced discourse on the resurrection:

a. The historical and the theological cannot be entirely separated.

b. The claim that Jesus was raised from the dead cannot be separated from his pre-Easter ministry. The stories about the pre-Easter ministry are deeply influenced by Easter, and Easter finds meaning and significance as the culminating peak of these stories.

c. The claim that Jesus was resurrected only seems to make sense when one believes in God—God as proclaimed and practiced by Jesus through his earthly ministry.

The New Testament witness, and all those who have struggled to interpret its ways of remembering Jesus display a multitude of abductive and retroactive reflections, and these continue to this day. It is against this backdrop that we also have identified in the previous sections elements that allow us to detect how present discussions of the resurrection still seem to revolve around questions of historicity and plausibility, on the one hand, and the questions of theological significance, on the other.[1] This is not surprising. As there is

---

1. Recent or still important contributions which are also open to the more problematic elements in the event of resurrection which is not dealt with here, but merit mentioning, are: D'Costa, *Resurrection Reconsidered*; various articles in Pannenberg, *Grundfragen Systematischer Theologie* vol. 2; Peters et al., *Resurrection*. Among the more apologetic we find Habermas and Craig, whose several publications all contribute in different forms to the attempt of making the resurrection historically plausible. E.g., Habermas, *Resurrection of Jesus*; Habermas, *Risen Jesus and Future Hope*; Habermas et al., *Resurrected?*; Habermas et al., *Did Jesus Rise from the Dead?* Habermas nevertheless fails to make plausible *what* resurrection is, in a way that settles the debate about how to understand it.

no way to secure finally the claim that Jesus did rise from the dead, is it still possible to make a case out of *this* fact? The fact that we cannot establish the resurrection *as a fact* and that no one has had access to it as a phenomenon needs to be affirmed by everyone wanting to address the issue of resurrection. The fact that there is no finally *established* fact is the only fact that we can certify. That is nevertheless not all there is to say.

The point just mentioned should, first and foremost, not be seen as one trying to avoid making claims about the historicity of the resurrection. From a logical point of view, there is no point in speaking about resurrection unless there is some type of historical reason for it. Nevertheless, our point is that one should be open to the fact that, although there is considerable emphasis on the resurrection in the New Testament, these facts are disputed and disputable—and that there might even be good theological reasons why this is the case.[2] The fact of the disputable fact is a fact that also those in favor of the resurrection should recognize. Moreover, we have suggested that what the New Testament itself writes on these matters is shaped by perceived objections to the resurrection, as are the ways in which later writers have developed their lines of argument on the topic as well.

It belongs to the critical task of theology to confront reductionist approaches to reality that asks only for the historical, empirical, or scientific *how* of the resurrection. Reality is more than what can be conceived by means of such questions.[3] Hence, to address the resurrection in a comprehensive way, one should take one's point of departure in how it is a manifestation of how God acts in history. This is well put by Ingolf Dalferth, who sees the Christian confession of the Easter message as one that is not about mere historical facts—it is not about AJ or ET, but about the act of *God* that raised Jesus from the dead. Thus, in his view, this confession is not primarily of a historical event, but about the act of God. This is in line with observations done throughout the presentation of the New Testament material; talks about resurrection, by its very nature, develop into talks about God. It is also not primarily an inference from historical events or facts, but the answer Christians have to an unsolvable experiential dilemma constituted by two contradicting experiences: that Jesus was dead, and that he appeared as being alive. This answer, Dalferth holds, is not independent of the message of Jesus himself. The Christians apply the message about God's salvation of Jesus himself, and sees God as the origin of his resurrected life. "Das christliche Auferweckungsbekenntnis—das

---

2. See Part II, The Easter Narratives, sec. Hole and Surplus and Part II, Towards a New Testament Theology of the Resurrection of Jesus, sec. The Resurrected Body: Admitting and Grappling with Vagueness.

3. Dalferth, "Volles Grab, Leerer Glaube?," 381.

ist die heuristische Hermeneutik der in ihm zur Sprache kommen den kreativen Abduktion—ist Ausdruck einer fundamentalen Erfahrungsintensivierung durch hermeneutische Selbstanwendung und als solches ein hermeneutisches Ereignis, das die Welt verändert hat."[4]

God changes the world through the resurrection of Jesus. Pannenberg and others who—rightly—argue that the future must be seen as determining the present, allow us to develop a theological approach in which the contingencies of what happens and the many things we experience cannot be adequately interpreted on the basis of the past. Instead, the future seems to hold more than what we can determine or anticipate. The resurrection is the event *par excellence* for this situation. Moreover, as the future holds this surplus compared to our explicit expectations, we cannot possibly be expected to have a concept that can contain all that this future implies. Thus, theology about the resurrection is a way of keeping humans open to new experiences.

The relationship between past and future is crucial for how one understands the relationship between the epistemological and the ontological dimension of the resurrection. To attribute an eschatological character to the event of Jesus's resurrection is to go beyond the abductive inferences that disciples and we ourselves can make on the basis of the VJ/ET with regard to the post-mortem state of Jesus. If we say that the resurrection of Jesus has an eschatological character, it does not only connect the past (of his resurrection) with the future (of our resurrection). It also means that the resurrection and the eschatological future that it reveals point to the transformation of the present world, and about which we presently do not know very much.

Thus, the very way we reason about the resurrection means that there are variables in play here that cannot be in our possession or control, and these make it hard to establish the resurrection as a fact among others. On the other hand, its eschatological character implies that the future reality that the resurrection reveals is already present and calls for our conceptual engagement. However, such engagement cannot exclude the fact that the very possibility of the resurrection remains elusive to us, and that it still remains an event marked and shaped by contingency. On the other hand, the future is not any longer a future, something underway, but something that Christians believe has been manifested and anticipated in this world, in space and time and history.

---

4. Dalferth, "Volles Grab, Leerer Glaube?," 401.

Resurrection and the Future: An Eschatological Event in the Present World

The relationship between past and present and future that manifests itself in Jesus's resurrection, here defined as eschatological, we can also see anticipated in the various elements of Jesus's ministry. In a previous volume on *Jesus as Healer*, we argued that the theological model of nature and grace provides us with a model for understanding his healings.[5] Something similar can now help us understand the resurrection. The link between Jesus's history and ministry and his resurrection suggests that Christianity is not only about Easter. It is about how death and destruction can be overcome, as the stories about Jesus as Healer testify to in a different way:

Resurrection and healing can both be seen as expressions of the grace of God, as this grace is manifest in the ministry of Jesus. Furthermore, both point to the embodied character of human existence, and how this is of relevance for understanding what it is to be human. All humans are, from a theological point of view, dependent on God's works and gifts through nature and grace both. As nature expresses itself in and through the human body, one can see the acts of grace for the healing of the body and the body transformed in the resurrection as something that engages with, presupposes, and also transcends the capacities of the body's natural conditions. Thus, the resurrection is the realization of nature in new ways that are beyond the measures and capacities that the body can provide by itself: the resurrected body is a body that is graced in ways hitherto unknown. Such becoming-graced is also visible in other ways in Jesus's own healings.

From a theological point of view, the transformative function of grace in relation to nature also means that the present conditions for human life that determine it as marked by sin are overcome. Sin is that which destroys life and distorts the free flow of life that articulates itself in the interplay between the different realms of human experience. When grace liberates from sin, it enables nature to realize itself more fully. From this perspective, it makes sense to speak of Jesus's resurrection as a manifestation of the victory over the sinful conditions, although such a victory is not yet fully realized in the reality of other humans. However, the ways in which Christians live in faith, hope, and love could be seen as manifestations of how they anticipate the life of resurrection—as these elements allow life to flourish already in the here and now. When grace works "against" nature, it is not against the underlying conditions for health, goodness, beauty, and love in the universe, but against the forces that, for different reasons,

---

5. Cf. Henriksen and Sandnes, *Jesus as Healer*, 231–34.

seem to impede and destroy the possibilities for these features of experience to occur. Resurrection is therefore not the overcoming of nature but is nature transformed by grace as the power to heal and to fulfill life's conditions for flourishing.[6]

The resurrection seen thus is a manifestation of how God works by means of both nature and grace in the actual transformation of Jesus's body, in order to create faith, hope, and love in his believers—something that was already part of Jesus's pre-Easter ministry. In classical theological sources, such as in Thomas Aquinas, nature and grace are perceived as working in interplay in a way that may shed light on the phenomenon of resurrection as an embodied reality. In the relationship between nature and grace, grace builds on nature and contributes to and conditions its perfection (*gratia non tollit naturam, sed perficit*—grace does not destroy nature, but perfects it).[7] At the same time, there would be no grace unless there was a nature in which and by which it could be realized.

We can develop this point further in a way that picks up on points that were also made by Allison in his presentation of the premises he have for his position on the resurrection: Christian faith sees this world as created by a God who loves life, beauty, and goodness, and has set for humans the goal of being like God in relating lovingly to the world. Resurrection is an expression of this love. To see humans as a composition of nature and grace is accordingly to see them as evolving from natural conditions in partly unpredictable ways. This is a manifestation of grace in nature, as it is this natural process that has offered us the chance and the embodied conditions for experiencing the world as a gift, for gratitude, flourishing, enjoyment, and deepening relationships with other humans. Grace thus opens a way

---

6. Against this backdrop, it also makes sense to underscore, with Stefan Alkier and in accordance with our presentation in Part II of this study, how the resurrection can be considered against the backdrop of a theology of creation: "The resurrection of Jesus Christ and the hope in the resurrection of the dead are impossible without a strong theology of creation. The theology of creation is the foundation upon which stands resurrection discourse, understood as the new creation." Alkier, *Reality of the Resurrection*, 234. Alkier supplies this line of reasoning a few pages later: "The biblical theology of creation becomes comprehensible as a disclosure of the cosmos as the creation coming to an appropriate self-understanding, wanted by God, intended by God, made possible creatively and only in relation to him. [. . .] [T]he world, all life, and also one's own life spring not from blind chance but rather from the intentional creativity of the God who establishes relationships in love, as he is portrayed in the Bible. Whoever does not share this hypothesis cannot speak of the resurrection of Jesus Christ and the hope in the resurrection of the dead, with the scriptures of the New Testament in their canonical connection with the Old Testament scriptures." Alkier, *Reality of the Resurrection*, 236.

7. Aquinas, *Summa Theologiae* 1, q. 1, a. 8, resp. 2. 3.

of being in the world that is caused by and oriented by more than natural conditions under human control.

A theology that takes God's interaction with the embodied human seriously, as this comes to the fore in experiences of healing as well as in the resurrection of Jesus, needs to see grace as conditioned by and building on, but not entirely determined by, nature in its present form. In the resurrection, we can identify the fulfillment of human life. God's transformative grace reveals new chances for nature, presenting it with new and surprising opportunities. This perspective is rooted in an understanding of God as the creative source of both nature and grace, and as such, God allows for both freedom and independence, for interplay and interaction. Resurrection is not about the miraculous or supernatural, but about nature becoming realized and fulfilled and redeemed from the powers of sin and death.

Christian theology that takes creation seriously cannot ignore that the natural conditions of human life are the basic conditions for all that God does and for all that befalls us. This also has implications for how we understand the resurrection. In it, grace builds on and is related to nature; without nature, there would be no place for grace; without a body there would be no body transformed by grace. Thus, it displays a loving and living God who without restrictions and limitations calls creation into love and life. Therefore, it is mistaken to see the resurrection as a mere sign of an other-worldly reality or of the mere spiritual dimension of reality. The resurrection manifests the transformation of God's creation and redeems it to flourishing and participation in life as God meant life to be.

John Webster's interpretation of the wonders of Jesus seems to be fitting for this theological interpretation as well and may point to further connections between the ministry of Jesus and his resurrection. He sees these as

> neither intrusions into processes of nature by a person with extraordinary powers nor a proof for the divinity of Christ in front of those who do not believe. They are the visible presence of the kingdom of God, in which God's good order realizes its shape and where God's final rule over all things is anticipated. It is not the natural laws that are contrary to the wonders, but the destructive forces of sin that will finally be overcome in the Eschaton. This understanding sees wonders as extraordinary acts performed by God in God's freedom, as testimonies to God's plan, and as a confirmation of the ordinary ways in which God upholds the world.[8]

---

8. Webster, "Wunder, Dogmatisch," 1728.

Webster's underscoring of the eschatological character of the wonders is of relevance in the present contexts as well, since it holds together the present and the future in a way that also allows for seeing both healings and the resurrection as both being significant elements in the realms of time and history. Furthermore, Webster here seems to share our interest in seeing the present and the future, nature and grace, the ordinary and everyday and the exceptional as being in consonance.

The above sketch of an interpretation of the resurrection provides us with a solid argument against any devaluation of the human embodied reality. Without the graceful transformative acts of God in and with and for the body in resurrection, the human being will not reach its final and eternal goal (*telos*) in terms of displaying the love, care, goodness, and beauty of God. Jesus's graceful interruptions of human life through his ministry already provided new opportunities for this goal to become present in, by, with, and under the conditions of human life: the concrete God becoming flesh in the incarnation therefore also connects incarnation, ministry, and resurrection.

However, having developed these rather "thick" reflections on the theological and eschatological dimensions that can be seen as inherent in a Christian understanding of the resurrection, we nevertheless also have to signal the need for some restraint or modesty with regard to the determination of the further content of the future reality of God. We also have to admit that although we in principle have to be open to future contingencies and events that we cannot predict, in itself this does not constitute an argument for claiming that all such things that we cannot predict do in fact happen. Even if we—ontologically—state that the future is open and cannot be determined based only on past and present events, this is different from saying that the future is something that entails *resurrection* as one of its possibilities. The only reason for this claim is the singular claim CR about Jesus's resurrection. To go beyond it in order to make the CR also include the future resurrection of all humans is to move beyond what we can assume that has happened towards something for which we can only hope. At this point, Wright, Pannenberg, and others who try to secure the plausibility of the resurrection based on the conception of contingency and an open future are making their case too quickly from the past to the future.

The theological reason for putting forward this type of argument is that Christian theology needs to build on the realization that the resurrection is not something we can possibly build a case for exclusively in terms of present, general conditions of argument or experience. We saw this clearly also in Allison, who more than any other of the authors we analyzed, nevertheless was careful in the inferences he drew from his material. When we, in the literature dealing with the possibility or impossibility of resurrection, see two different approaches—one starting with the generic conditions, and the other with the actual belief in the veracity of the resurrection of Jesus as the event on which to base further argument for its reality,[9] as well as a combination of the two—none of these approaches would have been entertained, however, had it not been that we are facing the actual claim that Jesus did rise from the dead (CR). Since CR implies a claim about something taking place in human history and the event is nevertheless something that we also lack adequate means to determine as part of that history, the claim faces some challenges, which we need to repeat:

- We have the *conceptual* difficulty: a dead human does not come to life again. This makes it essential to pose the question: what exactly does resurrection then mean? Some see the concept of resurrection as a metaphor for a new way of living in the presence of God, but as a metaphor that has little *explanatory* value. Its value in this regard lies in the way the metaphor points to the saturated phenomena that the disciples experience, and for which they struggle to find interpretative resources. But it seems difficult, indeed impossible, to define clearly the *concept* of resurrection. Accordingly, I would suggest that we see it as a *symbol* that allows us to see and experience the world differently, and to orient us in the world from other conditions than those given before Easter.[10] As a symbol in the Ricoeurian sense, it places us as interpreters in a situation of oscillation in which we constantly move between the symbol that gives rise to thought (in its many possible interpretations)—and back to the symbol.

---

9. This is fundamental to arguments of so different people as G. Habermas, W. Pannenberg, and W. L. Craig, just to mention a few of the most discussed figures in recent literature.

10. Cf. for this also how Markus Bockmuehl defines the function of resurrection as a metaphor: "The resurrection, in other words, is indeed a metaphor, as is often said—but its function is quite the opposite of conventional metaphors. From Plato's cave to Lewis's Narnia, ordinary religious metaphors tend to employ the literal and familiar to speak (however truthfully) of an otherworldly reality. The New Testament witness to the resurrection of Jesus, by contrast, redescribes earth in terms of heaven and history in terms of eschatology. For the early Christians, this marks the place in which God's world irreversibly invades the world of violence and corruption, planting here the flag of redemption. Heaven is no longer a metaphor of earthly bliss, or the world to come a pleasant postscript to mortality. Instead, Easter morning claims the redeemed cosmos as a metaphor of heaven, and transforms mortal life into the vestibule of paradise. The resurrection here constitutes the defining historical, moral and ecological reality that is the 'new creation.'" "Resurrection," 117.

- Then we have the assumed *ontological* impossibility of the resurrection, which is given with the predictions we can make on the basis of the past, as well as what we know about the biological conditions of life in general. This impossibility is, however, *in principle* softened by pointing to how the future is open and to the importance of being open to future contingencies and the newness of events. Nevertheless, when we speak of the resurrection, we speak of something that might be considered outside the scope of even future contingencies that may take place on the present and accessible conditions of nature: it is something which seems so ontologically impossible that it is hard to argue that *this event* (which we are only able to speak about metaphorically) possibly could take place at all, unless there was something that radically changed the conditions for life as we know it. In this respect, talk about the resurrection operates on other premises than does the rest of this world (as the post-Easter reports also indicate). This we have signaled above in the way we pointed to the resurrection as presupposing a graceful and transformative act of God—on and in nature.

The reports about resurrection visions (AJ/VJ) present us with the task that goes beyond the historical. These experiences are, *because they relate to the historical ministry of Jesus from Nazareth,* presenting us with the question of how we are, if at all, able to understand the reports in such a manner that these events are essential for the understanding of our own future.

The logical structure of everything that the resurrection reports open up to, is that the resurrection reality—so far—belongs uniquely to Jesus. No-one else has a part in this reality in the same manner. The reports nevertheless seem to be written in order to provide more than a foundation for the memory of this uniqueness. Instead they are attempts to inscribe in our world a foundation for understanding a possible future for ourselves as part of the community for which Jesus was the beginning. These stories provide reasons for conceiving that Jesus can be with his followers also in the future and as something more than a memory.

At this point, there is one element that can be taken from the possible parallels that Allison discusses, and which we also can see witnessed in similar material elsewhere: appearances of the dead often occur when there is a sudden, violent, or tragic death that leaves behind something as unaccomplished. If we interpret the VJ/AJ from that angle, they become instances that testify to the fact that Jesus wants his followers to continue his proclamation of the kingdom and reassures them that he is still with them. Thus, in this sense, although the AJ/VJ as generic phenomena are not totally different from what others may experience, their specific content in the context of Jesus's life and ministry takes on a significance that cannot be ignored or considered irrelevant—at least not for those who consider Jesus to be a relevant figure for how they orient their own lives. Thus, the element of Thirdness comes in for full in this regard, not only as pointing to those who interpret but as those who use their interpretations of the resurrection as means for orientation of their own lives.

The stories contribute to the awareness about *where* we are and under what conditions humans live, and as such, they contribute to establishing a point of orientation. If the resurrection is linked to the ministry of Jesus and the community he shaped, the reports about it show that Christians are part of a community of hope that is united with him through this hope. Nevertheless, the stories also uphold the difference between Jesus and his community. This maintaining of unity in difference is important to orient ourselves not only to the past but also to the promises about the future. The future promised through and by the resurrection cannot be understood as something for individual possession, but only as realizable in the presence of the community which Christians recognize themselves as participating in by sharing a common faith.[11]

The critical function of the resurrection is that it allows us not to totalize the present world and confront it with a consciousness of what happens as something that is still not fully captured by the powers of death. Thus, the resurrection can be seen as the ultimate gift which still only exists as a promise for us—but a promise that is nevertheless anticipated by the proclamation of Christ's resurrection. As a gift—indeed a gift of life—it also establishes a contrast between a gifting way of living and ways of living leading to death. As indicated already, this gift of life reveals that God is not letting the world surrender to the powers of death and that God wants to expose these powers as not mighty enough to have the last word. These powers are by the very instance of resurrection exposed as those that shall *not* be in the end, and as the powers which destruct both the gifts of life and life as a condition for gifting.[12]

---

11. Peter's case is illuminating here: After his denial of Jesus, his past demands that he recognizes himself as a betrayer, but his meeting with Jesus after the resurrection *heals* that memory and makes it possible for him to recognize himself from another point of view, from another orientation. The whole story of John 21 is about how Jesus's recognition of him and his love allows for him to have a future opened that is not determined by his ruined past.

12. In this sense, the memory of Jesus's resurrection provides a critical tool for evaluating the present. Williams, *Resurrection*, 25, points with regard to this to J. B. Metz's understanding of memory as "the means by which reason [can] become practical as freedom." Metz "refers to Marcuse's linking of memory with imagination, both being a means for the critical understanding of the present, 'a way of mediation that can

By establishing this contrast between what is (the end of life in death) and what is to be (the life in community with God and others), hope is founded. Hence, conceiving of resurrection primarily in individual terms is far too narrow. Moreover, this allows for living in the world with freedom based on the knowledge that a different world is *possible*, and that God is the one who ultimately not only supports this world, but will also bring it to its realization.

It is not without importance that this hope for what may appear, from a particular perspective as impossible, is based on *Christ's* resurrection. He was the one who suffered injustice, and who also claimed to be a witness to the kingdom of God. In the resurrection, not only is his claim about the coming kingdom vindicated, but his unjust suffering is also a sign that unjust suffering is not the end for those who suffer it. In this way, the resurrection is the reason for hope and for proclaiming that those who hunger and thirst for righteousness are blessed, because they will be filled (Matt 5:9). They need not think that death is their final defeat. This does not mean, however, that they should console themselves with the injustice they suffer, but rather that they should struggle against it in light of the final, eschatological vindication of their cause.

The social and ethical dimensions of the resurrection indicated here are developed further in Rowan Williams's treatise on the resurrection, where he sees the transformation of the world as more than a mere change in attitude: it provides us with a point of orientation from which we can see the world as a gift, as something to be given, and as the call to give. This, he says, has a "straightforwardly material dimension" as oppression and violence. The chains of destructiveness which occur socially, economically, and quite simply physically, always occur in connection with the possession of the world's resources. Williams sees this as ways of dealing with the world "that locks Christ out, and constitutes a denial of Christ's Lordship: it is a sign of unbelief in the resurrection. When convertedness is embodied in a transforming of economic relationships, material reality will have become charged with the life of Christ risen: the world will be revealed as his." [13]

Without trying to make it an argument *for* resurrection in the strict sense, it is worth considering the alternative here, as well. Had Jesus not

---

momentarily at least break through the omnipresent power of the given facts.' When the power of given present facts is challenged as we come to see the present situation as the issue of contingent processes and choices, we gain resources for new decision, and openness to new stages of process. We learn to act and to hope. Memory, at this level, can be the ground of hope, and there is no authentic hope without memory." Williams references to Metz is taken from Metz, *Faith in History and Society*, 193–95.

13. Williams, *Resurrection*, 103.

been resurrected, this would have meant that even the one who gave his life entirely to God and to other humans in order to proclaim the kingdom of God, in the end, had to see himself defeated by the powers of death. That would not only have meant that his own proclamation was a failure, but also that the God he witnessed to was not the one Jesus claimed God to be. In that sense, it is possible to see Jesus's resurrection not only as a consequence of him bearing a truthful witness to the true God. It is also possible to see that his resurrection allows for others to recognize him as the one in whom one can trust when it comes to how God relates to our future, when we in faith, hope, and love struggle for community, justice, and the distribution of the gifts of God. The alternative is to conclude that Jesus's witness was false and that those who struggle in faith, hope, and love for a just world might sometimes succeed, and sometimes fail. That is, of course, an option to be considered, but it is an option that is hard to make coherent with the affirmation that God is the God of life.

Concluding then, that although this last line of reasoning is not an argument for the reality of the resurrection, it is nevertheless an argument for the fact that the resurrection—if it took place—is in full accordance with the confession that God is the creator and sustainer of life and human community. In this way, we can also see the resurrection as a confirmation of Christ's identity as a witness to the God of life.[14] This study has revolved around the question of the resurrection of Jesus. As we now approach the end, we realize how deeply intertwined his resurrection is with the destiny of humanity. Hence, in spite of our concentration on Jesus's resurrection, the hopes that develop from there have constantly made themselves heard.

Remarks on the Resurrection, Individual Differences, and Disability

The New Testament reports that the disciples experienced Jesus after the resurrection with the wounds resulting from his crucifixion. This detail is important not only to make a clear link between the historical Jesus and the one they met after Easter, which we have underscored throughout this study. It also has some bearings on how we think about the resurrected body in general, pertaining not only to how we think about Jesus's body, but also the bodies of those for which the resurrection is still to come, i.e., the rest of humanity.

---

14. Cf. how this point is in accordance with Allison's as referred above in the previous chapter.

The wounds of the resurrected body suggest that the life-story of the resurrected one continues to be part of the identity of that person. We know from medicine and psychology that the significant events in a person's life-story leave traces not only in the mind but also in (and on) the body of the person. Experiences shape the body as well as the mind. The transformation in the resurrection thus does not seem to eradicate previous life experience and its significance for the person in question—a point that also expresses the continuation of creation in the new reality that the resurrection manifests. Identity is maintained in the resurrected—although there historically has been, and still are, different views on what this means.[15] However, despite this continuity, resurrection also seems to imply a transformation of the identity-shaping elements.

Moreover, given this fact, it is also possible to consider somewhat more a point we have only touched upon briefly earlier: what resurrection would mean for the one who has led a life under conditions of illness and disability.

As for illness, the resurrection connects to the healing ministry of Jesus insofar as the reality of the resurrection seems to imply that illness and suffering are no longer present. Thus, resurrection presents hope to those who suffer—and a Gospel for the body. This hope is grounded in his ministry as well as in his resurrection, since both point to the kingdom of God as the fulfillment of creation.[16]

With regard to the topic of disability, there are two different aspects to address: First, the experience that many who have led a life with some impairments, nevertheless have experienced that their so-called disability also has enabled them to develop competencies and provided for experiences and skills that they would not want to be without. To the extent that such traits represent positive elements in their identity, there is no reason to see the resurrection as overcoming those. Second, one also has to take into account that there are features that actually have impaired their chances for participation in the community, and which may be so painful or severe that they are not part of what that person wants to have as the basis of her identity.[17] About these features, the resurrection can be seen as a transformative process where

---

15. On the topic of identity in relation to features in life that may be seen as problematic for the person in question, and how this problem appears from the point of view of what the resurrection may entail, see Gould, "Hope of Heavenly Healing of Disability Part 1," 217–34; "Hope of Heavenly Healing of Disability Part 2," 98–116.

16. Extensively on this topic, see Henriksen and Sandnes, *Jesus as Healer*, 113–30.

17. This distinction between the two main aspects echo the now common distinction between impairment as a physiological condition that is essentially neutral, and disability engendered by social and cultural forces that render such impairment negatively and "disable" the person in his or her social context.

they no longer are part of their lives. The distinction between these two lines of identity-shaping is a crucial element in much of contemporary discourse about religion, disability, health, and healing. What resurrection means with regard to such issues should not be simplified or passed over too quickly, since many people who suffer from illness or disability—albeit not all—see the resurrection as their only hope for a full life.

In addition to these remarks, and contrary to what has been the case in much of the tradition, the wounds of Jesus reported in the New Testament can nevertheless also be read as a critique of the idealized, perfect body.[18] Furthermore, it can be read as a critique of what some scholars address as the violent imperative of healing, in which "the *imperative* to be healed—the assumption that disabled bodies and minds all desire and require healing—functions as a form of violence and a kind of imperialism." This view promotes "the assumption [. . .] that 'able' bodies and minds are so obviously and naturally desirable that everyone should have them, that everyone should want them, that there is, in fact, no other dignified way to live."[19] Thus, the wounds of the resurrected imply recognition of how also suffering contributes to what shapes and forms human life and identity—but simultaneously, the reality of the resurrection allows for seeing these features transformed in a way that overcomes the negative impact of suffering.

The interpretation suggested here implies that the healing inherent in the resurrection does then not mean the constitution of a body in accordance with human ideals about the perfect. Instead, it may be seen as the event in which the individual, with his or her life-story, become integrated into a common reality with God in which he or she can participate fully and without any form of impairment. In this reality, pain and lack are not present, and the individual differences that people have, including bodily ones, are recognized as enriching and valuable parts of the human experience for the whole community.[20] This interpretation thus points to a vision of the resurrection that is emphasizing concrete experiences of community, participation, goodness, and flourishing, instead of primarily being about fulfilling ideals of the perfect body (which, by the way, is what, exactly?).[21] Resurrection is therefore not to be understood as exclusively about the body: the main point of the resurrection is that it will reconstitute the *identity* of the human,

18. To read the stories in this way has not always been common in the Christian tradition. There are many examples of how bodily disability and impairment are seen as something to be overcome, transformed, and/or healed in the reality of the resurrection. For details, see Moss, "Heavenly Healing."
19. Belser, "Violence, Disability and the Politics of Healing," 178.
20. Cf. Belser, "Violence, Disability and the Politics of Healing," 181.
21. Cf. for an extensive discussion also the recent book by Lelwica, *Shameful Bodies*.

of which the embodied dimension is part. However, for some, their identity may be related positively and affirmatively to their body, whereas the body for others is something they may experience as in need of being transformed in order to overcome the impediments that it represents for the realization of their full identities. The latter will be the case for people struggling with chronic illness and pain, whereas the former can be the case for those who have learned to affirm their identity as part of what constitutes what they experience as a good way of living.

Moreover, the conception of the resurrection as one in which the human body's identity is preserved, contributes to another element that is of vital importance: that to be part of creation is to be a finite human being. As finite, humans are vulnerable, but they are also susceptible to influence from others in the community they participate—for good or for bad. Vulnerability is part of being human. T. E. Reynolds points to how it is "precisely such vulnerability that God embraces in Christ, entering fully into the frailty of the human condition, even unto a tragic death." He sees this vulnerable condition, which all humans including Christ share, as something that is taken up into, and not negated, by the redemptive act of God in the resurrection. Resurrection does not "negate vulnerable finitude by making humans inviolable and perfectly whole," but "transforms vulnerability into communion with God, prefiguring the final eschatological horizon to come when all things will become so transformed."[22] The resurrection does not imply the erasure of the wounds inflicted upon us, because the wounds are themselves an attesting to the trauma and to the transformation of it by the power of God, and thereby also to how resurrected life is a continuation of human life in its wounded forms and not the manifestation of idealized bodies without traces of trauma.[23]

Finally, it is important to recognize that all human beings are disabled in some way or at some stage in life. In this life, there will inevitably be impediments to how we can participate in community and flourish. Resurrection brings the hope that these features will nevertheless not prevent us from taking part in the fulfillment of life that the reality of God implies, and in realizing the identity which we have in God's eyes. Resurrection is the reality that allows us to be what we are, transformed for full participation in a community constituted by faith, hope, and love.

---

22. Reynolds, "Theology and Disability," 42.

23. A significant recent contribution to the relationship between trauma and resurrection wounds is found in Rambo, *Resurrecting Wounds*.

A Contemporary Approach to the Pauline Core Argument

We have seen in the former part of the book that in his first letter to the Corinthians, Paul makes some strong statements about the centrality of the resurrection for the belief of the Christian community. Paul's argument implies an explicit rejection of a position that tries to establish a foundation for the belief in Jesus only in the past. He indicates that unless Christian belief is a belief in the future opened by the resurrection, it is no good:

> If there is no resurrection of the dead, then Christ has not been raised; and if Christ has not been raised, then our proclamation has been in vain, and your faith has been in vain. We are even found to be misrepresenting God because we testified of God that he raised Christ—whom he did not raise if it is true that the dead are not raised. For if the dead are not raised, then Christ has not been raised. If Christ has not been raised, your faith is futile, and you are still in your sins. (1 Cor. 15:13–17)

The striking openness with which Paul presents his line of reasoning is worth considering: he argues that for our faith in Christ not to be futile, belief in the resurrection is necessary. His argument can—critically—be read in two ways:

- The resurrection is the condition for a faith that is not futile. Hence, the resurrection is the warrant for the reliability of the Christian faith, and the condition for its possibility. Thus, the resurrection is the necessary condition for the specific content of the Christian faith.

- Those who believe must, therefore, uphold their belief in the resurrection in order not to be proved wrong or admit to failure. Respectively, in order to not have to recognize themselves as "still being in their sins," the affirmation of the resurrection is necessary since the resurrection implies that the life of sin is something that can and will be overcome by the grace of God through the future resurrection of all.

Nevertheless, the resurrection faith is not primarily about human hope or the need for avoiding failure: Paul argues that the resurrection faith has first and foremost to do with how we perceive God—and Jesus. The belief in the resurrection is a way of specifying that Christians believe in a God that ultimately will let life, justice, and community reign—for others—instead of death and the injustice against innocent victims. The hope in this God is thus not hope for us and for the petty desires of humans, but for a world that is shaped by flourishing life, justice, and righteousness. The frankness of the Pauline way of reasoning suggests this. Paul admits openly that one must consider that there exists the possibility that the dead are not resurrected. But his concern is not primarily that this makes our faith futile (although he also admits that, of course), but rather, that this makes witnessing to God a *misrepresentation*. One could even argue that his concern about misrepresentation is the core of the Pauline argument: If Christ has not been raised from the dead by God—then God is different, God is other than the believers in Christ have assumed. Hence, it all comes down to the very question about who God is that raised Jesus from the dead. In other words: the resurrection is at the center of the Christian faith since it opens to an understanding that brings together creation, redemption, and new life; nature and grace; past, present, and future; faith, hope, and love.

Undeniably, the confession of the resurrection of Christ is part of a very risky enterprise: all is at stake with this confession, and the confessor must be aware of the risk precisely because of this. Attempts to make the resurrection a less risky affair will always be an attempt to trivialize the phenomenon of the resurrection into something less transforming, or something that can be delineated by precise definitions and contexts of interpretation that are seen as exclusive and exhaustive, or as something that can be controlled and possessed by our notions. The Pauline argument suggests otherwise: resurrection is what finally binds Christ and God together in a reality that is unconditioned by human effort or understanding; it is not possession but a future present as a promise, not yet fully realized.

The risky business of resurrection faith is underscored by the inconclusive and elusive stories about the resurrection in the New Testament. As we have argued throughout, the empty tomb is itself not an argument for the resurrection. The apparently (at least initially) unrecognizable Jesus in the appearances before the disciples also indicates that there is no immediate access to a secure conviction about the risen Lord. As it seems impossible to develop a clear statement about Jesus's whereabouts after the resurrection, the difficulties are even more present.[24] However, these uncertainties are not providing us with clear arguments *against* the resurrection. One can claim that the very same approach that tries to establish a secure historical foundation for the resurrection, also expresses itself negatively in the struggle for the opposite: in both instances, a conviction is expressed that this is a reality that we can more or less sufficiently access, control, or determine the content of. Given that the resurrection is the example *par*

---

24. Lüdemann, "Opening Statement," 40–41, observes that the question "where did he go afterwards?" is impossible to answer, and uses this to argue against resurrection faith. However, as Pannenberg indicates (Pannenberg, *Grundfragen Systematischer Theologie* 2:167–68), the vagueness of the New Testament in dealing with such questions cannot in itself be taken to provide reasons for rejecting the resurrection.

excellence of what Marion and others call the saturated phenomenon, this argument is hardly convincing. Hence, a more or less positivistic approach to the resurrection seems not only to fail to describe what characterizes that phenomenon, but also to deviate from Pauline admission that such faith involves risk. Paul openly admits to the fact that we will have problems with that which seems impossible in 1 Cor. 15. To pretend otherwise would be to ignore the fact that the resurrection cannot be firmly established as a historical truth among others.

Before we conclude this section, one more element needs to be addressed: Paul claims that resurrection means bodily resurrection. Thus, he sides in a fundamental way with Luke. Luke's report of Jesus as eating, and about the empty tomb, secure resurrection faith from two important challenges: the empty tomb is vital in order to establish that there is some kind of *continuity* between the risen Christ and the pre-Easter Jesus, while the eating is essential in order to avoid understanding the appearances of Jesus as those of a ghost. According to ancient understanding, ghosts were not able to eat and drink.[25] In both instances, *the body* is of utmost importance, because the body makes it possible to situate the risen Christ in time and space, but also to recognize him as risen. However, the body is also understood as something that has changed. How can this narrative trait be explained? From an exegetical point of view, it can be reasoned as Eckstein does in his treatment of resurrection in Luke:

> And if the "physical" existence of the earthly Jesus is not characterized negatively, but is in the context of the Old Testament-Jewish theology of creation connoted altogether positively, then for Luke as well as for the other New Testament witnesses it goes without saying that God at Jesus' redemption does not leave the *soma*, the mortal body, to the reign of death but transforms him physically.[26]

There is a tacit element in Eckstein's reasoning here that needs to be highlighted: Jesus—as a true human—has the same mortal body as the rest of humanity. That he was an embodied being was part of the fullness of incarnation. To be participating fully in the community with the God of life implies that this mortal body must—in some non-definable way—be transformed. It is nevertheless still a body (in Paul's words: a *soma pneumatikon*), but a body different from the one we have now.

---

25. Further on these points, see Eckstein, "Bodily Resurrection in Luke," esp. 118–20.

26. Eckstein, "Bodily Resurrection in Luke," 123.

This point illuminates the possibility for Christians to recognize in themselves a future that means and implies a concrete, embodied difference. Resurrection is not only about being in full communion with God and others, or about being fully able to receive the gifts of God. It is also to be given the bodily preconditions for this fullness, which implies that resurrection is manifesting a reality that exceeds the present also in bodily terms, and that the fullness of this reality implies a surplus over against what is currently present in the creation of God. Throughout our work, we have observed that the resurrection is a *gift* of God. The gift-character of the resurrection proved significant for grasping the nature of this event. Paul, the apostle, articulates this more emphatically than any other in the New Testament. In his recent *Paul and the Gift*, John M.G. Barclay demonstrates that Paul's theology on grace is properly understood against the backdrop of gifts; in fact, the Greek *charis* belongs within this domain of words.[27] Significant to Paul's concept of grace is what Barclay calls the misfit between the gift and its receiver. God's grace in Christ is incongruous, given to the unworthy—against all human expectations, previous worth, and contrary to reason. This is clearly to be seen in Romans 4, in which *charis* figures prominently. The misfit between Abraham and the grace given to him (Gen 15:6) is by Paul formulated thusly: God justified the ungodly (Rom 4:4–5). Likewise, according to Rom 5:6, God justifies the "ungodly." In Romans 4, Paul considers this act of giving to the unworthy an extension of God's power to give life to that which is dead: "God gives life to the dead and calls into existence the things that do not exist" (Rom 4:17). In other words, the misfit between Abraham's pagan past and God' election of him, between Paul, the former persecutor who became an apostle of Christ, between a barren woman (Sara) and the promise of a child, mirror God's power to give life to the dead. *Vice versa*, Paul's hope in the resurrection, against all ordinary expectancies and human possibilities is that this is a gift, graciously to be bestowed on the dead. Thus, resurrection is a gift repealing the misfit between death and life.

The Resurrection as a Basis for Christology: Dirk-Martin Grube

How can we think of the resurrection as a basis for Christology—the doctrine about the identity of Jesus Christ? Is it the event itself that serves as a foundation of Christian belief in Jesus as the Son of God / the Messiah, or it is something else? In a recent contribution to this topic, Dirk-Martin Grube[28]

27. Barclay, *Paul and the Gift*.
28. See Grube, "Christian Theology."

has pointed to the need for addressing it from an angle that allows for both historical and theological perspectives, by developing an epistemological approach based in Thomas S. Kuhn's theory about paradigm shifts. Grube's argument, here admittedly shortened, goes as follows:

The experiences of the risen Christ must be seen as a perceptual anomaly from the perspective of Kuhn. By defining these experiences as anomalies, it then is possible to see how they can trigger the theoretical modifications that is necessary for the interpretative context (in our words: the context of discovery as well as the context of justification) of those who experience the appearances. Then, the term "Messiah" undergoes a change in meaning, and this change is part of the paradigm shift that Christian faith represents. Against this backdrop, it is the new context of interpretation that constitutes the paradigm-shift that becomes the foundation of Christological theorizing: "Rather than basing Christology on what the 'historical Jesus' did or said, the reconstruction of Jesus as the Christ in the context of this shift is foundational for Christology." Accordingly, Grube sees the resurrection as crucial not primarily because it is a historical fact, but because it is an anomaly that leads to a change in how reality is perceived.[29]

It is important here that Grube acknowledges that for the contemporaries of Jesus, the fact that "a deceased person lives goes obviously in against deeply entrenched expectations and is thus anomalous."[30] Thus, they are no more credulous than we are when it comes to this matter.[31] However, one can ask if this is not also an indication that not only the interpretative context is foundational for Christology, but also which experiences people have and do not have. Grube is right that the anomaly of the risen Christ causes a reinterpretation of the scriptures that is foundational for Christology, but he nevertheless also—against the too restrictive view of Bultmann[32] regarding historical matters—underscores the role of the historical experiences:

> The observational anomaly that Jesus who has ceased appears is treated with the help of modified theoretical resources whereas

29. Grube, "Christian Theology," 4.
30. Grube, "Christian Theology," 6.
31. See Part II, Towards a New Testament Theology of the Resurrection of Jesus, sec. Not so Credulous After All.
32. On the relationship between his own view and Bultmann's, Grube writes: "There is no need to reject the quest for the 'historical Jesus' as zealously as Bultmann does. That is, Bultmann declares the entire quest for the 'was und wie' of Jesus' life as being part of the 'preconditions of doing theology' but not as being part of this theology itself. This is unnecessarily restrictive and to be explained with the discourse-constellation of the time in which Bultmann wrote. Yet, in today's constellation, there is no need to reject this quest in such a zealous fashion." Grube, "Christian Theology," 7.

the different theoretical modifications cohere with each other as well as with the observations. Modified theoretical resources and observations "fit together" to the effect that reality—respectively the relevant parts of it—are disclosed in a novel fashion. Thus the disciples can "see" now where they could not see before. Put in terms of Kuhn's above-mentioned phrase: The early Christians "live in a different world" after the paradigm shift they have undergone.[33]

Grube thereby shows how the interplay of the historical and the theological together engenders the paradigm-shift that opens up to the emergence of Christianity. Thus, the resurrection, defined as an experiential anomaly, can be addressed as the foundation of Christianity. The resurrection is the origin of a new paradigm in which Jesus as the suffering Messiah is at the center. It is against this backdrop that it is possible to understand how "The early Christian communities reconstructed Jesus' life and fate in the strict sense of the word. That is, they re-conceptualized them in accordance with the new paradigm they came to live in."[34]

From a hermeneutical point of view, Grube's approach shows the interplay between the theological and the historical in a way that implies that the resurrection *as such*, i.e., without an appropriate context of interpretation (or an adequate paradigm) cannot be identified as the foundation of neither Christianity nor Christology. Hence, he claims that "it is fair to suggest that Jesus cannot be reconstructed as being Jesus the Christ apart from a paradigm shift."[35] Furthermore, and accordingly, "The 'theology' of the early Christian communities provides the foundation of Christology, not the life, deeds, consciousness or whatever of the 'historical Jesus'. Only when the latter are reconstructed in light of the new paradigm makes it sense to speak of Christology proper, not before."[36]

Although Grube will not reject the quest for the "historical Jesus," he will not see it as foundational, because he sees it as integrated into a paradigm that *he* sees as foundational. Nevertheless, this does not mean that he will ignore historical questions, but he holds that it is necessary to "distinguish between the respects in which it is relevant and those respects in which it is not."[37] Hence, he affirms that insights about the historical Jesus are relevant in *an explanatory sense*. They help to explain "why the early Christians came

---

33. Grube, "Christian Theology," 7.
34. Grube, "Christian Theology," 7.
35. Grube, "Christian Theology," 7.
36. Grube, "Christian Theology," 7.
37. Grube, "Christian Theology," 7.

to believe that he was resurrected: They remembered after Jesus' death that he had an intimate relationship with God during his lifetime and remembering this helped them to come up with the idea that this relationship could prevail even through death. Remembering this helped them thus to form the idea that Jesus had been resurrected by God after his death."[38]

It is not clear from this account how Grube considers the historical content inherent in the CR. This notwithstanding, he points to how it is necessary from both a theological and a historical point of view to see the discourse about Jesus's resurrection as related to how his believers remembered him and his life. Against this backdrop, it also makes sense to consider belief in the resurrection as crucial: it is crucial "because of the function it has rather than because of its historical character." This function can be described in a Kuhnian context as an anomaly that is necessary "if we wish to explain the emergence of Christianity as a new religious paradigm." Thus, to insist only on the historicity of the resurrection is insufficient: "Even if this historicity could be proven, it would be insufficient to explain the emergence of Christianity. Being nothing more than a 'fact,' the resurrection of Jesus could have been perceived as just another miracle. Yet, its perception as a miracle cannot explain the emergence of a new religious paradigm."[39] It is as an anomaly that causes a radical paradigm shift that helps us explain the emergence of Christianity. Only against the backdrop of comprehensive changes in the interpretative context that "leads to large-scale theoretical modifications that are coherent with each other and disclose reality anew so as to make sense of the anomaly (of the appearances)" is it possible to "make sense of the emergence of Christianity as a new religious paradigm."[40]

Resurrection as Manifestation of Incarnation: Ingolf U. Dalferth

The preceding sections of this part have been developed in order to provide a backdrop for the dogmatically relevant construction of the relation between resurrection and incarnation. This relation has its historical warrant in how the first Christians identified the resurrected as the Jesus they had shared their lives with, and the New Testament's retroactive compositions of narratives about the resurrected suggest this close link in depictions of meals, etc. However, even though resurrection and incarnation are closely tied together, it also has to be maintained, as indicated, that the resurrection implies a

---

38. Grube, "Christian Theology," 8.
39. Grube, "Christian Theology," 10.
40. Grube, "Christian Theology," 10.

surplus in terms of being compared to what is manifested in the pre-Easter bodily incarnation of the Word as Jesus from Nazareth.

Among the most heated debates in modern Christology is the one that took place after the publication of the volume edited by John Hick about the Incarnation.[41] Dalferth[42] claims that almost everything is—and remains—unclear in the debate about this book: when it asks if the incarnation is a myth or a truth, it is not clear what either incarnation, myth, or truth means in this context.[43] In the following, we will present his more constructive responses to this volume, without going into detail about his more critical remarks. In general, however, his evaluation of this collection of essays is that it demands a more nuanced approach than the authors provide.

Dalferth suggests that one needs to distinguish between different elements in the discussion of the incarnation. If it is not clear which dimension one is discussing in approaching the incarnation, obscurity remains.[44] He describes the different dimensions as follows:

- The event of incarnation,
- Conceptions of incarnation,
- Confessions of incarnation,
- The doctrine of incarnation, and
- Theories of incarnation.

We can make similar distinctions with regard to the resurrection, all the way down this list. Accordingly, if we do not make them, the whole discussion becomes unclear. If we look back on what we have put the emphasis on in this volume, it is clear that we have put most emphasis on the event of the resurrection, and the conditions for our conceptions of it, and only in the more recent sections, we have made reflections that may be relevant for the confession and the doctrine.

Dalferth identifies the main problem with Hick's critical approach in his identification of the historical human being Jesus from Nazareth before Easter as the sole referent of Christological formulations. This approach, he holds, implies a theological under-determination, because it goes astray at a very decisive point: it misses the *confessional* element.[45] We could also add, on our own

---

41. *The Myth of God Incarnate* (1977). Recently re-issued as *The Metaphor of God Incarnate*.
42. Dalferth, *Crucified and Resurrected*.
43. Dalferth, *Crucified and Resurrected*, 6.
44. Dalferth, *Crucified and Resurrected*, 9–10.
45. Dalferth, *Crucified and Resurrected*, 21.

part, that it misses the point we have tried to make that the understanding of the resurrection needs to be related to the pre-Easter ministry of Jesus, and if that is the case, it also means that what we can say about that ministry cannot be assessed apart from the belief in the resurrection.

Moreover, Dalferth holds that it is necessary for the logical structuring of Christological formulations to see them as attempts to express something about the resurrected crucified. Hence, the formulations try to say something more than merely making statements about the identity of pre-Easter Jesus. Dalferth consequently argues that the resurrection implies that we are dealing with something that is excessive to what can be grasped as the pre-Easter reality of Jesus: the resurrection provides us with a surplus compared to what was at hand before. Hence, he says, the central theme in any *confession* about Jesus Christ is not his historical reality as such, but his existence as the one whom God rose from the dead.[46]

Against this background, Dalferth formulates "the grammatical" conditions of Christology in a way that holds together resurrection and cross, God and world. The connection between these different instances is one that is determinative for the identity of all, and in this sense, one can say that the Jesus story is not only a story about Jesus's identity, but also a story about the identity of God and the world:

> Thus, the resurrection must be interpreted with the cross in mind, the cross with God in mind, God with the message of Jesus in mind, and God's actions on the cross and in resurrection of Jesus with us and the world in mind—this is the line of argument that Christology and Christian theology should take in order to conform with the Christian confession of faith in Jesus Christ.[47]

Christian faith is first and foremost a confession of the life-giving power of God in the resurrection of Christ, according to Dalferth. Hence most important is the confession that Jesus is the first whom God has risen from the dead, and not *who* one confesses that Jesus is. It is the resurrection by God that allows us to see the witness he gave to God as final, irreversible and unsurpassable.[48] Due to this understanding, Dalferth holds as essential that the way one allows for Jesus to be the theme of Christological confession allows for more than one mode of thematization. He argues that, just as we have to differentiate between theme and content, and between theme and the formulation of the theme, the foundation for all reasoning about the

46. Dalferth, *Crucified and Resurrected*, 24.
47. Dalferth, *Crucified and Resurrected*, 27.
48. Dalferth, *Crucified and Resurrected*, 28.

resurrection must be that Jesus is the first one to be risen by God.[49] How one then formulates the content, the background, and the horizon of this event may vary, but prior to all these ways of formulating the content is the event itself, which is the basis and object of Christian faith.

It is against this backdrop that Dalferth argues that *the resurrection is the primary determination of the theme of Christological confessions*. It is not the incarnation! He sees, in our view rightly, the doctrines of incarnation as both historically and epistemically secondary interpretations of the primary determination of the resurrection.[50] Hence, everything that the Christological confessions say about Christ in terms of the incarnation is dependent upon the fact of the resurrection. The resurrection becomes, so to say, the axis of Christology. If it breaks, there is not much point in anything else we can say about the historical person Jesus from Nazareth, including the incarnation.

There are several important implications of this way of arguing, and Dalferth himself presents some of them. Before we present his conclusions, it is important to notice that by giving the resurrection such a crucial place in the theme of Christology, Dalferth is underscoring the possible failure as well as the extreme incoherence that every type of theology risks that does not take its point of departure in this event. This is not an argument for the resurrection as such, but it is an argument for the centrality of the resurrection (which must be distinguished clearly from the first). Hence, at the center of the Christian confession to Jesus as the savior of the world is an event that cannot be established as a fact, but which—as we have indicated—we can only approach as a gift and a promise.

The most important result of this way of reasoning for Dalferth himself, is that it allows him to see incarnation Christology as unnecessary: it is not the primary element in the confession of Jesus. Instead of bringing the central element of Christology to its expression, it contributes to the interpretation of the life of Jesus in light of his resurrection and contributes in different ways to the explication of the importance of that event. Christologies are, generically speaking, results of efforts to comprehend the work God did in resurrecting Christ. They are not the work of God but interpreting the works of God. On the other hand, the resurrection is to be seen as the event that precedes our interpretative work, and which we come to too late in order to grasp fully. Hence, we also need a plurality of different ways to access the life and death and resurrection of Christ. No content of a confession is able to exhaust the theme of the confession or

---

49. Dalferth, *Crucified and Resurrected*, 31.
50. Dalferth, *Crucified and Resurrected*, 30–31.

to take the place of that which is referred to with the name Jesus Christ—including the confession of him as the son of God. This is so because this confession as well does not give a conceptual clarification of the Christological thematic, but instead, it refers us back to the resurrected Jesus, and thereby also to the eschatological actions of God for our salvation. These actions are the basis that transcends every attempt of interpretation and, as such, is the basis of Christian faith.[51]

Dalferth thus makes a move that identifies the singular reality of the resurrection as the only indispensable foundation of belief in Jesus as the true witness to God, and at the same time, he allows for—even sees the necessity for—a plurality of different ways of explicating the content that has been possible to develop given the event of the resurrection. While he underscores that formulations about the resurrection of Christ cannot be interpreted only as reflective formulations (Reflektionsaussagen), he also holds that such formulations imply propositions and claims about our reality (Realitätsaussagen).[52]

The crucial function of the resurrection reveals itself in more than being a point of departure for reflections and confessional formulations. It reveals itself also as the final means by which identity is sufficiently revealed to become liberating for all the parties involved. Dalferth develops the establishment of Jesus's identity along the following lines, which also allows us to see the close relationship between God and Jesus that incarnation theology tries to explicate:

> We can start by asking "Who is it that God raised from the dead?" The answer would be "It is the crucified Jesus from Nazareth." This answer then allows for another question of identity: "Who is Jesus from Nazareth?" Here the answer turns back in the form "It is the one whom God raised from the dead." This answer then provokes the third and final form of the question: "Who is the one who was crucified and resurrected?" The answer to this final question is now opening the soteriological horizon in which we can find a way of recognizing ourselves: "He is the one with whom God has identified Godself irrevocably for our sake. He is the Christ, the Lord, the Son of God."[53]

The resurrection as the axis of Christology thereby reveals itself as the axis of Christian theology in general. When we contemplate on how the being of Christ for us is founded in a divine reality, the Trinitarian way of reasoning

---

51. Dalferth, *Crucified and Resurrected*, 31.
52. Cf. Dalferth, *Crucified and Resurrected*, 55–58.
53. Dalferth, *Crucified and Resurrected*, 84.

presents itself as the conclusion to this story.[54] And in Dalferth, it is evident that the precondition for his work is the result of the Trinitarian discussion and its final formulation. Without this, he would not be able to lay out how the different schemas of understanding Christ can be explicated from the point of view of resurrection. However, the argument for how this is the case must be carried out in another context than that of the present book.[55]

Resurrection as a Manifestation of God's Future for Creation

We are unable to explicate fully what "resurrection" means, but the interpretative contexts we have employed have indicated that it is a *saturated phenomenon* or a *phenomenon of surplus*. Moreover, resurrection is a symbol for a future that contains a surplus compared to the conditions of the present world and suggests in a profound manner how present life can be transformed by the creative grace of God. The resurrection is itself a witness to how God works in creation by grace, and how God's works cannot be separated. The resurrection is a testimony to a God that desires the good for the created world. It is not only about the future but is manifested in the life and death of Jesus and in the hope that makes worthwhile struggles for goodness and justice. It supplies humans with a point of orientation that allows them to recognize themselves as loved, cared for, and not lost to the destructive powers of this world.

From a Christological point of view (that is still linked to our experience), we can have an established hope, which helps us recognize how history goes on in a way that is not determined by death, but by the God of life, who sent God's Son for us. God is a gifting God, and as the infinite source of all gifts, God becomes apparent (revealed) in and by God's gifts. This God is life, sustains life, and confronts death as that which means the destruction of the life and the goodness of God's creation. The resurrection is a testimony to and an instance of the act of the God who can create good things out of nothing. In this sense, the mission of Jesus is also a mission that is in consonance with God's love for creation. However, as indicated, the resurrection implies a surplus compared to that of creation, as death is no more. Jesus—as the first who bears a true, ultimate, and unsurpassable witness to God as life and community—is the first to take part in the community of the new creation and thus to realize it. The point of confessing the

---

54. Cf. Dalferth, *Crucified and Resurrected*, 155.

55. An attempt to develop this line of thinking further towards a trinitarian position can be found in Henriksen, *Life, Love, and Hope*.

resurrection is not to look back to the events surrounding his death, but to recognize him as the one who is living—and who is manifesting the future of all creation. Resurrection implies a future in which God's life, justice, and goodness rule. In the future of God, there is no competing economy which leads to exclusion and injustice. Resurrection to life is to be re-given a gift and is the fulfilling of God's promise to the world.

Bibliography

Aarflot, Christine Henriksen. *God (in) Acts: The Characterization of God in the Acts of the Apostles*. Eugene, OR: Pickwick, 2020.
Alkier, Stefan. *The Reality of the Resurrection: The New Testament Witness*. Waco, TX: Baylor University Press, 2013.
Alkier, Stefan, and Annette Weissenrieder. *Miracles Revisited: New Testament Miracle Stories and Their Concepts of Reality*. Studies of the Bible and Its Reception 2. Berlin: De Gruyter, 2013.
Alkier, Stefan, and David Moffitt. "Miracles Revisited: A Short Theological and Historical Survey." In *Miracles Revisited: New Testament Miracle Stories and Their Concepts of Reality*, edited by Stefan Alkier and Annette Weissenrieder, 315–37. Studies of the Bible and Its Reception 2. Berlin: De Gruyter, 2013.
Allison, Dale C., Jr. *Constructing Jesus: Memory, Imagination, and History*. Grand Rapids: Baker, 2010.
———. "Explaining the Resurrection: Conflicting Convictions." *Journal for the Study of the Historical Jesus* 3 (2005) 117–33.
———. *Resurrecting Jesus: The Earliest Christian Tradition and Its Interpreters*. New York: T. & T. Clark, 2005.
Anderson, Kevin L. *"But God Raised Him from the Dead": The Theology of Jesus' Resurrection in Luke-Acts*. Paternoster Biblical Monographs. Milton Keynes: Paternoster, 2006.
Andresen, Carl. *Logos und Mythos: Die Polemik des Kelsos wider das Christentum*. Arbeiten zur Kirchengeschichte 30. Berlin: De Gruyter, 1955.
The Apocriticus of Macarios Magnes. Translated by T.W. Crafer. Translations of Christian Literature Series I. London, New York: Macmillan, 1919.
Aquinas, Thomas. *The "Summa Theologica" of St. Thomas Aquinas, Part I, QQ. L-LXXIV*. Charleston, SC: BiblioLife, 2010.
Athenagoras. *Athenagoras: Legatio and De Resurrectione*. Edited and translated by William R. Schoedel. Oxford Early Christian Texts. Oxford: Clarendon, 1972.
Austad, Anne. "'Passing Away—Passing By': A Qualitative Study of Experiences and Meaning Making of Post Death Presence." PhD diss., MF Norwegian School of Theology, 2015.
Bailey, Kenneth. *Poet and Peasant and Through Peasant Eyes: A Literary-Cultural Approach to the Parables of Luke*. Combined Edition. Grand Rapids: Eerdmans, 1983.

Baker, John Austin. *The Foolishness of God*. Atlanta: John Knox, 1975.
Barclay, John M. G. *Paul and the Gift*. Grand Rapids: Eerdmans, 2015.
———. "The Resurrection in Contemporary New Testament Scholarship." In *Resurrection Reconsidered*, edited by Gavin D'Costa, 13–30. Oxford: Oneworld, 1996.
Barnett, Paul W. "The Jewish Sign Prophets A.D. 40–70: Their Intention and Origins." *New Testament Studies* 27 (1981) 679–97.
Barton, Stephen C., et al. *Resurrection: Essays in Honour of Leslie Houlden*. London: SPCK, 1994.
Bauckham, Richard. *The Christian World Around the New Testament*. Grand Rapids: Baker, 2017.
———. *The Climax of Prophecy: Studies in the Book of Revelation*. Edinburgh: T. & T. Clark, 1993.
———. *Jesus and the Eyewitness Testimony: The Gospels as Eyewitness Testimony*. Grand Rapids: Eerdmans, 2006.
———. "Jesus and the Wild Animals (Mark 1:13): A Christological Image for an Ecological Age." In *Jesus of Nazareth: Lord and Christ: Essays on the Historical Jesus and New Testament Christology. In Honor of I. Howard Marshall*, edited by Joel B. Green and Max Turner, 3–21. Grand Rapids: Eerdmans, 1994.
Belser, Julia Watts. "Violence, Disability and the Politics of Healing: The Inaugural Nancy Eiesland Endowment Lecture." *Journal of Disability and Religion* 19 (2015) 177–97.
Bieringer, Reimund. "'I am Ascending to my Father and your Father, to my God and your God' (John 20:17): Resurrection and Ascension in the Gospel of John." In *The Resurrection of Jesus in the Gospel of John*, edited by Craig R. Koester and Reimund Bieringer, 208–35. Wissenschaftliche Untersuchungen zum Neuen Testament 222. Tübingen: Mohr Siebeck, 2008.
Black, David Alan. *Perspectives on the Ending of Mark: 4 Views*. Nashville: Broadman & Holman, 2008.
Bockmuehl, Markus. "Resurrection." In *The Cambridge Companion to Jesus*, edited by Markus Bockmuehl, 102–18. Cambridge: Cambridge University Press, 2001.
———. *Simon Peter in Scripture and Memory*. Grand Rapids: Baker, 2012.
Boeve, L. "Theology and the Interruption of Experience." In *Religious Experience and Contemporary Theological Epistemology*, edited by L. Boeve, Y. De Maeseneer, and S. Van den Bossche, 11–40. Leuven: Peeters, 2005.
Boeve, L., et al. *Religious Experience and Contemporary Theological Epistemology*. Bibliotheca Ephemeridum Theologicarum Lovaniensium. Leuven: Peeters, 2005.
Bultmann, Rudolf. "Jesus Christus und die Mythologie." In *Glauben und Verstehen*, 4:141–189. Tübingen: J. B. C. Mohr, 1993.
———. *Neues Testament und Mythologie: Das Problem der Entmythologisierung der neutestamentlichen Verkündigung*. Nachdruck der 1941 erschienenen Fassung herausgegeben von Eberhard Jüngel. München: Chr. Kaiser, 1988.
———. "Zur Frage des Wunders." In *Glauben und Verstehen*, 1:218–28. Tübingen: J. B. C. Mohr, 1993.
Bynum, Caroline Walker. *The Resurrection of the Body in Western Christianity, 200–1336*. New York: Columbia University Press, 1995.

Byrskog, Samuel. *Jesus the Only Teacher: Didactic Authority and Transmission in Ancient Israel, Ancient Judaism and the Matthean Community*. Coniectana Biblica New Testament Series 24. Stockholm: Almquist & Wiksell, 1994.

———. *Story as History—History as Story: The Gospel Tradition in the Context of Ancient Oral History*. Wissenschaftliche Untersuchungen zum Neuen Testament 123. Tübingen: Mohr Siebeck, 2001.

Caird, G. B. *New Testament Theology*. Oxford: Oxford University Press, 1995.

Carnley, Peter. *Resurrection in Retrospect. A Critical Examination of the Theology of N. T. Wright*. Eugene, OR: Cascade, 2019.

———. *The Structure of Resurrection Belief*. Oxford: Clarendon, 1987.

Coakley, Sarah. "'Not with the Eye Only.' The Resurrection, Epistemology and Gender." *Reflections* 5 (2002) 24–57.

Coleman-Norton, P. R. "An Amusing Agraphon." *Catholic Biblical Quarterly* 12 (1959) 439–49.

Cook, John Granger. *Empty Tomb, Resurrection, Apotheosis*. Wissenschaftliche Untersuchungen zum Neuen Testament 410. Tübingen: Mohr Siebeck, 2018.

———. *The Interpretation of the New Testament in Greco-Roman Paganism*. Peabody, MA: Hendrickson, 2002.

———. "Resurrection and Paganism and the Question of an Empty Tomb in 1 Corinthians 15." *New Testament Studies* 63 (2017) 56–75.

———. "The Use of *anistêmi* and *egeirô* and the 'Resurrection of a Soul.'" *Zeitschrift für die Neutestamentliche Wissenschaft* 108 (2017) 259–80.

Copan, Paul, and Ronald K. Tacelli, eds. *Jesus' Resurrection: Fact or Figment? A Debate Between William Lane Craig and Gerd Lüdemann*. Downers Grove, IL: InterVarsity, 2000.

Craffert, Pieter F. "'I Witnessed the Raising of the Dead': Resurrection Accounts in a Neuroanthropological Perspective." *Neotestamentica* 45 (2011) 1–28.

———. "Jesus' Resurrection in Social-Scientific Perspective: Is There Anything New to be Said?" *Journal for the Study of the Historical Jesus* 7 (2009) 125–51.

Craig, William Lane. "Wright and Crossan on the Historicity of the Resurrection of Jesus." In *The Resurrection of Jesus: John Dominic Crossan and N. T. Wright in Dialogue*, edited by Robert B. Stewart, 139–48. Minneapolis: Fortress, 2006.

Crossan, John Dominic. "Appendix: Bodily-Resurrection Faith." In *The Resurrection of Jesus: John Dominic Crossan and N. T. Wright in Dialogue*, edited by Robert B. Stewart, 171–86. Minneapolis: Fortress, 2006.

———. *The Birth of Christianity: Discovering what Happened in the Years Immediately after the Execution of Jesus*. San Francisco: HarperCollins, 1999.

———. "Bodily-Resurrection Faith." In *The Resurrection of Jesus: The Crossan—Wright Dialogue*, edited by Robert B. Stewart, 182–86. Minneapolis: Fortress, 2006.

———. *A Revolutionary Biography*. San Francisco: HarperCollins, 1994.

———. *Who Killed Jesus? Exposing the Roots of Anti-Semitism in the Gospel Story of the Death of Jesus*. San Francisco: HarperCollins, 1995.

Crossan, John Dominic, and J. L. Reed. *Excavating Jesus: Beneath the Stones, Behind the Texts*. San Francisco: HarperCollins, 2001.

Crossley, James G. "The Historical Plausibility of the Empty Tomb Story and the Bodily Resurrection of Jesus." *Journal for the Study of the Historical Jesus* 3 (2005) 171–86.

Dalferth, Ingolf U. *Crucified and Resurrected: Restructuring the Grammar of Christology*. Grand Rapids: Baker, 2015.

———. "Volles Grab, Leerer Glaube? Zum Streit Um Die Auferweckung Des Gekreuzigten." *Zeitschrift für Theologie und Kirche* 95 (1998) 379–409.

Dalton, William. *Christ's Proclamation to the Spirits: A Study of 1 Peter 3:18–4:6*. Analecta Biblica 23. Roma: Editrice Pontificio Istitutio Biblico, 1989.

D'Costa, Gavin. *Resurrection Reconsidered*. Oxford: Oneworld, 1996.

Deichgräber, Reinhard. *Gotteshymnus und Christushymnus in der frühen Christenheit: Untersuchungen zu Form, Sprache und Stil der frühchristlichen Hymnen*. Studien zur Umwelt des Neuen Testaments 5. Göttingen: Vandenhoeck & Ruprecht, 1967.

Douven, Igor. "Abduction." In *The Stanford Encyclopedia of Philosophy*, edited by Edward N. Zalta. 2017. https://plato.stanford.edu/archives/sum2017/entries/abduction.

Dunn, James D. G. *The Evidence for Jesus: The Impact of Scholarship on Our Understanding of How Christianity Began*. London: SCM, 1985.

———. *Jesus Remembered*. Grand Rapids: Eerdmans, 2003.

———. *Jesus and the Spirit: A Study of Religious and Charismatic Experience of Jesus and the First Christians as Reflected in the New Testament*. Grand Rapids: Eerdmans, 1997.

———. *Romans 1–8*. Word Biblical Commentary 38A. Dallas: Word, 1988.

———. *The Theology of Paul the Apostle*. Grand Rapids: Eerdmans, 1998.

Earman, John. *Hume's Abject Failure: The Argument against Miracles*. Oxford: Oxford University Press, 2000.

Eckstein, Hans-Joachim. "Bodily Resurrection in Luke." In *Resurrection: Theological and Scientific Assessments*, edited by Ted Peters et al., 115–23. Grand Rapids: Eerdmans, 2002.

———. "Die Wirklichkeit der Auferstehung Jesu. Lukas 24,34 als Beispiel früher formelhafter Zeugnisse." In *Die Wirklichkeit der Auferstehung*, edited by Hans-Joachim Eckstein and Michael Welker, 1–30. Neukirchen-Vluyn: Neukirchener, 2010.

Eckstein, Hans-Joachim, and Michael Welker, eds. *Die Wirklichkeit der Auferstehung*. Neukirchen-Vluyn: Neukirchener, 2010.

Ehrman, Bart D., ed. and trans. *The Apostolic Fathers*. Loeb Classical Library. Cambridge, MA: Harvard University, 2003.

Eikrem, Asle. *Being in Religion: A Journey in Ontology from Pragmatics through Hermeneutics to Metaphysics*. Religion in Philosophy and Theology 67. Tübingen: Mohr Siebeck, 2013.

Endsjø, Dag Øistein. "Immortal Bodies, before Christ: Bodily Continuity in Ancient Greece and 1 Corinthians." *Journal for the Study of the New Testament* 30 (2008) 417–36.

Engberg-Pedersen, Troels. "Complete and Incomplete Transformation in Paul: A Philosophical Reading of Paul on Body and Spirit." In *Metamorphoses: Resurrection, Body, and Transformative Practices in early Christianity*, edited by Turid Karlsen Seim and Jorunn Økland, 123–46. Ekstasis: Religious Experiences from Antiquity to the Middle Ages 1. Berlin: De Gruyter, 2009.

———. *Cosmology and Self in the Apostle Paul: The Material Spirit*. Oxford: Oxford University Press, 2010.

Eusebius. *Life of Constantine*. Edited and translated by Averil Cameron and Stuart G. Hall. Oxford: Oxford University Press, 1999.

———. *Gospel Problems and Solutions: Quaestiones ad Stephanum et Marinum*. Edited by Roger Pearse and translated by David J. Miller et al. Ipswich: Chieftain Publishing, 2010.

Evans, Craig A. "Jewish Burial Traditions and the Resurrection of Jesus." *Journal for the Study of the Historical Jesus* 3 (2005) 233–48.

Fee, Gordon D. *The First Epistle to the Corinthians*. The New International Commentary on the New Testament. Grand Rapids: Eerdmans, 1987.

Feldman, Louis H. *Judean Antiquities 1–4 Translation and Commentary*. Edited by Steve Mason. Flavius Josephus: Translation and Commentary 3. Leiden: Brill, 2000.

Feldmeier Reinhard, and Hermann Spieckermann. *Der Gott der Lebendigen: Eine biblische Gotteslehre*. Topics of Biblical Theology 1. Tübingen: Mohr Siebeck, 2011.

Festinger, Leon. *A Theory of Cognitive Dissonance*. Stanford: Stanford University Press, 1957.

Fetzer, Antje. "Auferstanden ins Kerygma? Rudolf Bultmanns existentiale Interpretation der Auferstehung." In *Die Wirklichkeit der Auferstehung*, edited by Hans-Joachim Eckstein and Michael Welker, 83–110. Neukirchen-Vluyn: Neukirchener, 2010.

Finsterbusch, Karin. *Die Thora als Lebensweisung für Heidenchristen: Studien zur Bedeutung der Thora für die paulinische Ethik*. Studien zur Umwelt des Neuen Testaments 20. Göttingen: Vandenhoeck & Ruprecht, 1996.

Fitzmyer, Joseph. A. *The Acts of the Apostles: A New Translation with Introduction and Commentary*. Anchor Bible 31. New York: Doubleday, 1998.

Fjärstedt, Björn. "Synoptic Tradition in 1 Corinthians: Themes and Clusters of Them Words in 1 Corinthians 1–4 and 9." Doctoral thesis, Uppsala University, 1974.

Fogelin, Robert J. *A Defense of Hume on Miracles*. Princeton: Princeton University Press, 2003.

Foster, Paul. *The Gospel of Peter: Introduction, Critical Edition and Commentary*. Texts and Editions for New Testament Study 4. Leiden: Brill, 2010.

Frenschkowski, Marco. "Antike kritische und skeptische Stimmen zum Wunderglauben als Dialogparther des frühen Christentums." In *Hermeneutik der frühchristlichen Wundererzählungen: Geschichtliche. Literarische und rezeptionsorientierte Perspektiven*, 283–308. Wissenschaftliche Untersuchungen zum Neuen Testament 339. Tübingen: Mohr Siebeck, 2014.

Gadamer, Hans-Georg. *Truth and Method*. Stagbooks. London: Sheed & Ward, 1989.

Gerhardsson, Birger. "Evidence for Christ's Resurrection according to Paul: 1 Cor 15:1–11." In *Neotestamentica et Philonica: Studies in Honor of Peder Borgen*, edited by David E. Aune et al., 73–91. Novum Testamentum Supplementum 106. Leiden: Brill, 2003.

Gibson, Simon. *The Final Days of Jesus: The Archaeological Evidence*. New York: HarperCollins, 2010.

Gould, James Barton. "The Hope of Heavenly Healing of Disability Part 1: Theological Issues." *Journal of Disability and Religion* 20 (2016) 317–34.

———. "The Hope of Heavenly Healing of Disability Part 2: Philosophical Issues." *Journal of Disability and Religion* 21 (2017) 98–116.

Goulder, Michael. "The Baseless Fabric of a Vision." In *Resurrection Reconsidered*, edited by Gavin D'Costa, 48–61. Oxford: OneWorld, 1996.

———. "The Explanatory Power of Conversion-Visions." In *Jesus' Resurrection: Fact or Figment? A Debate Between William Lane Craig and Gerd Lüdemann*, edited by Paul Copan and Ronald K. Tacelli, 86–103. Downers Grove, IL: InterVarsity, 2000.

Grube, Dirk-Martin. "Christian Theology Emerged by Way of a Kuhnian Paradigm Shift." *International Journal of Philosophy and Theology* 79 (2018) 178–93.

Gschwandtner, Christina M. *Degrees of Givenness: On Saturation in Jean-Luc Marion*. Bloomington: Indiana University Press, 2014.

Habermas, Gary R. *The Resurrection of Jesus*. Lanham, MD: University Press of America, 1984.

———. *The Risen Jesus and Future Hope*. Lanham, MD: Rowman & Littlefield, 2003.

Habermas, Gary R, et al. *Did Jesus Rise from the Dead? The Resurrection Debate*. San Francisco: Harper & Row, 1987.

———. *Resurrected?: An Atheist and Theist Dialogue*. Lanham, MD: Rowman & Littlefield, 2005.

Hayes, Jacqueline. "Experiencing the Presence of the Deceased: Symptoms, Spirits, or Ordinary Life?" ProQuest Dissertations Publishing, 2011.

Hayes, Jacqueline, and Ivan Leudar. "Experiences of Continued Presence: On the Practical Consequences of 'Hallucinations' in Bereavement." *Psychology And Psychotherapy* 89 (2016) 194–210.

Hays, Richard B. *Echoes of Scripture in the Gospels*. Waco, TX: Baylor University Press, 2016.

Henriksen, Jan-Olav. *Christianity as Distinct Practices: A Complicated Relationship*. London: Bloomsbury, 2019.

———. *Desire, Gift and Recogniton*. Christology and Postmodern Philosophy. Grand Rapids: Eerdmans, 2009.

———. *Finitude and Theological Anthropology: An Interdisciplinary Exploration into Theological Dimensions of Finitude*. Leuven: Peeters, 2011.

———. *Life, Love, and Hope: God and Human Experience*. Grand Rapids: Eerdmans, 2014.

———. *Religion as Orientation and Transformation: A Maximalist Theory*. Religion in Philosophy and Theology. Tübingen: Mohr Siebeck, 2017.

Henriksen, Jan-Olav, and Karl Olav Sandnes. *Jesus as Healer: A Gospel for the Body*. Grand Rapids: Eerdmans, 2016.

Hick, John. *The Metaphor of God Incarnate*. 2nd ed. London: SCM, 2005.

Hoffmann, Matthias Reinhard. *The Destroyer and the Lamb: The Relationship Between Angelomorphic and Lamb Christology in the Book of Revelation*. Wissenschaftliche Untersuchungen zum Neuen Testament 2.203. Tübingen: Mohr Siebeck, 2005.

Hoffmann, Paul. "Auferstehung II/1." In *Theologische Realenzyklopädie*, edited by G. Krause and G. Müller, 4:478–513. Berlin: De Gruyter, 1979.

Hurtado, Larry W. "Earliest Expression of a Discrete Group-Formation among Christ-Believers." *Estudios Biblicos* 75 (2017) 451–70.

Hvalvik, Reidar, and Karl Olav Sandnes. "Prayer and Identity Formation: Attempts at a Synthesis." In *Early Christian Prayer and Identity Formation*, edited by Reidar Hvalvik and Karl Olav Sandnes, 371–81. Wissenschaftliche Untersuchungen zum Neuen Testament 336. Tübingen: Mohr Siebeck, 2014.

Johnston, Jeremiah J. *The Resurrection of Jesus in the Gospel of Peter*. Jewish and Christian Texts 21. London: T. & T. Clark, 2016.

Johnstone, Brian V. "The Resurrection in Phenomenology: Jean-Luc Marion on the 'Saturated Phenomenon Par Excellence.'" *Pacifica* 28 (2015) 23–39.

Juel, Donald H. *Messianic Exegesis: Christological Interpretation of the Old Testament in Early Christianity*. Philadelphia: Fortress, 1988.

Justin Martyr. *Apologiae Pro Christianis*. Edited by Miroslav Marcovoch. Patristische Texte und Studien 38. Berlin, New York: De Gruyter, 1994.

———. *Iustini Martyris, Dialogus cum Tryphone*. Edited by Miroslav Marcovich. Patristische Texte und Studien 47. Berlin: Walter de Gruyter, 1997.

Justin: Philosopher and Martyr. Edited with a Commentary on the text by Denis Minns and Paul Parvis. Oxford: Oxford University Press, 2009.

Kannaday, Wayne C. *Apologetic Discourse and the Scribal Tradition: Evidence of the Influence of Apologetic Interests on the Text of the Canonical Gospels*. Text-Critical Studies 5. Atlanta: Society of Biblical Literature, 2004.

Kartzow, Marianne Bjelland. *Gossip and Gender: Othering of Speech in the Pastoral Epistles*. Beihefte zur Zeitschrift für die Neutestamentliche Wissenschaft 164. Berlin: Walter de Gruyter, 2009.

Keener, Craig S. *Acts: An Exegetical Commentary: Volume 3: 15:1–23:35*. Grand Rapids: Baker, 2014.

Kelhoffer, James A. *Conceptions of "Gospel" and Legitimacy in Early Christianity*. Wissenschaftliche Untersuchungen zum Neuen Testament 324. Tübingen: Mohr Siebeck, 2014.

———. *Miracle and Mission: The Authentication of Missionaries and Their Message in the Longer Ending of Mark*. Wissenschaftliche Untersuchungen zum Neuen Testament 2.112. Tübingen: Mohr Siebeck, 2000.

Kienzler, Klaus. *Logik Der Auferstehung: Eine Untersuchung Zu Rudolf Bultmann, Gerhard Ebeling Und Wolfhart Pannenberg*. Freiburger Theologische Studien. Freiburg: Herder, 1976.

Kim, Seyoon. *The Origin of Paul's Gospel*. Wissenschaftliche Untersuchungen zum Neuen Testament 4. Tübingen: Mohr Siebeck, 1981.

Koester, Craig R. *Revelation and the End of All Things*. Grand Rapids: Eerdmans, 2001.

———. *Revelation: A New Translation with Introduction and Commentary*. Anchor Bible 38A. New Haven, CT: Yale University Press, 2014.

Küchler, Max. *Jerusalem: Ein Handbuch und Studienreiseführer zur Heiligen Stadt*. Orte und Landschaften der Bibel IV 2. Göttingen: Vandenhoeck & Ruprecht, 2007.

Küng, Hans. *On Being a Christian*. Translated by Edward Quinn. New York: Doubleday, 1974.

Kvalbein, Hans. "The Lord's Prayer and the Eucharist Prayer in the *Didache*." In *Early Christian Prayer and Identity Formation*, edited by Reidar Hvalvik and Karl Olav Sandnes, 233–66. Wissenschaftlcihe Untersuchungen zum Neuen Testament 336. Tübingen: Mohr Siebeck, 2014.

Labahn, Michael. "The Resurrection of the Followers of the Lamb: Between Heavenly 'Reality' and Hope for the Future: The Concept of Resurrection within the Imagery of Death and Life in the Book of Revelation." In *Resurrection of the Dead: Biblical Traditions in Dialogue*, edited by Geert van Oyen, 319–42. Bibliotheca Ephemeridum Theologicarum Lovaniensium 249. Leuven: Peeters, 2012.

Lampe, Peter. "Jesu DNS-Spuren in einem Ossuar und in einem Massengrab seine Gebeine? Von medialer Pseudowissenschaft und zuweilen unsachgemässen Expertenreaktion." *Zeitschrift für Neues Testament* 19 (2007) 72–76.

Larsen, Matthew D. *Gospels Before the Book*. Oxford: Oxford University Press, 2018.

Lehtipuu, Outi. *Debates over the Resurrection of the Dead: Constructing Early Christian Identity*. Oxford Early Christian Studies. Oxford: Oxford University Press, 2015.

Lelwica, Michelle Mary. *Shameful Bodies: Religion and the Culture of Physical Improvement.* London: Bloomsbury, 2017.

Licona, Michael R. *The Resurrection of Jesus: A New Historiographical Approach.* Downers Grove, IL: InterVarsity, 2010.

Lindemann, Andreas. *Der Erste Korintherbrief.* Handbuch zum Neuen Testament 9.1. Tübingen: Mohr Siebeck, 2000.

———. "The Resurrection of Jesus: Reflections on Historical and Theological Questions." *Ephemerides Theologicae Lovanienses* 93 (2017) 557–79.

Lona, Horacio E. *Die "Wahre Lehre" des Kelsos: Übersetzt und erklärt.* Kommentar zu frühchristlichen Apologeten 1. Freiburg: Herder, 2005.

Lüdemann, Gerd. "Opening Statement." In *Jesus' Resurrection: Fact or Figment? A Debate Between William Lane Craig and Gerd Lüdemann,* edited by Paul Copan and Ronald K. Tacelli, 40–45. Downers Grove, IL: InterVarsity, 2000.

———. *The Resurrection of Christ: A Historical Inquiry.* Amherst, NY: Prometheus, 2004.

———. "The Resurrection of Jesus: Fifteen Years later." In *Resurrection of the Dead: Biblical Traditions in Dialogue,* edited by Geert van Oyen and Tom Shepherd, 535–57. Bibliotheca Ephemeridium Theologicarum Lovaniensium 249. Leuven: Peeters, 2012.

———. *The Resurrection of Jesus: History, Experience, Theology.* Minneapolis: Fortress,1994.

———. *What Really Happened to Jesus? A Historical Approach to the Resurrection.* Louisville: Westminster John Knox, 1995.

Lunn, Nicholas P. *The Original Ending of Mark: A New Case for the Authenticity of Mark 16:9–20.* Eugene, OR: Pickwick, 2014.

Macarios de Magnésie. *Macarios de Magnésie: Le Monogénès, Édition Critique et Traduction Française I–II. Introduction Génerale.* Edited and translated by Richard Goulet. Textes et Traditions 7. Paris: J. Vrin, 2003.

MacDonald, Dennis R. *Mimesis and Intertextuality in Antiquity and Christianity.* Harrisburg, PA: Trinity, 2001.

MacDonald, Margaret Y. *Early Christian Women and Pagan Opinion: The Power of the Hysterical Woman.* Cambridge: Cambridge University Press, 1996.

Mackinlay, Shane. "Eyes Wide Shut: A Response to Jean-Luc Marion's Account of the Journey to Emmaus." *Modern Theology* 20 (2004) 447–56.

Macquarrie, John. *Jesus Christ in Modern Thought.* London: SCM, 1990.

Magness, Jodi. *Stone and Dung, Oil and Spit: Jewish Daily Life in the Time of Jesus.* Grand Rapids: Eerdmans, 2011.

Marion, Jean-Luc. *Being Given: Toward a Phenomenology of Givenness.* Cultural Memory in the Present. Stanford: Stanford University Press, 2002.

———. *In Excess: Studies of Saturated Phenomena.* Perspectives in Continental Philosophy 27. New York: New York University Press, 2002.

———. "'They Recognized Him; and He Became Invisible to Them.'" *Modern Theology* 18 (2002) 145–52.

Martin, Dale B. *The Corinthian Body.* New Haven, CT: Yale University Press, 1995.

Mason, Steve. *Life of Josephus.* Edited by Steve Mason. Flavius Josephus 9. Leiden: Brill, 2001.

Melito of Sardis. *On Pascha and Fragments.* Oxford Early Christian Texts. Edited and translated by Stuart G. Hall. Oxford: Clarendon, 1979.

Metz, Johannes Baptist. *Faith in History and Society: Toward a Practical Fundamental Theology*. New York: Seabury Press, 1980.
Moffitt, David M. *Atonement and the Logic of Resurrection in the Epistle to the Hebrews*. Supplements to Novum Testamentum 141. Leiden: Brill, 2011.
Molnar, Paul D. *Incarnation and Resurrection: Toward a Contemporary Understanding*. Grand Rapids: Eerdmans, 2007.
Moss, Candida R. "Heavenly Healing: Eschatological Cleansing and the Resurrection of the Dead in the Early Church." *Journal of the American Academy of Religion* 79 (2011) 991–1017.
Nanos, Mark D., and Magnus Zetterholm, eds. *Paul within Judaism: Restoring the First Century Context to the Apostle*. Philadelphia: Fortress, 2015.
New Testament Apocrypha Volume One: Gospels and Related Writings. Edited by Wilhelm Schneemelcher and R. McL. Wilson. Louisville: Westminster John Knox, 1991.
Niehoff, Maren R. *Jewish Exegesis and Homeric Scholarship in Alexandria*. Cambridge: Cambridge University Press, 2011.
Novakovic, Lidija. *Raised From the Dead According to Scripture: The Role of Israel's Scripture in the Early Christian Interpretation of Jesus' Resurrection*. Jewish and Christian Texts. London: T. & T. Clark, 2012.
———. *Resurrection: A Guide for the Perplexed*. London: Bloomsbury, 2016.
O'Connell, Jake. "Jesus' Resurrection and Collective Hallucinations." *Tyndale Bulletin* 60 (2009) 69–105.
Origen. *Contra Celsum*. Translated with an Introduction and Notes by Henry Chadwick. Cambridge: Cambridge University Press, 1953.
———. *Origène Contre Celse*. Source Chrétienne 132. Edited and translated by Marcel Borret. Paris: Cerf, 1967.
Pannenberg, Wolfhart. "Die Auferstehung Jesu und die Zukunft des Menschen." In *Grundfragen Systematischer Theologie* 2:207–25. Göttingen: Vandenhoeck und Ruprecht, 1980.
———. "The Concept of Miracle." *Zygon* 37 (2002) 759–62.
———. *Grundfragen Systematischer Theologie*. Göttingen: Vandenhoeck und Ruprecht, 1980.
———. "Hermeneutic and Universal History." In *Basic Questions in Theology: Volume 1*. Minneapolis: Augsburg Fortress, 2008.
———. "History and the Reality of the Resurrection." In *Resurrection Reconsidered*, edited by Gavid D'Costa, 62–72. Oxford: Oneworld, 1996.
———. *Jesus—God and Man*. SCM Classics. London: SCM, 2002.
———. *Systematic Theology*. 3 vols. Grand Rapids: Eerdmans, 1991.
Peirce, Charles S. *Collected Papers*. Cambridge, MA: Belknap, 1978.
———. *The Essential Peirce: Selected Philosophical Writings*. 2 vols. Edited by Peirce Edition Project. Bloomington: Indiana University Press, 1992.
Peters, Ted, et al. *Resurrection: Theological and Scientific Assessments*. Grand Rapids: Eerdmans, 2002.
Popper, Karl Raimund. *Conjectures and Refutations: The Growth of Scientific Knowledge*. New York: Basic, 1962.
Quarles, Charles L. "The Gospel of Peter: Does It Contain a Precanonical Resurrection Narrative?" In *The Resurrection of Jesus: John Dominic Crossan and N. T. Wright in Dialogue*, edited by Robert B. Stewart, 106–20. Minneapolis: Fortress, 2006.

———. "Matthew 27:51–53: Meaning, Genre, Intertextuality, Theology, and Reception History." *Journal of Evangelical Theologies Society* 59 (2016) 271–86.
Rambo, Shelly. *Resurrecting Wounds: Living in the Afterlife of Trauma*. Waco, TX: Baylor University Press, 2017.
Ravnå, Per Bjarne. *Jesus fra Nasaret: Mislykket profet eller guds sønn?* Oslo: Dreyer, 2017.
Read-Heimerdinger, Jenny, and Josep Rius-Camp. *A Gospel Synopsis of the Greek Text of Matthew, Mark and Luke: A Comparison of Codex Bezae and Codex Vaticanus*. New Testament Tools, Studies and Documents 45. Leiden: Brill, 2014.
Reemts, Christiana. *Vernunftgemässer Glaube: Die Begründung des Christentums in der Schrift des Origenes gegen Celsus*. Hereditas 13. Bonn: Borengässer, 1997.
Reynolds, T. E. "Theology and Disability: Changing the Conversation." *Journal of Religion, Disability and Health* 16 (2012) 33–48.
Riley, Gregory. *Resurrection Reconsidered. Thomas and John in Controversy*. Minneapolis: Fortress, 1995.
Ringleben, Joachim. *Wahrhaft Auferstanden: Zur Begründung der Theologie des lebendigen Gottes*. Tübingen: Mohr Siebeck, 1998.
Risser, James. *Hermeneutics and the Voice of the Other: Re-Reading Gadamer's Philosophical Hermeneutics*. Suny Series in Contemporary Continental Philosophy. Albany: State University of New York Press, 1997.
Robinette, Brian D. *Grammars of Resurrection: A Christian Theology of Presence and Absence*. New York: Herder & Herder, 2009.
Robinson, Andrew. *God and the World of Signs: Trinity, Evolution, and the Metaphysical Semiotics of C.S. Peirce*. Philosophical Studies in Science and Religion. Leiden: Brill, 2010.
Sandnes, Karl Olav. "Ancient Debates on Jesus as Miracke Worker: Emic and Etic Persepctives." In *Healing and Exorcism in Second Temple Judaism and Early Christianity*, edited by Mikael Tellbe and Tommy Wassermann, 197–218. Wissenschaftliche Untersuchungen zum Neuen Testament 2.511. Tübingen 2019.
———. *Belly and Body in the Pauline Epistles*. Society for New Testament Studies 120. Cambridge: Cambridge University Press, 2002.
———. *The Challenge of Homer: School, Pagan Poets and Early Christianity*. Library of New Testament Studies 400. London: T. & T. Clark, 2009.
———. *Early Christian Discourses on Jesus' Prayer at Gethsemane: Corageous, Committed, Cowardly?* Supplements to Novum Testamentum 166. Leiden: Brill, 2016.
———. "Ekklêsia at Corinth: Between Public and Private." *Tidsskrift for Teologi og Kirke* 78 (2007) 248–65.
———. "Justification and Abraham: Exegesis of Romans 4." In *God's Power for Salvation: Romans 1,1–5,11*, edited by Cilliers Breytenbach, 147–81. Colloquium Oecumenicum Paulinum 23. Leuven: Peeters, 2017.
———. *A New Family: Conversion and Ecclesiology in the Early Church with Cross-Cultural Comparisons*. Studies in the Intercultural History of Christianity 91. Bern: Peter Lang, 1994.
———. *Paul—One of the Prophets? A Contribution to the Apostle's Self-Understanding*. Wissenschaftliche Untersuchungen zum Neuen Testament 2.43. Tübingen: Mohr Siebeck, 1991.
———. *Paul Perceived: An Interactionist Perspective on Paul and the Law*. Wissenschaftliche Untersuchungen zum Neuen Testament 412. Tübingen: Mohr Siebeck, 2018.

———. "Seal and Baptism in Early Christianity." In *Ablution, Initiation, and Baptism: Late Antiquity, Early Judaism, and Early Christianity*, edited by David Hellholm et al., 1441–81. Beihefte zur Zeitschrift für die Neutestamentliche Wissenschaft 176/ II. Berlin: De Gruyter, 2011.

Schneiders, Sandra M. "Touching the Risen Jesus: Mary Magdalene and Thomas the Twin in John 20." In *The Resurrection of Jesus in the Gospel of John*, edited by Craig R. Koester and Reimund Bieringer, 153–76. Wissenschaftliche Untersuchungen zum Neuen Testament 222. Tübingen: Mohr Siebeck, 2008.

Schulz, Heiko. "The Concept of Miracle and the Concepts of Reality. Some Provisional Remarks." In *Miracles Revisited: New Testament Miracle Stories and Their Concepts of Reality*, edited by Stefan Alkier and Annette Weissenrieder Alkier, 351–76. Berlin: De Gruyter, 2013.

———. "Das Ende Des Common Sense. Kritische Überlegungen Zur Wunderkritik David Humes." *Zeitschrift für Neuere Theologiegeschichte / Journal for the History of Modern Theology* 3 (1996) 1–38.

Schurz, G. "Patterns of Abduction." *An International Journal for Epistemology, Methodology and Philosophy of Science* 164 (2008) 201–34.

Schweitzer, Don. "Jesus' Resurrection as a Saturated Phenomenon." *Studies in Religion* 44 (2015) 501–15.

Segal, Alan F. "The Resurrection: Faith or History?" In *The Resurrection of Jesus: The Crossan-Wright Dialogue*, edited by Robert B. Stewart, 121–38. Minneapolis: Fortress, 2006.

Seland, Torrey. *Establishment Violence in Philo and Luke: A Study of Non-Conformity to the Torah and Jewish Vigilante Reactions*. Biblical Interpretation Series 15. Leiden: Brill, 1995.

———. "Saul of Tarsus and Early Zealotism: Reading Galatians 1,13–14 in Light of Philo's Writings." *Biblica* 83 (2002) 449–71.

Sheehy, Benedict C. *The Arguments of Apocriticus: A Re-Evaluation of the Apology of Macarius Magnes*. MA diss., Wilfried Laurier University, 1989. http://scholars.wlu.ca/etd/101.

Shepherd, Thomas R. "Narrative Analysis as a Text Critical Tool: Mark 16 in Codex W as a Test Case." *Journal for the Study of the New Testament* 32 (2009) 77–98.

Siliezar, Carlos Raúl Sosa. *Creation Imagery in John*. Library of New Testament Studies 546. London: Bloomsbury, 2015.

Sluga, Hans. "Family Resemblance." *Grazer Philosophische Studien* 71 (2006) 1–21.

Smith, Daniel A. *Revisiting the Empty Tomb: The Early History of Easter*. Minneapolis: Fortress, 2010.

———. "Seeing a Pneuma(tic) Body): The Apologetic Interests of Luke 24:36–43." *Catholic Biblical Quarterly* 72 (2010) 742–72.

Smith, Jonathan Z. *Drudgery Divine: On the Comparison of Early Christianities and the Religions of Late Antiquity*. Chicago: University of Chicago Press, 1990.

Stanton, Graham. "Early Objections to the Resurrection of Jesus." In *Resurrection: Essays in Honour of Leslie Houlden*, edited by Stephen Barton and Graham Stanton, 79–94. London: SPCK, 1994.

Stendahl, Krister. *Paul Among Jews and Gentiles*. Philadelphia: Fortress, 1976.

Stewart, Robert B., ed. *The Resurrection of Jesus: John Dominic Crossan and N. T. Wright in Dialogue*. Minneapolis: Fortress, 2006.

Stordalen, Terje. *Echoes of Eden: Genesis 2 and 3 and Symbolism of the Eden Garden in Biblical Hebrew Literature*. Contributions to Biblical Exegesis and Theology 25. Leuven: Peeters, 2000.

Tappenden, Frederick S. *Resurrection in Paul: Cognition, Metaphor, and Transformation*. Early Christianity and its Literature 19. Atlanta: SBL, 2016.

Taves, Ann. *Religious Experience Reconsidered: A Building Block Approach to the Study of Religion and Other Special Things*. Princeton: Princeton University Press, 2009.

Tertullian. *Treatise on the Resurrection*. Edited and translated by Ernest Evans. London: SPCK, 1960.

Theophilus of Antioch. *Ad Autolycum*. Text and Translation by Robert M. Grant. Oxford Early Christian Texts. Oxford: Clarendon, 1970.

Thiselton, Anthony C. *The First Epistle to the Corinthians: A Commentary on the Greek Text*. Grand Rapids: Eerdmans, 2000.

Thomas, Günther. "'Er ist nicht hier'! Die Rede vom leeren Grab als Zeichen der neuen Schöpfung." In *Die Wirklichkeit der Auferstehung*, edited by Hans-Joachim Eckstein and Michael Welker, 183–220. Neukirchen-Vluyn: Neukirchener, 2010.

Victor, U. *Lukian von Samosata: Alexandros oder der Lügenprophet*. Leiden: Brill, 1997.

Wahlberg, Mats. *Revelation as Testimony: A Philosophical-Theological Study*. Grand Rapids: Eerdmans, 2014.

Walker, Peter. *The Weekend that Changed the World: The Mystery of Jerusalem's Empty Tomb*. San Francisco: HarperCollins, 1999.

Ware, James. "Paul's Understanding of the Resurrection in 1 Corinthians 15:36–54." *Journal of Biblical Literature* 103 (2014) 809–35.

———. "The Resurrection of Jesus in the Pre-Pauline Formula of 1 Cor 15:3–5." *New Testament Studies* 60 (2014) 475–98.

Watson, Francis. "'He is not here': Towards a Theology of the Empty Tomb." In *Resurrection: Essays in Honour of Leslie Houlden*, edited by Stephen Barton and Graham Stanton, 95–107. London: SPCK, 1994.

Webster, John. "Wunder, Dogmatisch." In *Die Religion in Geschichte und Gegenwart: Handwörterbuch für Theologie und Religionswissenschaft*, edited by Hans Dieter Betz et al., 8:1727–29. Tübingen: Mohr Siebeck, 2005.

Welker, Michael. "Wright on Resurrection." *Scottish Journal of Theology* 60 (2007) 458–75.

Wenz, Gunther. *Introduction to Wolfhart Pannenberg's Systematic Theology*. Göttingen: Vandenhoeck & Ruprecht, 2013.

Wiebe, Phillip H. *Visions of Jesus: Direct Encounters from the New Testament to Today*. Oxford: Oxford University Press, 1997.

Williams, Rowan. *Resurrection: Interpreting the Easter Gospel*. Cleveland: Pilgrim, 2002.

Winter, Bruce W. *Seek the Welfare of the City: Christians as Benefactors and Citizens*. Grand Rapids: Eerdmans, 1994.

Wright, N. T. *The Resurrection of the Son of God*. Minneapolis: Fortress, 2003.

Wright, N. T., and John Dominic Crossan. "The Resurrection: Historical Event or Theological Explanation? A Dialogue." In *The Resurrection of Jesus: John Dominic Crossan and N. T. Wright*, edited by Robert B. Stewart, 16–47. Minneapolis: Fortress, 2006.

Yong, Amos. *Theology and Down Syndrome: Reimagining Disability in Late Modernity*. Waco, TX: Baylor University Press, 2007.

Zeller, Dieter. "Religionsgeschichtliche Erwägungen zur Auferstehung." *Zeitschrift für Neues Testament* 19 (2007) 15–23.

Author Index

Alkier, Stefan, 28–32, 53n1, 96, 110, 135, 192
Allison Jr., Dale C., 2, 42, 97, 105, 181, 222–23, 235, 247–55, 260, 262, 264
Althaus, Paul, 224
Anderson, Kevin L., 66–69, 134
Austad, Anne, 102–4

Baker, John Austin, 170, 248
Barclay, John M. G., 93, 274
Barth, Karl, 230–32
Bieringer, Reimund, 142
Bynum, Caroline Walker, 115
Bultmann, Rudolf, 39–40, 43, 207–213, 222, 230–32, 275
Byrskog, Samuel, 51, 122

Caird, G. B., 54–55, 117
Carnley, Peter, 185n67, 219–34
Cook, John Granger, 98
Crossan, John D., 1, 2, 42–43, 50, 73, 93, 252
Crossley, James G., 103, 180

Dalferth, Ingolf, 5, 216, 257, 277–82
Deichgräber, Reinhard, 78
Dunn, James D. G., 64, 80, 101, 171

Eckstein, Hans-Joachim, 273
Engberg-Pedersen, Troels, 110–11, 114, 116
Evans, Craig A., 93–94

Festinger, Leon, 81
Fjärstedt, Björn, 105
Frenschkowski, Marco, 162

Gadamer, Hans-Georg, 11–13
Gerhardsson, Birger, 89n1, 99, 106–7
Goulder, Michael, 80n17, 86, 123
Grube, Dirk-Martin, 5, 274–77

Habermas, G., 233
Hays, Richard B., 136
Heidegger, Martin, 209
Hick, John, 278
Hume, David, 199, 202, 205
Hurtado, Larry, 75n1

Juel, Donald H., 179

Kannaday, Wayne C., 128
Kartzow, Marianne Bjelland, 146
Kähler, Martin, 170
Kienzler, Klaus, 211
Koester, Craig R., 71, 73
Kuhn, Thomas S., 275, 277
Küng, Hans, 2, 168, 172

Lampe, Peter, 168–69
Licona, Michael R., 116, 156
Lindemann, Andreas, 40–41, 91, 97–98, 169, 171
Lona, Horacio E., 84
Lüdemann, Gerd, 1, 40–41, 80–84, 91, 167, 169
Luther, Martin, 59

Marion, J.-L., 5, 32, 192–98, 221, 273
Martin, Dale, 109–111, 114, 116
Metz, J. B., 265n12

Novakovic, Lidija, 146, 155–56, 159–60, 164, 179–80

O'Connell, Jake, 160

Pannenberg, Wolfhart, 27, 199–201, 204–5, 212–19, 222–23, 226–28, 230, 233–34, 258, 262
Peirce, C. S., 3, 18, 21–25, 28–31

Quarles, Charles L., 181

Ravnå, Per Bjarne, 123n10, 153n57
Reynolds, T. E., 270
Ricoeur, Paul, 171, 263
Risser, James, 13
Robinette, Brian D., 123, 159, 167, 174, 177, 184
Robinson, Andrew, 21, 24

Schneiders, Sandra, 142
Schulz, Heiko, 202–5
Schurz, G., 19–20
Segal, Alan F., 41
Siliezar, Carlos Rosa Sosa, 144
Smith, Daniel A., 137n13, 153–55
Smith, Jonathan Z., 43
Stordalen, Terje, 145

Tappenden, Frederick S., 60–61, 63, 112, 114
Taves, Ann, 32–37, 200, 202
Thiselton, Anthony, 92
Troeltsch, Ernt, 157

Wahlberg, Mats, 16–17
Ware, James, 98, 105–6, 110, 114–15
Watson, Francis, 129, 157, 173–74
Webster, John, 261–62
Welker, Michael, 244–45
Williams, Rowan, 198, 266
Wright, N. T., 1, 2, 27, 42, 44, 112, 175, 185, 223–24, 233–47, 255, 262

Yong, Amos, 188

Subject Index

abduction, 3–4, 10, 14–19, 23, 44, 158, 167, 195–96, 206, 234, 255, 258
absence and presence, 122, 127, 130, 158, 174, 198, 222
analogies, 42–43
angels, 48–49, 122, 126, 129
apologetic, 50, 53, 99, 101, 130, 138, 140, 156, 165
appearances/apparitions/visions, 8–9, 12, 25, 40, 102–4, 153, 178, 213, 215–18, 223, 228, 237–43, 247, 250–55, 257–58, 264
Augustine, 199–200, 205

baptism, 60–63, 89
burial, 93–95

camera, 2–4, 169–70
"conference table approach", 55, 90, 126, 138–39
Celsus, 128, 148–49, 162–63, 175, 184

deduction and induction, 15, 18, 195
disability, 188–89, 268–70
discovery and justification, 4, 17–18, 24–26, 122, 124, 127–29, 136n11, 163, 179–80, 203, 242
doubt/credulity, 138, 152, 162–65

egeirein, 93, 96–98, 107, 111, 133, 155
emotions, 129–30, 134
empty tomb, 8–9, 25, 40–41, 53, 89–94, 99, 105, 108, 129, 153–55, 158, 168–73, 178–79, 213, 215–18, 223, 226, 228, 237–43, 247, 257–58
eschatological event/uniqueness, 210, 222, 235, 258
exaltation/ascension, 44, 65, 71, 97–98, 102, 127, 136, 154–55, 171, 177–78
experiences, 3–4, 8–14, 20, 32–33, 36, 42, 203, 221, 233, 235

faith, 196, 209, 232, 234, 242, 271, 280
Firstness-Secondness-Thirdness, 22–23, 25, 29–31, 100, 103, 108, 124, 127, 129, 163, 209–210, 235

gap/hole/ambiguity/elusiveness, 46–47, 50–52, 59, 158, 167, 221, 225, 227, 245
gift/grace, 4, 136, 139, 160, 170, 175, 190, 197, 259–61, 265, 274, 282
God Creator/theocentric, 5, 56–58, 60, 67, 90, 96, 127, 130, 139, 157, 169, 174–75, 180, 183–85, 191, 199, 208, 249, 256, 265, 282–83
Gospel of Peter, 47–51, 121, 150

hope, 266, 271, 274

identity, 267–70
incarnation, 278, 280–81
interpretative category, 7, 229

299

Julian the Emperor, 49

Lamb (the Book of Revelation), 70–73

Mary Magdalene, 47, 121, 125, 127–29, 141–43, 149, 153
metaphor, 21, 44, 171
miracles, 198–205, 207
mission, 131
mythology, 210

narrative, 4, 105, 107, 127, 156, 166–68, 170–71, 177
nature, 259, 261
New Jerusalem, 72–73

orientation, 3, 10–11, 35–36, 190–91, 265–66, 282

Paul, 29, 79–80, 101–2, 106
Peter, 79, 101, 123, 135, 140
Phantasma, 137
Physicality/body, 67, 102, 105–6, 109, 111–19, 128–29, 137–39, 143, 164, 168, 185–86, 214–15, 240–41, 244–45, 261, 269–70, 273
pre-Easter ministry or life of Jesus, 5, 131, 135, 158, 171, 175, 254, 256, 264, 267–68, 278–79
proofs/evidence, 30, 65–67, 138, 183, 224–25, 227
psychological explanations, 1, 41–42, 80–84, 157–58, 163

recognition, 134–38, 175, 179, 245
reductionism, 257
relative indeterminacy, 14, 22, 27–28, 225, 235
religious imagery, 10–11
restoration theology, 68–69
resuscitation, 214
running, 129, 134, 140, 156–57

Sadducees, 126, 163
saturated phenomenon, 5, 32, 159, 186, 197, 221, 273
Scripture, 67–68, 92–93, 99–100, 111, 119, 127, 131, 135–36, 138–39, 147, 156, 179–80, 183
Spirit, 68, 117
surplus/excess, 131, 157–58, 166, 190–91, 194, 274, 278–79, 282

theophany, 128
"third day", 98–99, 108, 133
Thomas, 142–43, 246
Thomas Aquinas, 260
tradition criticism, 40–41, 91–92, 104–5, 152
transformation/glorification, 11, 35, 58, 106, 160, 214, 229, 241, 259–60, 270

universal history, 212, 226

witnesses, 49, 51–52, 68, 101, 123, 157
women, 121, 122–23, 126, 128–30, 133–35, 146–52

Scripture Index

Old Testament

Genesis

1:26–27	113
2:7	60, 111–12, 143, 145–47
3:17–19	60, 64
12:7	100
15:6	57, 274
17:1	100
18	159
18:1	100
19:1–11	159

Numbers

25	83

Judges

6:11–24	159

Psalms

15LXX	66–67
33:9	57
91:13	127
110	171
110:1	43, 70, 97, 127

Deuteronomy

6:20–24	90
19:15	147
26:5–11	90

Joshua

24:2–13	90

2 Kings

6:17	136

Isaiah

7:3	131
7:14	131
8:1–4	131
8:10	131
11:1–10	181
23:17LXX	69
26:9	179, 180
48:13LXX	57
58:11	145
61:11	145
65:17	72
66:12	72

Jeremiah

27:19LXX	68
29:6LXX	68

Ezekiel

16:55LXX	69
17:23LXX	68
36:35	145
37	9
37:9	143
37:12	179

Hosea

1–2	131
6:2	99

Daniel

12:2	179, 181

Apocrypha and Pseudepigrapha

2 Baruch

49–51	160

2 Maccabees

7	58, 60, 113, 137–38
7:9	58
7:11	58
7:14	58
7:23	58
7:28	57
7:29	58

Jubilees (Jub.)

23.31	97

Testament of Job

52	98

New Testament

Matthew

1:23	131
2	182
2:11	130
5:9	266
9:36	131
10:19	131
10:29–31	131
17:2	128
17:11	68
18:18	142
18:20	131
22:23–33	160
26:49	130
27:8	130
27:52–53	180–82
27:61	128
27:62–66	41, 130
28:1	76–77, 128, 145
28:2	46
28:2–4	128
28:6	46
28:8	130, 152
28:9	130, 188
28:10	152
28:13	49, 152
28:16–20	129–30
28:17	126, 130, 138, 152
28:18	130

Mark

1:10parr	49
1:12–13	181–82
4:12	122, 126
5:29–30	188
5:42	123
6:49parr	102, 137
6:52	126
7:18	126
8:16–18	126
8:21	126
8:29parr	79
9:3	124
9:11–12	68

SCRIPTURE INDEX

9:28–29	126
10:27parr	162
10:51	142
12:18–27	160, 177, 188
12:25	118, 126
14:26	137
14:28	123
14:28–31	79
14:54	79
14:66–72	79
14:72parr	79
15:39	49
15:40	121
15:47	121
16:1	76
16:1–8	120, 125, 127, 154
16:3–4	121
16:4	46, 121
16:5–7	120–22
16:7	122–23, 125, 153–54
16:8	123n10, 124, 152
16:9	76–77, 125
16:9–20	127, 131
16:10	125
16:12	48, 125, 137
16:12–13	125, 126
16:14	126
16:14–15	127
16:15–18	127
16:18–22	127
16:19–20	127

Luke

2:19	133
2:51	133
9:16	136
9:22	133
9:44–45	133
13:32–33	133
15:24	78
17:25	133
18:12	75
18:31–34	133
20:27–39	160
20:36	126
22:15–38	133
22:19	136
22:61	133
23:55	133
24	30–31, 43, 67, 73, 79, 117, 143, 153, 164, 170–71, 177, 179, 193–96
24:1	76
24:5–6	135
24:6	133
24:6–8	133
24:1–12	133
24:9	126
24:11	138, 152
24:12	134
24:13	134
24:13–35	125, 134
24:13–38	66, 102
24:15–16	134–35
24:16	48
24:21	135
24:22–24	135, 139
24:23	135
24:25	126, 138
24:25–27	73, 93, 135, 179
24:30–32	125, 136
24:31	125, 134, 136
24:32	31, 133, 136
24:33	126, 137
24:34	79, 137
24:35	126
24:36–49	102
24:36–43	126, 134
24:37	138
24:38–43	66
24:39	116, 138, 253
24:39–40	188
24:40–42	138
24:41	138
24:42–43	188
24:44	93
24:45–46	179
24:46	133
24:46–49	73
24:51	65, 134, 136

John

1:1–5	145
2:22	133n2
2:23	140–41
3:1	145
3:19–21	145
4:23	142
4:34	145
5:36	145
6:30	140–41
7:8	141
7:39	141
7:53—8:11	144
8:12	145
9:4	145
11	213
11:9	145
11:40	140
12:16	133n2
13:30	145
14:16	133n2
17:20	142
19:34	143
19:41	141, 145
20	170, 246
20:1	76, 145
20:1–10	79, 140
20:2	142
20:7	140, 144
20:8	141
20:8–9	141
20:9	140
20:10	140
20:11–18	140
20:13	141, 152
20:15	41, 141, 145, 152
20:17	141–42, 186
20:18	142
20:19	48, 126, 145
20:19–29	140
20:22	143–45
20:23	142
20:24–27	188
20:24–29	126
20:25	50, 143
20:27	50, 138
20:29	142–43
20:30–31	142
21:1	143
21:1–14	79
21:15–23	79

Acts

1	177
1:1–2	65
1:3	65–66
1:3–4	185
1:6	68–69, 72, 135
1:8	68
1:21–22	65, 68, 102
2:14	79
2:24–32	66
2:27	67
2:31	67
2:32	68, 174
2:33	65
2:36	174
2:38	127
3:13	135
3:13–15	65, 67–68
3:15	174
3:20–21	68–69
4:10	67, 174
5:30–31	67
5:32	68
7:51–56	65
9:41	66
10:38	105
10:38–40	170
10:39	68
10:39–40	174
10:40–41	175
10:41–42	102
10:43	67
13:26–31	174
13:30–31	68
13:31	177
13:32–38	66
13:34–37	67
13:37–38	67
16:15	127
16:31	127
16:33	127

17:18	68
17:31	66–67
18:8	127
20:7	76
22:3	83
23:6–10	118, 177
26:8	68
26:18	78
26:23	68
26:23	67
28:20	68

Romans

1:3–4	57
3:1–3	63
3:8	60
3:30	57
4	57, 59, 274
4:4–5	274
4:17	57, 2
4:18	57
5:2	57
5:12–21	60
5:20	60
6:1	60
6:1–11	60–63
6:4–8	60
6:5	61
6:8	61
7:14–25	83
7:22	62n20
8:9–11	62
8:11	112, 117
8:12–13	63
8:17	63
8:18–23	63
8:19–22	64
8:23	117
8:24	59
8:29	117
10:7	107, 117
10:9	56
10:9–13	90
11:36	57
13:13	62

1 Corinthians

1:18	92
2:9	14, 173
2:14–15	112–13, 116
6:2–3	160
6:10	116
6:13	117, 188
7:17	61
8:6	57
9:1	79
9:1–2	101
9:14	105
11:20	75
11:23	104
12:12	142
12:27	142
15	40, 67, 117, 123, 153n57, 172
15:1–2	90–91
15:1–3	104
15:1–11	90
15:3	96
15:3–5	40, 65, 77, 90, 91–92, 97, 100, 106
15:3–8	91, 108, 253
15:3–11	4, 101
15:4	76, 97, 99
15:5	41, 79, 137
15:5–8	49
15:6	104
15:7–8	41
15:8	79, 90, 101
15:8–9	40
15:11	78, 90–91
15:12	89–90, 177
15:12–15	90
15:12–19	96–97
15:13–17	271
15:15	90
15:20–23	187
15:22	60, 89
15:29–34	110n6
15:35	97, 109, 125, 187
15:35–58	89
15:36	110, 113
15:36–37	111

1 Corinthians (continued)

15:36–41	110
15:42	67, 110
15:42–44	111, 113
15:42–49	111
15:44	89, 137n13
15:45	111
15:45–49	60
15:47–48	111
15:49	113, 117
15:50	67, 109, 115–16, 163, 165, 169
15:50–54	113
15:52	117
15:53–54	113, 117
15:54	67
15:54–57	110
16:2	75–77

2 Corinthians

1:9	58
3:18	117
4:6–18	115
4:16	62n20
4:10	61
5:1	67n, 117
5:1–5	114
5:1–10	117, 169
5:2	115
5:3	115
8–9	75
12:1	101–2

Galatians

1:11–16	101
1:13–14	107
1:14	83
1:15–16	79, 100
2:2	101
2:10	75
3:28	188
5:16	61

Ephesians

2:1–3	78
3:16	62n20
4:7–10	78
4:23	62n20
5:8–14	78

Philippians

3:5–11	80
3:6	83
3:21	63, 80, 117

Colossians

1:12–14	78
1:13	182
1:16–17	57
1:18	182
2:12–13	61n17
3:1	61n17

1 Thessalonians

1:9–10	56, 96
4:1	61
4:13–18	56
4:18	56

1 Timothy

4:7	146

2 Timothy

2:18	177

Hebrews

1–2	48

1 Peter

1:3	87
1:4	67
2:9–10	78
3:19	49–50
4:6	49

Revelation

1:5	70
1:17–18	71
1:18	70
2:8	70
5:5–6	70
5:7	70
5:9	70
5:12–13	70
7:10	70
7:17	70
18–20	71
18:23	73
19	71–72
19:7	73
19:9	73
21–22:5	72
21:1–4	188
21:4	170
22:1–3	70, 72

Greco-Roman Writings

Josephus

Jewish Antiquities (Ant.)

1.196–98	159n81
4.219	147–48

Jewish War (Bell.)

4.137	93n14

Against Apion (C. Ap.)

2.211	93n14

Life

256	148

Philo

On the Life of Abraham (Abr.)

114–18	159n81

On the Life of Joseph (Jos.)

22–23	94n14
26–27	94n14

Qumran

11QT 64.7–13	94n14

Aristotle

Rhetoric (Rhet.)

1.1.3	66
1.2.16–18	65

Cicero

De Natura Deorum (Nat. Deor.)

3.5.12–13	147

Tusculanea disputationes (Tusc.)

3.29.72	147

Lucian of Samosata

Alexander the false prophet (Alex.)

1	85
5	85
7–8	85
15–19	85
20	85–86
23–31	85

Philostratus

Vita Apolonii (Vit. Apoll.)

1.16.2	147n34

Plato

Gorgias (Gorg.)

527A	146

Laws (Leg.)

10.887D	146

Pliny the Younger

Epistles (Ep.)

10.96.7	78

Quintilian

Institutio oratoria (Inst.)

5.9.3–4	66

Early Christian Writings

Athenagoras

De resurrection (Res.)

3	189
25.3	188

Augustine

The City of God (Civ.)

22.15,19–20	188

Didachê (Did.)

8:1	76n4
14:1	75

Eusebius

Gospel Problems and Solutions

10.147–84	156

Ecclesiastical history (Hist. eccl.)

3.39.3–4	51

Life of Constantine

3.25–40	94–95
4.40–47	94

Gospel of Peter

8.28	48
9.34	47
9.34–37	47–48, 77
10.38	49
10.38–42	48
12.50	47
13.55	47

Hermas the Shepherd

Similitudes (Sim.)

9.16.2	61n15
9.16.4	61

Mandates (Mand.)

4.3.1	61n15

Ignatius

To the Magnesians (Magn.)

9:1–2	75–76

To the Smyeneans (Smyrn.)

2–3	164

Jerome

Epistles (Ep.)

53	151

Justin Martyr

First Apology (1 Apol.)

19	163
67.3	77
67.8	77

Dialogue with Trypho (Dial.)

108.2	130

Macarius of Magnesia

Apocriticus

2.25.1	150
2.25.2	151
2.30.1–13	151, 176
2.30.12–13	151, 176
3.1–2 (51)	150

Minucius Felix

Octavius (Oct.)

8.4	151
20:3–4	147

Origen

Against Celsus (Cels.)

1.68	86
1.8	85
2.11–12	79n11
2.45	79n11
2.48–54	86
2.55	84, 148–49
2.57	184
2.59	86, 149
2.59–60	149
3.22	84n28
3.24	85
3.43	84n28
3.50	86
5.14	162, 184
5.20	149
5.23	184
6.74	149
8.22	75
8.49	184–85

Protoevangelium of James

16	50
19.3	50
19.3–20.3	50

Tatian

Address to the Greeks (Orat.)

30.1	146

Tertullian

The Resurrection of the Flesh (Res.)

32	189
48.1	115n18
57	163, 188
60–61	188

Theophilus of Antioch

To Autolycus (Autol.)

1.8	183
1.13	182–83
1.14	182–83
2.10	183
2.13	183
2:14	183
8	182
3.2	182